THE HANDLING OF INTERNATIONAL DISPUTES
BY MEANS OF INQUIRY

The Royal Institute of International Affairs is an unofficial body which promotes the scientific study of international questions and does not express opinions of its own. The opinions expressed in this publication are the responsibility of the author.

The Institute gratefully acknowledges the comments and suggestions of the following who read the manuscript on behalf of the Research Committee: Sydney Bailey, Professor Geoffrey Goodwin, and Dr Rosalyn Higgins.

THE HANDLING OF INTERNATIONAL DISPUTES BY MEANS OF INQUIRY

NISSIM BAR-YAACOV, M.A., Ph.D.

Associate Professor of International Relations
The Hebrew University of Jerusalem

Published for

THE ROYAL INSTITUTE OF
INTERNATIONAL AFFAIRS

by

OXFORD UNIVERSITY PRESS
LONDON   NEW YORK   TORONTO
1974

Oxford University Press, Ely House, London W. 1

GLASGOW   NEW YORK   TORONTO   MELBOURNE   WELLINGTON
CAPE TOWN   IBADAN   NAIROBI   DAR ES SALAAM   LUSAKA   ADDIS ABABA
DELHI   BOMBAY   CALCUTTA   MADRAS   KARACHI   LAHORE   DACCA
KUALA LUMPUR   SINGAPORE   HONG KONG   TOKYO

ISBN 0 19 218302 8

© Royal Institute of International Affairs, 1974

*Printed in Great Britain by
Robert MacLehose & Co. Ltd
Printers to the University of Glasgow*

To Dina

CONTENTS

Note: I am indebted to Brigadier R. A. Gardiner of the Royal Geographical Society for indicating the Egyptian Red grid reference system for the Suez Canal sector. The Israeli grid reference system is used for the rest of the map.

ACKNOWLEDGEMENTS

I am very grateful to the Royal Institute of International Affairs for publishing this study under its distinguished auspices. The institute's staff has been most kind and helpful in handling both the academic and technical aspects of publication. I am particularly indebted to Mr J. E. S. Fawcett and to Dr R. Higgins who read the typescript and offered valuable suggestions. It was a great pleasure to exchange views with two scholars of such high standing.

The typescript was edited initially by the late Mrs G. Lyons to whom I cannot, unfortunately, convey my gratitude. Mrs Lyons edited my books for many years and my sessions with her were most rewarding. Shortly before her death she suggested that her daughter-in-law, Mrs A. Lyons, barrister-at-law, might prepare the index of this book. Mrs A. Lyons has performed this task with scholarly precision.

Hermia Oliver, of Chatham House, edited the final version of this study, and I am indebted to her careful attention which, I am confident, has reduced errors and discrepancies to a minimum.

Several colleagues have been impressed with the neatness of the typescript. The credit must go, first of all, to Miss C. Clayton who typed the bulk of the material. Subsequently, Mrs M. Ben-Dor and my wife, Claire, typed various additions and revisions. (Naturally, I have benefited from Claire's English background in many other ways.)

Mrs B. Joseffia drew most of the maps and charts with her usual devotion and skill. I am indebted to the draughtsmen of the Oxford University Press for the preparation of the map depicting the general area of the *Red Crusader* incident and for making the necessary technical adjustments to other maps or charts. Regarding the spelling of place-names in the map of the Faroe Islands, I was helped by the first secretary of the Royal Danish embassy in Tel-Aviv, Mr K. Due, who spared no effort in seeking professional advice from the 'Geodætisk Institut' in Copenhagen.

I also wish to thank the research committee of the Hebrew University faculty of social sciences for approving my recurrent annual applications for research grants.

Finally, my gratitude is extended to my former teacher, Professor Emeritus N. Feinberg, who followed with sympathetic interest the progress of my research and, in the best of tradition, offered his competent advice.

Jerusalem, February 1974   N. Bar-Yaacov

A2

ABBREVIATIONS

a.i.   agenda item
AFDI   Annuaire français de droit international
AJIL   American journal of international law
Annuaire   Annuaire de l'Institut de Droit International
Arch. dip.   Archives diplomatiques
BYIL   British yearbook of international law
C, Cd, Cmnd   Command papers (Great Britain)
ECOSOC   Economic and Social Council
ESCOR   Economic and Social Council Official Records
FAO   Food and Agriculture Organization
FO   Foreign Office (UK)
FRUS   Foreign Relations of the United States
GAOR   General Assembly Official Records
Hague Recueil   Hague Academy, *Recueil des cours*
HC Deb.   House of Commons Debates
i.a.   inter alia
ICJ   International Court of Justice
ICLQ   International and comparative law quarterly
ICRC   International Committee of the Red Cross
ILC   International Law Commission
Int. aff.   International affairs
Int. conc.   International conciliation
Int. org.   International organization
LNOJ   League of Nations Official Journal
LN *Survey*   League of Nations, *Arbitration and security; systematic survey of the arbitration conventions and treaties of mutual security deposited with the League of Nations,* 2nd edn (1927)
LNTS   League of Nations Treaty Series
Moore, *International arbitrations*   J. B. Moore, *History and digest of the international arbitrations to which the United States has been a party* (1898)
NAR   North American review
Ned. tijd. int. recht   Nederlands tijdschrift voor internationaal recht
OAS   Organization of American States
PCA   Permanent Court of Arbitration
PCIJ   Permanent Court of International Justice
Pol. Sci. Q.   Political science quarterly
RBDI   Revue belge de droit international
RGDIP   Revue générale de droit international public
SCOR   Security Council Official Records
Scott, *Proceedings 1899/1907*   J. B. Scott, *Proceedings of the Hague Peace Conferences,* (1) *The Conference of 1899;* (2) *The Conference of 1907* (see Bibliography)

xi

TCIA   Treaties, conventions, international acts, protocols and agreements between the United States of America and other powers (see Bibliography)

TCOR   Trusteeship Council Official Records

UKTS   UK Treaty Series

UN *Survey*   UN, *Systematic survey of treaties for the pacific settlement of international disputes, 1928–48* (1948)

UNCIO   UN Conference on International Organization

UNCIP   UN Commission for India and Pakistan

UNIPOM   UN India and Pakistan Observation Mission

UNITAR   UN Institute for Training and Research

UNMOGIP   UN Military Observer Group in India and Pakistan

UNOGIL   UN Observer Group in Lebanon

UNSCOB   UN Special Commission on the Balkans

UNSCOP   UN Special Commission on Palestine

UNTEA   UN Temporary Executive Authority

UNTS   UN Treaty Series

UNTSO   UN Truce Supervision Organization

UNYOM   UN Observation Mission in Yemen

YBUN   Yearbook of the United Nations

CHAPTER 1

Introduction

States have in recent years displayed a growing unwillingness to rely on the UN for the peaceful settlement of international disputes. The reasons for this attitude must be sought both in the inability of the great powers to achieve unanimity with regard to many issues relating to the maintenance of international peace, and in the fear of individual states that the organs of the UN, motivated by political considerations, may interfere in disputes which could otherwise be settled outside the international organization. The widely felt need to remove the political element from the existing machinery for the settlement of disputes has led to emphasis on the responsibility of individual states to seek 'first of all' a solution to their dispute by 'peaceful means of their own choice' (Art. 33(1) of the UN Charter). Among the traditional means of settlement of international disputes, increased interest has been focused on the method of inquiry. Efforts have been made, within and outside the UN, to promote the application of this method by the establishment of machinery designed first and foremost to assist states in employing commissions of inquiry of their own choice.[1]

[1]The activities of the UN in the matter will be examined in ch. 8 below. Mention should here be made of the resolution adopted at the 44th conference of the Inter-Parliamentary Union (1955), in which the Union expressed the wish that, without prejudice to the action of the UN regarding the maintenance of peace, states divided by differences and believing that they cannot have recourse to arbitration or judicial settlement, should at least seek a solution by means of commissions of inquiry and conciliation. (See Union Interparlementaire, *Compte rendu de la XLIVe conférence tenue à Helsinki du 25 au 31 août 1955* (1956), p. 1130.)

Professor Rolin, rapporteur of the Committee on Juridical Questions, introducing the draft-resolution on the subject, pointed out the shortcomings of negotiation as a method for the peaceful settlement of disputes; the failure of states to accept the compulsory jurisdiction of the ICJ; and the limitations of the League of Nations and the UN, whose members had been motivated in their votes by their own interests rather than by the merits of the case. In such a 'period of defiance' he urged recourse to 'the method of conciliation and inquiry', which did not entail the sacrifice of sovereignty (ibid., pp. 721–2).

The same line of thought must have guided the members of the Institute of International Law when they undertook in the years 1958–61 a thorough study of bilateral conciliation. Their deliberations have proved most useful in the clarification of the role of inquiry in the process of bilateral conciliation.

Cf. also the recommendations of the Commission to Study the Organization of Peace (chairman: Professor L. B. Sohn), *Twentieth report: The United Nations: the next twenty-five years* (New York, 1970), p. 21.

Sydney Bailey has recently expressed the view that inquiry as a means of settlement deserves more attention than it has hitherto received: see *Peaceful settlement of disputes*, published under the auspices of UNITAR (1970), p. 29. See also below, p. 10.

The present study was conceived in the midst of these efforts, and its purpose is to analyse some of the pertinent issues. Before defining these issues, we propose to clarify the conceptual framework.

Two basic meanings have been attributed to the term 'inquiry' in the literature dealing with the peaceful settlement of disputes: (*a*) as denoting a specific category of investigation conducted by an international body; and (*b*) as one of the universally recognized methods for settlement of disputes, such as mediation, conciliation, arbitration, and judicial settlement. These two meanings may overlap in so far as one specific category of investigation is considered to be *the* method of inquiry. Let us now examine the concept of 'inquiry' in terms of these two meanings.

The different categories of inquiry employed in the settlement of international disputes. These categories may be distinguished both with regard to the type of the investigating organ and the scope of the investigation. Another distinguishing criterion relates to the aim of the inquiry, namely, is the inquiry envisaged as an exclusive method intended to provide the basis for the solution of the dispute, or is it a part of a wider range of procedures to be employed to that end?

The following categories of inquiry are particularly relevant for our purposes:

1. Inquiry in the sense of the institution of inquiry as defined in the Hague Conventions of 1899 and 1907. These conventions lay down that states which are involved in a dispute affecting neither honour nor vital interests, and arising from a difference of opinion on points of fact, agree to establish a commission of inquiry whose task is to facilitate a solution of the dispute by an impartial and conscientious investigation. The report of the commission is to be confined to a finding of facts,[2] and is in no way to have the character of an arbitral award. The parties have complete freedom of action as to the effect to be given to the finding.[3]

2. The overall investigations conducted by an international tribunal, acting on its own or through persons designated by it, for the purpose of ascertaining the materiality of alleged facts, their nature, and the circumstances accompanying them. These investigations may be effected by examination of witnesses, visits on the spot, requests for documentary evidence or other means at the disposal of the tribunal.[4]

[2] The *Oxford English Dictionary* gives, i.a., the following meanings of the word 'fact': '4. Something that has really occurred or is actually the case; something certainly known to be of this character; hence, a particular truth known by actual observation or authentic testimony, as opposed to what is merely inferred, or to a conjecture or fiction; a datum of experience, as distinguished from the conclusions that may be based upon it. . . . (*Law*) 7. The circumstances and incidents of a case, looked at apart from their legal bearing.'

[3] See generally chs 2 & 4 of the present study. For the relevant texts of Part III of the two conventions see below, pp. 31–3, and App. I, pp. 330–8.

[4] Cf. *Dict. de la terminologie du droit international* (1960), p. 253.

Lauterpacht points out that a substantial part of the task of international judicial tribunals consists in the examination and weighing of the relevance of facts for the purpose of determining liability and assessing damages. As the *Corfu Channel Case*

3. The examination to be conducted by commissions established by virtue of the Bryan treaties (below, pp. 114 ff.). These commissions are empowered to deal with disputes of any nature and the scope of their 'investigation' extends to all aspects of the dispute, whether factual or legal. The commissions are called upon to submit to the parties a report embodying the results of their investigation. The Bryan commissions are generally designated in the legal literature as commissions of inquiry, although they are not so named in the treaties themselves.

4. The elucidation of the questions in dispute by commissions of conciliation. As in the previous instance, the examination is not confined to the factual aspects of the dispute, but extends also to the legal issues involved.[5]

5. Inquiry by the Council of the League of Nations, that is, the all-embracing examination of a dispute submitted to the 'inquiry' of the Council by virtue of Articles 12 and 15 of the Covenant (below, p. 120).[6]

6. Inquiry in the sense of Article 34 of the UN Charter, which empowers the Security Council to investigate any dispute, or any situation which might lead to international friction or give rise to a dispute. The purpose of such an inquiry is to determine whether the continuance of the dispute or situation is likely to endanger the maintenance of international peace and security.[7]

7. The conduct of investigations, whether or not confined to the facts of the dispute, by special commissions appointed by the League of Nations, the UN, or regional organizations, e.g. the Lytton Commission in the Manchurian conflict and UNSCOP. The distinguishing characteristic of such commissions is that, unlike the Hague commissions, they may recommend a solution of the dispute. As far as their designation is concerned, here again the title of 'commissions of inquiry' has commonly been assigned to commissions which were not so named by the appointing organ.

8. Any one of a number of specific techniques employed by competent bodies for the purpose of ascertaining the facts of a dispute,

---

showed (below, p. 4, n. 8), the ICJ is in a position to perform that task with exacting care (*The development of international law by the International Court* (1958), p. 48).

Arbitral tribunals have often been specifically requested to inquire into the facts of the dispute submitted to them. Thus in the *Casablanca Case* between Germany and France (1908) the tribunal was charged with 'the settlement of questions of fact and of law' concerning the forcible removal of deserters from the French Foreign Legion, who were under the protection of the German consul in Casablanca (see Scott, *The Hague Court reports* (1916), p. 117).

According to Art. 36 of the ICJ Statute, states parties to the Statute may at any time accept the jurisdiction of the Court in all legal disputes concerning, i.a., 'the existence of any fact which, if established, would constitute a breach of an international obligation.'

[5]As shown in ch. 7 below, most disputes submitted to commissions of conciliation entail legal questions.

[6]While Art. 15 of the Covenant conferred on the Assembly powers concurrent with those of the Council, emphasis is usually placed on the 'inquiry' function of the Council.

[7]On the application of Art. 34 by the Security Council, see Kerley, 'The powers of investigation of the Security Council', 55 *AJIL* (1961), 892–918.

notably examination of witnesses, explanations by counsel, opinions of experts and visits on the spot.[8]

The above classification reveals two basic dichotomies: first, inquiry confined to the ascertainment of facts, as opposed to inquiry intended to clarify all aspects of the dispute, whether factual, legal, or political; and secondly, inquiry conducted by commissions set up by the states concerned and being in the direct service of these states, as opposed to inquiry conducted by the League of Nations, the UN, or regional organizations.

[8]Foster analyses the following 'specific techniques of fact-finding' used by the ICJ: (1) Documentary evidence; (2) Enquiries and expert evidence; (3) Testimonial evidence; (4) Third party evidence; (5) Judicial notice; and (6) On-site visits ('Fact-finding and the World Court', 7 *Canadian yearbook of international law* (1969), 150–91). Cf. in particular Art. 62 of the Rules of Court, relating to inquiries and expert opinions (ICJ, *Acts and documents concerning the organization of the Court*, No. 2: *Rules of Court* (1972)).

Inquiry in the sense of examination of witnesses is envisaged by Witenberg, who enumerates among the means of information most frequently mentioned in treaties of arbitration 'les enquêtes, les expertises, le transport sur les lieux' (see Witenberg, 'La théorie des preuves devant les juridictions internationales', in 56 *Hague Recueil* (1936), (ii), p. 53). Cf. Stroud's *Judicial dict. of words and phrases*, ii (3rd edn by Burke, 1952), at p. 1465: 'an "inquiry" in an action is not limited to what a man can see with his own eyes; it signifies a judicial inquiry with witnesses; therefore in a reference "for inquiry and report" under s. 56, Judicature Act, 1873 (36 & 37 Vict., c. 66—see now s. 88 Judicature Act, 1925 (15 & 16 Geo. 5, c. 49)—the referee may, and it is the invariable practice to, hear counsel and witnesses (*Wenlock* v. *River Dee Co.*, 19 Q.B.D. 155).' One of the meanings of 'enquête', given in Quemner's *Dict. juridique Français–Anglais, Anglais–Français* (1969), at p. 93 is 'hearing of witnesses before trial'.

With regard to opinions of experts, see the order of 13 September 1928 made by the PCIJ in the *Chorzow Factory Case* whereby an 'expert enquiry' was to be held with a view to enabling the Court to fix 'with a full knowledge of the facts' the amount of indemnity to be paid by the Polish government to the German government for the expropriated factory. A committee of three experts was appointed by the Court for that purpose (PCIJ, ser. A, no. 17, p. 99).

So far as visit on the spot is concerned, it may first be noted that the expression 'descente sur les lieux' is synonymous with 'enquête sur les lieux'. See *Dict. de la terminologie du droit international*, p. 207. In the case concerning the *Diversion of Water from the Meuse* (1937) the PCIJ visited the scene and saw the various installations involved (see PCIJ, ser. A/B, no. 70). The most notable recent use of inquiry on the spot in the practice of the ICJ took place in the *Corfu Channel Case* (1949) between Albania and the UK. The case arose from an incident which occurred on 22 October 1946 in the Corfu Channel. Two British warships were damaged by mines and forty-four British officers and men were killed. By a decision of 17 January 1949 'regarding an inquiry on the spot' (ICJ *Reports 1949*, p. 151), the Court requested a Committee of Naval Experts to proceed to the Albanian coast in order to investigate fully the question whether the minefield alleged to have caused the disaster could have been laid without the knowledge of the Albanian authorities. Relying heavily on the committee's report, the Court came to the conclusion that the laying of the minefield (found by the Court to have caused the explosions on 22 October 1946) could not have been accomplished without the knowledge of the Albanian government (ibid., p. 22). See Ch. De Visscher, *Aspects récents du droit procédural de la Cour Internationale de Justice* (1966), p. 206, and Rosenne, *The International Court of Justice* (1957), p. 158.

For the practice of 'Visit to the Place (descentes sur les lieux)' of international arbitral tribunals and of the PCIJ, see Sandifer, *Evidence before international tribunals* (1939), pp. 241–2. See also Hudson, 'Visits by international tribunals to places concerned in proceedings', 31 *AJIL* (1937), 696–7. As appears from the last two studies, the device of visit to the place had been practised before the establishment of the Hague institution of inquiry.

An additional criterion for classification relates to the subject of the inquiry, *stricto sensu*. The promoters of the Hague institution primarily had in mind the appointment of inquiry commissions in connection with border incidents, acts of sabotage or, perhaps, the persecution of minorities. The diversified purposes of international organizations have widened the scope of the application of inquiry. The ascertainment of facts by international organizations has been employed, as we shall shortly see, in a wider set of circumstances pertaining to military operations, subversive activities or violations of human rights, and more particularly in the so-called 'technical', socio-economic spheres of state intercourse.

The various conceptions of inquiry as a method for the settlement of international disputes. With regard to the concept of inquiry as a single and separate method for settling disputes, the question arises: is inquiry limited to the Hague system or has it acquired a more diversified character, including several or all of the categories of inquiry enumerated above? Opinions on this subject are extremely varied.

The widest conception of the institution of international inquiry has been expressed in two studies by the UN Secretary-General, published in 1965 and 1966 respectively, under the title *Report of the Secretary-General on methods of fact-finding*.[9]

The first study was prepared in pursuance of General Assembly resolution 1967 (XVIII) of 16 December 1963, entitled 'Question of Methods of Fact-Finding'.[10] The Assembly pointed out in the Preamble to the resolution that inquiry is mentioned in Article 33 of the Charter (for text see below, p. 134) as one of the peaceful means of settlement of disputes, and that 'inquiry, investigation and other methods of fact-finding are also referred to in other instruments of a general or regional nature'.[11] Considering, i.a., the important contribution which impartial fact-finding could make in the peaceful settlement and prevention of disputes, the General Assembly requested the Secretary-General to study the relevant aspects of the problem and to report on the results of such study, both to the Assembly and to the Special Committee on Principles of International Law.[12]

The study submitted by the Secretary-General describes the practice of states and some international organizations, principally the League of Nations and the UN, in the use of 'international inquiry as a peaceful

---

[9]The two studies are dated 1 May 1964 and 22 Apr. 1966 (see A/5694, GAOR, 20th sess., a.i. 90 & 94, Annexes (1965) & A/6228, ibid., 21st sess., a.i. 87, Annexes (1966)).

[10]This resolution marked one stage in the Assembly's endeavours to promote the principles of international law concerning friendly relations and co-operation among states, particularly the principle that 'states shall settle their international disputes in such a manner that international peace and security and justice are not endangered' (res. 1815 (XVII) of 18 Dec. 1962).

[11]For comment on the terms used in the last-quoted passage see below, p. 320.

[12]This committee was established under GA res. 1966 (XVIII), adopted on the same day. For the text of res. 1967 (XVIII) see below, p. 300.

means for settling disputes or adjusting situations'.[13] After an outline of the relevant provisions of the Hague Conventions and of the work of certain commissions of inquiry established in conformity with their provisions, the study discusses the Bryan treaties as the 'second milestone' in the evolution of the 'international inquiry procedure'. (The commissions envisaged in the Bryan treaties are designated by the Secretary-General as 'commissions of inquiry' (see para. 51) although the treaties themselves do not employ this term.) The next stage in the evolution of the institution is marked by the Covenant of the League of Nations. Article 12 and, in particular, Article 15 of the Covenant, states the author of this study (para. 82), were to give considerable impetus to the use of the inquiry procedure, which, since the Bryan treaties, had already become linked to the conciliation procedure. Under the Covenant, which at least implicitly entrusted conciliatory functions to the Council and the Assembly, the inquiry procedure ceased to be an independent process and became a means of providing those organs with information aimed at assisting them to assemble the facts and data which they needed to fulfil those functions (see para. 379). The study discusses in this connection the functions of the 'commissions of inquiry' established by the Council of the League in the dispute between Great Britain and Turkey concerning the frontiers in Iraq (1924), in the Demir-Kapu dispute between Bulgaria and Greece (1925), and in the Sino-Japanese dispute (1931).[14]

There follows an outline of 'international inquiry' under 'treaties of inquiry, conciliation, conciliation and arbitration, or conciliation, arbitration and judicial settlement' concluded between 1919 and 1940 (see para. 104). The study relates that, while there are only a few treaties of inquiry properly so-called—i.e. treaties instituting commissions with the sole task of 'inquiry' or 'investigation'—the procedure of inquiry is closely linked with the procedure of conciliation provided for by other treaties which charge the commission, for instance, to investigate and settle the dispute by conciliation, or to promote the settlement of the dispute by an 'impartial and conscientious examination of the facts and by submitting proposals with a view to settling the case', or 'to elucidate the questions in dispute, to collect with that object all necessary information by means of inquiry or otherwise, and to endeavour to bring the parties to an agreement'.

A large part of the study is devoted to the use of the 'inquiry procedure' (see para. 384) by the Security Council, the General Assembly, and the Secretary-General of the UN.

The following 'fact-finding bodies' established in pursuance of General

---

[13]See para. 5 of the first study. On the role of inquiry in the adjustment of situations see below, p. 314, n. 169.

[14]The dates in parentheses following the designation of particular bodies refer to the year in which the decisions concerning their establishment had been adopted.

Assembly resolutions are briefly discussed: the Interim Committee (1947), UNSCOP (1947), UNSCOB (1947), the UN Temporary Commission on Korea (1947), the Panel for Inquiry and Conciliation (1949), the Peace Observation Commission (1950), the UN Commission to Investigate Conditions for Free Elections in Germany (1951), the UN Commission on the Racial Situation in the Union of South Africa (1952), the UN Plebiscite Commissioner in Togoland (1955), the UN Emergency Force (1956), the investigatory group on the situation in Hungary (1956), the UN Special Committee on Hungary (1957), the Special Representative of the Secretary-General in Amman (1958), the UN Commission of Investigation into the death of Mr Lumumba (1961), the Sub-Committee on the Situation in Angola (1961), the UN Commission for Ruanda-Urundi (charged, i.a., with investigating the assassination of the Prime Minister of Burundi) (1961), the UN commission to investigate the circumstances of the death of Mr Hammarskjöld (1961), the Special Committee for South-West Africa (1961), the Special Committee on the Policies of *Apartheid* of the Government of the Republic of South Africa (1962), and the UN Fact-Finding Mission to South Viet Nam (charged with ascertaining facts relating to alleged violations of human rights) (1963).

Within the purview of the study fall, in addition, the following bodies established by the Security Council: the Security Council Sub-Committee on the Spanish Question (1946), the UN Commission of Investigation concerning Greek Frontier Incidents (1946), the Security Council Sub-Committee on Incidents in the Corfu Channel (1947), the Security Council Consular Commission in Batavia (1947), the Security Council Committee of Good Offices on the Indonesian Question (1947), UNCIP (1948), UNMOGIP (1948), UNTSO (1948), UNOGIL (1958), the Security Council Sub-Committee on Laos (1959), and UNYOM (1963).

The study goes on to discuss the 'fact-finding missions' (para. 147) conducted under the authority of the Secretary-General by his special representatives in Cambodia and Thailand (1962) and Oman (1962), as well as by the UN Malaysia Mission (1963), and the Personal Representative of the Secretary-General in Cyprus (1964). The section dealing with the relevant activities of the UN ends with a reference to the provision of Article 50 of the Statute of the International Court of Justice, according to which the Court may entrust any individual body, bureau, commission, or other organization that it may select with the task of carrying out an inquiry or giving an expert opinion.

The Secretary-General then mentions the various fact-finding activities of the Council of the OAS, e.g. the appointment of committees to investigate allegations of border incursions or armed conspiracies in the cases of Costa Rica and Nicaragua (1948, 1955, and 1959), Haiti and the Dominican Republic (1950), Honduras and

Nicaragua (1957), Panama and Cuba (1958), and Venezuela and the Dominican Republic (1960). Attention is also drawn to the provisions of the Pact of Bogotá (1948) dealing with the 'procedure of investigation and conciliation', the provisions of the Charter of the Organization of African Unity (1963) on the Commission of Mediation, Conciliation and Arbitration, as well as provisions of certain treaties concluded since 1940, e.g. the European Convention for the Peaceful Settlement of Disputes (1957).

The second study by the Secretary-General was prepared in pursuance of a resolution of the General Assembly of 20 December 1965, also entitled 'Question of Methods of Fact-Finding'. By the terms of the resolution, the Secretary-General was requested to supplement his earlier study 'so as to cover the main trends and characteristics of international inquiry, as envisaged in some treaties as a means for ensuring their execution . . .'. The first chapter of the study deals with fact-finding conducted by UN bodies in relation to human rights, narcotic drugs, and trust and non-self-governing territories. The second chapter covers fact-finding activities conducted by the specialized agencies and the International Atomic Energy Agency, while the third and final chapter is devoted to fact-finding conducted by other international bodies, e.g. the Benelux Economic Union, the Council of Europe, the European Atomic Energy Community, and the ICRC. The Secretary-General calls attention, i.a., to the annual reports submitted by the Administering Authorities on political, economic, social, and educational conditions in territories placed under trusteeship, as well as to the dispatch of visiting missions and plebiscite commissions. We learn, in addition, that in 1950 the governing body of the ILO set up a special procedure with regard to complaints alleging interference with freedom of association. (Complaints may be submitted to the Fact-Finding and Conciliation Commission on Freedom of Association, a body of ten independent members established in the same year in agreement with ECOSOC.) Reference is also made to the 'reporting system', whereby ECOSOC invites states which are members of the UN and the specialized agencies to supply information on human rights and fundamental freedoms in territories subject to their jurisdiction; the obligation of states members of the FAO to communicate to the Organization upon request all laws and regulations, as well as official reports and statistics, concerning nutrition, food, and agriculture; and the right of the International Atomic Energy Agency to send into the territories of 'a recipient State' inspectors with broad powers of access.

The application of 'international inquiry', as described in the second report of the Secretary-General, has been singled out in UN debates as proving the usefulness of inquiry in preventing, rather than settling, disputes (below, pp. 313 ff).

The two studies by the Secretary-General reveal a tendency to conceive any permanent or ad hoc arrangement for the supply of information as an embodiment of the method of inquiry. Such an approach has far-reaching theoretical implications, since there is hardly any phenomenon of intercourse among nations which does not involve the communication of information.

The complexity of the problem may be discerned from the following fundamental changes in the conception of the method of inquiry emerging from the above studies:

1. Extension of the 'inquiry' from investigation into the facts only into investigation of all aspects of the dispute, whether factual, legal or political.

2. Employment of 'inquiry' by international organizations, rather than directly by the parties to the dispute.

3. Use of 'inquiry' in conjunction with other bilateral methods of settlement, e.g. conciliation or judicial settlement.

4. The power of 'commissions of inquiry' to make recommendations (e.g. UNSCOP).

5. Application of 'inquiry' in some specific, technical spheres, as a matter of routine practice for the purpose of preventing, rather than settling, disputes.

6. Routine supervision by military observation groups or peace-keeping forces.

7. Extension of the method to 'adjustment of situations', in addition to the settlement of disputes.

While most of these traits have found particular expression in the work of international organizations, the extension of 'inquiry' into all aspects of the dispute and its employment in conjunction with conciliation have also been prominent in bilateral arrangements.

An approach very similar to that of the Secretary-General was adopted by the study group set up in 1963 by the David Davies Memorial Institute of International Studies in London. The chairman and rapporteur of the group was Sir Humphrey Waldock. The results of the discussions were published in 1972 under the title *International disputes; the legal aspects.* This volume contains the report of the group and the ten memoranda on which it is based.[15] The first memorandum is in the nature of a general introduction; the others deal respectively with negotiation, mediation and good offices, conciliation, arbitration, the International Court of Justice, fact-finding and commissions of inquiry,[16] the UN and peaceful settlement, settlement of disputes in special fields, and a case study of the Argentine–Chile boundary dispute.

'Fact-finding and inquiry' (the difference between the two terms is not explained) are considered in the final report of the group as an integral

[15]A previous version of the report and the accompanying eight memoranda were published in 1966 under the title *Report of a study group on the peaceful settlement of international disputes.*

[16]A memorandum on this subject was not included in the original report.

part of the judicial function (p. 22). Similarly, fact-finding and inquiry are normally an essential part of the function of an 'arbitral or conciliation tribunal'. Fact-finding and inquiry are no less essential for the effective handling of disputes by organs of international organizations, especially by the Security Council and the General Assembly. The 'methods' of fact-finding and inquiry used by each organ necessarily depend on the nature of the competence conferred upon it.

In a section entitled 'Arbitration and fact-finding through the machinery of the Permanent Court of Arbitration' (pp. 24–5), the report notes that the Hague Conventions provide general machinery for arbitration and fact-finding centred on the facilities of the Bureau of the Permanent Court of Arbitration, but outside the framework of any political organization. As to fact-finding in particular, attention is drawn to several relevant articles of the Convention of 1907.

'Fact-finding (inquiry) as a separate procedure' is considered in the final section of the report, devoted to suggestions for improving the machinery for the peaceful settlement of disputes. The group expresses the opinion that the system of 'bilateral fact-finding Inquiries', i.e. the establishment of fact-finding commissions by the parties to the dispute, 'deserves much more attention as a means of settlement than it has hitherto received' (p. 44).

Bilateral inquiry is discussed in Darwin's memorandum on 'Fact-finding and commissions of inquiry'. As to the activities of the UN in the field of fact-finding, Darwin refers the reader to the memorandum on 'The United Nations and peaceful settlement', written by D. W. Bowett. This memorandum contains a section entitled 'Establishment of fact-finding body' (pp. 186–7), in which the author emphasizes the specific power of the Security Council to set up a subsidiary organ for the purpose of investigating 'any dispute or any situation which might lead to international friction or give rise to a dispute' (Art. 34 of the Charter). He distinguishes between fact-finding bodies dispatched to the country concerned, e.g. the 'Commission of Inquiry' to Laos (1959), and fact-finding bodies whose task is 'to investigate the evidence produced before the Security Council', e.g. the 'fact-finding sub-committee' established during the discussions of the Corfu Channel dispute in 1947, or the Spanish sub-committee set up in 1946. The latter 'technique', observes Bowett, lacks many of the advantages of 'on-the-spot' investigation, and in some cases may be quite useless.[17] However, there may be considerable advantage in a greater use of this 'impartial' (quotation marks in the original) investigation of evidence within the Security Council itself, for there will at least be an attempt to elucidate the facts and to set aside, for a time, the barrage of political propaganda.[18]

[17]Thus it would be difficult to see how an investigation of the nature of the Cuban missile sites could have been undertaken except by an 'on-the-spot' investigation (ibid., p. 187).

[18]Bowett points out that 'a good deal of investigation and fact-finding' can occur as

As to the General Assembly, he asserts that its power to engage in fact-finding is undisputed (p. 194). This was perhaps the primary role—it also included conciliation—of the Special Committee on Palestine established in 1947. Mention is also made of the special mandate of the Interim Committee to investigate disputes. Depending upon how one defines a 'dispute', it might be argued, according to the author, that bodies such as the Special Committee on Information for Non-Self-Governing Territories or the 'Committee of 24' are bodies with powers of investigation into 'disputes' with colonial powers.[19]

With regard to the role of the Secretary-General, it is stated (pp. 196–197) that he has been specifically directed to lend his good offices to governments engaged in a dispute or to enter into negotiations with governments in order to bring to an end a particular dispute. Referring to the Special Representative of the Secretary-General in Jordan, who was entrusted with the task of conducting consultations and negotiations regarding the withdrawal of foreign troops from Lebanon and Jordan, the author stresses that the 'additional function served by such Representatives of the Secretary-General is to keep him informed of the facts of a situation'. Accurate, first-hand knowledge of the facts would be essential not only to his own role in negotiating with governments, but also in advising the UN organs. Moreover, in connection with the apartheid issue with South Africa, it happened that the Secretary-General was able to visit the Union in January 1961, at a time when the South African government would not admit any UN committee into its territory. After recalling the numerous activities of the Secretary-General undertaken on his own initiative, e.g. the Peking visit in 1955 and the discussions with Israel and the Arab states in 1956, the author observes that this independent activity has in practice taken the form of fact-finding coupled with good offices or conciliation. The Malaysia Mission set up by the Secretary-General in 1963 is described in this connection as 'a fact-finding mission to ensure compliance with the principle of self-determination'.[20]

---

part of a broader peacekeeping operation, especially where observation or supervision is the primary task of the body concerned (ibid.). Reference is made to observer groups, used for two purposes: (1) to verify the facts and thus adduce the evidence on a complaint by one state against another—as with UNSCOB's investigation of Greece's charges of violation of her frontiers, or UNOGIL's investigation of the Lebanese allegation against Arab states; and (2) to verify the degree to which the parties have complied with the terms of their own agreements or the terms of a Security Council resolution designed to prevent or end hostilities, e.g. UNTSO in Palestine, UNMOGIP in Kashmir, UNYOM in Yemen, and to some extent UNTEA in West Irian (ibid., p. 200).

[19]The last-mentioned committee was charged by virtue of GA res. 1810 (XVII) of 17 Dec. 1962 to seek means for the speedy application of the Declaration on the Granting of Independence to Colonial Countries and Peoples, adopted by the Assembly on 14 Dec. 1960.

[20]On 5 Aug. 1963 the heads of government of Indonesia, Malaya, and the Philippines expressed their wish that the Secretary-General or his representative should ascertain, prior to the establishment of the Federation of Malaysia, the wishes of the people of Sabah (North Borneo) and Sarawak. This aim was to be achieved by a 'fresh approach', which in

It appears that, like the UN Secretary-General, the David Davies Study Group conceives the method of inquiry as an elastic phenomenon which finds expression in any device for acquiring information on factual matters, regardless of the existence or non-existence of a dispute. The method of inquiry is regarded as comprising a multiplicity of methods of fact-finding.

The approach adopted in Oppenheim's *International Law* (vol. ii, 7th edn, by Lauterpacht, 1952) stands in marked contrast with the studies by the Secretary-General and the David Davies group inasmuch as inquiry is not considered as a single institution which has acquired different characteristics from the period of the Hague Conferences up to the present. 'Inquiry' is treated in Oppenheim's chapter on amicable settlement of state differences in a piecemeal manner, either as a phase of negotiation, or as a stepping stone to conciliation, or as a device used by UN organs.[21] Thus, in the discussion on the method of negotiation, it is pointed out (p. 7) that one of the commonest obstacles preventing successful settlement of a dispute by means of negotiation is the difficulty of ascertaining the precise facts which have given rise to the dispute. Herein lies the value of bodies such as the International Commission of Inquiry under Hague Convention I, or the 'Permanent Commissions of Inquiry' under the Bryan treaties.

We find, in addition, two paragraphs—'International commissions of inquiry' and 'Bryan permanent commissions of inquiry'—inserted in the section on conciliation (pp. 13–16). The system envisaged in the Hague Convention and in the Bryan treaties is treated incidentally, as it were, in order to explain the growth of conciliation. In the words of the author: 'Historically, conciliation may be regarded as a development out of the International Commissions of Inquiry and the Permanent Commissions of the so-called Bryan 'cooling-off' treaties' (p. 12).[22] As regards the use of inquiry commissions, examples are given of commissions established by the parties, to the exclusion of commissions

---

the opinion of the Secretary-General was necessary to ensure complete compliance with the principle of self-determination within the requirements embodied in Principle 9 of the Declaration on the Granting of Independence to Colonial Countries and Peoples (see above p. 11, n. 19). The Secretary-General, or his representative, was to take into consideration the propriety of the elections which had taken place shortly before in Sabah and Sarawak, by examining, verifying and satisfying himself, i.a., as to whether Malaysia was a major issue and whether the elections were free. The heads of government requested, in addition, that the Secretary-General should send working parties to carry out the above task (see Joint Statement of the Heads of Government of the Republic of Indonesia, the Federation of Malaya and the Republic of the Philippines, *International legal materials*, Sept. 1963, pp. 871–2).

[21]This chapter (I) contains separate sections on 'Negotiation', 'Good offices and mediation', 'Conciliation', 'Arbitration', 'Judicial settlement', 'Conciliation in conjunction with arbitration and judicial settlement', and 'The United Nations and the settlement of disputes'. There is no section on 'inquiry'.

[22]Conciliation is defined as the process of settling a dispute by referring it to a commission whose task it is to elucidate the facts and to make a report containing proposals for a settlement.

appointed by international organizations. However, in the section on the UN and the settlement of disputes, mention is made of the powers of the Security Council to set up 'commissions of inquiry' or 'commissions of inquiry and investigation', such as the Commission of Investigation concerning Greek frontier incidents. In connection with the wide competence of the General Assembly in the settlement of disputes, it is pointed out that the Assembly, like the Security Council, is empowered to conduct investigations and to set up permanent or temporary bodies for that purpose (pp. 104–5 & 110–11).

Oppenheim's treatise does not disclose any comprehensive, independent notion of inquiry as a peaceful method for the pacific settlement of international disputes. While mediation, good offices, and conciliation are each conceived as single methods which take different forms, both in direct settlement and in the activities of permanent or ad hoc UN bodies, no parallel conception emerges with regard to inquiry. The main discussion of what seems to be inquiry as a method for the peaceful settlement of disputes is submerged in an extensive treatment of conciliation and is limited to the Hague and Bryan commissions. The appointment of commissions of inquiry by UN organs is mentioned exclusively in connection with the competence of those organs in the settlement of disputes. No distinction is drawn, as in the case of conciliation, between 'ordinary' commissions of inquiry and commissions of inquiry appointed by the UN (p. 20).

As to the meaning of 'inquiry', it is significant that the Bryan commissions are considered as commissions of inquiry, in spite of the fact that they were not so designated in the Bryan treaties themselves, and in spite of their larger competence to investigate all aspects of a dispute.[23]

The approach of Fenwick (*International law*, 4th edn, 1965) is different in several aspects. He singles out 'Commissions of inquiry' for separate treatment, along with 'Negotiation', 'Good offices' and 'Mediation', 'The procedure of conciliation', 'Arbitration', 'Provisions of the Covenant of the League of Nations', 'The Permanent Court of International Justice', 'The Charter of the United Nations', 'The International Court of Justice', and 'Inter-American regional agreements'. The author confines his short comment on 'the international institution' of commissions of inquiry to the provisions of the Hague Convention of 1899, the Dogger Bank incident, and the Hague Convention of 1907 (pp. 609–610). No mention of any possible development of the institution is made in this context. The Bryan treaties are discussed in connection

---

[23]Like Oppenheim–Lauterpacht, Stone treats the Hague commissions of inquiry and the Bryan treaties in connection with 'Growth of the methods of conciliation' (*Legal controls of international conflict* (1959), pp. 165, 171–3). The difference is that Stone points out the role of inquiry with reference to 'collective conciliation' rather than with reference to bilateral conciliation. A chapter devoted to the 'Traditional Methods of Settlement of International Disputes' is confined to the analysis of negotiation, good offices and mediation. 'Inquiry' is not treated in this chapter.

with arbitration. Contrary to Oppenheim–Lauterpacht, the commissions envisaged in these treaties are not designated as 'Commissions of Inquiry' (pp. 618–19). Fenwick notes that in contrast with the Hague commission of inquiry, the commissions under the Bryan treaties were given jurisdiction not only over the facts of the case, but over the whole question submitted.

'Inquiry' by the Council or the Assembly of the League of Nations is conceived by Fenwick in terms of the general treatment of a given dispute. No mention is made of the establishment of special 'inquiry' bodies by these two organs. While the traditional procedures of good offices and mediation are deemed to have been extended in the framework of the Covenant, no similar extension or development is noted with regard to the Hague system of inquiry.[24] The 'adaptation' of 'inquiry' from the Bryan treaties seems to have been inspired, in the author's view, by the 'cooling-off' principle of those treaties, rather than by the influence of the institution of the Hague commissions of inquiry. The failure of the author to establish any causal link between the Hague and Bryan commissions tends to support this interpretation. It would seem in the final analysis that Fenwick's conception of inquiry as a method for the peaceful settlement of disputes is narrowly confined to the system of inquiry commissions envisaged in the Hague Conventions.[25]

Guggenheim's attitude stands out by his simultaneous examination of 'inquiry' and 'conciliation', often conceived as one and the same method. His treatise (*Traité de droit international public*, vol. ii, 1954) contains a chapter entitled 'La procédure d'enquête et de conciliation', which is divided into two parts: 'Les procédures d'enquête et de conciliation en dehors des organisations internationales' and 'Les procédures de conciliation et l'enquête dans le cadre de l'organisation internationale' (ch. 3, pp. 197 ff.). In the first part the author points out that the Hague Conference of 1899 established a new method (*mode*) of settlement of international disputes, namely 'the commission of inquiry' (p. 202).[26] Once the procedure of inquiry deprived of political character had been established, the United States endeavoured to extend this solution to the procedure of mediation, the intention being to substitute for the state mediators, international commissions presided

[24]Similarly, conciliation is conceived strictly as a bilateral procedure. According to Fenwick (p. 624), the obligation of submitting disputes to inquiry by the Council gave a new impulse to what came to be known as the procedure of 'conciliation', which might be defined as 'the submission of disputes to a previously constituted commission, enjoying the confidence of the States in controversy, whose duty it was to examine all aspects of the dispute and to submit to the parties a solution based upon equity and mutual concession which they were free to accept or reject'.

[25]The treatment of pacific settlement under the Charter is confined to a summary of relevant provisions (ibid., pp. 626–7).

[26]The author then states that the Second Hague Conference regulated the procedure of inquiry, and mentions two cases handled in conformity with the Convention of 1907.

over by independent persons. Such commissions envisaged in the Bryan treaties could submit to the parties proposals for the prevention of war based on the state of facts established by the inquiry.[27] Consequently, the Bryan treaties contained at the same time elements of the procedure of inquiry and of the procedure of mediation (p. 204).

So far as the League of Nations is concerned, the Council could make proposals for a settlement and also had the right, with the consent of the parties concerned, to send a commission to the place to elucidate the state of facts (p. 221). Discussing the procedure of conciliation and inquiry followed by the UN Security Council, Guggenheim notes (p. 228) that, in conformity with Article 34 of the Charter, the Council, before entering into the merits of the dispute, must ascertain that peace is threatened. It is absolved from that obligation if it charges a commission of inquiry with this function (p. 233). With regard to the General Assembly, the author states that the provisions of Articles 10 and 14 of the Charter do not in any way limit its powers of inquiry and of recommendation (p. 238).[28] Thus, on 15 May 1947, the Assembly gave to a 'commission of inquiry' (UNSCOP) wide powers permitting it, i.a., to make proposals for the settlement of the Palestine problem.

In sum, Guggenheim distinguishes between two forms of the method of inquiry: inquiry conducted by the Hague commissions in direct service of the states in dispute, and inquiry conducted by international organizations. The latter type does not seem to be confined to commissions of inquiry established as subsidiary organs. It appears that the examination of the dispute by the Security Council itself, by virtue of Article 34 of the Charter, is conceived as an application of the method of inquiry. The same is probably true with regard to the examination of a dispute by the General Assembly in plenary meetings.

The constantly recurring simultaneous reference to both conciliation and inquiry prevents the reader from acquiring a clear understanding of the author's definition of inquiry. The problem becomes more involved in view of Guggenheim's opinion, expressed before the Institute of International Law (session of 1961), that the procedure of inquiry elaborated by the Hague Conventions is one of the three types of the procedure of conciliation, the other two being the Bryan procedure and that envisaged in the agreement between Germany and Switzerland of 1921.[29]

[27]The texts of the Bryan treaties do not suggest that the commissions have any powers of recommendation at the end of the examination.

[28]This is in contrast with the limited powers of the Security Council or its commissions to ascertain only whether the continuance of the dispute or situation is likely to endanger the maintenance of international peace and security.

[29]See 49 (ii), *Annuaire, 1961*, pp. 252–3. On the German-Swiss agreement see below, p. 123.
Like Guggenheim, Starke employs the term 'conciliation' in a wide meaning, comprising the Hague institution of inquiry. He writes (*An introduction to international law*, 6th edn (1967), p. 405) that 'Conciliation Commissions were provided for in the Hague Conventions of 1899 and 1907 for the Pacific Settlement of International Disputes'. The author

The approach of Rousseau (*Droit international public*, 1968) is different both as regards the independent status of the method of inquiry and as regards its nature after 1907. Rousseau's section on diplomatic means ('modes') of settlement contains three sub-sections, on mediation, inquiry, and conciliation, respectively.[30] With regard to inquiry, the author explains the classical system of the Hague Conventions, the resort to 'commissions of inquiry' as envisaged in the Bryan treaties, and the 'evolution' of the procedure of inquiry in the contemporary period (pp. 482–6). He relates that the procedure regulated in the Convention of 1907 consists in submitting the dispute to investigating commissioners whose sole task is 'to establish the materiality of the facts', without making any finding on responsibilities. After giving a few examples of the application of the Hague Conventions, he points out that the procedure of inquiry is also envisaged in the framework of Pan-American institutions and in certain bilateral treaties. The system of the Bryan treaties is definitely treated by Rousseau as a system of inquiry.

Under a subtitle, 'The evolution of the procedure of inquiry in the contemporary period', Rousseau deals with the use of the procedure by the League of Nations and the UN. He emphasizes that the inquiry conducted by these organizations differs from the classical inquiry of the Hague Conventions in three respects: (1) while the inquiry of 1907 is a self-sufficient, autonomous procedure, the inquiry of the League and of the UN is one element of a larger settlement—it is a means of enlightening the international organs; (2) the commission is almost always sent to the spot; and (3) the commissions established by the two organizations may not only present the facts but also propose a solution.[31]

Rousseau's conception of inquiry as an independent method clearly embraces the use of inquiry by the League and the UN as an integral part of one and the same method. The emphasis is on the 'evolution' of the classical system, special attention being paid to the differences from the original set-up. The examples are confined to commissions. Other devices of 'fact-finding' which appear abundantly in the studies

---

here refers to the respective Title III and Part III of these conventions, which provide for the establishment of 'Commissions of Inquiry', the term 'conciliation' not being used at all.

[30]These are preceded by two paragraphs on negotiations and good offices, respectively.

[31]Rousseau states that the procedure of inquiry had been utilized by the League in the Åland Islands dispute between Finland and Sweden, when a commission of rapporteurs appointed by the Council in 1920 was charged with preparing the bases for solution and with ascertaining the wishes of the population of the archipelago; in the Mosul dispute between Britain and Turkey (1924, 1925); in the Greco-Bulgarian dispute (1925); and in the Sino-Japanese dispute (1931) (ibid., p. 485). As regards the UN, the procedure of inquiry found expression in the appointment of UNSCOP (1947); in two commissions charged with investigating Greek frontier incidents (1947); in the consular commission charged with supervising the cessation of hostilities in Indonesia (1947); and in the commission charged with inquiring into the conditions for free elections in Germany (1951) (ibid., pp. 485–6).

by the Secretary-General and the David Davies study group are not mentioned. Contrary to Guggenheim, Rousseau does not seem to regard the Hague system of inquiry as an embodiment of the conciliation method. He states that conciliation is a method introduced after 1919 and notes that the task of the conciliation commissions is wider than that of the 'old commissions of inquiry', whose role was limited to ascertaining the facts (p. 487).[32]

Lastly, reference should be made to the opinion of Cot (*La conciliation internationale*, 1968), who has given close attention to the subject of our study in his section on the origins of international conciliation. He asserts, on the basis of the experience of commissions of inquiry established in accordance with the Hague Conventions, that inquiry is not a method for the pacific settlement of disputes but an instrument in the service of various possible methods. As a result, the nature of inquiry changes in accordance with the particular method which it is called upon to serve, e.g. mediation, or arbitration (p. 45).[33] If Cot's analysis is correct—a question which will be of particular interest in the course of our study—it will be difficult to arrive at a clear, unequivocal conception of 'inquiry'.

The above examination reveals a variety of approaches. On the one hand, all possible devices for ascertaining facts, or 'methods of fact-finding', are regarded as an application of the method of inquiry. (This applies equally to the use of specially appointed commissions, investigation by the permanent organs of international organizations without the help of such commissions, and routine techniques for the supply of information designed to facilitate the supervision of compliance with treaty stipulations.) On the other hand, the institution of inquiry is regarded as being confined to specially appointed commissions. Inquiry is sometimes envisaged as a method for ascertaining the facts only, while in other instances it is held to comprise the examination of all aspects of the dispute, including legal issues.

---

[32]The last statement should not be taken as referring to the Bryan commissions, since their competence went beyond the ascertainment of facts.

Rousseau's section on conciliation does not deal with any 'evolution' of the institution within the framework of the League and the UN. There is no mention of any conciliatory functions of these organizations, nor are commissions of conciliation established either by the League or by the UN included in the examples relating to the application of the method.

[33]A distinction of a somewhat different order between 'inquiry' and other 'procedures' for the pacific settlement of disputes is made by Goodrich, Hambro, and Simons (*Charter of the UN*, 3rd edn, 1969). Inquiry, according to these writers, is not, strictly speaking, a method of settlement, but rather a means for finding a basis for a settlement. The criterion of the distinction here seems to be the finality of the settlement. Thus, 'negotiation' is described as a 'method' whereby states settle their differences, and arbitration is defined as a 'method' of pacific settlement in which the parties obligate themselves in advance to accept the decision of an arbitrator or arbitral tribunal. As far as 'mediation and conciliation' are concerned, the authors do not enter into the question whether these are methods of settlement or means for finding a basis for a settlement. Mediation and conciliation are described as procedures by which third parties seek to assist the disputants to reach a settlement (see ibid., pp. 261–2).

As far as the relationship between inquiry and other methods is concerned, many authors tend to assign to inquiry a subordinate status. Inquiry is conceived either as a stepping-stone to conciliation, or as a particular form of conciliation, or as a subsidiary device designed to facilitate the solution of the dispute by other established methods. On a slightly different plane, inquiry and conciliation are treated as one and the same method, without any attempt to bring out the distinction between them.

Faced with the diverse approaches exemplified in the preceding analysis, we are confronted with a problem of definition. In view of the manifold forms and uses attributed to the method of inquiry, it would seem that there is a need to draw a line between the evolution of the institution and the loss of its identity through the addition or substitution of certain characteristics which transform it into a completely different phenomenon. While it is not our purpose to take up this challenge in its entirety, it is hoped that the present study will contribute to the clarification of the notion of inquiry as a means for the settlement of international disputes, by analysing the theory and practice of the resort to inquiry by commissions of inquiry and commissions of conciliation established by the parties to the dispute.

One of the questions to which our attention will be drawn is whether the method of inquiry should be regarded as including the power of the commission to examine all aspects of a dispute—in the sense of the Bryan treaties—as opposed to the mere ascertainment of facts—in the sense of the Hague Conventions.

So far as the employment of inquiry in conjunction with conciliation is concerned, we shall try to evaluate the role of inquiry in the work of conciliation commissions established by the parties to the dispute. It will be of interest to know, in particular, whether or to what extent inquiry into the facts and inquiry into all aspects of the dispute have become submerged in the process of conciliation.

Our attention will be focused, in addition, on the legal aspects of inquiry. The promoters of inquiry at the Hague Conferences made every effort to keep it distinct from the arbitral or judicial settlement of disputes.[34] However, practice has shown that the ascertainment of a 'simple' fact, such as the location of an incident, may have unequivocal legal implications. Moreover, certain facts, e.g. the actions of commanding officers, may have legal aspects which it may be difficult to ignore without prejudicing the thoroughness of an 'impartial and conscientious examination'. We shall examine the theory and practice in

---

[34]It is noteworthy, in this respect, that in Fauchille's treatise the discussion of commissions of inquiry appears in the chapter on 'Moyens juridiques' of pacific settlement, along with the treatment of arbitration. The chapter on 'Moyens diplomatiques' deals with diplomatic negotiations, congresses or conferences, and good offices and mediation. See *Traité de droit international public*, 8th edn. of Bonfil's *Manuel de droit international public*, i, pt 3 (1926), pp. 513 ff.

the matter, keeping in mind the changes which the Hague institution has undergone with regard to the competence of commissions of inquiry.[35]

Closely connected with the above issue is the question whether the resort to commissions of inquiry has led, or is likely to lead, to the final settlement of the dispute. Since one of the distinguishing characteristics of the Hague system of inquiry has been that the parties to the dispute are entirely free as to the effect to be given to the commission's findings on the facts, it is of interest to ascertain to what extent the recourse to a commission of inquiry is sufficient, in itself, to produce the basis of a settlement. The practice has been quite illuminating in this respect.

Another problem relating to the usefulness of commissions of inquiry bears on the nature of the disputes suitable to be handled by such commissions. The Hague institution, as we shall shortly see, was born among strong fears that it would jeopardize the independence of small states. To alleviate these fears the promoters of the inquiry method made sure that the relevant provisions of the two conventions should exclude serious disputes involving either honour or vital (subsequently 'essential') interests. Practice has indicated that states have not always adhered to the letter of these provisions. In this connection it is pertinent to assess the contribution of commissions of inquiry to the maintenance of world peace.

Our study also pays attention to the organization and procedure of commissions of inquiry and commissions of conciliation in the light of the available material. The view has been widely held that the application of rules regarding the organization and procedure of arbitral tribunals to the organization and procedure of commissions of inquiry or commissions of conciliation has had an influence going beyond strictly technical matters. We shall attempt to follow up this issue on all suitable occasions.

While our analysis will be centred on the use of inquiry by commissions established by the states in dispute and responsible to those states alone, we shall also examine the relationship between relevant bilateral arrangements, on the one hand, and the League of Nations and the UN on the other hand. A question of special interest is to what extent the two organizations responsible for the maintenance of international peace have hindered or encouraged the direct resort to inquiry by the states involved. We shall also devote our attention to the application of inquiry techniques by UN bodies, and to the theoretical significance of relevant UN deliberations.

[35]According to Schwarzenberger (*A manual of international law*, 5th edn (1967), p. 241) an inquiry conducted by an international institution serves to elicit the facts of a dispute and, occasionally, also the law applicable thereto. It appears from the context that the author has in mind inquiry conducted by commissions set up on the Hague model.

CHAPTER 2

The Institution of Inquiry under

the Hague Convention of 1899

The Russian government presented to the Hague Peace Conference of 1899 a draft convention dealing with the settlement of international disputes by means of good offices, mediation, arbitration, and international commissions of inquiry.[1] The section of the draft entitled 'International Commissions of Inquiry' reads as follows:

Article 14. In cases which may arise between the signatory States where differences of opinion with regard to local circumstances have given rise to a dispute [litige] of an international character which cannot be settled through the ordinary diplomatic channels, but wherein neither the honour nor the vital interests of these States is involved, the interested Governments agree [conviennent] to form an international commission of inquiry in order to ascertain the circumstances forming the basis of the disagreement [dissentiment] and to elucidate the facts of the case by means of an impartial and conscientious investigation [et d'éclaircir sur les lieux par un examen impartial et consciencieux toutes les questions de fait[2]].

Article 15. These international commissions are formed as follows:

Each interested Government names two members and the four members together choose the fifth member, who is also the president of the commission. In case of equal voting for the selection of a president, the two interested Governments by common agreement address a third Government or a third person, who shall name the president of the commission.

Article 16. The Governments between which a serious disagreement [dissentiment grave] or a dispute [conflit] under the conditions above indicated has arisen, undertake [s'engagent] to supply the commission of inquiry with all means and facilities necessary to a thorough and conscientious study of the facts of the case.

Article 17. The international commission of inquiry, after having stated the circumstances under which the disagreement or dispute has arisen, communicates its report to the interested Governments, signed by all the members of the commission.

[1]See Scott, *Proceedings, 1899*, pp. 797–800. The translation of the proceedings of both conferences appears in 4 volumes (as listed in the bibliography below). The original French text likewise appears in 4 volumes published at The Hague by the Netherlands Ministry for Foreign Affairs (see bibliography). Quotations from the proceedings rely, as a rule, on the English translation, but the original French terms are sometimes added in parentheses or in footnotes in order to make the intention of the drafters or speakers clearer.

[2]It will be noticed that the translation is somewhat inaccurate inasmuch as the words 'sur les lieux' have not been translated. The intention of the draftsmen obviously was that the investigation should be made 'on the spot'. For a subsequent version to that effect, see below, p. 24.

Article 18. The report of the international commission of inquiry has in no way the character of an award; it leaves the disputing Governments entire freedom either to conclude a settlement in a friendly way on the basis of the above-mentioned report, or to resort to arbitration by concluding an agreement ad hoc, or, finally, to resort to such use of force as is accepted in international relations.

The Russian initiative for the adoption of universal rules regulating the settlement of disputes by international commissions of inquiry provoked lively debates at both Hague Conferences and in the legal literature. The main issue was whether the Russian government meant to introduce a novel institution, which might perhaps be useful in the promotion of international peace but which might, at the same time, be detrimental to the independence of states. A series of more specific questions were raised in this respect: Should the recourse to commissions of inquiry be obligatory or voluntary? What should be the degree of gravity of the dispute to be submitted to a commission of inquiry? Was the reservation regarding honour or vital interests (Art. 14) to be retained? Should the inquiries be limited to 'local circumstances' verified by investigations 'on the spot' (Art. 14 & p. 20 n. 2 above), or should the scope of the inquiry be extended? To what extent, if any, were states to be bound by the report of the commissions? Should the international inquiry be an independent institution, or only a preliminary step to compulsory arbitration?[3] Was the procedure to be followed by the commissions of inquiry to be identical, similar, or different from the procedure of arbitral tribunals? Was it possible to give a finding on facts without giving a finding in law?

The Russian draft convention served as a basis for the discussions of the Committee of Examination[4] appointed by the Third Commission of the conference.[5] At the meeting of the committee held on

[3] Art. 7 of the Russian draft provided that, with regard to controversies concerning legal questions, and especially with regard to those concerning the interpretation or application of treaties in force, arbitration was recognized as being the most effective and at the same time the most equitable means for the friendly settlement of such controversies. In Art. 8 the contracting parties agreed to have recourse to arbitration in disputes involving questions of this character, so far as they did not concern the vital interests or national honour of the litigant powers.

According to Art. 10, arbitration should be obligatory in the following cases, provided that they did not concern the vital interests or national honour of the contracting states: (1) In case of differences or disputes relating to pecuniary damage suffered by a state or its nationals, as a consequence of illegal actions or negligence on the part of another state or its nationals; (2) in case of disagreement relating to the interpretation or application of treaties and conventions concerning posts, telegraphs, navigation on international rivers, inheritance, and marking of boundaries, so far as they concerned purely technical and non-political questions.

[4] The countries represented on the committee were Austria-Hungary, Belgium, France, Germany, the Netherlands, Russia, Switzerland, and the USA.

[5] This commission was charged with examining the subjects contained in point 8 of the Russian circular of 30 Dec. 1898, proposing the programme of the conference. Point 8 read: 'Acceptance, in principle, of the use of good offices, mediation, and voluntary arbitration, in cases where they are available, with the purpose of preventing armed

21 June 1899,[6] the delegate of Austria-Hungary expressed reservations with regard to the proposed obligatory character of the inquiry commissions. He recognized their beneficial value, but to declare them obligatory was, in his view, to make an innovation in the law of nations, and thus go very far indeed. The duties which Article 14 imposed on states were serious, especially when compared with the obligations of Article 16 relating to the facilities to be given to the commissions. These obligations implied an abnegation of national sovereignty and, for that reason, he suggested that the provisions of Article 14 should be made voluntary. The US and German delegates supported the above thesis and, in the absence of the Russian principal delegate, Martens (who was prevented from attending the meeting), the Committee of Examination revised Article 14 to the effect that 'the signatory States have agreed *to recommend* to the interested Governments the constitution of an international commission of inquiry (emphasis added).

A change concerning the composition of the commission of inquiry was proposed by the US delegate. In his view there should be three neutral members in addition to the four members appointed by the parties. Such a composition would strengthen the authority of the commission in the eyes of the public. Moreover, if the president was the only neutral member, he would not have much authority to make the two opposing sides accept his opinion. The committee adopted a compromise solution by qualifying the provision in Article 15 regarding the composition of the commission by the phrase 'unless otherwise stipulated'. The parties to the dispute would thus be free, in special circumstances, to agree on a composition different from that provided for in the convention.

The discussion of Article 16, providing for the duty of states to supply the commission with all the means and facilities necessary for the performance of its functions, revealed the fear of certain delegates that the commissions might interfere unduly in the internal affairs of states. The US, French, and German delegates asked who was to judge what were necessary means and facilities. It would seem difficult and dangerous, they claimed, to subscribe to such an obligation, because a state might be faced with the alternative of having to furnish or to refuse information relating to its own security. The committee accepted this reasoning and amended Article 16 to the effect that states would furnish the commission of inquiry with the said facilities '*as fully as they may think possible*' (emphasis added).[7]

---

conflicts between nations; understanding in relation to their mode of application and establishment of a uniform practice in employing them' (see Scott, *The reports to the Hague Conferences of 1899 and 1907* (1917), p. 3).

[6]See Scott, *Proceedings, 1899*, pp. 727–8.

[7]The US delegate, Holls, explains the reservation by the fear that 'an ill-advised or secretly hostile commission might demand information directly compromising the security of the state' (see Holls, *The Peace Conference at The Hague* (1900), p. 218).

The reference in the Russian draft to 'accepted' resort to force (Art. 18) subsequent to the submission of the commission's report, raised apprehensions among the members of the Committee of Examination. In order to avoid any suggestion of a right of war, the committee decided to delete the final proviso of Article 18. Thus, the three ways open to states after the filing of the report of the commission of inquiry were either to conclude a settlement in a friendly way on the basis of the report, or to have recourse to mediation, or to submit their dispute to arbitration.

At the meeting of the Committee of Examination held on 23 June 1899,[8] Martens vigorously attempted to secure the reversal of the decision, adopted in his absence, that the commissions of inquiry should be established on a voluntary basis. He maintained that international commissions of inquiry were not an innovation. They had already proved that they might be of service in controversies between two states acting in good faith, for example in boundary disputes. In such instances public opinion was aroused, especially if the dispute occurred suddenly and people were ignorant of its origins and real cause. There was a danger, he said, that because of this ignorance the dispute would become embittered. That is why the Russian delegation wished to provide for the contingency of the commission of inquiry having for its purpose first and foremost to seek and make known the truth as to the cause of the dispute and as to the materiality of the facts. The commission would be set up in order to make a report, and not to make decisions which might in any way bind the parties. But while it would be working for the purpose of making a report, time would be gained, and that was the second object which the Russian delegation had in view. Emotions would become calmer and the dispute would cease to be acute.

Martens asserted that this double and important practical result could not be obtained unless the interested governments agreed to bind themselves reciprocally to appoint these commissions—with the reservation, of course, that vital questions and the honour of states would not be affected thereby. If the committee limited itself to the mere utterance of a platonic wish, it would miss its goal.

The Committee of Examination was obviously impressed by the above arguments, but it was not prepared to restore in full the relevant provision of the Russian draft of Article 14. In a compromise solution, suggested by the delegate of Belgium, the article was revised to read that the interested governments 'agree to form, *so far as circumstances allow*' (emphasis added), an international commission of inquiry. This reservation was not accepted without some feeling of regret on the part of several members, who pointed out that, since a restriction regarding vital interests and national honour already appeared in the proposed

[8]See Scott, *Proceedings, 1899*, pp. 730–1.

provision, the grafting of a second reservation upon the first would appear to be unnecessary and difficult to explain.[9]

Following a second reading of the Russian draft on 3 July 1899, the Committee of Examination submitted to the Third Commission a revised draft of the whole section on international commissions of inquiry, as part of a general revised draft convention.[10] The crucial Article 14 of the Russian draft became Article 9 of the draft convention. At this stage the article read as follows:

In disputes of an international nature arising from a difference of opinion as to facts which may be verified by local examination, and furthermore not involving the honour or vital interests of the interested Powers, these Powers, in case they are not able to come to an agreement by means of diplomacy, agree to have recourse, so far as circumstances allow, to the institution of international commissions of inquiry in order to elucidate on the spot all the facts of the case by an impartial and conscientious investigation.[11]

At the meeting of the committee held on 18 July 1899, the US delegate reopened the discussion on the voluntary or obligatory character of the inquiry commissions.[12] He suggested that it would be best to be content with recommending the establishment of these commissions. The delegate of Austria-Hungary supported this suggestion and explained that since the speech by Martens in favour of the obligatory character of the commissions of inquiry, the principle of obligation had met with serious objections outside the Committee of Examination. It was to be feared, he said, that in the forthcoming discussion in the Third Commission certain members would ask for the omission of Article 9 entirely, and thus the whole institution would be imperilled. He proposed, therefore, to 'omit the word *obligation*'.[13] Martens replied that the proviso according to which recourse to commissions of inquiry would be had only 'if circumstances allow', furnished every guarantee. However, if there was a possibility of the text not being adopted, he would make a sacrifice and renounce the obligation.

The US delegate wished it to be explained in the report of the Committee of Examination to the Third Commission that a commission of

[9]See statement of Chevalier Descamps (Belgium), president of the committee, before the Third Commission on 7 July 1899 (Scott, *Proceedings, 1899*, p. 595).

[10]For text see ibid., p. 851.

[11]Ibid. The French text of Art. 9 read: 'Dans les litiges d'ordre international provenant d'une divergence d'appréciation sur des faits qui peuvent être l'objet d'une constatation locale, et n'engageant d'ailleurs ni l'honneur ni les intérêts vitaux des Puissances intéressées, ces Puissances, pour le cas où elles ne pourraient se mettre d'accord par les voies diplomatiques ordinaires, conviennent de recourir, en tant que les circonstances le permettent, à l'institution de Commissions internationales d'enquête, afin d'éclaircir sur place, par un examen impartial et consciencieux, toutes les questions de fait' (see Netherlands, *Conférence Internationale de la Paix, La Haye, 18 mai–29 juillet 1899* (1899), p. 259).

[12]See Scott, *Proceedings, 1899*, pp. 780–2.

[13]The word 'obligation' did not appear in the draft. The speaker was obviously referring to the legal meaning of the provision in question.

inquiry is not a form of arbitration. There was nothing in its operation which might be called 'judicial'. The parties were not represented by lawyers, and members of the commission were not judges but simply investigators.

The vice-president of the conference, the Netherlands delegate, who attended the meeting ex officio, had reservations of a different order. He noted that the inquiries of the commissions might be dangerous and embarrassing in certain circumstances, notably in the case of colonies.

In the view of the French delegate, strong opposition to the committee's proposals would come from the states which were badly administered. Such states feared that commissions of inquiry would reveal the defects of administration and thus humiliate the governments concerned. Further, they feared that, following such revelations, public opinion would be brought to bear upon them. The French delegate asserted that in these circumstances the committee should make concessions in order to attain its purpose.

A different explanation of the opposing states' motives was offered by the Swiss delegate. These states feared, he said, that obligatory international commissions of inquiry would be used as a pretext by the state which was right on the facts, to exercise moral compulsion on the state which was wrong to resort to arbitration. As a result, the commissions of inquiry would in fact be instruments of compulsory arbitration.

The alleged arguments of the so far anonymous 'opposition' brought about a change in the attitude of the German delegate. While reasserting that the text of Article 9 did not imply the principle of obligatory arbitration, he proposed that, in order to avoid a troublesome debate, the commissions of inquiry should be purely voluntary. He emphasized that international commissions of inquiry would have a varying degree of importance, depending upon the state involved: for a small state they might be dangerous, while for a large state they were not.

Following a suggestion by the president of the Third Commission (the French delegate), the committee decided to reserve its decision on the proposal to omit any reference to obligation, until after the discussion in the commission.

The confrontation which took place in the Third Commission during its first reading of Section 3 [International Commissions of Inquiry] of the draft convention was described in the following manner by the president of the US delegation, White:

July 19. Field day in the arbitration committee. [The reference is to the Third Commission.] A decided sensation was produced by vigorous speeches by my Berlin colleague, Beldiman, of the Roumanian delegation, by Servian and other delegates, against the provision for *commissions d'enquête*—De Martens, Descamps and others making vigorous speeches in behalf of them. It looked as if the Balkan states were likely to withdraw from the conference if the *commissions d'enquête* feature was insisted upon: they are evidently afraid that such 'examining commissions' may be sent within their boundaries by some of their big neighbours—Russia, for example—to spy out the land and start intrigues. The whole matter was put over. . . .[14]

The attack on the provisions concerning international commissions of inquiry was led, indeed, by the Romanian delegate, Beldiman, who was supported by the Serbian and Greek delegates. Beldiman declared that the Romanian government was not prepared to adhere to the articles which comprised Section 3. There was an essential difference, he said, between the mixed commissions of inquiry which had frequently been resorted to in practice, especially between neighbouring states, and the institution of international law which was proposed. Romania, for example, had on many occasions had recourse, in its neighbourly relations with Russia, Austria-Hungary, and Bulgaria, to such mixed commissions, whose mission was to ascertain, or clear up on the spot, facts which had given rise to an incident or controversy. These commissions had often been very serviceable by furnishing the governments concerned with the data necessary to settle together differences provoked by certain facts of a local character. From this point of view there was no innovation in the institution proposed. But the obligatory principle and the composition of the proposed commissions were an innovation. If the new principle were to be adopted for cases of local investigation which were so frequent and which hitherto had been left entirely to the unrestricted judgement of the governments, it was to be feared that the practical application of the obligatory provision, far from facilitating the solution of the dispute in question, would, on the contrary, give rise to serious difficulties. For to be obliged in certain cases to accept an international investigation by virtue of a treaty provision, instead of having, as in the past, complete freedom of action, might at a particular moment confront a state with serious political complications.

With reference to the composition of the inquiry commissions, Beldiman noted that if the draft were to become public law, membership in such commissions would not, as hitherto, be restricted exclusively to representatives of the states directly interested in the dispute, but the door would be thrown open to the intervention of third powers.

Another Power may propose a commission of inquiry in circumstances that do not suit us [he said]. Numerous cases may arise that are very important to our kingdom but not appropriate to invoke honour or vital interests. . . . And will it not frequently happen that various powers in dispute are unevenly matched?

The Serbian delegate was prepared to recognize that in exceptional circumstances international inquiry represented a useful assertion of authority. However, in the relations between great powers on the one

[14]See *Autobiography of Andrew Dickson White*, ii (1922), p. 336. See also Scott, *Proceedings, 1899*, pp. 627–43.

hand, and small states on the other, the question arose whether in practice the great powers would always show a disposition to recognize that small states had the same susceptibilities in the matter of honour and vital interests as they themselves would certainly not fail to have. Would not the small states be drawn into humiliating discussions as to whether in such and such a case their national honour was really involved, while, on the other hand, it would frequently suffice for the great powers to invoke the argument of national honour to make it impossible for small states to bring the subject to discussion?

Asking for the omission of Section 3, the Serbian delegate further asserted that public opinion in small states would no longer regard inquiry commissions as a means for impartial ascertainment of the real facts with a view to facilitating the work of justice, but as an outward sign of inferiority and dependence. Public opinion in the small states would therefore never accept such commissions.[15]

Martens maintained that the international commissions of inquiry had no political aim and did not meddle with the policies of either big or small states. He took the opportunity of further elaborating his conception of the task and importance of the commissions. Suppose, he said, the authorities at a frontier arrested somebody on foreign territory. A most serious dispute might arise. The more obscure the circumstances remained, the more would popular feeling be inflamed. Newspaper articles and questions in parliament might force the hand of governments and involve them in conduct that was the very opposite of their intentions. One might compare these commissions of inquiry to a safety valve, as the governments concerned would be able to say to an over-excited and ill-informed public opinion: 'Wait. We shall organize a commission which will go to the spot and secure all the necessary information.' In that way time would be gained, and in international life a day gained might save the future of a nation.

Support for the draft of the Committee of Examination was also expressed by Rolin, the delegate of Siam. He saw the value of the inquiry method not only in preventing governments from falling into error and public opinion from being led astray, but also in promoting arbitration between states. In his view, a controversy between states would very rarely have to do with a question of fact. The ascertaining of facts would generally be nothing more than a natural and necessary prelude to a legal argument. He believed, therefore, that arbitration must necessarily follow upon investigation, in default of an immediate

---

[15]The motion for the deletion of Section 3 was also supported by the Greek delegate, on grounds similar to those outlined above.

The Bulgarian delegate, however, had apparently no political reason to fear the consequences of the Russian initiative. He objected to the reservations made by the delegates of the three states bordering on Bulgaria. However, in order to allay any apprehensions regarding the possible violation of the independence of states, he suggested an amendment to Art. 13 (formerly Art. 18), to the effect that the parties might consider the report as never having been made. See below, p. 30.

agreement. The Siamese government, he declared, would consider the prior conclusion of a *compromis* as the principal condition on which it would be able to consent to an investigation of disputed facts on its territory by an international commission of inquiry.

At this stage of the discussion the Third Commission was not prepared to take a decision on the proposals for deletion or amendment of draft Section 3. The Commission adopted the draft on first reading,[16] leaving the Committee of Examination to draw its conclusion from the preceding debates.

The next meeting of the Committee of Examination, which took place on the same day (19 July, 1899),[17] was attended by the representatives of Bulgaria, Greece, Romania, and Serbia.[18] Martens declared that he was prepared to accept the sacrifice of agreeing to the voluntary character of the international commissions of inquiry on the understanding that the states concerned would be under a moral obligation to resort to such commissions. That moral obligation would be similar to the one incurred by states which are reminded to have recourse to the Permanent Court of Arbitration, in accordance with Article 27 of the draft convention.[19] As to the alleged discrimination against small states, Martens wondered why such states did not wish to profit by the guarantees provided in the text. Weak states could invoke the clause on vital interests in the smallest dispute with great powers, while it would be difficult to understand the action of a great power in arguing about its own vital interests in order to avoid an inquiry asked for by a small state.

The president and rapporteur of the committee, Descamps (Belgium), shared in particular the latter view: 'Every time that an international court is established in the world, there are more chances for it to serve as a defence to the weak than to the strong', he said.[20]

Following Martens's retreat, the committee agreed on the following revised text of Article 9:

[16]Two different English versions of the text submitted to the Third Commission appear in Scott's *Proceedings, 1899*. The text of Art. 9 adopted by the Third Commission on first reading (without changes) appears in the record of the meeting of 19 July 1899 in the following terms: 'In disputes of an international nature arising from a difference of opinion regarding facts which may form the object of local determination, and besides involving neither the honour nor vital interests of the interested powers, these powers, in case they cannot come to an agreement by the ordinary means of diplomacy, agree to have recourse, so far as circumstances allow, to the institution of international commissions of inquiry, in order to elucidate on the spot, by means of an impartial and conscientious investigation, all the facts' (ibid., p. 644). For the other English version and for the French version see above, p. 24.

[17]Scott, *Proceedings, 1899*, pp. 790–4.

[18]These representatives were not members of the Committee of Examination. For the composition of the committee see above, p. 21, n. 4.

[19]For text see Scott, *Proceedings, 1899*, p. 135.

[20]By using the expression 'international court' Descamps appears to have assimilated commissions of inquiry to courts of law.

In disputes of an international nature arising from a difference of opinion regarding facts, the signatory powers *deem it expedient*, to facilitate the solution of these disputes, that the parties who have not been able to come to an agreement by means of diplomacy should institute international commissions of inquiry in order to elucidate all the facts by means of an impartial and conscientious investigation (emphasis added).

The obligation expressed in the original text having been suppressed, the committee thought that there was no reason to retain the reservation entitling a state to refuse inquiry if its *honour* and *vital interests* were involved, or if particular circumstances warranted, in its opinion, such refusal. Moreover, the committee deleted the expressions 'which may form the object of local determination' and 'on the spot', as being inexact.[21]

The question of the similarity of international commissions of inquiry to arbitral tribunals was discussed by the committee in connection with the provisions on procedure. The delegate of Luxembourg proposed an amendment to Article 10 to the effect that the procedure of inquiry should be governed by the principles relating to arbitral procedure, so far as these principles were applicable to the institution of international commissions of inquiry. The German delegate responded that the commissions of inquiry should remain distinct from arbitration, and that they should themselves determine their procedure. Martens shared this view. The purpose of the commissions of inquiry was neither to provoke an arbitration nor to prevent one. They had an entirely separate existence and their purpose was '*to state*', by common agreement between the parties, the material causes of the dispute. The parties might take advantage of the inquiry in order to have recourse to arbitration, or, on the contrary, they might settle the matter in a friendly manner.[22] The Netherlands delegate supported Martens on the distinction between inquiry and arbitration, but suggested that the rules of procedure be formulated in Article 10 itself.

As a result, the Committee of Examination agreed to include in Article 10 the following basic rules: (1) the act instituting the inquiry should state explicitly the facts to be examined; (2) both sides should be heard, each party being informed of all statements of the opposing party;[23] (3) the commission of inquiry should determine the forms and periods to be observed.

[21]See statement of the president of the committee before the Third Commission on 22 July 1899 (Scott, *Proceedings, 1899*, p. 670). The two omitted expressions are from the English version given at p. 28, n. 16, above.

[22]Mérignhac (*La Conférence Internationale de la Paix* (1900), p. 286) notes that the reasoning of the delegates of Germany and Russia was questionable. The delegate of Luxembourg had no intention of putting on the same plane two institutions, different in their aim and in their result; he simply wanted—bearing in mind that in both cases there was a 'procès', i.e. a contest—that the commissions of inquiry should utilize those parts of the arbitral procedure which, upon examination, could be applied.

[23]For the final text of Art. 10 in English and French see below, p. 32. According to

With regard to Article 13, dealing with the report of the commissions, the Bulgarian delegate suggested an amendment to the effect that the parties would be entitled to consider the report 'as not having been made'. He was clearly in favour of commissions of inquiry, because he thought that one should increase the 'juridical means' to be opposed to the direct diplomatic contacts between two states—contacts in which the *ultima ratio* was always reliance upon armed force. However, in order to allay the apprehensions of certain Balkan states, he proposed the above amendment. While the Greek delegate supported the motion, the Belgian and Russian delegates objected. The Belgian delegate asserted that the report of the commissions of inquiry would simply state the facts and could not result in imposing obligations upon the parties. Martens, on his part, claimed that it was not necessary to go so far as to accept a text which would permit a power to ignore the statement of facts. The committee was not prepared to accept the far-reaching Bulgarian proposal and took no action on it.

The second reading of the Russian draft by the Third Commission, on 22 July 1899,[24] revealed that Romania was still not satisfied with the concessions made to her. While the Greek and Serbian delegations accepted the revised text of Section 3 without reservations, the Romanian delegation submitted for approval the following text of Article 9 communicated by the Romanian government:

In disputes of an international nature *involving neither honour nor essential interests*, and arising from a difference of opinion on points of fact, the signatory powers deem it expedient that the parties who have not been able to come to an agreement by means of diplomacy, should, *as far as circumstances allow*, institute an international commission of inquiry to facilitate a solution of these disputes by elucidating the facts by means of an impartial and con- scientious investigation.[25]

The object of the Romanian amendments obviously was to emphasize the purely optional character of the recourse to an international com- mission of inquiry, by restoring the reservations with regard to honour, interests, and circumstances, and by strengthening the reservations about 'interests' to embrace not only 'vital' interests but also interests which are considered by the state concerned as 'essential'.

In the face of the determined stand of the Romanian delegation, the Third Commission saw no other way of obtaining results in its delibera- tions on Section 3 than by accepting the Romanian text of Article 9 in its entirety. According to La Pradelle, the delegates of Great Britain,

---

Gasc's *Dict. of the French and English languages* (1945) the term 'contradictoirement' in the context of legal proceedings means that both sides must be heard in the presence of each other.

[24]See Scott, *Proceedings, 1899*, pp. 669–73.
[25]Ibid., p. 116 (emphasis added).

Italy, and Austria supported Beldiman's proposal since the great powers understood that international commissions of inquiry could be more embarrassing for big states than for small ones.[26] The only consolation for those who yielded grudgingly to Romania's pressure was that Romania did not insist on retaining the provision to the effect that the commissions of inquiry should deal only with local incidents. As pointed out by the Netherlands delegate, the omission of the expressions 'which may form the object of local determination' and 'on the spot' gave the institution a more general scope, by extending it to all questions concerning points of fact.[27]

The text of Section 3, as agreed upon by the Third Commission, was adopted by the seventh plenary meeting of the conference on 25 July 1899. The doubts and apprehensions which underlay the debate of the Committee of Examination found expression even at this last stage, when the delegate of Turkey declared that the recourse to international commissions of inquiry was purely facultative, and that the imperial government would be the sole judge in deciding whether Turkey should or should not accept the establishment of an international commission of inquiry in pursuance of Section 3. In his view, the provisions on inquiry were not to be applied to the internal regulations of the states concerned. As we shall see presently, Turkey had special reasons to fear the universal endorsement of international commissions of inquiry (cf. below, p. 35).

To sum up, the final text of Part III (formerly Section 3) of the Convention of 1899 for the Pacific Settlement of International Disputes reads as follows:[28]

Part III. International Commissions of Inquiry

Art. 9. In disputes of an international nature involving neither honour nor essential interests, and arising from a difference of opinion on points of fact, the signatory powers deem it

Titre III. Des Commissions internationales d'enquête

Art. 9. Dans les litiges d'ordre international n'engageant ni l'honneur ni des intérêts essentiels et provenant d'une divergence d'appréciation sur des points de fait, les Puissances

[26]See La Pradelle, 'La conférence de la Paix (La Haye, 18 mai–29 juillet 1899)', in 6 *RGDIP* (1899), 775. The author notes that even in the USA there were expressions of anxiety lest Europe should intervene in the affairs of America under cover of commissions of inquiry (ibid., p. 771).

[27]The president of the commission noted that in maritime disputes examination on the spot was not practicable (Scott, *Proceedings, 1899*, p. 673).

[28]See Scott, *Proceedings, 1899*, pp. 237–8. (For a list of the parties to the convention see the note at pp. 338–9 below.) The English text used by the PCA differs from that published in Scott's *Proceedings* (see the pamphlet published by the Court under the title *Convention for the pacific settlement of international disputes, concluded at The Hague on July 29th 1899* (May 1957). I am grateful to Baron E. O. van Boetzelaer, Secretary-General of the Court, for sending me the English text of the 1899 and 1907 Conventions used by the Court. For the French text see Netherlands, *Conférence Internationale de la Paix* (1899), pp. 224–34; Martens, *Nouveau recueil général de traités*, 2nd ser., xxvi (1901), pp. 920–49. It was also published by the PCA in 1901.

expedient that the parties who have not been able to come to an agreement by means of diplomacy, should, as far as circumstances allow, institute an international commission of inquiry, to facilitate a solution of these disputes by elucidating the facts by means of an impartial and conscientious investigation.

Art. 10. The international commissions of inquiry are constituted by special agreement between the parties in dispute.

The inquiry convention defines the facts to be examined and the extent of the powers of the commissioners.

It settles the procedure.

At an inquiry both sides must be heard.

The form and the periods to be observed, if not stated in the inquiry convention, are decided by the commission itself.

Art. 11. International commissions of inquiry are formed, unless otherwise stipulated, in the manner determined by Article 32 of the present Convention.[30]

Art. 12. The Powers in dispute undertake to supply the international commission of inquiry as fully as they may think possible, with all means and facilities necessary to enable it to become completely acquainted with and to accurately understand the facts in question.

signataires jugent utile que les Parties qui n'auraient pu se mettre d'accord par les voies diplomatiques instituent, en tant que les circonstances le permettront, une Commission internationale d'enquête chargée de faciliter la solution de ces litiges en éclaircissant, par un examen impartial et consciencieux, les questions de fait.[29]

Art. 10. Les Commissions internationales d'enquête sont constituées par convention spéciale entre les Parties en litige.

La convention d'enquête précise les faits à examiner et l'étendue des pouvoirs des commissaires.

Elle règle la procédure.

L'enquête a lieu contradictoirement.

La forme et les délais à observer, en tant qu'ils ne sont pas fixés par la convention d'enquête, sont déterminés par la Commission elle-même.

Art. 11. Les Commissions internationales d'enquête sont formées, sauf stipulation contraire, de la manière déterminée par l'article 32 de la présente Convention.

Art. 12. Les Puissances en litige s'engagent à fournir à la Commission internationale d'enquête, dans la plus large mesure qu'elles jugeront possible, tous les moyens et toutes les facilités nécessaires pour la connaissance complète et l'appréciation exacte des faits en question.

[29]It should be pointed out that the phrase 'les Puissances signataires jugent utile' is incorrectly translated in the version published by the PCA as 'the signatory Powers recommend'. As we have seen, the use of the term 'recommend' was particularly opposed by certain delegates at the conference and it was therefore replaced by 'deem it expedient'.

[30]Art. 32 provides (in part):

'. . . Failing the constitution of the [arbitral] tribunal by direct agreement between the parties, the following course shall be pursued:

'Each party appoints two arbitrators, and these together choose an umpire.

'If the votes are equally divided the choice of an umpire is entrusted to a third Power selected by the parties by common accord.

'If an agreement is not arrived at on this subject, each party selects a different Power, and the choice of the umpire is made in concert by the Powers thus selected.'

Art. 13. The international commission of inquiry communicates its report to the Powers in dispute, signed by all the members of the commission.

Art. 14. The report of the international commission of inquiry is limited to a finding of facts, and has in no way the character of an award. It leaves to the Powers in dispute entire freedom as to the effect to be given to this finding.

Art. 13. La Commission internationale d'enquête présente aux Puissances en litige son rapport signé par tous les membres de la Commission.

Art. 14. Le rapport de la Commission internationale d'enquête, limité à la constatation des faits, n'a nullement le caractère d'une sentence arbitrale. Il laisse aux Puissances en litige une entière liberté pour la suite à donner à cette constatation.

The above examination has enabled us to trace the main issues relating to the institution of international commissions of inquiry as they emerged from the various texts and statements. We can now proceed to a clarification of these issues with the help of other sources.

An article written by Martens[31] soon after the Hague Conference of 1899 is particularly valuable for an understanding of the ideas of the Russian delegate with regard to the nature of the institution of inquiry. Martens asserts the practical value of the Russian proposal by reference to the cases of Schnaebelé and the *Maine*. In addition, he supports his claim that international commissions of inquiry are not innovations, by reference to the inquiry concerning the massacre of Armenians in Turkey.[32] The first two cases were not submitted to international commissions of inquiry, but are given as examples of suitable instances in which disputes could have been satisfactorily settled, or at least dealt with, by such commissions.

M. Schnaebelé, a French police inspector, was arrested in 1887 by the German authorities on the Franco-German frontier, as he was proceeding to Ars-sur-Moselle to have an interview with the German police inspector there. He was accused of transmitting information on German fortifications to the French government. A dispute followed between the two countries as to whether the arrest had taken place on French or on German soil. Shortly after, M. Schnaebelé was released by order of the German emperor. In a dispatch forwarded to the French ambassador in Berlin, Prince Bismarck explained that, although the German government considered that, in view of the proofs of his guilt, M. Schnaebelé's arrest was fully justified, it had found it expedient to set him at liberty on the general principle that business meetings of frontier officials 'must always be regarded as protected by a mutually assured safe-conduct'.[33]

The second incident which seems to have prompted Martens to

[31]'International arbitration and the Peace Conference at the Hague,' *NAR*, 169 (1899), pp. 604–24.
[32]Ibid., pp. 612–13.
[33]See *Annual Register, 1887*, p. 247.

develop his 'safety valve' theory, concerns the incident involving the US battleship *Maine*. An explosion which took place on 15 February 1898 in the harbour of Havana, destroyed the vessel and caused the death of 259 of her officers and crew.[34] In view of the tense relations between the United States and Spain at that period, suspicions were widespread in the United States that the Spanish government was responsible for the explosion. The Spanish government proposed an international inquiry into the incident, but the US government declined the 'offer'[35] and set up a commission of inquiry consisting of three US naval officers. The commission found that the vessel had been destroyed by a submarine mine, but that there was no evidence then obtainable to fix the responsibility.

The Spanish government indignantly denied any responsibility for the disaster, and also held a commission of inquiry, which found that the explosion had come from an internal cause. The two opposing conclusions reached by the inquiry commissions established by each party increased the international tension. 'Excitement was aroused to fever heat' by the American press. 'Violent scenes' took place in the Congress.[36] On 18 March 1898 President McKinley transmitted to the Congress the report of the *Maine* commission of inquiry. On 11 April he issued a message reviewing the 'intolerable' state of affairs in Cuba since the beginning of the Cuban insurrection. On 20 April the United States forwarded an ultimatum to Spain, demanding the withdrawal of Spanish forces from Cuba. The Spanish Cortes formally recognized a state of war on 24 April, and on the next day the US Congress voted that war had existed between the United States and Spain from 21 April, for on that day the president had proclaimed a blockade of the Cuban coast.

The *Maine* incident has been generally regarded as the immediate cause of the Spanish-American War. In the words of T. J. Lawrence, it was an article of faith in the United States that the battleship had been treacherously blown up by the Spaniards and 'this belief on a matter of fact was one of the most potent causes of the war which soon afterwards broke out . . .'.[37]

The incident is illustrative of the likelihood that when each of the disputing states appoints a commission of inquiry from among its own nationals, the findings of the two commissions will contradict each other.[38] Furthermore, if a mixed inquiry commission based on parity

[34]For a description of the incident and subsequent developments see ibid., *1898*, pp. 362–363.

[35]See Low, 'The International Conference of Peace', *NAR*, 169 (1899), p. 635.

[36]Ibid., p. 362.

[37]*International problems and Hague conferences* (1908), p. 56.

[38]Lawrence explains the diametrically opposite findings of the two *Maine* commissions by the fact that one was appointed by the US government and the other by the Spanish authorities, 'and thus the elements of passion and bias were not eliminated' (ibid.).

had been established, it would certainly have reached a deadlock, because of the uncompromisingly opposed views of the national commissioners. On the other hand, a single commission with a neutral president has a better chance of establishing the real facts. From the practical point of view it is doubtful whether an international commission of inquiry could possibly have been established following the *Maine* incident. The general opinion is that the United States was determined, prior to the incident, to start a war against Spain, and that she used the incident as a convenient pretext to pursue her aim.[39]

The only historical precedent for international commissions of inquiry cited by Martens in his article is the inquiry, conducted jointly by three great powers and Turkey, into the circumstances of the Armenian massacres of 1894. Taking account of an intensive public movement on behalf of the persecuted Armenians of Turkish Anatolia, the British government invited the other five great powers to deal with the problem. France, Italy, and Russia acceded to the request, while Austria and Germany appeared uninterested. The four powers, France, Great Britain, Italy, and Russia, suggested the establishment of a mixed commission of inquiry composed of their own representatives and those of Turkey. As a result the Ottoman government appointed a commission of five members, all Turks,[40] 'and obtained from the Powers represented at Erzerum authority for their Consuls to be represented by Delegates attached to the Commission'.[41] Three delegates were designated respectively by the French, British, and Russian consuls at Erzerum. The commission thus composed was charged with determining the origins of the massacres, the facts relating to the killings and the destruction of property, and the responsibilities involved.

During 1895 the commission held 107 sittings and heard 190 witnesses.

[39]See, for instance, Pillet, *La cause de la paix et les deux conférences de La Haye* (1908), p. 14: 'Si une commission d'enquête [the author refers to international commissions on the Hague model] avait été réunie et avait décidé que l'accident avait été purement fortuit—pense-t-on que cette décision aurait détourné les Etats-Unis de leurs projets belliqueux contre l'Espagne? Il faudrait toute la naïveté du bon abbé de Saint Pierre pour penser ainsi. Les Etats-Unis voulaient mettre la main sur Cuba. Ils ont profité de l'occasion qui s'offrait à eux. Si cette occasion avait fait défaut, ils en auraient attendu et, au besoin, suscité une autre, et le résultat aurait été le même.'
Scott, on the other hand, makes a more optimistic appraisal of a possible international inquiry into the *Maine* incident. He writes: '. . . It cannot be doubted that its existence [of an international commission on the Hague model] in the year 1898 would have brought pressure upon Spain and the United States to submit the question of the Maine to an international commission of inquiry, in order that the facts be established by means of an impartial, that is to say, international, and conscientious investigation. It can not be said that the explosion of the Maine was the direct or proximate cause of the war with Spain; but the elimination of the incident might have prompted the two nations to adjust their other difficulties without an appeal to the sword' (*The Hague Peace Conferences of 1899 and 1907* (1909), p. 268).
[40]The president of the commission was Shefik Bey. One of the five members withdrew a week after the beginning of the commission's work.
[41]See C. 7894, No. 252. Inclosure: Report of the Consular Delegates attached to the Commission appointed to inquire into the Events at Sassoon (Eng. trans. at pp. 161–89). The quotation is from p. 161.

The delegates of the powers participated actively in the inquiries, in spite of the uncooperative attitude of their Turkish colleagues. The commission visited the region of Sasun affected by the events of the preceding year. In a report adopted on 20 July 1895, and presented by the British government to parliament in September 1895,[42] the representatives of the three great powers estimated that some 900 deaths had been caused by the bloody events of August and September 1894 in the region of Sasun. They found, in addition, that a certain number of Armenian refugees were massacred, without distinction of age or sex, by Turkish soldiers and policemen and by Kurds. The three representatives also established that much destruction of property had taken place in the Armenian regions.

The results of the inquiry were considered of great importance as they made possible a better appreciation of the subsequent intolerable policy of the Turkish government towards the Armenian population. In fact, the inquiry itself stimulated all six great powers to undertake intensive diplomatic interventions with the purpose of bringing about administrative reforms in the Armenian provinces of the Ottoman empire. At the end of 1895 these interventions, supported by a naval demonstration at Constantinople, compelled the sultan to promulgate reforms entailing the reorganization of the gendarmerie and police forces and the improvement of the administrative and judicial services in the Armenian provinces.[43]

While Martens relates in his article that he referred at the Hague Conference of 1899 to the cases of Schnaebelé and the *Maine*, it is not clear whether he also relied at the conference on the 'example'[44] of the inquiry in Turkey. In any event, his speeches as recorded summarily in the records of the conference contain no reference to the inquiry in Anatolia. Moreover, the circumstances which he described in his speeches as suitable for the establishment of international commissions of inquiry are almost identical with those surrounding the Schnaebelé and *Maine* cases, but they are in direct contrast to those of the Armenian investigation. While the Hague institution is based upon a genuinely voluntary agreement between two states to submit a dispute to an international commission of inquiry, the agreement of Turkey was secured by political pressure exercised by three great powers. As regards the subject of the inquiry, the Hague records do not reveal any intention that

[42]See text ibid., pp. 161–89.

[43]See 'Chronique des faits internationaux: Turquie; La question arménienne; Intervention européenne', 3 *RGDIP* (1896), 88–128.

By Art. 61 of the treaty between Austria, France, Germany, Great Britain, Italy, Russia, and Turkey for the settlement of affairs in the east, signed at Berlin on 13 July 1878, the Sublime Porte undertook to carry out 'without further delay, the improvement and reforms demanded by local requirements in the provinces inhabited by Armenians, and to guarantee their security against the Circassians and Kurds'. For the text of the treaty see 2 *AJIL* (1908), Official Documents, pp. 401 ff.

[44]*NAR*, 169 (1899), p. 613.

inquiry commissions should deal with disputes relating to a state's treatment of its own citizens. The evidence is that the treatment by one state of the citizens of another state could not be the subject of an international inquiry. To the extent that the subject of internal policies was raised at the conference, express reservations were made to the effect that the commissions should not deal with such policies (pp. 22, 25 26, & 31 above). As regards composition, there is no indication whatsoever that the draftsmen of the convention envisaged a commission composed, as in the Armenian case, of three representatives from one side and four representatives from the other side. The rule unanimously adopted at The Hague was that of equal 'representation' of both sides, in the sense that each appoints an equal number of members to the commission. To this equal number is added a single, neutral, president, or, in the case of the US proposal, three neutral members. There is no doubt that in the Turkish case the three great powers assumed the role of neutral members, a position wholly inconsistent with that which emerged at The Hague. This peculiar composition of the commission which inquired into the Armenian massacres led to action based on a report by the minority. The great powers, far from letting Turkey have 'entire freedom as to the effect to be given' to the findings of the report,[45] put diplomatic and physical pressure on her to introduce the internal reforms necessitated by the factual state of affairs as revealed in the report presented by the three 'Delegates' who were, in effect, minority members of the commission. In sum, the inquiry in Turkey is entirely different from the institution of inquiry as conceived at the First Hague Peace Conference.

It is likely that, if Martens avoided mentioning the Armenian inquiry in his speeches at the conference, his purpose was to prevent raising the suspicions of small states that the Russian proposal aimed at ensuring the institutionalization of intervention by the great powers in the internal affairs of small states. The Turkish example was still very fresh in the minds of the delegates from Eastern Europe.[46]

Another instance of great power intervention—associated both with a naval demonstration and with an international inquiry—which might have underlain the apprehensions of the Greek delegation in particular, is that concerning Don Pacifico.[47] The commission established in this case had been regarded as the only known example prior to 1899 of an international commission of inquiry comprising a neutral element, which resembles the Hague commissions of inquiry.[48] In 1847 a riotous

---

[45]Art. 14 of the Hague Convention of 1899.

[46]Cf. Beaucourt, *Les commissions internationales d'enquête* (1909), p. 94; and above, p. 3.

[47]See Whiteman, *Damages in international law*, ii (1937), p. 839; Stuyt, *Survey of international arbitrations, 1794–1970* (1972), p. 46; La Pradelle & Politis, *Recueil des arbitrages internationaux*, 2nd edn, i: *1798–1855* (1957), pp. 580–97; Oppenheim, ii, 137–8.

[48]Politis, 'Les commissions internationales d'enquête', 19 *RGDIP* (1912), 152 n. 1.

mob, aided by Greek soldiers, plundered the house of Don Pacifico, a British subject living in Athens. Britain claimed damages from Greece for the losses sustained. Greece refused to comply, maintaining correctly[49] that Don Pacifico should have first sought redress in the Greek courts. Britain continued to press her claims[50] and, following a 24-hour ultimatum issued on 18 January 1850, blockaded the Greek coast. As a result of French mediation the blockade was lifted and the two disputing governments concluded, on 18 July 1850, an agreement[51] in which the Greek government undertook to indemnify Don Pacifico after 'a full and fair investigation' ('une enquête complète et de bonne foi') had proved that he had suffered injury as a result of the destruction or loss of certain documents. (These documents related to Pacifico's claims against Portugal for losses sustained by him during the civil war in Portugal, and for salary and expenses while he was Portugal's consul-general in Greece.) The agreement provided that, for the purpose of conducting the investigation, 'two arbiters, with an umpire to decide between them in case of difference' were to be appointed by the joint agreement of the governments of France, Britain, and Greece, and that this 'Commission of Arbitration'[52] was to report to the British and Greek governments whether any, and if any what amount, of real injury had been sustained by Don Pacifico by reason of the alleged loss of the documents.

The commission[53] stated in its report[54] that it had discovered in the archives of the Cortes at Lisbon the original and certified copies of the documents containing the most important of Pacifico's claims against Portugal. Pacifico was still able to present these claims if they were properly founded, although he had apparently neglected to present them promptly. In the opinion of the commission, Pacifico had sustained no actual pecuniary loss on account of the destruction in Greece of documents bearing on these claims. However, taking into consideration the possibility that a few documents of no great importance might have been lost when his house in Athens was pillaged and also the expenses which he had incurred during the investigation, the commissioners were of the opinion that he was entitled to receive the sum

[49]See Oppenheim, ii, 138.

[50]While Britain also insisted on the payment of previous claims on behalf of other British subjects, it was clear that she was specially concerned with that of Don Pacifico. The other claims were subsequently settled by diplomatic negotiations between France, Britain, and Greece.

[51]See *Hertslet's commercial treaties*, ix (1856), pp. 497–501 (Eng. & French texts); La Pradelle & Politis, i. 589 (French text).

[52]Politis describes the commission as 'commission arbitrale d'enquête' (see La Pradelle & Politis, i. 590).

[53]The members of the commission were Patrick Francis Campbell Johnston, for Britain; George Torlades O'Neill (Greek consul-general at Lisbon), for Greece; and Léon Béclard (umpire) (secretary of the French legation at Lisbon), for France.

[54]For the English text see *Hertslet's commercial treaties*, ix. 501–3, and for the French text La Pradelle & Politis, i. 593–5.

of £150 from the Greek government. In conclusion, the commissioners expressed their opinion that Britain 'has had but one object in view in this inquiry, namely, a fair, impartial, and honest solution of a difficult question'.

It will be noted that while the above commission resembles the Hague commissions of inquiry in so far as its main task was to establish certain facts and to report its findings to the parties, it is distinguished by its obviously arbitral character, as witness the designation of the commission and of the commissioners in the agreement, as well as the advance undertaking of the parties to accept the findings of the commission.

In addition to the above concrete examples, which the participants in the First Hague Conference had, or might have had, in mind, we may point out another instance, which was discovered by historical research after the conference, and which was considered as a 'precedent' for the Hague commissions of inquiry.[55] As early as the sixteenth century England and Scotland observed periodically a 'Day of Trewes' on which the English Warden of the Marches met the Scottish Warden of the Marches at an appointed place. Each side undertook to cease pursuing its feuds for a period of twenty-four hours. The English Warden then nominated six Scots and the Scottish Warden six Englishmen to examine with them the 'Bills of Complaint' received from citizens of both sides. The 'commission' conducted an inquiry into each case, and decided whether the bill was 'foul' or 'clear'. Anyone found 'culpable in bills' was ordered to pay compensation for the loss or damage caused, and the Warden of his nationality had to see that on the next 'Day of Trewes' he was handed over to the opposite Warden for punishment, if necessary.

It is doubtful whether the practice of England and Scotland could be regarded as a precedent for the Hague institution, because the groups of fourteen members set up by the two countries issued binding decisions and because of the absence of a neutral element in the composition of these groups.

We propose to refer now to the following general observations concerning a possible controversy suitable for settlement by the Hague institution of inquiry. James Brown Scott[56] envisages a situation where two neighbouring states claim the right to exercise exclusive jurisdiction over a certain region, and each is unwilling to yield to the other. The question of jurisdiction would be settled if some machinery could be established to ascertain the exact boundary. While the ascertainment of the facts would thus decide the controversy, the value of the finding must depend upon the care and accuracy with which it is made. It would

---

[55]See Lawrence, p. 60.
[56]*Hague Peace Conferences*, p. 265. The author was US technical delegate to the Second Peace Conference at The Hague.

therefore seem that a commission charged with sifting the evidence and establishing the facts should include a member or members from third states.

In Scott's view, serious disputes are suitable for submission to international commissions of inquiry. In moments of excitement, he says, states are not unwilling to resort voluntarily to a commission if, by so doing, they may escape 'grave consequences'. It is evident that independent sovereign nations could, if they so desired, submit differences involving both honour and vital interests.[57]

Bustamente[58] explains that the Russian project for international commissions of inquiry was inspired by the practice followed by different states in the settlement of questions raised by frontier incidents or for rectification of frontiers. That is why the Russian draft, which was the basis of the present Article 9, envisaged differences of opinion with regard to local events which should be clarified at the place of their occurrence. Subsequently, on the initiative of the prominent Dutch jurist Asser, a new practical orientation was given to the inquiry commissions—they were extended to cover all questions of fact and were no longer limited to local circumstances.

In our endeavour to determine whether the institution of inquiry commissions provided for in the Hague Convention of 1889 was an innovation, and in order to ascertain its main traits as distinguished from those of similar institutions, it is proposed to compare the Hague commissions with the mixed commissions of inquiry and the mixed arbitral commissions which were set up before 1899.

As far as mixed commissions of inquiry are concerned, it may be recalled that the Romanian delegate referred to them as having been useful in settling disputes between his country and its neighbours (above, p. 26).[59] The essential characteristics of these commissions are that they are composed solely of the representatives of the states in dispute, and that their task is to enlighten the interested governments on contested facts.[60] The reports of such commissions in no way restrict the liberty of action of the parties. The work of these commissions is rarely publicized. They are usually designated according to the nature of their work, e.g., mixed naval commission, mixed commission of delimitation.[61] Thus, Italy and Switzerland tried to resolve a centuries-long dispute on their frontier at the Alp of Cravairola by resorting to

[57]Ibid., p. 266.

[58]See Bustamente y Sirvén, *La Seconde Conférence de la Paix réunie à La Haye en 1907* (1909), pp. 111–12.

[59]Cf. also Bustamente above.

[60]Such 'mixed commissions' are to be distinguished not only from the mixed arbitral commissions, but also from preparatory diplomatic mixed commissions, e.g. the commission composed of five Americans and five Britons who negotiated the Treaty of Washington of 1871, and from purely administrative mixed commissions, such as repatriation commissions dealing with the execution of treaty provisions.

[61]See Politis, p. 152.

frontier inquiry commissions. In 1861 a mixed commission 'visited the spot, examined new documents, but could reach a definite agreement only on one thing, i.e. that it was impossible to agree'.[62] In 1869 a new mixed commission met, visited the places, and examined documents, but reached no result. A third mixed commission met without result in 1872. Seeing that the dispute could not be settled by 'ordinary diplomatic procedures',[63] Switzerland then proposed recourse to an arbitral tribunal (below, n. 65).

It would seem that the Hague commissions of inquiry are almost identical with the last-mentioned commission of inquiry, both with regard to their object and to the effect of their findings. The only difference is the addition, in the Hague commissions, of a neutral element.

So far as mixed arbitral commissions are concerned, the primary difference between them and the Hague commissions of inquiry is that the former render obligatory decisions, based on law and equity, whereas the latter issue a non-binding report on the facts of the case.[64] For that reason, mixed arbitral commissions cannot be regarded as the forerunners of the Hague institution. We have noted how sensitive were most of the delegates at The Hague to any notion of inquiry commissions which might imply arbitral powers. The emphasis during the debates on the voluntary character of the commissions' report, and the express provision of Article 14 of the convention that the report 'has in no way the character of an award' and that it leaves to the powers in dispute 'entire freedom' as to the effect to be given to the findings contained in it, show that the powers assembled at The Hague sought to draw a clear distinction between commissions of inquiry and arbitral commissions. It is in the matter of their composition that the two institutions are similar. In this respect one could say that the promoters of the Hague commissions drew upon the experience of the arbitral commissions, for in their minds the inclusion of a neutral element was the primary condition for an 'impartial and conscientious investigation'.[65]

[62]La Pradelle & Politis, iii (1954), p. 471.

[63]Ibid., p. 472.

[64]Modern arbitration by mixed arbitral commissions, often designated only as 'mixed commissions', has its origin in the Jay Treaty of 19 November 1794 between Great Britain and the USA. The commissions established by that treaty and under subsequent treaties dealt mainly with frontier disputes and with claims for damages by individuals and companies.

Art. 7 of the Jay Treaty provided that the commissioners 'shall decide the claims in question according to the merits of the several cases, and to justice, equity and the laws of nations' (see 1 TCIA, 590).

[65]The mixed arbitral commissions established prior to the First Hague Conference may be classified in the following main types as regards their composition:

(1) Commissions composed of an unequal number of members, all of whom are nationals of the parties, e.g. the *Saint Croix river arbitration. Mixed commission under article V of the treaty between Great Britain and the United States of November 19, 1794,* in 2 vols of Moore, *International adjudications,* modern ser., i (1929) & ii (1930).

Bearing in mind the historical antecedents of the Hague commissions of inquiry, we may conclude that the institution embodied in the Hague Convention of 1899 was an innovation, designed to enlarge the means for the pacific settlement of international disputes.[66] The question has, however, been asked—by Politis in particular—whether the commissions of inquiry envisaged in the convention were not, in effect, disguised arbitral tribunals.[67] From the theoretical point of view, he states, arbitration is concerned with questions of law, and results in a binding award, while inquiry deals only with questions of fact, and results only in a report with regard to which the parties reserve entire freedom of action. However, the links between the disputed elements of fact and the elements of law are so close that it is impossible to give a finding on the former without touching upon the latter; sometimes the legal aspect of the controversy is so simple that its solution reveals itself as soon as the facts are determined. Moreover, the parties may take advantage of the provision in paragraph 2 of Article 10 entitling them to define the 'extent of the powers of the commissioners', and may turn the inquiry into an arbitration.

As to the effect of the report, claims Politis, the parties would be bound in practice to draw the conclusions which emerge from the report. Although the report 'has in no way the character of an award'

---

(2) Commissions composed of an equal number of nationals of each party; if the commissioners disagreed on the award to be given, the case was to be referred to a foreign head of state, e.g. the mixed commissions under the Treaty of Ghent, 24 Dec. 1814, between Great Britain and the USA (1 TCIA, 612).

(3) Commissions composed of an equal number of nationals; if the commissioners disagreed, the case was to be referred to a foreign national appointed by, and acting on behalf of, a foreign sovereign, e.g. the Claims Convention of 11 Apr. 1839 between the USA and Mexico. For the work of the commission see Moore, *International arbitrations*, ii. 1209–359.

(4) Commissions composed of an equal number of nationals from each party; if the commissioners disagreed, they were to choose a foreign national as an umpire, e.g. convention of 31 Dec. 1873 regarding the dispute between Italy and Switzerland over their frontier at the Alp of Cravairola (see La Pradelle & Politis, iii. 464–514, and Moore, *International arbitrations*, ii. 2027–50).

(5) Commissions composed of an equal number of nationals from each party and a foreign national, chosen by the parties and participating in the deliberations. See Treaty of Washington of 8 May 1871 (1 TCIA, 700; see also Moore, *International arbitrations*, i. 683–702, and La Pradelle & Politis, iii. 41–440).

(6) Commissions composed of an equal number of nationals of each party and an unequal number of foreign nationals who form the majority, e.g. *Alabama Claims* under the Treaty of Washington of 8 May 1871 (see Moore, *International arbitrations*, i. 495–682).

(7) Commissions composed entirely of foreign nationals, e.g. the commission established by the Anglo-Brazilian compromis of 22 Apr. 1873 in the *Dundonald Case* (see La Pradelle & Politis, iii. 441–63).

[66]Cf. Mérignhac, p. 279: 'Les articles 14 à 18 du projet russe organisaient ... un nouveau rouage pacifique intermédiaire entre la médiation et l'arbitrage ...'.

Martens's assertion that the institution was not an innovation was apparently designed to dispel the fears of those states who were not prepared to subscribe to a new institution which might impair their sovereignty. Cf. Beaucourt, p. 17.

[67]See Politis, pp. 154–6.

(Art. 14), the findings of the commissioners with regard to the facts are final, and have the same juridical value as those emanating from a judge. There also remains the moral obligation to bring the dispute to an end after the findings of the inquiry have been made known. If the legal implications of the findings on the facts are simple, the parties can readily arrive at a settlement on the basis of the findings. If the implications are complicated, there is the possibility of recourse to mediation or arbitration. The actions of the mediator or the arbitrator would necessarily be considerably influenced by the findings of the commission of inquiry.[68]

Finally, the provisions of the Convention of 1899 concerning the organization and work of commissions of inquiry are inspired by arbitration. As in arbitration (Art. 39), the inquiry is preceded by a preliminary agreement (Art. 10) which has the same object—to define the questions to be examined and to determine the powers of the members of the commission. The arbitral tribunal and the inquiry commission are composed in the same manner (Art. 11 referring to Art. 32).[69] Like the arbitrators, the commissioners are competent, if no mention is made in the preliminary agreement, to decide the form and the periods to be observed (Arts 10 & 49). In both cases the procedure requires that both sides be heard (Arts 10 & 40). In both cases the parties must, in principle, furnish all necessary information (Arts 12 & 44). The commissioners' report has to be signed by all the commissioners (Art. 13), just as the arbitrators' award has to be signed by all the arbitrators (Art. 52(1)).[70] Moreover, in addition to the above stipulations, there was a tacit agreement that the commissions of inquiry should adopt the arbitral procedure in all details of their work.

[68]Cf. Scott, *Hague Peace Conferences*, p. 267: 'The differences of opinion regarding the effect of the fact as found upon the liability of either party are in no ways concerned; for the parties may arrange the difficulty by diplomatic negotiations, or, if they choose, they may submit the question of responsibility to arbitration. Of the proceedings to be taken, they are the sole competent judges. It cannot be denied, however, that the mere ascertainment of the fact goes far in itself to establish responsibility, and a direct, although moral pressure, is thus brought upon the parties to settle the difficulty in accordance with the fact found.'
Cf. Cot, who asserts (p. 44) that the Hague Conventions confer on international commissions of inquiry two functions: one—quasi-arbitral—to say what the fact is, and one—quasi-mediatory—to assist the settlement of the dispute.

[69]Cot points out (p. 46) that the adoption of the provisions on the composition of arbitral tribunals gives to international commissions of inquiry a definite arbitral character which influences the behaviour of the commissioners. A commission composed in such a way naturally follows the example of arbitral commissions.

[70]A comparison of the text of Part III (International Commissions of Inquiry) and Part IV (International Arbitration), led Smith & Sibley to enumerate eleven 'most important differences between an International Commission of Inquiry and the Permanent Court of Arbitration'. These eleven concern (1) the effect of the report, (2) way of constituting the body, (3) nature of the question to be decided (law, fact), (4) instrument for submission of the case, (5) recourse to settlement, (6) basis of forms and procedure, (7) seat of the court or the commission, (8) choice of language, (9) replacement of deceased arbitrators or commissioners, (10) revision of award or report, (11) rules on evidence or expenses (*International law as interpreted during the Russo-Japanese war*, 2nd edn (1907), pp. 266–8).

The foregoing analysis of the juridical and practical implications of the provisions concerning international commissions of inquiry led Politis to conclude (p. 156) that the Hague institution was, in essence, arbitration in disguise. In order to be accepted, the institution had to appear as entailing less of a political danger than mediation, and fewer juridical consequences than arbitration. Thus, in calming the susceptibilities of states, the institution could better serve the cause of peace.

Indeed, as we have seen, the promoters of the institution spared no effort to secure the support of the members of the conference. They accepted many amendments to meet the apprehensions of certain states, so that even the platonic declaration that the commissions of inquiry were useful was surrounded by numerous reservations.[71]

The compromises made by the supporters of the inquiry method showed their confidence in its practical application. This confidence proved to be not unwarranted—at least so far as the immediate future was concerned—when two great powers, Russia and England, had recourse to the new institution in order to resolve the serious Dogger Bank dispute. The development, solution, and implications of this dispute for the conception of international inquiry are the subject of our next chapter.

[71]After enumerating the reservations contained in Art. 9, Bokanowski wrote: 'Nous croyons que si l'audace n'avait pas manqué, on aurait écrit: au bon vouloir des Parties' (*Les commissions internationales d'enquête* (1908), p. 46).

CHAPTER 3

The Dogger Bank Incident:
Great Britain–Russia, 1905

HISTORICAL BACKGROUND

The Dogger Bank incident, in which a number of English fishing-vessels were damaged by the Russian Baltic fleet, occurred during a period of strained relations between Great Britain and Russia. The tension resulted from the alliance of Great Britain with Russia's enemy, Japan, and from Russian interference with British shipping.

The beginning of the century had been marked by two conflicting alliances among the great powers: France and Russia on the one hand, and Great Britain and Japan on the other. In 1901 France agreed to help Russian expansion towards India by subsidizing the building of a railway to Tashkent. The two countries signed a convention for joint military action against Britain, and proceeded with plans (never completed) for naval cooperation against that country. It seems that the practical objective of the French was to extract British concessions with regard to Morocco in exchange for French neutrality in the Far East.[1]

Apprehensive of Russian designs in Asia, Britain sought to achieve a direct settlement with Russia. However, the negotiations failed owing to Russia's request for a port on the Persian Gulf, in addition to control of Northern China. Japan, for her part, was interested in eliminating the Russian presence in Korea and thus ensuring the security of her coast. To attain this objective, in the autumn of 1901 she took a twofold initiative: negotiations with Russia and negotiations for an alliance with Britain. Japan thought that if the negotiations with Russia failed, the British navy could hold France in check. The British reacted favourably to Japan's approach, not only because of their common interest in containing Russia, but also because they feared that the Russo-Japanese negotiations might result in an anti-British combination of the two powers.

On 30 January 1902 Great Britain and Japan signed an agreement[2] in which they expressed their desire to maintain the status quo and general peace in Eastern Asia and to maintain, in particular, the independence and territorial integrity of the empire of China and the empire of Korea. The two countries defined their special interests as follows: those of Britain related principally to China, while Japan, in addition

---

[1]See Taylor, *The struggle for mastery in Europe, 1848–1918* (1954), p. 399.
[2]For text see Cd 914 (3 UKTS (1902)); 1 *AJIL* (1907), Official Documents, pp. 14–15.

to the interests which she possessed in China, was interested 'in a peculiar degree, politically as well as commercially and industrially, in Korea'. They agreed that in the event of one of them becoming involved in war with another state in defence of its interests, the other contracting party would remain neutral. However, if a fourth state joined the war against the contracting party, the other contracting party was to join its ally in waging war against the common enemy. Britain succeeded in inserting an article to the effect that neither party would, without consulting the other, enter into separate arrangements with another state 'to the prejudice of the interests above described'. The agreement was for five years,[3] and was still in force when the Dogger Bank incident occurred.

Both Japan and Britain achieved their short-term objectives by means of the agreement of 1902: Japan received recognition of her special interests in Korea and the assurance that Britain would keep France neutral in case she went to war with Russia; Britain prevented a Russo-Japanese alliance and strengthened her defence against further Russian encroachments in Asia.[4]

France and Russia reacted by publishing on 17 March 1902 a declaration in which 'the two allied Governments' undertook to consult each other on the means of safeguarding their interests, in case the aggressive actions of third powers or new troubles in China, endangering the integrity and free development of that country, became a threat to their interests.[5] Faced with the Anglo-Japanese alliance, Russia adopted a more cautious attitude, and in April 1902 made an agreement with China to withdraw from Manchuria by annual stages. In 1903 the Russians put forward, as a condition for implementing the second stage of withdrawal, such demands as would have perpetuated their control of Manchuria. Following Japanese, British, and US protests, the Russians abandoned their demands, but refused to withdraw. The Far East crisis became more acute and the danger of war came nearer. This danger put France in a delicate position, which was reflected in her role in the settlement of the Dogger Bank dispute. If a war broke out between Japan and Russia, the latter would appeal for French support. Then France would have either to forsake her alliance with Russia, or wage war against Britain. The solution was to seek a reconciliation with Britain in the hope of isolating her from Japan or at least of bringing to bear on the disputing parties in the Far East joint Franco-British pressure for moderation. France approached Britain with a proposal to

[3]On 12 Aug. 1905 (just before the signing of the Treaty of Portsmouth which ended the Russo-Japanese War), the treaty was renewed for another five years. This time Britain pledged herself to give help to Japan if she was attacked even by only one state instead of by two (see Grant & Temperley, *Europe in the nineteenth and twentieth centuries (1789–1950)*, 6th edn (1952), p. 335).

[4]See Taylor, p. 400.

[5]See Hershey, *The international law and diplomacy of the Russo-Japanese war* (1906), pp. 28–9.

settle all colonial differences, in the hope that such a general settlement would contribute to the creation of a more peaceful atmosphere in the Far East. Negotiations began in July 1903. In January 1904 France had to mediate simultaneously between Russia and Japan. By that time Russia had established the principle that Korea was essential to her security and was not prepared to make any significant concessions in her negotiations with Japan. The Japanese lost patience, and on 8 February 1904 launched the war by an attack on the Russian ships at Port Arthur.[6]

The outbreak of the Russo-Japanese War served to accelerate the Anglo-French negotiations. On 8 April 1904 France and Britain concluded a series of agreements which marked the birth of the so-called entente cordiale. These agreements settled all outstanding colonial differences, particularly with regard to Egypt and Morocco, and expressed the desire of both France and Britain to limit the sphere of the Russo-Japanese War. The Dogger Bank incident, which occurred shortly afterwards, was a serious challenge to the peaceful policy of the two countries.

From the outset of the war the sympathies of Britain were on the side of her ally, Japan. During the hostilities, public opinion took a decisively anti-Russian course as a result of the seizure of British ships by Russian men-of-war. 'A terrible storm of indignation arose in England' in July 1904, when the British liner *Malacca* was arrested in the Red Sea by the Russian cruiser *Peterburg*,[7] on a charge of carrying contraband, and was brought to Port Said in the custody of a Russian prize crew and flying the Russian flag. The Russian government, acting on the advice of the French government, consented to the release of the *Malacca* after having received the assurance of the British government that the munitions of war on board the vessel were British government stores, and after a perfunctory pro forma examination of the cargo by a British and a Russian consul.[8] Another 'storm of indignation' followed the sinking,

---

[6]On 6 Feb. 1904 Japan informed the Russian government that in view of the 'obstinate rejections by Russia of Japan's proposals respecting Korea' and of the 'obstinate refusal of Russia to enter into an engagement to respect China's territorial integrity in Manchuria', and in view of 'Russia's repeated delays to reply without intelligible reasons and of her naval and military activities, irreconcilable with pacific aims', the Japanese government had 'no other alternative than to terminate the present futile negotiations'. In adopting this course, the Japanese government reserved to itself the right to take 'such independent action' as it deemed best to defend its 'menaced position' as well as 'to protect the acquired rights and legitimate interests of the Empire'. Two days later the Japanese navy opened hostilities (see Hershey, p. 60).

[7]Ibid., p. 139. The *Peterburg* and the *Smolensk*, belonging to the Russian 'volunteer fleet' in the Black Sea, made their way out of the Bosphorus and the Dardanelles into the Mediterranean as merchantmen (flying a commercial flag), passed through the Suez Canal and proceeded to stop and seize neutral vessels in the Red Sea.

[8]After consenting to the release of the *Malacca*, Russia agreed to instruct the officers of her 'volunteer fleet' to cease interfering with neutral shipping on the ground that 'the present status of the volunteer fleet was not sufficiently well defined, according to International Law, to render further searches and seizures advisable'. There was no agreement in

in July the same year, of the British steamer *Knight Commander* by the Russian Vladivostok squadron. In this instance, the British secretary of state for foreign affairs, Lord Lansdowne, instructed his ambassador at St Petersburg, Sir Charles Hardinge, to make it clear to the Russian government that should it act upon its extreme contentions with regard to contraband of war and the treatment of vessels accused of carrying it, 'His Majesty's Government will be constrained to take such precautions as may seem to them desirable and sufficient for the protection of their commerce'.[9]

DIPLOMATIC NEGOTIATIONS

On 24 October 1904 Lord Lansdowne informed Sir Charles Hardinge[10] that during the night of 21 October, suddenly, and without the slightest warning, the Russian Baltic fleet had fired upon the 'Gamecock' steam fishing fleet of Hull which was fishing off the Dogger Bank in the North Sea. At least one vessel was sunk, two persons were killed, and a number seriously wounded. The whole action seemed to have been of the most deliberate character: signals were made ordering the fleet to change formation, after which fire was opened and maintained for a considerable time. When the firing ceased the Russian fleet, without making the slightest attempt to save life or to ascertain the amount of damage that it had done, continued its voyage. One small vessel of the Baltic fleet remained on the scene of the incident for about six hours, and then also, without making any effort to save life, steamed after the fleet. Lord Lansdowne further stated that all the distinguishing lights required by

---

principle on the broader question of the right of passage through the Straits by these vessels (ibid., pp. 140–2).

Foreign men-of-war were excluded from the Straits by a series of international agreements, the first of which was the Convention of London of 13 July 1841, between Austria, France, Great Britain, Prussia, Russia, and Turkey. The Peace Treaty of Paris of 30 March 1856 and Convention No. I annexed to it confirmed this rule. According to the Treaty of London of 13 March 1871, the Sublime Porte could open the Straits in time of peace to the men-of-war of friendly and allied powers, for the purpose, if necessary, of securing the execution of the provisions of the Treaty of Paris (see Oppenheim, i, 8th edn by Lauterpacht (1955), pp. 513–14). During the period under discussion, Russia did not attempt to send her Baltic Sea fleet through the Straits for fear that Britain would enforce the treaty provisions, which were in the interest of her Japanese ally (see Taylor, p. 422).

[9]Hershey, p. 145. The Russian government justified its right to sink the *Knight Commander* on the grounds that the vessel carried contraband of war, i.e. railway material and machinery, and because her captor was unable to bring her to the nearest Russian port without manifest danger to the squadron, since she did not have enough coal. Owing to the strong line taken by the British government, the Russian government agreed to have the case reviewed by a special admiralty court at St Petersburg. This court reversed the decision of the Vladivostok Prize Court, which had condemned the *Knight Commander*, and Russia paid an indemnity of approximately £100,000 to Britain (ibid., pp. 146–7). The Russian policy with regard to the visit, search, and sinking of neutral vessels was also applied to other British vessels, as well as to the vessels of other neutral states, e.g., Germany, Denmark. See generally ibid., pp. 138–46.

[10]See Cd 2350 (Russia No. 2, 1905).

international regulations were shown by the fishing-vessels; in addition, they were illuminated by searchlights of the Russian squadron.[11] That, in these circumstances, they could have been mistaken for anything but what they were, could only have been due to 'the most culpable negligence'.

The British ambassador was instructed to inform the Russian minister for foreign affairs, Count Lamsdorff, of what had occurred, and to say that the indignation provoked by this incident could not possibly be exaggerated. The action of the Russian commanding officer, Admiral Rojdestvensky, in leaving the scene of the disaster without offering assistance had aggravated this feeling. While the British government preferred not to formulate its demands before receiving explanations from the Russian government, it requested 'ample apology and complete and prompt reparation, as well as security against the recurrence of such intolerable incidents'.

On the same day the Russian chargé d'affaires told Lord Lansdowne that, in the absence of any information from Russian sources, he could only conjecture that the incident was due to an unfortunate mistake.[12] The Russian government had received numerous reports that Japanese agents were visiting England for the purpose of organizing attacks on the Russian Baltic fleet, and it was perhaps not unnatural that the captains of the Russian ships should have been alarmed at finding the foreign vessels in close proximity to their men-of-war. The chargé d'affaires imagined that if any Japanese torpedo-boats had attempted to attack the Baltic fleet, they would have endeavoured to do so under the guise of innocent fishing-boats.

Before receiving the instructions of Lord Lansdowne, Sir Charles Hardinge had asked Count Lamsdorff, also on 24 October, whether he could offer any explanation with regard to reports in the Russian press to the effect that the Baltic fleet had attacked British fishing-vessels.[13] Count Lamsdorff replied that the news in the press had moved him very much and that the Ministry of the Marine had so far received no information from the commander of the fleet, Admiral Rojdestvensky. Hardinge advised the minister, 'with a view to maintaining friendly relations between the two countries', to lose no time in making a declaration that if, 'after careful inquiry, any officers of the fleet were proved to have been in fault, they would be severely punished and full reparation made to the victims and their families'. Count Lamsdorff assured the British ambassador that a full inquiry would be made into the circumstances of the occurrence and that if any persons were found on investigation to be guilty, adequate punishment would follow, and full reparation would be made to all the unfortunate people who had suffered.

On the next day Count Lamsdorff informed the British ambassador

---

[11]The terms 'squadron' and 'fleet' were used interchangeably.
[12]Ibid., No. 6. [13]Ibid., Nos 3 & 36.

that the Russian emperor, Nicholas II, had asked him to convey to the British king, Edward VII, and to the British government, his sincere regrets for the sad loss of life.[14] The emperor, having received no news from the commander of the Baltic fleet, could only attribute the incident to a most regrettable misunderstanding, but, as soon as light had been thrown on the circumstances surrounding the incident, complete reparation would be made to the victims. No mention was made in the emperor's message of possible punishment of those who might be found guilty.

In London the Russian ambassador, Count Benckendorff, told Lord Lansdowne on the same day that no difficulty would be experienced with regard to the question of compensation.[15] The question of responsibility was more complicated. It would be difficult to establish responsibility without a full report from the naval authorities, and this might take time. However, no pains would be spared to ascertain where the blame lay. Lord Lansdowne formulated to the ambassador the following demands: (1) an ample apology and disclaimer by the Russian government (the regrets of the emperor had apparently not yet been received); (2) fullest reparation to the victims; (3) a searching inquiry with a view to ascertaining 'who was to blame for what, if the circumstances were as stated, could only be regarded, not only as a blunder, but as a culpable blunder'; (4) adequate punishment of the persons who proved to be responsible; (5) security against the repetition of such incidents.

By 26 October the British government had become seriously concerned that no word of explanation had been heard from Admiral Rojdestvensky and that no attempt had been made to stop the voyage of his fleet to the Far East in order to disembark the persons implicated in the incident. On that day Lord Lansdowne addressed a note to Count Benckendorff[16] stating, i.a., that it seemed to him absolutely incomprehensible that the officers of the fleet should have left the Russian minister of the marine without information on so grave an event, and that the fleet should be pursuing its way to the East, carrying with it all those who were able to give an account of the incident. 'I presume,' wrote Lord Lansdowne, 'that an effort was made to intercept it with a view at least to obtaining from the authors of the attack such explanations and such evidence as they may be able to furnish'.

In talks with Count Benckendorff, held on the same day, Lord Lansdowne stated that if the Russian fleet 'were allowed to continue its journey without calling at Vigo [in Spain], *we might find ourselves at war before the week was over*' (emphasis added).[17] During a second talk on the same day he reiterated that the departure of the persons responsible for the North Sea incident would not only enable them to elude justice, but would also make it impossible to obtain conclusive results from the inquiry which the Russian government had promised to undertake.

[14]Ibid., Nos 8 & 36.   [15]Ibid., No. 10.   [16]Ibid., No. 12, Annex 2.   [17]Ibid., No. 12.

Lord Lansdowne warned that unless the British demands in this respect were met, it might be necessary for the British government to take measures to enforce them.[18] These statements were reinforced by the issuing of preliminary orders by the Admiralty for the mobilization of the British fleets. The Channel, Mediterranean, and Home squadrons were ordered to meet at Gibraltar in readiness to intercept the Russian fleet on its way southward if such action became necessary.[19] The firm attitude of the British government had the desired effect, and the Russian government instructed Admiral Rojdestvensky to stop at Vigo.

On 27 October Count Lamsdorff communicated to Sir Charles Hardinge the long-awaited account by Admiral Rojdestvensky. It was contained in two telegrams.[20] The first related that the squadron had met many hundreds of fishermen and had treated them with every consideration except on the occasion of the Dogger Bank incident. At that time the fishermen were in the company of two foreign torpedo-boats, one of which had disappeared while the second, according to the statements of the fishermen themselves, remained near them till morning. The fishermen had taken the second torpedo-boat for a Russian ship, but it had been of a different nationality. That boat had remained behind in order either to find its consort or to repair the damage it had sustained. It evidently feared to betray its origin to those who were not its accomplices. If there were also fishermen on the spot who were unwisely drawn into the incident, the admiral wished to express his most sincere regrets to the unfortunate victims. In the circumstances, he concluded, no warship could have acted otherwise, even in time of complete peace.

The account in the second telegram was more specific. The incident, it said, was provoked by two torpedo-boats which, without lights and under cover of darkness, prepared to attack the leading vessel of the Russian squadron. When the squadron began to show war signals and then to fire, several other steamers resembling fishing-vessels were discovered. The squadron tried to spare these vessels, and stopped firing as soon as the torpedo-boats had disappeared. The admiral reiterated that the boat which remained on the scene was one of the enemy torpedo-boats, and went on to say that the squadron could not render assistance to the small steamers, since they could have been suspected of complicity in view of their obstinate attempts to break the line of the Russian ships. He added that some of the boats had not shown any lights at all, and others did so very late.

In a slightly different version, contained in a telegram dated 26 October from Admiral Rojdestvensky to the Russian naval attaché in London, the admiral asserted that the incident was occasioned by the action of two torpedo-boats which 'steamed at full speed under cover of the night, and showing no lights, towards the ship which was leading

[18]Ibid.   [19]See Hershey, p. 220.   [20]Cd 2350, Nos 14, 15 & 37 (Inclosure).

our detachment'.[21] With regard to the role of the fishing-vessels, the admiral stated: 'Our ships refrained from giving assistance to the trawlers on account of their apparent complicity, which they manifested by their persistence in attempting to pass through our line.' When on 27 October Count Benckendorff related to Lord Lansdowne[22] the contents of the telegram, the British foreign secretary replied that the version given by the admiral would not carry the slightest conviction in England. How was it possible that Japanese torpedo-boats should have been found in the middle of the North Sea? Where had they come from?[23]

Count Benckendorff asked Lord Lansdowne whether the admiral's statement did not entirely alter the situation. Lord Lansdowne replied that the British government still demanded a thorough investigation, with a view to ascertaining where the responsibility lay and in order to secure the punishment of the culprits. Count Benckendorff said that it was evident that an investigation had already taken place; the admiral had arrived at Vigo the previous day and had no doubt already instituted an inquiry. Lord Lansdowne replied that the inquiry, if there had been one, must obviously have been of a very hurried nature and that it was idle to suppose that the British government could regard it as disposing of the facts of the case. The whole incident must form the subject of a complete and searching investigation, and such an investigation could not take place without the presence of the persons who were responsible for the attack upon the fishing fleet. The British government adhered to its demand that these persons should be recalled and placed on trial.

Having discussed the matter with the prime minister, Mr Balfour, and other colleagues, Lord Lansdowne met Count Benckendorff again on the same day and explained the position to him as follows:[24] It was absolutely necessary that before the Russian fleet left Vigo steps should be taken by the Russian authorities to ascertain who were the persons responsible for the attack. These persons should be left behind, as well as any others whose testimony was regarded by the Russian naval authorities as essential to the elucidation of the facts. An inquiry should then be held as to the facts. In the view of the British government such an inquiry could best be entrusted to an independent court possessing

[21]Ibid., No. 16.   [22]Ibid., No. 19.

[23]On 27 Oct. Lord Lansdowne asked the British representatives in Denmark, France, Germany, the Netherlands, Norway, and Sweden to ascertain whether any torpedo-boats or destroyers belonging to the governments to which they were accredited were in the vicinity of the Dogger Bank at the time of the incident. They were also asked whether any information was available with regard to Japanese agents having acquired and equipped any torpedo-boats or destroyers along the coast (ibid., No. 18). All answers were in the negative (ibid., Nos 24, 25, 26, 38, 44, 46, 47, 63). It was also ascertained that no British torpedo-boats or destroyers were near the Dogger Bank at the time of the incident (ibid., Nos 20 & 40). The Japanese government, for its part, informed the British foreign secretary that no Japanese war vessels were in the vicinity at that time (ibid., No. 48).

[24]Ibid.

an international character. 'Articles IX to XIV of the Hague Convention on International Commissions of Inquiry' seemed to provide for such an inquiry. The commission might in this instance be formed of naval officers of high rank representing the two powers concerned and three of the other great powers. It would, of course, be a sine qua non that the British government should receive an assurance from the Russian government that the latter would adequately punish the persons, if any, who might be found guilty by the international commission.

Two dispatches from Sir Charles Hardinge, dated 28 October,[25] showed that the two opposing parties had reached the same conclusion regarding the method by which the dispute could be solved. First, he informed Lord Lansdowne that the Russian minister of the marine had ordered the admiral to remain at Vigo with those ships which had witnessed the incident. Secondly, Hardinge quoted the following telegram sent by Count Lamsdorff to the Russian ambassador in London:

Being desirous of throwing as much light as possible on all that has occurred in the North Sea, the Emperor thinks it would be useful to refer the question for careful investigation to an International Commission of Inquiry, as contemplated by the Hague Convention. By order of His Majesty, your Excellency is requested to propose this method of solution to the Government of His Britannic Majesty.[26]

While the two separate proposals of Britain and Russia for the submission of the dispute to an international commission of inquiry created the impression of two independent initiatives, the original initiative came from France.[27] On 26 October the French ambassador in London, M. Cambon, had an interview with Lord Lansdowne concerning the crisis, and on the following day M. Cambon attended the meeting between Lord Lansdowne and Count Benckendorff at which the proposal for an inquiry commission was put forward. The London *Times* reported on 29 October that France had played an important role in the negotiations which made a satisfactory solution possible. As an ally of Russia and a friend of England, she was well placed to make her counsel of wisdom and moderation heard with equal force in St Petersburg and in London.[28]

Further negotiations between the parties concentrated on the terms

---

[25]Ibid., Nos 21 & 22.

[26]The wording of the emperor's proposal implies that he had no knowledge of Lord Lansdowne's proposal. According to one view the emperor must have known of it, since Count Lamsdorff's proposal was made before noon on 27 Oct. and the emperor's is dated 28 Oct. The difference in time between London and St Petersburg was not sufficiently great to account for such a delay. Moreover, it appeared that Count Lamsdorff at least had knowledge of Lord Lansdowne's proposal before his audience with the emperor on 28 Oct. (see Hershey, p. 225).

[27]See Scott, *The Hague Court reports* (1916), p. 403. See also below, p. 87.

[28]See La Penha, *La commission d'enquête sur l'incident anglo-russe de la mer du Nord* (1906), pp. 55, 194–6.

c

of reference of the proposed commission of inquiry. From the outset the Russian government took exception to Lord Lansdowne's insistence that the commission should establish who were the guilty persons. When Sir Charles Hardinge conveyed to Count Lamsdorff, on 28 October,[29] the request of the British government that the Russian government should give an assurance that it would adequately punish the persons, if any, who might be found guilty by the commission, Count Lamsdorff stated that he could not discuss the question of punishment until the results of the inquiry were fully known; he could not admit that, after the statement made by Admiral Rojdestvensky, any blame could be attached to the Russian officers. When 'the Court of Inquiry' had completed its work and had made a report on the circumstances of the incident, he said, then would be the moment to apportion responsi- bilities and their consequences, in whatever direction they might lie. The inference clearly was that the establishment of 'responsibilities' and, above all, of guilt, was to be outside the competence of the proposed commission.

Count Lamsdorff said on the same occasion that the peaceful turn which had at that stage been given to the question was largely due to the carefully moderated tone of Lord Lansdowne as compared with the menacing attitude of the British press. The state of public feeling in Russia was such that any sign of threats by the British government would have been deeply resented, and could hardly have failed to bring about a disastrous war.

On the same day the Russian ambassador in London called on Lord Lansdowne[30] in order to convey the emperor's message regarding the institution of an international commission of inquiry. Lord Lansdowne commented that the message dealt only with a part of the question, and that it was necessary to avoid misunderstanding with regard to the remaining points. He asked the ambassador 'for an authority' to authorize the prime minister to make a statement that 'any persons found guilty by this Tribunal, will be tried by the Russian Government and punished adequately'. Count Benckendorff agreed, on the under- standing that any other government would act likewise with regard to its own subjects or officers who might be found guilty.[31]

Lord Lansdowne also stressed the need to issue special instructions to the Russian fleet with the object of avoiding a recurrence of such incidents. He was disturbed by Admiral Rojdestvensky's statement that even in time of peace no warship could have acted differently. According to the French press, the admiral claimed to have acted in conformity with instructions given to him before the voyage. It was stated that the

[29]Cd 2350, No. 45.
[30]Ibid., No. 28.
[31]There was apparently some discrepancy between the views of the Russian minister for foreign affairs and his ambassador on the question of the commission's competence to establish guilt.

officers in command of the fleet knew that they had to fire upon any boat that came near their squadron.[32] Lord Lansdowne pointed out that if instructions of this kind had been issued, and remained in force, the presence of the Russian fleet was a menace to neutral commerce in any seas through which it might pass.[33]

In a speech made on the evening of 28 October, the prime minister, Mr Balfour, summed up the result of the negotiations between the two countries, saying, i.a.: 'Any persons found guilty by this tribunal will be tried by the Russian Government and punished adequately.' On the same occasion Mr Balfour ridiculed Admiral Rojdestvensky's version of the incident by expressing disbelief in the existence of the 'phantom Japanese ships' which had allegedly attacked the Russian fleet.

The Admiral's story [he said] is really an attack upon our national honour, and implied that we are not doing our duty as neutrals. . . . In an island kingdom like Great Britain the nationality of every craft is known. It is inconceivable that we should be harbouring Japanese sailors and warships without Russia and, indeed, the whole civilized world knowing it. I enter a most emphatic protest against such an allegation.[34]

On 31 October Lord Lansdowne insisted, in a conversation with Count Benckendorff, that the terms of reference of the proposed commission of inquiry should be settled immediately, and he submitted to the Russian ambassador a 'Draft of Proposed Agreement for reference to International Commission of Inquiry', containing a preamble and six articles.[35] The Preamble stipulated that the elucidation of the questions in dispute should be referred to an international commission of inquiry 'analogous' to that provided for in Articles 9–14 of the Hague Convention of 1899, while Article 2 read as follows:

[32]On 25 Oct. the Russian chief of staff, Rear-Admiral Wirenius, told the British naval attaché that the Russian admiralty had for a considerable time been in possession of completely reliable information that the Japanese had been elaborating methods of attacking the squadron under cover of fishing and other vessels, and that no doubt Admiral Rojdestvensky had sailed with serious warnings on this subject impressed on his mind (ibid., No. 32 (Inclosure)).

[33]In a further conversation, on 29 Oct., Lord Lansdowne gave the ambassador a 'friendly warning' against the wholesale seizure by the Russian fleet of vessels suspected of carrying contraband. If, during their long voyage to the East, the Russian captains considered themselves justified in such wholesale seizure, public feeling in England would become uncontrollable. Lord Lansdowne recalled that important questions of international law connected with this subject were at that moment being discussed between the two governments. It would be deplorable if, at such a time, a multitude of British prizes were seized upon the assumption that the Russian, and not the British, interpretation of the law was to prevail, and were sent up the channel and past British shores for adjudication in Russian prize courts (ibid., No. 35).

On 2 Nov. Count Benckendorff made the following announcement to Lord Lansdowne: 'Before the Russian Admiral left Vigo, special instructions were given to him that the Russian fleet, during its voyage to the Far East, is to observe the utmost caution in order to avoid occasioning injury or inconvenience to any neutral shipping which they may encounter' (ibid., No. 54).

[34]See Hershey, p. 227, quoting the London *Times* (weekly edn) of 4 Nov. 1904.

[35]Cd 2350, Nos 41 & 43 (with Inclosure).

The Commission shall inquire into and report upon all the circumstances attending the disaster in the North Sea, and particularly as to where the responsibility for the disaster lies, and the degree of blame which attaches to those upon whom that responsibility is found to rest.

Lord Lansdowne explained that it was essential for the commission to apportion responsibility and blame. This was indeed a necessary condition, as it was understood by the British government that the Russian government had promised to punish adequately 'any persons who might be found by the Commission to have been responsible for the disaster, and to whom, in their opinion, blame attached'.[36]

When the ambassador expressed objections to the emphasis put by Lord Lansdowne on the need to ensure the punishment of the Russian officers, Lord Lansdowne explained that the stipulation was not one-sided, for the defence made by the Russian admiral was 'an imputation on the manner in which British neutrality had been observed, as well as upon the conduct of the fishing fleet'.

The question of the 'responsibility', 'blame', and 'punishment' of the persons involved in the incident was so important, in the view of the British government, that Lord Lansdowne sent a cable on the same day to Sir Charles Hardinge urging him to discuss it immediately with Count Lamsdorff.[37] Lord Lansdowne stated that Count Lamsdorff and Count Benckendorff had indicated 'the desire of the Russian Government to exclude altogether from the consideration of the Commission the question of "responsibility" '. In the view of the British government this was wholly inadmissible. The British government would be satisfied to receive the official assurance of the Russian government that the officers detained were those who were specially implicated in the incident and upon whom the blame, if blame there was, must fall. Hardinge was instructed to inform Count Lamsdorff that the British had no desire to press for any form of words which prejudged the culpability or innocence of those concerned, whatever their nationality might be. It would be for the commission 'to determine the question of responsibility and justification or blame, as the case may be'.

Count Lamsdorff replied[38] that the commission of inquiry alone should determine responsibility for the incident. (This was a change from his previous position, to the effect that responsibilities would be apportioned after the submission of the report.) He could not admit the responsibility or guilt of the officers waiting at Vigo until it was proved by that body, but since those officers who were actually implicated would be in the best position to give evidence, the selection of certain individuals as witnesses did not exclude the possibility of their having been responsible in the matter. The Count assured the British

[36]In the context of Art. 2, the expression 'in their opinion' should be understood as referring to the opinion of the commission.

[37]Cd 2350, No. 55.   [38]Ibid., No. 57.

ambassador that the consequences of responsibility would indubitably have to be suffered by the Russian officers, in accordance with Russian law, if it could be shown to fall upon them; and in the event—which at that stage he equally declined to admit—of the complicity of the fishermen in the attack on the fleet being proved, he was absolutely convinced that similar action would be taken in their case by the British government.

Having obtained the views of Count Lamsdorff, Lord Lansdowne cabled to Hardinge on 4 November[39] that a misunderstanding of the use of the word 'responsibility' seemed to be causing the difficulty. 'The International Tribunal alone can determine whether responsibility is equivalent to guilt or is in itself deserving of punishment,' he stated. 'We do not regard this as necessarily the case, but in our view the persons who are responsible are those on whom blame would fall, if blame there was.'

On the same day Count Lamsdorff accepted 'integrally' the draft convention proposed by the British government.[40] (By 8 November the parties agreed on three additional articles proposed by the British.)[41] However, on 12 November Count Lamsdorff submitted to Hardinge a different version of the crucial Article 2, which omitted the expression 'and the degree of blame', relating to the competence of the commission.[42] Count Lamsdorff explained that his ministry had worded Article 2 in a somewhat altered form as compared with the English text, assuming that the 'present version, expressing as it does the selfsame idea, will not give rise to any objection on the part of His Majesty's Government'. The text submitted read: 'The commission shall investigate all circumstances connected with the North Sea incident and particularly elucidate the facts relating thereto, and give a decision on the question of responsibility, in accordance with the results of the inquiry.'[43]

Count Lamsdorff's expectation that the British government would accept the omission of 'blame' from the terms of reference was not warranted. Indeed, it provoked strong feelings in London. On 14 November Lord Lansdowne expressed his deep regret[44] that Count Lamsdorff 'should have thought it necessary to recommence a discussion which we regard as definitely closed . . .'. The British government could not consent to a controversy as to the terms of the agreement, and desired to adhere to the original text. On the same day Hardinge received a note from Count Lamsdorff[45] to the effect that, after consultation

---

[39]Ibid., No. 58.   [40]Ibid., No. 65 (Inclosure).
[41]For the final text see below, p. 59. [42]Cd 2350, No. 72.
[43]Ibid., No. 79, Inclosure 2. The French text submitted by the Russian ministry read as follows: 'La Commission devra examiner toutes les circonstances ayant trait à l'incident de la Mer du Nord, notamment, élucider les faits y relatifs, et se prononcer sur la question de responsabilité selon les résultats de l'enquête' (ibid.). The English translation incorrectly employs the term 'decision'.
[44]Ibid., No. 75.   [45]Ibid., No. 76.

with the best Russian jurists, with Martens at their head, he had come to the conclusion that the original text of Article 2 was contrary to the sense of the provisions of the Hague Convention, and that his sole object in proposing a more exact text 'was to maintain *integrally* the idea of the Article'.

The British government was not prepared to compromise. On 15 November Lord Lansdowne took up the argument in a cable to Hardinge.[46] The objection that the British version of Article 2 was contrary to the sense of the Hague Convention might also be urged, he stated, against the Russian draft, 'for it cannot possibly be contended that the question of responsibility is a question of fact but that the question of blame is not'. In any case, the British ambassador was to remind Count Lamsdorff that 'what we contemplated was a Convention "analogous" to, and not identical with, those recommended by the Hague Convention'. And to make his position still clearer, Lord Lansdowne sent another message to Hardinge on the same day,[47] stating that 'in our opinion, question of responsibility and question of blame are both questions of fact'.

In view of this determined stand, the Russian government decided to give way. On 17 November Count Lamsdorff addressed a note to the British ambassador[48] stating that the whole misunderstanding consisted in the fact that the imperial government was, from the outset, convinced that the provisions of the Hague Convention would be the sole basis of the agreement, while the British government wished the commission of inquiry to have wider powers. Count Lamsdorff enclosed a revised draft of Article 2, which conformed to the original English text and which reflected, in addition, the understanding of the parties that the commission would deal with the conduct of all persons concerned and not merely with that of the Russian officers. The revised draft read:

The Commission shall inquire into and report on all the circumstances relative to the North Sea incident, and particularly on the question as to where the responsibility lies, and the degree of blame attaching to the subjects of the two High Contracting Parties or to the subjects of other countries in the event of their responsibility being established by the inquiry.

In recommending to Lord Lansdowne the acceptance of this version,[49] Hardinge noted: 'The fact that subjects of Great Britain, Russia and other countries have been mentioned has apparently removed a feeling underlying the opposition of the Russian Government that the word "blame" was aimed at Russian officers alone.'

The British government accepted the new draft, subject to Russian agreement that, should the instrument to be signed prove to be in any way inconsistent with the provisions of Articles 9–14 of the Hague

[46]Ibid., No. 77.   [47]Ibid., No. 78.
[48]Ibid., No. 88 (Inclosure 1).   [49]Ibid., No. 83.

Convention, the articles of the instrument should be held to override those of the convention.[50] The Russian government accepted the proviso,[51] and on 25 November 1904 Sir Charles Hardinge and Count Lamsdorff signed the following Declaration:[52]

His Britannic Majesty's Government and the Imperial Russian Government, having agreed to intrust to an International Commission of Inquiry, assembled conformably to Articles IX to XIV of The Hague Convention of the 29th (17th) July, 1899, for the pacific settlement of international disputes, the task of elucidating by means of an impartial and conscientious investigation the questions of fact connected with the incident which occurred during the night of the 21st–22nd (8th–9th) October, 1904, in the North Sea (on which occasion the firing of the guns of the Russian fleet caused the loss of a boat and the death of two persons belonging to a British fishing fleet, as well as damage to other boats of that fleet and injuries to the crews of some of those boats), the Undersigned, being duly authorised thereto, have agreed upon the following provisions:

Article I
The International Commission of Inquiry shall be composed of five members (Commissioners), of whom two shall be officers of high rank in the British and Imperial Russian navies respectively. The Governments of France and of the United States of America shall each be requested to select one of their naval officers of high rank as a member of the Commission. The fifth member shall be chosen by agreement between the four members above mentioned.
In the event of no agreement being arrived at between the four Commissioners as to the selection of the fifth member of the Commission, His Imperial and Royal Majesty the Emperor of Austria, King of Hungary, shall be invited to select him.
Each of the two High Contracting Parties shall likewise appoint a legal Assessor to advise the Commissioners, and an Agent officially empowered to take part in the labours of the Commission.

Article II
The Commission shall inquire into and report on all the circumstances relative to the North Sea incident, and particularly on the question as to where the responsibility lies, and the degree of blame attaching to the subjects of the two High Contracting Parties or to the subjects of other countries in the event of their responsibility being established by the inquiry.

Article III
The Commission shall settle the details of the procedure which it will follow for the purpose of accomplishing the task with which it has been intrusted.

[50] Ibid., No. 84.
[51] Ibid., No. 89.
[52] Ibid., No. 96, and Inclosure 1, containing the original French text and the English translation. For the English text see also 2 *AJIL* (1908), 929, and Scott, *Hague Court reports* (1916), p. 410.

Article IV

The two High Contracting Parties undertake to supply the International Commission of Inquiry, to the utmost extent which they may find possible, with all the means and facilities necessary, in order to enable it to acquaint itself thoroughly with and appreciate correctly the matters in dispute.

Article V

The Commission shall assemble at Paris as soon as possible after the signature of this Agreement.

Article VI

The Commission shall present its Report to the two High Contracting Parties signed by all the members of the Commission.

Article VII

The Commission shall take all its decisions by a majority of the votes of the five Commissioners.

Article VIII

The two High Contracting Parties undertake each to bear, on reciprocal terms, the expenses of the inquiry made by it previous to the assembly of the Commission. The expenses incurred by the International Commission, after the date of its assembly, in organizing its staff and in conducting the investigations which it will have to make, shall be shared equally by the two Governments.

THE WORK OF THE COMMISSION OF INQUIRY

On 22 December 1904 the four commissioners—Admirals Beaumont, Kaznakov (who was replaced by Admiral Doubassoff during the second session, on 9 January), Davis, and Fournier, selected respectively by Britain, Russia, the United States, and France—decided to ask that Admiral Baron Spaun of the Austro-Hungarian fleet be designated by the emperor of Austria, king of Hungary, as the fifth commissioner. The emperor complied with their request. The full commission, meeting on 9 January 1905, elected Admiral Fournier, of the French navy, as president.[53] Each of the two parties was represented by a legal assessor and by an agent. The agents were assisted by counsel and advocates.

In the course of ten sessions, from 9 to 25 January, the commission elaborated and adopted the rules of procedure. Thirteen sessions, from 25 January to 2 February, were devoted to the examination of witnesses (the British called for twenty-seven and the Russians for four witnesses). On 19 January the two agents read their recital of facts at a public meeting, and on 13 February they presented their observations and

[53]The full procès-verbaux of the sessions (in French) are to be found in FO Confidential Paper No. 8376. An abridged version which does not include the procès-verbaux of the sessions held in private and the depositions of the witnesses appears in *Arch. dip.*, 94, 3rd ser., No. 4 (ii, 1905), pp. 450–95.

conclusions. On 23 February the president communicated to the agents the report of the commission and two days later he read the report at a public meeting.

The rules of procedure[54]

According to the rules of procedure, the president of the commission was to be assisted by a secretary-general, whose function would be to ensure the drawing up of stenographic records of the sessions, to supervise the execution of all necessary translations, to keep all documents submitted to the commission in the archives, to contact the embassies with regard to all questions that might interest the commission, to issue communiqués to the press, and to ensure generally, under the direction of the president, the auxiliary services of the commission. Each of the contracting parties could authorize a person to assist in the work of the secretariat.

During the discussion of the draft rules of procedure presented by the agents of the parties, a debate took place on the desirability of holding meetings in public. The British agent, Sir Edward Fry, asserted that for Britain the subject of inquiry was of national interest and that the British public would passionately follow the work of the commission. There was nothing to fear from wide publicity. The Russian agent, Baron Michael Taube, claimed, on the other hand, that nothing could better ensure the veracity of the evidence than closed doors. The witnesses needed an atmosphere of calm in order to give evidence on facts which were already remote. Moreover, public discussion might reveal to third powers items of a confidential nature. Baron Taube pointed out, in addition, that the Hague Convention adopted the principle of closed doors with regard to arbitration (Art. 41).[55]

It was finally agreed that the sessions were to be public or 'not public' according to their object. Public sessions were to be those in which the agents of the parties gave their recitals of facts and in which the witnesses were examined, the session at which the agents presented their conclusions, and the last session, at which the commission would make known the results of its deliberations. All other sessions in which the deliberations of the commission would take place would not be public. The following persons were authorized to attend the non-public sessions: the assessors to the commissioners, the agents of the parties and their counsellors, the persons authorized or summoned by the commission, the members of the secretariat-general, and the aides and secretaries of the commissioners.[56]

[54]For the text of the rules, see the full procès-verbaux (referred to in the previous note), pp. 23–33; *Arch. dip.*, 93, 3rd ser., No. 1 (i, 1905), pp. 102–7; and 'De quelques règles de procédure appliquées en matière d'enquête internationale', in *Journal du droit international privé et de la jurisprudence comparée*, 33 (1906), Annex, pp. 335–40.

[55]*Arch. dip.*, 94, 3rd ser., No. 4 (ii, 1905), p. 452.

[56]Mandelstam states, with reference to the degree of publicity, that the sessions of the

The official language of the commission was French. However, witnesses could give evidence in their own language.

The commissioners were to retire to the Council Hall at any time they thought desirable. In principle, only the assessors were authorized to attend meetings in the Council Hall. The commissioners could decide to invite to the Council Hall any persons whose information or advice they considered might be useful. No publicity whatsoever was to be given to the deliberations among the commissioners and the assessors in the Council Hall. As to the decisions reached, they were to be announced in the Meeting Hall.

The agents were to present a statement of facts. They could be assisted by legal advisers, counsellors, or advocates, whose names were previously to be notified to the commission and approved by it.

Witnesses were to be summoned ex officio, or by request of the parties. They were to take an oath, or to declare on their word of honour to tell the truth, or to make a solemn declaration. Written evidence was to be accepted from witnesses whose prompt appearance could not be secured. A witness who refused or was unable to appear could give evidence before the competent authorities at his place of residence. The assessors and agents could proceed freely to examine witnesses. Legal advisers, counsellors, and advocates could ask questions directly, but only after having submitted them to the president. No witness could give evidence more than once on the same facts, except with the approval of the commission or in order to be confronted with another witness whose evidence contradicted his. Witnesses were not to be allowed to read from a text. However, they could be authorized by the president to help themselves with notes or documents if the nature of the alleged facts necessitated their use.

When the commissioners had exhausted all possible sources of information, the agents were entitled to submit their conclusions and observations in writing. The conclusions and observations were to be read by the agents at public sessions. Following the reading, the commissioners were to proceed in the Council Hall with deliberations on the conclusions to be drawn from the discussions, and with the drafting of their report.

---

commission were of three kinds: (1) public, i.e. open to a certain number of strangers, e.g. press correspondents—such were all sessions devoted to the reading of the exposition of facts and conclusions, and the report, as also the interrogation of witnesses; (2) not public, i.e. open only to persons in some way connected with the commission—such were all sessions held for purposes of deliberation; (3) sessions in the Council Hall, in which, in principle, only the commissioners and assessors participated (see Mandelstam, 'La commission internationale d'enquête sur l'incident de la mer du Nord', 12 *RGDIP* (1905), 374).

The statement of facts[57]

The British agent related in his statement of facts that, a few hours before the Dogger Bank incident, a vessel of the Russian fleet was sighted by the Swedish merchant vessel *Aldebaran*. The Russian vessel illuminated the *Aldebaran* with her searchlights and then fired on her for some time. As far as the Dogger Bank incident itself was concerned, the Russian vessels involved seemed to starboard their helms to pass to the southward or windward of all except a few of the British trawlers. All the trawlers exhibited at that time the regulation fishing lights as well as a white stern light, and most of them had deck lights burning brightly. As the Russian men-of-war neared the fishing fleet they were observed to be going slow or to have stopped. They then made signals and shone their searchlights on the trawlers, and subsequently fired on them from their starboard and port sides, there being two or three trawlers on their port side. The firing commenced and was continued after the searchlights of the firing ships had been turned on the trawlers long enough to enable those on board the Russian vessels to distinguish the character of the trawlers as peaceful fishing craft. The British agent pointed out, i.a., that the Russian vessel *Aurora* was hit by projectiles fired from other Russian vessels.

Apparently referring to previous Russian allegations of an attack by Japanese torpedo-boats, the British agent affirmed that, apart from the Russian men-of-war, there were no other men-of-war of any kind among the fishing vessels or in the vicinity during the night of the incident. No man-of-war had been noticed by any of the fishing-vessels for a considerable length of time. None of the fishing vessels carried any kind of war material. No Japanese man-of-war of any kind was at that moment in the North Sea, nor were there any Japanese on board the vessels of the fishing fleet. As regards losses, 2 men were killed and 6 wounded by the gun-fire; 1 vessel was sunk, and damage was caused to 5 more. Other vessels were damaged by the vibrations caused by explosions nearby.

In conclusion, the British agent stated that fishing-vessels which were pursuing their lawful occupation in fishing grounds in the North Sea, generally known as such and situated outside the route usually followed by vessels navigating between Skagen and the Straits of Dover, were without warning or provocation fired upon by men-of-war of the Imperial Russian Navy.

The Russian agent said that, according to information received by his government, the Japanese planned to take advantage of the passage of the Baltic fleet through Danish waters and to attack it there. Consequently, the Russian government adopted a series of security measures.

[57]See *Arch. dip.*, 93, 3rd ser., No. 1 (i, 1905), pp. 97–102. For the English text of the statement of the British agent, see *North Sea Incident; International Commission of Inquiry: Statement of Facts submitted on behalf of His Britannic Majesty's Government*, FO Confidential Paper No. 8319.

After the squadron left Skagen, on 7 October 1904, on its way to Cherbourg, alarming news concerning the appearance of suspicious ships was received. On the night of 8–9 October, at 12.55 a.m., the leading vessel of the last echelon perceived the silhouettes of two small boats, with all lights extinguished, approaching at great speed towards the Russian men-of-war. The whole squadron immediately shone its searchlights, and at the moment when the two suspicious boats were in the area of the projected rays they were recognized as torpedo-boats. The Russian vessels promptly opened fire on them. Immediately afterwards, small boats resembling fishing-vessels were noticed in the vicinity of the Russian ships and in the zone illuminated by their searchlights. Some of these boats did not show their lights, some showed them late, while others barred the route taken by the Russian ships. As it was clear that in these conditions the fire directed against the torpedo-boats could also hit the fishing-vessels, measures were taken to guarantee their safety as far as possible: the searchlight of the leading Russian vessel was alternately projected on to the fishing-boats and then lifted to 45°, which signified an order not to fire on a vessel so designated. However, in view of the danger of attack from the torpedo-boats, the men-of-war were compelled to continue firing in spite of the risk of hitting not only the fishing-vessels but also those vessels of the Baltic fleet itself which might be—and indeed were (as demonstrated by the presence, immediately established, of the *Dmitri Donskoi* and the *Aurora*)—in the line of fire.

Meanwhile, according to the Russian agent, the two torpedo-boats moved away and shortly afterwards disappeared. At that moment, by order of the leading Russian vessel, fire was stopped. Firing lasted for ten minutes in all. Although apprehensive that some of the fishing-boats might have been damaged by the fire of his fleet, but not being sure, on the other hand, that all danger from the two (or perhaps more) torpedo-boats was completely over, Admiral Rojdestvensky judged it essential that the whole squadron should continue its voyage without stopping.

The Russian agent concluded that, in the circumstances, Admiral Rojdestvensky, who held the great responsibility of ensuring the safety of his forces, not only had the right but, what is more, was under the absolute obligation to act as he did, i.e. while realizing that he might harm innocent fishermen, subjects of a neutral power, at the same time he was forced to use all means at his disposal to destroy the torpedo-boats which had attacked his squadron.

It will be noted that in justifying the actions of Admiral Rojdestvensky the Russian agent did not mention the possible complicity of the British vessels in the alleged Japanese attack. On the contrary, he referred to 'innocent (*inoffensifs*) fishermen'. It seems that the Russian government had decided not to endorse the version given by the admiral in his first reports on the incident (above, pp. 51–2).

Conclusions and observations presented by the agents[58]

The agent of the British government drew the following conclusions from the evidence of the witnesses and documents.

I. That on the night of the 21st–22nd (8th–9th) October, 1904, there was in fact no torpedo-boat or destroyer present among the British trawlers or in the neighbourhood of the Russian fleet, and that the Russian officers were mistaken in their belief that such vessels were present, or in the neighbourhood, or attacked, or intended to attack, the Russian fleet.

II. (*a*) That there was no sufficient justification for opening fire at all.

(*b*) When opened, there was a failure to direct and control the fire so as to avoid injury to the fishing fleet.

(*c*) The firing upon the fishing fleet was continued for an unreasonable length of time.

III. That those on board the Russian fleet ought to have rendered assistance to the injured men and damaged vessels.

IV. That there was no fault of any kind in the conduct of those on the British trawlers or those connected with their management.

In his observations the British agent made the following analysis of certain pertinent events: on the morning of 21 October the transport *Kamtchatka* which, with the cruisers *Dmitri Donskoi* and *Aurora*, formed the fourth division of the Russian fleet, had fallen behind these cruisers—a delay which was aggravated by an accident in her engines to such an extent that by 8 o'clock in the evening she was some 30–35 miles behind Admiral Rojdestvensky's division, instead of 50 miles ahead of it, as she should have been. In accordance with wireless telegrams transmitted to the flagship *Souvoroff* at about 8.30 in the evening, the crew on board the *Kamtchatka* believed that it was being subjected to an attack by torpedo-boats. In fact the *Kamtchatka* was not attacked but, on the contrary, opened fire herself on the German fishing-boat *Sonntag*, and then bombarded the Swedish vessel *Aldebaran* for a considerable time. The reports received from the *Kamtchatka* caused a state of alert to be ordered in Admiral Rojdestvensky's division at nightfall. The officers of that division redoubled their vigilance since they expected that an attack would be delivered at or about the place where the incident occurred.

When the Dogger Bank incident started, at about 1 o'clock in the morning, the *Aurora* and the *Dmitri Donskoi*, which the admiral and his staff thought were at least fifteen miles ahead of the admiral's division, were in fact in a position somewhere before the beam of the leading ship of his division, and within the range of its guns. In these circumstances the silhouette of a vessel could be seen in front of the *Souvoroff*. According to Admiral Rojdestvensky's report, two silhouettes were seen. The

[58]See *Arch. dip.*, 94, 3rd ser., No. 4 (ii, 1905), pp. 474–89. For the English text of the observations and conclusions of the British agent see *North Sea Incident; International Commission of Inquiry: Conclusions and Observations presented on behalf of His Britannic Majesty's Government*, FO Confidential Paper No. 8341.

probable explanation of what followed was that the *Aurora*, unknown to those on board the *Souvoroff*, went on ahead of her to a distance of 1½–2 miles, and it was the *Aurora's* silhouette that was first taken for a torpedo-boat. The searchlights of the *Souvoroff* were turned in the direction of the silhouette but it was impossible to illuminate an object at such a distance. A luminous veil was thus formed, behind which the silhouette disappeared; and two fishing boats, which were only partly illuminated, were mistaken, in the state of haste and expectation which reigned, for torpedo-boats. Order was given on the *Souvoroff* to open fire, and her example was immediately followed by the other vessels of the squadron.

As a result of the bombardment, the *Aurora* was struck in five places. Although this fact was known to Admiral Rojdestvensky shortly after the accident, it was not mentioned in the copy of the admiral's cable given to the representatives of the British government, and was not revealed by the Russian government until six weeks after the event. Moreover, no officer from the *Aurora* or from the *Dmitri Donskoi* was cited as a witness before the commission. Nor were the log-books, order-books, or signal-books of any of the vessels produced before the commission up to the end of the public sittings on 2 February.

The British agent stressed that, according to the Russian evidence, one of the torpedo-boats was seriously damaged and was on the verge of sinking: in fact it was a fishing-vessel that was thus damaged and sunk. According to the same evidence, the so-called torpedo-boat to port succeeded in escaping, despite the fire directed at it; this was exactly what happened to the fishing-boat *Mino*. It was well known that a vessel of another kind and size could be mistaken at first sight, at night, for a torpedo-boat. In such circumstances it was the duty of experienced officers to wait a moment and to watch closely before starting to fire. Had the officers done so, they would have seen that the so-called torpedo-boats were either Russian vessels or harmless trawlers.

The British agent insinuated that the attack on the fishing-vessels was deliberate. It appeared, he stated, from the telegraphic reports on the incident sent by Admiral Rojdestvensky and communicated to the British government, that the Russian officers at the time suspected that the trawlers were assisting in the supposed attack, and, in these circumstances, it must be inferred that the fire of the Russian fleet was, to some extent, directed upon the fishing-boats. This indeed could hardly be disputed, in view of the statement in one of the admiral's telegrams that he respected all fishing-boats during the voyage, except those which were in the company of foreign torpedo-boats.

Appraisal of the facts revealed by the inquiry led the agent of the Russian government to state the following findings: (1) that the firing by the squadron was exclusively caused by the dangerously close approach of two torpedo-boats proceeding under cover of night, without lights and at full speed, towards the division which included the vessel flying Admiral Rojdestvensky's flag; (2) that the squadron's fire was directed exclusively against those torpedo-boats and that the English fishing-boats were hit as a result of unavoidable accident; (3) that the squadron did everything in its power to minimize, as far as possible, the risk of hitting the fishing-vessels.

After giving reasons for each of the above findings, the Russian agent drew two conclusions: (1) that the firing by the Russian squadron on the night of 21–22 October 1904 was ordered and carried out in legitimate execution of the military duties of the commander of the squadron; (2) that, consequently, no responsibility could possibly rest upon Admiral Rojdestvensky or any of his subordinates.

In support of his contentions, he stated that the facts alleged by his government were actually witnessed by authoritative naval officers of high moral standing, whereas those alleged by Great Britain were supported only by official notes of a certain government to the effect that there were no torpedo-boats at the place of the incident, and by the evidence of fishermen who were under such unfavourable conditions that they could not properly have appreciated the course of events.

With regard to the *Kamtchatka* incident, the agent asserted that the alarm sounded by that vessel made little impression on board the *Souvoroff*. If the squadron expected an attack, it was by reason of information received since the time of its departure, notably at Skagen. He said in this connection that the order to start firing was given by Admiral Rojdestvensky himself, 'en pleine connaissance de cause'.

The allegation that the fishing-vessels were mistaken for torpedo-boats was inadmissible in his view, not only because of the different shape and structure of the two kinds of ships but because the simultaneous presence of torpedo-boats perceived in the distance and the group of numerous fishing-boats permitted a comparison which excluded any confusion between them. Any allegation that the suspected boats were in fact certain cruisers of the squadron was also unfounded. The sailing orders which they had to follow, and which they regularly followed, were such that these cruisers sailed many hours ahead of Rojdestvensky's division on the same route. They reached Cherbourg long before the arrival of the other echelons. Any mistake with regard to the other vessels of the squadron was also impossible. In particular, the *Aurora* could not have been involved, because her position was different from that of the two (Japanese) torpedo-boats and because it was not possible to confuse a cruiser of 6,000 tons with a torpedo-boat of 200 or 300 tons. The object of the firing was clear from the evidence of one of the Russian officers, who stated that the torpedo-boat, target of the fire, was lit up as if by magnesium, by the glow of burning projectiles.

The Russian agent also noted that the fishing-vessels were not the only innocent boats that Admiral Rojdestvensky had been unable to avoid firing upon. Certain ships of his own squadron also suffered damage.

At the end of his observations the Russian agent expressed the sincere regret of his government that the incident had caused injury to innocent parties. While refusing to admit the responsibility of the commander of the squadron, he stated that the imperial government in no way intended to avoid paying material reparation, and would be ready to compensate the innocent victims of the fleet's fire and make good the damage caused. The fixing and the distribution of the compensation could be referred to a tribunal chosen from the Permanent Court of Arbitration.

The report of the commission[59]

In their report of 26 February 1905 the commissioners reached the following findings.

The accidental delay of the *Kamtchatka* may incidentally have been the cause of the events which followed. This transport did, in fact, meet the Swedish vessel *Aldebaran* and other unknown vessels, and opened fire on them, no doubt as a result of her anxiety caused by her momentary isolation, her damaged engines, and her poor fighting ability. The commander of the *Kamtchatka* sent a message to his commander-in-chief regarding this encounter, stating that he was 'attacked on all sides by torpedo-boats'.[60] In order to understand the effect of this news on Admiral Rojdestvensky's subsequent decisions, it should be remembered that, in his opinion, the torpedo-boats (of whose presence fifty miles to the rear of his division he had been informed, rightly or wrongly) might overtake and attack him at about 1 o'clock in the morning. The information received led Admiral Rojdestvensky, at about 10 o'clock in the evening, to signal to his ships to redouble their vigilance and to look out for an attack by torpedo-boats. Moreover, the admiral's standing orders to the officer of the watch on board all the ships were to open fire in the event of an obvious and imminent attack by torpedo-boats. If the attack came from ahead, he was to open fire on his own initiative; if from astern, he should refer to his commanding officer.

With regard to these orders, the majority of the commissioners considered that they were in no way excessive in time of war, and particu-

[59]For the English text see Cd 2352 (Russia No. 3, 1905) and Scott, *Hague Court reports* (1916), pp. 404–10. For the original French text see the procès-verbaux referred to at p. 60, n. 53 above; Scott, *Hague Court reports* (1916), App., p. 609; and 12 *RGDIP* (1905), Documents, p. 4.

[60]There was abundant evidence, not included in the report of the commission, to show that Admiral Rojdestvensky and other officers of the Baltic fleet were extremely nervous and that they were in great fear of mines and attacks by Japanese torpedo-boats. A dispatch to the Berlin *Lokal Anzeiger* of 27 Oct. stated that a German fishing-vessel was fired on off the Dogger Bank on 21 Oct. The master of a Norwegian steamship reported that he was fired on by a Russian ship on 23 Oct. in the English Channel. The skipper of a Swedish steamer stated that on 21 Oct. his vessel was chased in the Skagerak by a foreign cruiser, apparently Russian. It was also reported that a Danish torpedo-boat was fired upon (see Hershey, p. 223).

larly in the circumstances then obtaining, which Admiral Rojdestvensky had every reason to consider very alarming.

As for the British fishing-vessels, it appeared from the concordant testimony of the British witnesses that all these boats carried their proper lights and were trawling in accordance with their usual rules.

The incident started when the look-out men on board the *Souvoroff* discovered, on the crest of the waves on the starboard bow, at an approximate distance of 18 to 20 cables, a vessel which aroused their suspicions because they saw no light and because she appeared to be bearing down on them. When the suspicious-looking vessel was shown up by the searchlight, the look-out men thought they recognized a torpedo-boat proceeding at great speed. It was on account of these appearances that Admiral Rojdestvensky ordered fire to be opened on this unknown vessel. The majority of the commissioners expressed the opinion that the responsibility for this action and the results of the fire to which the fishing fleet was subjected were to be attributed to Admiral Rojdestvensky.

The report stated further that, in order to prevent fire from being directed at a fishing-vessel situated very close to the *Souvoroff*, the searchlight was immediately raised to an angle of 45°. At the same time the look-out men on board the *Souvoroff* perceived to port another vessel, which aroused their suspicions because it presented the same features as those of the object of their fire to starboard. Fire was immediately opened on this second object.

According to the standing orders of the fleet, the admiral indicated the objects at which fire should be aimed by directing his searchlight upon them; but as every vessel swept the horizon in every direction with her own searchlights to avoid being taken by surprise, it was difficult to prevent confusion.

The firing, which lasted for ten to twelve minutes, caused great loss to the trawlers. Two men were killed and 6 others wounded; 1 boat was sunk and 5 were damaged to a greater or lesser extent. The Russian cruiser *Aurora* was also hit by several shots.

The majority of the commissioners observed that they did not have precise enough details to determine what was the object fired on by the ships; but the commissioners unanimously recognized that the vessels of the fishing fleet did not commit any hostile act. The majority were of the opinion that there were no torpedo-boats either among the trawlers or anywhere nearby, and that the opening of fire by Admiral Rojdestvensky was not justifiable. The Russian commissioner, not considering himself justified in sharing this opinion, expressed his conviction that it was precisely the suspicious-looking vessels approaching the squadron with hostile intent which provoked the fire.

In the view of the majority, the fact that the *Aurora* was hit by several 47 mm. and 75 mm. shells led to the supposition that this cruiser, and perhaps some other Russian ships left behind on the route followed by the *Souvoroff*, but unknown to that vessel, might have provoked and been the target of the first few shots. This mistake might have been due to the fact that the *Aurora*, seen from astern, was apparently showing no light, and by a nocturnal optical illusion which deceived the look-out on the flagship. According to the conjectures of the commissioners, certain distant trawlers could have been mistaken for the Russians' original objectives, and thus were fired upon directly. Others, on the contrary, might have been struck by fire apparently aimed at more distant objectives. These considerations, the commissioners went on, were not in contradiction with the impressions formed by certain of the trawlers which, finding that they had been hit, and remaining in the glare of the searchlights, apparently believed that they were the target of direct fire.

The time during which the firing lasted on the starboard side, even taking into account the Russian version, seemed to the majority of the commissioners to have been longer than was necessary. The majority considered, at the same time, that they did not have enough data to enable them to determine why the fire on the port side was continued. In any case, the commissioners took 'pleasure in recognizing unanimously that Admiral Rojdestvensky personally did everything he could, from the beginning to the end of the incident, to prevent trawlers, recognized as such, from being fired upon by the squadron'. They also recognized unanimously that, after the circumstances which preceded the incident and those which caused it, there was, at the cessation of fire, sufficient uncertainty with regard to the danger to which the division of vessels had been exposed to induce the admiral to proceed on his way. Nevertheless, the majority regretted that Admiral Rojdestvensky, when passing through the Straits of Dover, did not take care to inform the authorities of the neighbouring maritime powers that, since he had been led to open fire near a group of trawlers, these boats stood in need of assistance.

In concluding their report the commissioners declared that their findings 'are not, in their opinion, of a nature to cast any discredit upon the military qualities or the humanity of Admiral Rojdestvensky, or of the personnel of his squadron'.

Following the submission of the report to the parties, Russia made a payment, by way of damages, of £65,000,[61] and the dispute was thus closed.

CONCLUSIONS

The nature of the dispute

The Dogger Bank Commission of Inquiry (also referred to as the Paris Commission) departed from the model established by the Hague

[61]Ibid., p. 238.

Convention of 1899 as regards the kind of dispute with which it dealt. While the convention provided for the submission to international investigation of disputes which did not involve the essential interests or the honour of the parties, the Dogger Bank dispute certainly involved such interests and honour. Britain saw in the action of the Russian fleet an attack on her neutral rights and interests. Russia, on the other hand, based her case on her rights and interests as a belligerent power anxious to ensure the security of her armed forces against enemy attack. As far as honour was concerned, the diplomatic correspondence preceding the formation of the inquiry commission provides ample evidence of considerations of honour and prestige. The Russian allegations of complicity on the part of British fishing-vessels in a Japanese attack on the Russian fleet were a serious challenge to the honour of neutral Britain (above, p. 55), while the Russian government was particularly sensitive to British demands, made under threats, for the searching out of the persons responsible, for the punishment of the guilty ones and for guarantees against the repetition of similar incidents above, pp. 50–1, 54). British accusations that the Russian fleet abandoned defenceless fishermen after having fired upon them without the slightest justification were regarded as an attack on Russian honour. Moreover, the fact that the British prime minister had ridiculed the attack as one by 'phantom' Japanese torpedo-boats could only be interpreted as an insult to the professional capabilities of the Imperial Russian Navy. According to one view, the British government sought a finding by an international commission that no Japanese torpedo-boats were involved, in order to make the Russians look ridiculous and thus inflict an 'ironic vengeance' on their adversary.[62]

Paradoxically, it may be thought, it is precisely because the dispute was of a different nature from that envisaged in Article 9 of the Hague Convention that it came within the kind of dispute which the promoter of that institution, Martens, thought as most suitable for submission to inquiry. Britain's susceptibilities were so hurt, British public opinion was so roused—especially after the conflicting Russian version of the incident became known—that the two countries were on the verge of war within a week from the occurrence of the incident.

The Dogger Bank incident seemed also to justify Martens's prognosis with respect to the futility of conducting two independent national inquiries. Russia agreed to order her admiral to conduct an inquiry, but she objected to interference in it. And to ensure her freedom of action she declined the invitation to be officially represented at the British inquiries opened at Hull by the coroner and by the Board of Trade.[63]

[62]See La Penha, p. 188.

[63]While the talks on the constitution of an international inquiry were proceeding, the British Board of Trade prepared to conduct its own inquiry into the Dogger Bank incident, and Lord Lansdowne informed Count Benckendorff on 26 October 1904 that every facility would be given to any representative whom the Russian embassy might appoint for the

The holding of two parallel national inquiries entailed the risk of contradictory findings, which might lead to an irreparable misunderstanding. It was to forestall such an eventuality that the Hague Convention offered a solution. France, being interested in this conflict, took advantage of her alliance and friendship with both parties to offer her good offices. She suggested recourse to an international commission of inquiry, and the offer was immediately accepted.[64] Tension was at once relaxed, and the crisis averted, the moment the two governments decided to have recourse to an international commission of inquiry.

The competence of the commission. Inquiry and judicial functions

The Declaration of St Petersburg (above, p. 59) charged the Dogger Bank Commission with the general task, set out in the Preamble, of elucidating, by means of an impartial and conscientious investigation, the questions of fact connected with the incident. The more specific task of the commission, formulated in Article 2, was to inquire into 'all the circumstances relative to the incident'. These circumstances were to include 'the question as to where responsibility lies, and the degree of blame attaching to the persons found responsible'. The obvious departure from the model of inquiry commissions established by the Hague Convention of 1899 was the power of the commission to examine questions of responsibilities and blame generally regarded as falling within the purview of judicial tribunals.

The nature of both the inquiry and the judicial functions of the commission, as well as the relationship between them, have been the subject of academic discussions which may assist us in defining the proper functions of a genuine inquiry commission.

Mandelstam claims (pp. 406–8) that many of the articles of the commission's report combined an exposé of facts with 'appreciations' of their causes and responsibilities; other articles were in the nature of findings of a judge or, rather, of a jury, pronouncing whether there was or was not a violation of international law (délit international). To the first category belong the two findings that the accidental delay of the *Kamtchatka* was, perhaps, the cause of the incident, and that the responsibility for opening fire and the results of the firing to which the fishing fleet was exposed were to be attributed to Admiral Rojdestvensky.

The judicial function, on the other hand, is expressed in the following findings: The minute precautions taken by Admiral Rojdestvensky

---

purpose of observing the proceedings. On 1 Nov. the Russian ambassador advised the FO that the Russian government did not consider it essential that their embassy should be represented at the inquiry to be held at Hull (see Cd 2350, Nos 12 & 52). A British lawyer followed the proceedings at Hull on behalf of the Russian embassy.
[64]See Politis, p. 158.

seemed to be justified by numerous reports regarding possible hostile attacks; the standing orders given by the admiral to the officer of the watch to open fire in case of an evident, imminent attack by torpedo-boats were in no way excessive in time of war and, particularly, in the circumstances surrounding the incident; the vessels of the fishing fleet did not commit any hostile act; since there were no torpedo-boats, the opening of fire by Admiral Rojdestvensky was not justifiable; the time of firing on the starboard side seemed to have been longer than was necessary; the admiral did everything he could to prevent trawlers, recognized as such, from being fired upon by the squadron; there was sufficient uncertainty with regard to possible danger to induce the admiral to proceed on his way, without rendering assistance to the injured fishermen; it was regrettable that Admiral Rojdestvensky did not take care to inform the authorities of the neighbouring powers of the need to assist the trawlers.

Mandelstam concludes that, in sum, the commissioners fulfilled their role of judges—as opposed to investigators—by recognizing that the British ships did not commit any hostile act, and also by their findings that the opening of fire was unjustified, that it lasted too long, and that the admiral failed to inform neighbouring states of the incident. The last three findings did not, he states, amount to imputing blame. This followed from the concluding observation of the report, that none of the findings was of a nature to cast discredit upon the military qualities or the humanity of Admiral Rojdestvensky or of the personnel of his squadron.

Mandelstam's conception of the judicial functions of the commission is closely followed by Pillet (p. 25). The 'pretended findings of fact' concerning the unjustifiable opening of fire, the duration of the firing and the failure to inform, writes Pillet, were also judgments regarding the conduct of Admiral Rojdestvensky and his officers. What more would one have found in an arbitral sentence, except a condemnation for which all the grounds already existed in the report? Pillet concludes, therefore, that the only application made of the innovation initiated at the Hague Conference resulted in falsifying the meaning of this innovation to make it fit into the traditional framework of international arbitration.

According to Politis (pp. 162–3), the commission's report contains an analytical exposé of the facts, their causes and consequences, and of the responsibilities which are to be deduced from them. With regard to the facts, the most important finding was that there was no torpedo-boat on the spot. As regards the appreciation of facts and responsibilities, they were divided into three categories. First, no reproach could be addressed to the British trawlers—they trawled in conformity with their usual regulations and had not committed any hostile act. Secondly, Admiral Rojdestvensky had engaged his responsibility in three ways—

by opening fire unjustifiably, since there was no enemy torpedo-boat nearby; by the excessive duration of the fire; and by the failure to inform. Thirdly, if he committed faults, these implied neither intention nor culpable negligence.[65] Thus, after admitting his responsibility, the commission recognized unanimously that there was no room to blame him. That was the final conclusion of the report—the findings did not cast any discredit upon the military qualities or the humanity of the admiral or of his men.

The parties, continues Politis, immediately drew the practical conclusion that, as no one incurred blame, there was no room for a criminal prosecution. However, since Russia was held responsible for the incident, the Russian government hastened to carry out the obligation, which it had accepted in advance, to compensate the victims.

Unlike Mandelstam, Politis (pp. 166–7) makes no attempt to separate the fact-finding (inquiry) functions of the Dogger Bank Commission from its judicial functions. In his opinion the case proved that the distinction between facts and law could not always be made. Logical analysis permitted the conflict to be confined to:

(1) A difference of appreciation with regard to a fact: had the Russian admiral really seen the Japanese torpedo-boats or was he justified in the circumstances in believing in their presence?

(2) A difference of appreciation with regard to a point of law: had Russia, because of the conduct of her agents, a responsibility towards Britain, from the double point of view of reparation for damage caused and punishment of the guilty? The question of fact conditioned the question of law. To resolve the latter, one had to begin by answering the former. Theoretically these questions were distinct, and it is conceivable that the inquiry could have been limited to the question of fact, in which event its result would help the parties to resolve the second, either by amicable agreement or by recourse to arbitration. But, as the parties realized, this was not possible in practice. At the end of the negotiations Russia accepted the British approach and in the

[65]Politis offers the following interpretation: Rojdestvensky's knowledge before he sailed of the danger of an attack in the North Sea made him anxious; the message announcing that one of his vessels was being attacked on all sides by torpedo-boats heightened this to the point of alarm; excessive precautions followed, including the use of searchlights at night that provoked confusion in the firing from which the fishermen had suffered. On the other hand, a series of events—the damage to a vessel, the delay of one of the divisions of the squadron, a nocturnal optical illusion caused by a ship seen from astern showing no visible light—tended to prove that the bombardment suffered by the fishing fleet was a simple accident which, with a little more presence of mind, could have been avoided, but which was in no way due to negligence, still less to culpable negligence; on the contrary, many facts, e.g. the manoeuvre of one of the units of the fleet to avoid damaging an innocent fishing-boat and the order given, as soon as the trawlers were recognized as such, not to fire on them, showed that the admiral had done everything in his power to prevent trawlers, recognized as such, from being fired upon by the squadron. As to his failure to help the victims, one had to recognize that the circumstances at the time of the cessation of fire seemed sufficiently uncertain to induce the admiral to proceed on his way (ibid., p. 163).

Declaration of St Petersburg both parties seemed to regard the questions of responsibility and blame as questions of fact.[66]

It should be stressed that in the above analysis Politis imputes to the commission certain deductions which do not in fact appear in the report. The commission did not state that no fault could be imputed to the British trawlers. It said only that they trawled in conformity with their usual regulations and that they had not committed any hostile act. The report did not state that Admiral Rojdestvensky had incurred responsibility in three ways. It said only that he was responsible for the opening of fire and the ensuing damage. It did not state that his responsibility was involved in its other findings on the unjustified opening of fire,[67] on the duration of the fire, and on the failure to inform. Similarly, nowhere in the report was it said that Russia was responsible for the incident. Moreover, the commissioners did not state that the admiral committed 'faults' and that these 'faults' did not imply either 'intention', or 'negligence', or 'culpable negligence'. They also did not state that there was no room to apportion 'blame'. All these statements and terms are used by Politis in order to convey what is, in his opinion, the commissioners' interpretation of the events and of their own functions.

Let us now examine how the commissioners interpreted their task of investigating the questions of fact and the surrounding circumstances, including the questions of responsibility and blame.

To use their own words, the commissioners proceeded in their report to analyse the facts in 'their logical sequence'; they considered that by making known the prevailing opinion of the commission on each important or decisive point of the report, they thus made sufficiently clear the causes and consequences of the incident, as well as the deductions which were to be drawn from them with regard to the question of responsibility (section 1 of the report).

It appears that the commissioners considered their report to be confined to an analysis of facts. While this analysis makes clear the causes and the consequences of the incident, it does not follow that these causes and consequences are explicitly stated in the report. The same holds true with regard to the question of responsibility. The analysis of facts, in their opinion, made clear the deductions 'which are to be drawn' from the causes and the consequences of the incident with regard to the question of responsibility. It does not follow that the commissioners themselves stated in the report the deductions which they had drawn in the matter. Did they mean that the deductions were to be made by the parties on the basis of the report?

In the report, which consists of seventeen sections, there is only one—

[66]Reference is made here to the Preamble of the declaration. In the view of Politis, it is only by an abuse of language that one can say of the search for responsibility, even with regard to simple reparation for damage, that it constitutes a question of fact.

[67]It will be recalled that the commission dealt with the opening of fire on two occasions (see above, pp. 69 f.).

section 11—in which the commission specifically makes a finding on responsibility. In that section the majority of the commissioners express the opinion that the responsibility for the order to fire and for the results of the fire was to be attributed to Admiral Rojdestvensky. Bearing in mind the context within which the majority of the commissioners reached this finding, it would seem that they intended to convey a statement of fact, without expressing any opinion on the possible legal responsibility involved. It will be noted that only after this finding did the commissioners state that the fishing fleet had not committed any hostile act and that the opening of the fire was not justified as there were no enemy torpedo-boats nearby.

The foregoing examination is intended to enlighten us on the nature of the commission's task, particularly on the question whether a differentiation could be made between its fact-finding and its judicial functions. This question is central to our study, since we are seeking to understand the nature of a genuine commission without a judicial mandate. For this purpose we must first define the term 'responsibility'. Two interpretations are possible: factual responsibility and legal responsibility. A person who has performed a certain act may or may not be legally responsible for a violation of international law. The answer depends on whether or not the act performed is held to entail such a violation. The finding that Admiral Rojdestvensky was responsible for giving the order to fire and for the resulting damage is in itself a finding of fact. If the parties, or an arbitral tribunal, held that the factual responsibility for giving the order to fire which caused the damage entailed legal responsibility, since it constituted a violation of international law, we could say no more than that the above finding of fact had a certain legal effect. For that reason it is not transformed into a finding of law. Conversely, if the parties, or an arbitral tribunal, held that the order to fire would not entail legal responsibility in case it were proved that the fishing-boats were in collusion with attacking Japanese boats, then the finding of fact regarding the order to fire would not entail legal consequences, such as payment of damages.

It is generally accepted that it is within the competence of a genuine inquiry commission to establish who were the authors of the act which is the subject of the investigation.[68] In the oft-quoted *Maine* case, the principal task of an international inquiry commission would have been to establish whether the Spanish authorities caused the explosion on the *Maine*. If the inquiry commission established that Spanish officials

---

[68] Cf. Hyde, *International law* (2nd edn, 1947), ii, 1568 (with reference to the Hague Conventions): '. . . As a fact-finding body, a commission of inquiry, especially when composed chiefly of nationals of states other than those at variance, should be competent to make a report that is entitled to respect. Hence its conclusions on any of the factual aspects of a dispute, for instance, the causes of events, or the authorship of acts, or the consequences of what may have taken place, may be of first importance as a means of enabling the parties to a controversy to reach accord . . .'.

blew up, or were responsible for blowing up, the vessel, would such a finding be defined as legal simply because it entailed legal consequences? Would such a commission be designated as a court by virtue of such a finding? Similarly, if one of the main tasks of the inquiry commission concerning the massacres of the Armenians was to establish whether or not Turkish soldiers participated in the massacres, and if the commission ascertained the fact of such participation or if it reported that Turkish soldiers were responsible for the massacres in the sense that they participated in them, would that be a finding of a judicial character?

It is submitted that an inquiry commission should be charged with the establishment of factual responsibility in the sense of the authorship of the acts subject to the inquiry. It is for the parties or an arbitral tribunal, and not for an inquiry commission, to evaluate the legal consequences of such a finding.

We come now to the central issue: with regard to the competence to establish the guilt of the persons found 'responsible', had the Dogger Bank Commission exercised an inquiry function or a judicial function, or both? We frame the question in this way because, in spite of its mandate to establish 'blame', the commission made no finding as to the existence of 'blame' or 'guilt'. It made a finding regarding the humanity and military qualities of the Russian officers, which some writers consider equivalent to a verdict of 'not guilty'.

We would here suggest that the entire analysis of facts made by the commission for the purpose of making clear whether the Russian officers were guilty, falls properly within the competence and functions of a genuine inquiry commission established in accordance with the Hague Convention of 1899.

As inquiry commissions are not charged simply with stating the facts but with elucidating 'questions' of fact by an impartial and conscientious investigation, the search for the causes of an incident is generally considered as part of the fact-finding function. Thus, if an inquiry is to be made into a border incident, the governments involved would be interested in receiving a report not only on certain facts, but also on the causes underlying those facts. The commission of inquiry is required to enlighten the parties, not by supplying them with a list of unrelated facts but by providing them with an intelligible account of the chain of events.[69] In the circumstances described during the deliberations of the Hague Conference of 1899, it was thought likely that a tense situation might develop if people in one state believed that the neighbouring state had deliberately caused a border incident. If the incident was due to a mistake, or a misunderstanding, the state whose

---

[69]Witenberg (p. 6) defined the functions of commissions of inquiry as follows: 'Il s'agit de reconstituer des faits litigieux, *d'en établir la relation exacte*, sans tirer, d'ailleurs, aucune conséquence' (emphasis added).

soldiers had caused it might well agree to the submission of the dispute to an inquiry commission. The primary task of such a commission would be to determine the origins of the incident, and particularly whether the persons involved had acted in good or in bad faith. It is pertinent that the appreciation of the good or bad faith of the author of an act was considered by French jurisprudence as a simple question of fact.[70]

The Dogger Bank case is a perfect example of an incident suitable for a genuine inquiry commission with no judicial function. Public opinion in Britain saw in the incident the expression of a ruthless and deliberately injurious policy on the part of the Russian navy. A genuine inquiry commission would have been entrusted with the elucidation of all the relevant facts which would enable it to conclude whether Admiral Rojdestvensky had acted in good or in bad faith. In essence, such a commission should have approached its task by the same route—by ascertaining the causes and the consequences of the different actions involved in the incident, including the motives of the principal persons concerned. A commission of this kind would have been bound to find out whether the fishing-boats had or had not committed a hostile act. Why should a finding to that effect be regarded as a judicial finding? What is an inquiry commission required to do when it investigates a shooting incident, if not to establish who were the authors of the shooting and, if the case arises, their accomplices? Such a commission would have been bound, similarly, to find out whether Admiral Rojdestvensky was 'justified' in fact in giving the order to fire, i.e. it would have been expected to find out whether there were or were not Japanese boats in the vicinity. In this respect, the finding of the Dogger Bank Commission is a simple finding of fact. And to avoid any impression to the contrary, the commission stated that the order to fire was unjustified since there were no Japanese torpedo-boats nearby. The report of the commission —and for that matter the report of any inquiry commission—would have lost none of its intrinsic value if the commissioners had omitted their finding on the 'unjustifiable' opening of fire and had confined themselves to a finding that there were no Japanese torpedo-boats in the vicinity. If one side claims that an order was given to fire at Japanese boats and the commission finds that there were no Japanese boats there, the parties themselves could draw the obvious conclusion that the order was not justified in fact (even though the admiral may have had cogent reasons to believe in the presence of enemy boats).

A finding of fact that the incident was caused because the admiral gave the order to fire when he mistook one or more of his own vessels for enemy boats, would have fulfilled the same purpose as an allegedly

[70] See Pillet, p. 13. Cf. Politis (above, pp 74–5), who writes that the conflict could have been confined to a question of fact, i.e. whether the Russian admiral really saw Japanese torpedo-boats or *whether he had any grounds in the circumstances for believing in their presence.*

judicial finding that the admiral was responsible for unjustified opening of fire. All the other findings of the commission, regarding the background, development, and consequences of the incident, would have had their place in a report of a genuine inquiry commission not exercising a judicial mandate. This includes the 'verdict' regarding the humanity and military qualities of the Russian officers. If the commission were charged with establishing whether the officers acted in good or in bad faith, it would be perfectly normal for it to express its appraisal of the conduct of the officers. (In view of the mistakes that were made by the Russian officers, perhaps the commission should have taken care not to create the impression of praising them.) As regards the failure of the admiral to give assistance to his victims, it will be recalled that British public opinion saw in this failure unequivocal evidence of bad faith on his part (above, p. 49). It follows that an inquiry commission legitimately charged with establishing whether there was or was not bad faith was entitled to deal with this aspect of the question and to present a clear appraisal of the admiral's motives. If the commission were to find that the admiral had good reasons not to render assistance, it should so report. And if it was convinced that in the circumstances the admiral could have been more helpful, there was no reason to conceal such an opinion. The same observations are valid with regard to the finding that the admiral did everything he could to prevent trawlers, recognized as such, from being fired upon.

It is further submitted that the following two findings should not be treated as judicial in contrast to investigatory: that the minute precautions taken by Admiral Rojdestvensky seemed to be justified by numerous reports regarding possible hostile action; and that the standing orders to the officers of the watch to open fire in the event of an evident and imminent attack by torpedo-boats were in no way excessive in time of war and, more particularly, in the circumstances surrounding the incident.

There seems to be an inclination among writers to regard any finding in which the term 'justify' appears, as a judicial finding. However, if our analysis is to proceed on the assumption that a genuine inquiry commission would have been charged with determining whether Admiral Rojdestvensky was justified in believing in an attack by Japanese boats, and if we do not see in this a judicial task, there is no reason to regard prima facie the use of the word 'justified' as implying a judicial function, or a judicial finding.

The above two findings were intended to clarify the origins of the incident and should, therefore, be seen as lying within the proper purview of a function of inquiry. They explain that Admiral Rojdestvensky expected to be attacked, and bear directly therefore on the reasons which prompted him to give the order to fire. The second finding represents an expert opinion designed to convey that the incident was not caused by irresponsible and careless orders on the part of the admiral. When two disputing states appoint admirals to 'elucidate' or, according to the Concise Oxford Dictionary (4th edn, 1950), to *explain* a naval incident, these admirals are expected to give them the benefit of their professional experience and knowledge. This is what the commissioners did in the present case.[71]

The admirals on the commission did not give a ruling whether the orders were or were not in conformity with international law. If the parties, upon receipt of the report, considered that the finding suggested the existence of legal questions concerning the legality of the standing orders, they would have been free to submit such a question to arbitration. When the authors of the Hague Convention stipulated that the powers in dispute had entire freedom as to the effect to be given to the findings of the report (above, p. 33, Art. 14), they meant, i.a., that the report on the facts might reveal some legal questions which the parties might regard as requiring solution by a competent judicial tribunal.

Similar considerations could be advanced concerning the last 'judicial' finding, i.e. that the duration of the firing on the starboard side seemed to the majority of the commissioners to have been longer than necessary. This is an expert opinion bearing on the question whether the admiral was careless or irresponsible. The report contains many findings (which we consider factual) to the effect that the admiral was not careless or irresponsible. One would expect the Dogger Bank Commission—and, again, a genuine inquiry commission—to bring to light any observation likely to qualify any of these findings. The inquiry must, according to Article 9 of the Hague Convention, be 'impartial and conscientious'. It should include both positive and negative aspects of the conduct of the persons concerned, so long as these aspects emerge clearly and are relevant to the purpose of the inquiry. Bearing in mind the aims of our 'model' inquiry commission, there seems to be no doubt that such professional appraisals would be relevant.

The difficulties inherent in Mandelstam's differentiation between judicial and non-judicial functions can be illustrated in the following manner. If Britain and Russia had agreed to constitute an inquiry commission in strict accordance with the Hague Convention, and if such a commission were devoid of all judicial competence, as defined by Mandelstam, it would have summed up its work in the following three findings: the accidental delay of the *Kamtchatka* was perhaps the cause of the incident; Admiral Rojdestvensky was responsible for opening fire and for damaging the fishing fleet; there were no Japanese torpedoboats on the scene of the incident.

[71]Cf. Le Ray, who asserts that the Declaration of St Petersburg gave a position of secondary importance to the legal assessors by asking the commissioners to determine responsibilities, thus appealing to the technical qualifications of the admirals rather than to the principles of law of the assessors (*Les commissions internationales d'enquête au XXe siècle* (1910), pp. 78–9).

Such a narrow conception of the scope of the inquiry commission would hardly have justified its existence. The commission would not have answered the main question which interested the parties, namely, was Admiral Rojdestvensky justified in believing that his fleet was about to be attacked by Japanese torpedo-boats and did he act in bad faith with regard to the fishing-boats? These questions fall into the category of those which the Hague institution was primarily called upon to solve. The Dogger Bank Commission provided evidence which enabled the parties to find an answer to such questions, and it thus acted as a genuine inquiry commission. Our discussion should show that the commission could have achieved the same result without having the competence to determine legal responsibilities. What was needed was a bona fide intention by the parties to draw the legal consequences arising from the elucidation of pertinent questions of fact.

Organization and functioning of the commission
The commission's organization and method of work very much resembled those of an arbitral tribunal. In accordance with the best type of arbitral tribunal, the commission comprised a majority of neutral members.[72] The parties were represented by agents and counsellors. The procedure started with a recital of facts, similar to the introductory memorials of arbitral tribunals. The sittings of the commission, like those of an arbitral tribunal, were in principle public. With regard to evidence and opinions of experts, the procedure was modelled on judicial procedure. And, if there were no pleadings, the discussions ended with the presentation of conclusions.

While, according to the provisions of the Hague Convention, the report was not to have the character of an arbitral award and the parties enjoyed complete freedom as to the effect to be given to it, the report of the commission did have the effect of an award, since the parties accepted its findings in advance and agreed to act accordingly.

The references to 'independent court' (above, p. 52), 'the Court of Inquiry' (above, p. 54), 'tribunal' (above, pp. 54–5), 'International tribunal' (above, p. 54), 'trial',[73] used alternatively by the negotiators on both sides seem to show that the parties had no doubts about the

[72]The predominance of neutral members enhances the prestige of a commission. Moreover, the president is released from the task of using his casting vote should he be the only neutral member (see above, p. 22 & below, p. 96).

In the following arbitrations which took place shortly before the Dogger Bank incident, the tribunal was composed entirely of neutral members: the *Pious Fund* case (Mexico and USA, 1902), the *Venezuelan Preferential Claims* case (Germany, Italy, UK, and Venezuela, 1904), and the *Muscat Dhows* case (France and UK, 1905).

In the *Alabama* case (above, p. 42) and in the *Behring Sea Seal Fishing* case (UK and USA, 1892), the neutral members were in the majority.

[73]On 27 Oct. 1904 the Russian ambassador in London told the British foreign secretary that he had made it quite clear to his superiors that the British government insisted upon a trial. The ambassador proceeded to ask whether he might add that if this demand were conceded, the crisis would no longer remain acute (see Cd 2350, No. 19).

character of the commission to be established.[74] This attitude followed from the agreement of the parties to confer on the commission the power to establish the criminal responsibility of the persons involved.

The judicial powers of the Dogger Bank Commission give rise to questions of an organizational and procedural nature, on which Mandelstam (p. 409) offers the following comments. As regards the qualifications of the commissioners, it would have been reasonable to choose high naval officers if the task of the commission were confined to an inquiry. It would seem that the authors of the Declaration of St Petersburg took into account the juridical function of the commission, by providing for the appointment of two legal assessors to assist the commissioners. Perhaps the opposite should have been done—jurists appointed as commissioners, with naval officers as expert assessors. However, a commission of five naval officers, with a predominantly neutral element, could not profit more from the differing opinions of two jurists appointed by the parties to the dispute, than would a commission of five jurists from the technical explanations of two admirals who disagreed between themselves. To be rationally organized, the number of legal assessors or naval experts should have been equal to that of the naval commissioners or jurist commissioners. Only thus would the preponderance of the neutral element have been re-established. Such considerations appear to have led the commissioners in the Dogger Bank case to draft their report without the co-operation of the two legal assessors, although the rules of procedure authorized the participation of the assessors in the drafting of the report.

According to the diplomatic correspondence, the agents of the parties were intended to be simple intermediaries between the parties and the commission.[75] In fact, they took part in the discussions on the rules of procedure, were invited to almost all the meetings in the Council Hall, and participated in all the private talks between the commissioners and the assessors. (According to the rules of procedure, they could only be called to the Council Hall as and when they were required.)

[74] This observation is not negated by a subsequent formal reservation as to the use of the term 'tribunal'.

At the meeting on 13 February 1905, the Russian agent noted that in his conclusions the British agent referred to Russian officers called before the 'tribunal'. The Russian agent recalled that in the Declaration of St Petersburg the term 'international commission of inquiry' was used. The British agent declared that he would be prepared to take this remark into consideration (*Arch. dip.*, 94, 3rd ser., No. 4 (ii, 1905), p. 474).

[75] The emperor of Russia accepted the British draft article dealing with the appointment of agents 'on trust', since Count Lamsdorff was unable to explain to him the duties and attributes of the agents. Count Lamsdorff suggested to the British ambassador that the agents should be selected from the British and Russian embassies in Paris, unless their duties were to be of a very special character (Cd 2350, No. 66). Lord Lansdowne informed his ambassador that the agents would not perform duties of any very special character: they would merely act as intermediaries between the commission and the governments concerned, and they could, therefore, be selected from the staff of the two embassies (ibid., No. 68). The British agent was Hugh O'Beirne, first secretary at the British embassy in Paris, and the Russian agent was Anatole Nekludow, counsellor at the Russian embassy.

At public meetings they rose to the position of real advocates of their governments. They presented the exposé of facts, communicated the list of witnesses, examined witnesses personally or through counsel, read conclusions and observations, made declarations and protests—in a word, the agents were the guardians of the interests of their country before the commission. In view of the competence of the commission to determine guilt, it would have been preferable, according to Mandelstam (p. 185), to appoint as agents jurists or diplomat-jurists.

As to procedure, the parties should have been allowed full freedom to prove their thesis by pleading orally, instead of being limited to simultaneous presentations of conclusions and observations.[76] This view is supported by Politis. It was not reasonable, he asserts, that an enlarged inquiry, which approached arbitration, should not offer the guarantees of arbitration. The commissioners were given the formidable power of establishing the guilt of certain persons but, since the parties were reluctant to transform the commission into a true tribunal, the accused were deprived of the right of defence. Moreover, there is nothing in theory to prevent the delivering of pleadings in an inquiry. Politis concedes at the same time, however, that even in arbitration the procedure may, without inconvenience, omit pleadings (p. 168). Apparently he, as well as Mandelstam, would have preferred the inclusion of oral pleadings in the Dogger Bank inquiry because of the especially serious—that is, criminal—aspect of the case.

The experience of the Dogger Bank inquiry shows that the time spent by the commission in the preparation of the rules hindered its work on the merits of the case. Inquiry into facts should be done as soon as possible after their occurrence, while memories are fresh and material evidence is still available. It will be recalled that the representative of the Netherlands had proposed at the Hague Conference the inclusion in the section on inquiry commissions of detailed rules of procedure; this would assist the commissioners, who would often not be jurists (above, pp. 29 & 32). However, the conference confined itself to singling out the requirement that the procedure take place 'contradictoirement' (above, p. 29, n. 23). It remained for the Second Hague Conference to draw conclusions from the Dogger Bank incident and draft more comprehensive rules of procedure, which would be immediately available to the parties.

Criticism of the report

Different opinions were expressed regarding the soundness of the report. The commissioners were accused of inconsistency for having failed to 'blame' the Russian officers after finding that they were responsible for wrongful acts.[77]

---

[76]Mandelstam, pp. 399 & 410.
[77]An editorial in the *New York Press* of 26 Feb. 1905 intimated that the 'decision' of the

John Basset Moore answered this criticism[78] by drawing a distinction between civil law and criminal law. It was not improbable, he stated, that if the commissioners had been lawyers instead of admirals, they would have brought out more clearly the distinction, which doubtless was present in their minds, 'between justification in fact and apparent justification'. They found that the attack was not in fact justified, and from this finding there arose an obligation to make compensation. But when we pass from the domain of civil law to that of penal law, when we pass from the question of paying compensation for a wrongful act to that of undergoing punishment for it, the element of intent becomes material. The commissioners were therefore not guilty of inconsistency because, while they found that the firing was unjustified, they also held that Admiral Rojdestvensky had not incurred liability to punishment.

For his part, Mandelstam (p. 407) explains the 'apparent' inconsistency by what he terms 'extreme confusion' of the functions of the commissioners, who, after having established the facts and the responsibilities, had to declare, like a real jury, whether the British vessels or the Russian officers had committed culpable acts.

This explanation is refuted by Politis (p. 171) by reference to the Declaration of St Petersburg, which specifically empowered the commission to make findings on blame. If, instead of the decision which the logic of their findings seemed to have imposed on them, they preferred a contrary solution, it was not for fear of acting ultra vires, but because of the very legitimate concern not to compromise the peaceful effect already produced by recourse to an inquiry. The contradictory statements of the witnesses did not completely dissipate the obscurity which surrounded the incident. Having no other basis for their deliberations than these statements, the admirals were unable to throw light on the incident. Since the truth escaped them, they strove to formulate—on the basis of uncertain findings—appraisals acceptable to both disputing parties. The commission understood the extreme danger of a categorical decision which, if entirely favourable to one of the parties, would necessarily have been met with protests from the other, and it wisely abstained from giving such a decision. Doubts and prudence imposed a middle solution, whose conciliatory tendencies compensated for the inevitable faults of logic. Thus explained, the report deserves only approval. It brought a peaceful procedure to a happy conclusion by implementing the ideas which inspired the French intervention. The

commission was prompted by a desire to conciliate the parties rather than to mete out justice, and that the commissioners did not wish to lay such blame upon the Russian admiral as would render his trial and punishment by Russia necessary. The article is quoted by Hershey, p. 239.

The question was asked in the British press: how could Admiral Rojdestvensky, who had fired for no reason, be a credit to the Russian navy? (see Beaucourt, p. 167).

[78] See 'The North Sea incident', in *The collected papers of John Basset Moore*, iii (1944), pp. 200–1.

report assured 'to the British the reparation due to them, and to the Russians the benefit of all the circumstances which could mitigate the crime caused by their error'.

The example of 1905 shows, according to Politis, how illusory it was to hope that an inquiry would result in all cases in the discovery of the truth. The commissioners were not always assured of having either the possibility of being completely informed on all matters or, above all, the independence necessary for their delicate functions. However, it would be too extreme to conclude that the role of the inquiry was not serious. It was of small importance, from the point of view of peace, whether the truth were established. It sufficed for the inquiry to furnish a suitable means for dissipating animosity and putting an end to controversies. From this point of view the Dogger Bank precedent was entirely successful. The inquiry did not discover the complete truth; nevertheless, it preserved the peace.

The view that the commissioners were prevented by the nature of their task from blaming the Russian officers, was forcefully put forward by Pillet (p. 14). In his opinion, commissioner-inquirers did not enjoy the independence necessary for their delicate functions. The circumstances in which they were placed would often prevent them from deciding freely. The commission, he writes, was eager to declare that the officers under Admiral Rojdestvensky were the victims of an excusable error, and the incident was terminated by the payment of compensation to the victims and their families. The commissioners would certainly not have been able to declare with the same composure that there could have been no error and that there was no excuse for the officers' conduct. What kind of an investigator is he, asks Pillet, who can come to a conclusion in one sense, but cannot do so in the opposite direction?

La Penha (p. 189) has no doubt that an arbitral sentence, handed down by a true tribunal, would have confirmed the British charges against the commander of the Russian Baltic fleet. He attributes the refusal of the commissioners to pronounce blame to their 'courtoisie'.[79]

The observations of Politis and Pillet do not seem to be substantiated.[80] The commission discovered all the important relevant facts

---

[79]The author's view seems to be based on his analysis of the evidence given by the English fishermen. The testimony established beyond doubt the fact that a very short distance separated the Russian vessels from the fishing boats. Moreover, the Russian vessels moved very slowly and directed the beams of their searchlights for the whole of the twenty minutes during which the firing lasted. In these circumstances it seemed difficult to accept the Russians' assertion that they caused damage to the fishermen while firing on the mysterious torpedo-boats which they had allegedly discovered in the mists of the North Sea during the night of 21 Oct.

The only excuse they could give was that since their look-out men were alerted by the appearance of the torpedo-boats, they fired on the English fishing-boats thinking that there was some complicity between them. (It will be recalled that no charge of complicity was raised by the Russian agent in his recital of facts, conclusions, and observations.)

[80]The analysis by Politis seems somewhat inconsistent as he maintains, on the one hand, that the logic of the commissioners' findings should have led them to blame Admiral

D

which allowed it to present a comprehensive picture of the origin, development, and results of the incident, as well as the motives underlying the actions of the persons involved. The merits of the issue depended on the question whether Admiral Rojdestvensky had good reason to believe that he was being attacked by Japanese torpedo-boats. The commission reported weighty evidence showing that the admiral had reasons for such a belief, and the parties in dispute drew the logical conclusion that his mistake implied neither intention nor negligence nor, still less, culpable negligence. Certain British authorities unequivocally confirmed the existence of extenuating circumstances or otherwise justified Admiral Rojdestvensky's actions. Lawrence states 'in fairness'[81] that although the Russians had no justification for firing, still less for continuing their fire for the length of time that they did, their suspicion that they might be attacked was not altogether groundless, since they possessed information—which did not all come from tainted sources—of the presence of hostile vessels not far away.

The British admiral, Sir John Fisher, was quoted as saying that mistakes like those made by Admiral Rojdestvensky were possible,[82] and the prevailing opinion in British naval circles was expressed by an officer in the following terms:[83]

The opinion is strongly held by officers of our own and other European navies that a fleet of warships at sea in time of war should not allow any war vessel it can not identify as a neutral to approach it. It is generally held, too, that a merchant vessel should be kept off unless it is known to be well disposed, for otherwise there is nothing to prevent a belligerent from chartering a merchant vessel and doing a lot of damage with her to the enemy's fleet.

No doubt the Russian Commander thought two of his small cruisers, which suddenly appeared, were Japanese torpedo-boats, and if he did, his only proper course was to fire on them. It is really nothing remarkable that cruisers should be taken for torpedo-boats, for there isn't a navy in the world in which the same blunder has not been made. I counted up sixteen authenticated cases the other day, involving the best navies in the world, the British and American not excepted.[84]

The contribution of the commission to the maintenance of peace

Opinions are unanimous as to the positive role played by the commission with regard to the maintenance of international peace. Some

---

Rojdestvensky, while, on the other hand, he asserts that the commissioners were incapable of establishing the truth, which escaped them, and that their findings were uncertain.

[81] *International problems*, p. 58.
[82] See Beaucourt, p. 118.
[83] See Hershey, p. 243.
[84] In his account of the incident, written five years later, the president of the commission concluded as follows: 'Le fait que les arrières non éclairés de deux des croiseurs russes l'*Aurora* et le *Dimitri-Donskoi*, marchant devant l'escadre à son insu, à vitesse réduite, furent atteints par des projectiles, permet de supposer que l'apparition subite et confuse de ces bâtiments, à portée limite de visibilité, avait pu être l'object de cette regrettable méprise?' (F. E. Fournier, *La politique navale et la flotte française* (1910)).

authors indulge in exalted praise, while others offer more moderate observations. Beaucourt states (at p. 184) that the result of the commission was to avoid a great European war. Myers asserts,[85] with reference to the commission, that the Hague Convention had doubtless prevented going to war. According to Lawrence (p. 57), the wisdom of the First Hague Conference was demonstrated in a most striking manner. Its work led to the peaceful settlement of a dispute which, but for it, would in all probability have resulted in a terrible war. The acceptance of the 'award' of the 'tribunal' showed, according to Scott,[86] that the First Peace Conference had created a practical and efficient means of ascertaining facts in a heated controversy, and prevented a resort to arms which in the inflamed state of public feeling might have occurred.

The above appraisals appear somewhat exaggerated, unless they are interpreted as meaning that the parties to the dispute decided not to go to war but instead to submit their differences to an international commission of inquiry. In this sense should be interpreted the statement of the president of the commission in his opening speech, that the establishment of the commission had the happy effect of immediately appeasing the conflicting national susceptibilities.[87] Both Britain and Russia felt that once the agreement for recourse to a commission of inquiry was reached, the 'acute character of crisis would disappear'.[88] Indeed, when the Declaration of St Petersburg was signed, there was a widespread feeling that the peace was saved. The inquiry was followed with great interest, but its result was awaited without anxiety.

The presence of mind of the British and Russian leaders and the friendly intervention of France permitted the disputing sides to discern their real interests in time. If the war had extended to England, it would have necessarily degenerated into a general conflagration. The essential interests which, at the outset of the Russo-Japanese conflict, had brought France and England together into an 'entente cordiale' and had dictated to them, in spite of their alliances, mutual abstention, would have been irreparably compromised by an extension of the hostilities, from which neither of them could gain. The British wished to remain out of the war and they hoped to be able to contain Russia in Persia and Afghanistan without a serious dispute. The Russians were not strong enough to fight Britain alone, and help from France was by no means certain. In any event, Russia was weary of the Far East. By the time of the Dogger Bank incident, the extremist 'Korean Circle' had lost all influence in Russian politics. The Ministry for Foreign Affairs and moderate officers and capitalists were again in control, and they

[85]*The commission of inquiry: the Wilson-Bryan peace plan* (1913), p. 11.
[86]*Hague Peace Conferences*, p. 268.
[87]*Arch. dip.*, 94, 3rd ser., No. 4 (ii, 1905), p. 452.
[88]See Cd 2350, No. 17.

were anxious, far from extending the war, to end it on any terms not blatantly humiliating.[89]

In such circumstances there was no other way but to look for an honourable method of resolving the Dogger Bank dispute. The Hague Convention provided that method. It can also be asserted that the very existence of the institution of international commissions of inquiry was likely to elicit the good will of the parties, if they had not decided in advance to resort to arms.[90]

It should be added, however, that the substantive findings of the commission and the moderate language in which they were formulated, had a peaceful effect. Had the commission condemned in unequivocal terms the conduct of the Russian officers, had it issued a verdict of guilty of a criminal offence, and had Russia been expected, as a consequence, to punish Admiral Rojdestvensky and other officers, the 'acuteness' of the crisis would have re-emerged. Violent reactions could have been provoked in Russia to what might have been considered as a new attack on the honour of the Imperial Navy. The commissioners were undoubtedly aware of such possible consequences. But our analysis of their work does not suggest that this awareness blurred their sense of justice.

Whether the commission made a large or a small contribution to the peaceful settlement of the dispute, its positive role cannot be denied. For the purpose of our study, the question also arises whether the credit should not be given to the institution of international commissions of inquiry established by the Hague Convention of 1899. Pillet (p. 25) is sceptical on this point. He finds it curious that the commission reached the desired result only by denying the true character of the institution of inquiry commissions and functioning as an arbitral commission would have functioned. Our examination tends to challenge this opinion. The commission in fact suppressed its judicial mandate and functioned as a genuine inquiry commission. It is perhaps for that reason that the delegates to the Second Hague Conference drew inspiration from the experience of the Dogger Bank Commission in their efforts to improve the institution of international commissions of inquiry.

[89]See Politis, p. 158; and Taylor, p. 425.

[90]Bourgeois, president of the First Commission of the Second Hague Conference, stated at the opening meeting of the commission on 22 June 1907 that from the immediate practical point of view the institution of commissions of inquiry had been able in less than ten years to justify its introduction into the modern law of nations. A serious conflict was feared between two of the world's greatest powers; appeal was made to the Convention of 1899, and the conflict was prevented by recourse to a commission of inquiry. The very existence of this agency of justice in positive international law, and the flexibility of the provisions which established it, enabled two great states, without the slightest injury to their national dignity, to secure within scarcely five months the peaceful settlement of a dispute which, in other times, might have led to the most serious consequences (see Scott, *Proceedings, 1907*, ii. 3).

CHAPTER 4

The Institution of Inquiry under
the Hague Convention of 1907

The purpose of the Second Hague Peace Conference was to improve upon the arrangements adopted in 1899 in the light of the experience of the intervening years. Stimulated by the fact that two of the most powerful nations in the world had found the commission of inquiry to be a sure, honourable, and expeditious method of settling a serious dispute,[1] the Russian government included in its circular of 3 April 1906, at the head of the suggested programme for the Second Peace Conference, a provision calling for improvements to be made in the Convention of 1899 with regard to international commissions of inquiry.[2]

Since the Second Peace Conference met shortly after the Dogger Bank Commission completed its work, it was to be expected that the three powers which had organized the commission would contribute towards the improvement of the system of international inquiry. Indeed, Great Britain, France, and Russia respectively submitted to the conference a series of draft amendments, based on their recent experience. Moreover, the bodies which dealt with the subject[3] included among their members Sir Edward Fry, who had acted at the Dogger Bank inquiry as legal assessor appointed by the British government; M. Fromageot (delegate of France at the conference of 1907), who had been deputy to the Russian agent; and M. Martens, whose advice had carried such weight in the formulation of the agreement for inquiry into the Dogger Bank incident.

The Russian proposal for amendment of the 1899 Convention envisaged the substitution of an undertaking to submit disputes to a

---

[1]See report of Baron Guillaume on behalf of the First Commission of the Conference of 1907, in Scott, *Proceedings, 1907*, i, 399.

[2]See text of the letter of the Russian ambassador in Washington to the Secretary of State, in Scott, *Reports to Hague Conferences*, p. 186. The Russian government called at the same time for improvements in the provisions of the Convention of 1899 relating to the court of arbitration.

[3]The First Commission of the conference dealt with 'Improvements to be made in the provisions of the Convention relative to the peaceful settlement of international disputes; International commissions of inquiry and questions relating thereto; Questions relative to maritime prizes'.

The First Sub-Commission of the First Commission dealt with the improvement of the Convention of 1899, including the question of inquiry commissions, while the Second Sub-Commission dealt with questions relating to maritime prizes.

The First Sub-Commission appointed a Committee of Examination A, which dealt exhaustively with the question of international commissions of inquiry.

commission of inquiry ('. . . the signatory Powers agree [conviennent] to institute . . .') for the simple declaration on the utility of such commissions contained in the convention.[4] Disputes involving neither the honour nor the independence of the parties were excluded from the undertaking. According to the Russian proposal, the competence of the commission of inquiry was in principle to be enlarged. The commission was to elucidate the facts and to establish, if necessary, 'responsibility therefor'. As regards the effect of the commission's report, the Russian government suggested dispensing with the 'entire freedom' left to the parties, and providing instead that states are free either to conclude a friendly settlement or to resort to the Permanent Court of Arbitration at The Hague. The experience of the Dogger Bank Commission further prompted the Russian government to suggest that the commission of inquiry should be constituted within two weeks after the date of the incident which had prompted its formation, and that it should sit, if possible, in the place where the incident had occurred.

The rest of the Russian proposals dealt with the composition of the commission, representation of the parties before the commission, voting, functions of the president, hearing of the parties, the role of the commissioners and agents, communication of documents, summoning and examination of witnesses, arguments or statement of conclusions, character and scope of the report, signing of the report, and minority opinion.

Britain and France were of the view that past experience did not impose any changes regarding either the voluntary recourse to the commissions or the extent of their powers or the effect of the report. Accordingly, their proposals, which were combined during the conference in a single draft,[5] were confined to detailed rules designed to facilitate the organization and working of the commissions. These rules related to the manner of formation of the commission, replacement of members, place of meeting, choice of languages, appointment and duties of agents, counsel or advocates, registry, publicity of meetings, submission of statements of fact and documents, examinations of locality, requests for explanations and information, summoning of witnesses or experts, conclusions of agents, examination of witnesses, termination of the inquiry, decisions by a majority, signing of the report, reading of the report, effect of the report, and sharing of expenses.[6]

[4]For the Russian 'Draft intended to replace Part III of the Convention of July 29, 1899, for the Pacific Settlement of International Disputes', see Scott, *Reports to Hague Conferences*, pp. 458–9.

[5]See text in Scott, *Proceedings, 1907*, ii, 861 ff.

[6]Bourgeois (France), president of the First Commission, said at the opening meeting of the commission on 22 June, with regard to commissions of inquiry, that experience had shown that the provisions of Part III of the 1899 Convention would be advantageously completed by adding some general rules of procedure, easily applicable, to which either the states could refer when agreeing to their *compromis* of inquiry, or the investigating

The final text of the convention was based primarily on the joint Franco-British proposal.[7] Among other proposals submitted to the conference,[8] that of the Netherlands provided, like the Russian proposal, for the replacement in Article 9 of the Convention of 1899 of the words 'deem it expedient' by 'agree'.[9]

We shall now examine the main problems discussed at the conference, with the object of understanding the ideas underlying the relevant provisions of the Convention of 1907.

Obligatory or voluntary recourse to commissions of inquiry

The idea of making the inquiry obligatory in principle did not find any support. Martens, and after him the Netherlands delegate, de Beaufort, tried in vain to diminish the importance of their governments' proposals by claiming that the adoption of their version of Article 9 would not in any way change the voluntary character of the inquiry. Martens explained that there was no juridical obligation in the text proposed by Russia. In the presence of the reservations concerning the honour and independence of states, of which the parties remained the sole judges, the very idea of an obligation seemed to him to be excluded. The Russian delegation merely wished to recommend strongly the use of such commissions when such use was found to be possible.[10] De Beaufort, for his part, stated that without wishing to touch on the optional nature of the international commission of inquiry, he would favour its use 'in all cases where the circumstances might not be opposed to it'.[11]

The rest of the delegates showed the same apprehensions as were so prominent during the First Hague Conference. Baron von Bieberstein (Germany) recalled that the same Russian proposal was rejected at the first conference. If the second conference accepted it, this would be interpreted as a change of real importance.[12] Sir Edward Fry was also against any innovation in this respect. The amendment proposed by the Russian delegate would, in his view, under certain conditions, give the commissions an obligatory character, whilst it seemed very desirable to have them retain their optional character. The operation of the Dogger

---

commissioners could refer in the course of their mission (ibid., p. 4). For the meaning of the phrase 'rules of procedure' see below, p. 100, n. 56.

[7] For the authentic French text, and an unofficial English translation, of Part III of the convention, see below, App. I, pp. 330–8. For a list of the states parties to the convention, see the Note following the English version of Part III, at pp. 338–9.

[8] The Haitian delegate, bearing in mind the role played by France in the Dogger Bank incident, proposed adding to Art. 9 of the 1899 Hague Convention a provision to the effect that the signatory powers might suggest to the parties in dispute recourse to international commissions of inquiry (Scott, *Reports to Hague Conferences*, p. 463). The conference did not adopt this proposal. It seemed useless to draw attention to a self-evident right, and its affirmation could have raised susceptibilities (see Politis, p. 177).

[9] See Scott, *Reports to Hague Conferences*, p. 459.

[10] See Scott, *Proceedings, 1907*, ii. 218–20.

[11] Ibid., p. 220.　　　　　　　　　　　[12] Ibid., p. 221.

Bank Commission proved a great success for the institution of international inquiry and a great benefit to peace. One should not compromise it.[13] As far as the delegations of Romania and Turkey were concerned, it was only natural for them to put on record their opposition to any attempt to reverse their achievements of 1899.[14]

Most of the delegates agreed that the text of 1899 was defective, but the proposed improvement seemed dangerous since it risked compromising the agreement reached at the first conference. That is why the Russian and Netherlands delegations had to give way. The general feeling, however, was in favour of the wider use of the commissions. As stated by the Portuguese delegate, d'Oliveira, if two powers agreed to establish a commission of inquiry, they would know well how to interpret Article 9 in a liberal manner. It was only in case they could not agree that they would interpret it in a restrictive sense. The example of the Paris Commission was decisive. D'Oliveira submitted that the more important a new institution, the more one should avoid stipulations which might alienate general confidence from it, and the greatest care must be exercised not to impose it on both governmental and public opinion. Obligation in this matter would be a retrograde step. It was within the field of arbitration that one must generalize the obligation, and not within the field of commissions of inquiry.[15]

The president of the Committee of Examination, L. Bourgeois, suggested a compromise formulation to the effect that recourse be made to commissions of inquiry *especially* in disputes involving neither honour nor essential interests.[16] However, d'Oliveira preferred the retention of the former text, and this was the view of the majority. Nevertheless, the committee adopted a slight modification to Article 9 by adding the words 'and desirable' to the word 'expedient', seeing that the same addition had already been adopted in Article 3, dealing with mediation.[17] The insertion of these words was designed to bring moral pressure to bear on the parties to submit their controversy to an international inquiry.[18]

In appraising the results of the conference on the topic under consideration, Bustamente states that the solution arrived at was logical, not only because the controversies of 1899 were fresh in mind, but because any other solution would have given certain powers a very easy means to intervene in the affairs of others. Certain 'juridical institutions' which are theoretically unassailable, he writes, would serve perfectly the instincts of domination of big states, by furnishing a constant pretext for coercing small states.[19]

---

[13]Ibid., p. 220.
[14]See statements of Beldiman and Turkhan Pasha (ibid., p. 221).
[15]Ibid., p. 383.   [16]Ibid.   [17]Ibid.
[18]Cf. Scott, *Hague Peace Conferences*, p. 273.
[19]See Bustamente, p. 115.

Nature of the dispute

The Russian proposal that the disputes to be submitted to an inquiry commission should involve neither the honour nor the *independence* of the parties—and not, as hitherto, neither the honour nor the essential interests of the parties—was designed to increase the number of disputes suitable for settlement by the method of inquiry. According to Martens, there was general agreement that the incident in the North Sea seemed to affect the honour and the essential interests of two great nations and that the Paris Commission was set up *despite* the text of Article 9. In the event of such a serious dispute arising between other powers, the latter must not be exposed to the danger of being stopped in their recourse to an international inquiry by the defective text of the Convention of 1899.[20]

On the other hand, Sir Edward Fry and the Austro-Hungarian delegate (Lammasch) suggested that the example of the Paris Commission proved that the text of former Article 9 could not be interpreted in the restrictive sense adopted by Martens.[21] The Brazilian delegate (Barbosa), for his part, objected to the Russian proposal by pointing out that one could imagine disputes engaging neither honour nor independence but affecting essential interests.[22]

In view of the still prevailing apprehension of a possible prejudicial use of inquiry commissions, it is not surprising that the Russian proposal met the same fate as that designed to increase the obligation of states to settle their disputes by means of inquiry. Martens submitted to the will of the majority, but he did not fail to express, on the eve of the adoption of the Convention of 1907, his disappointment at the attitude of his colleagues. He said that the conference seemed desirous of disregarding the most remarkable historical lesson which had resulted from the celebrated Dogger Bank case. The conference did not wish to declare recourse to commissions of inquiry ' "useful and desirable" *in all cases*' (emphasis in the original).[23] This statement would show that, so far as Russia was concerned, no reservation whatsoever should have been formulated with regard to the nature of the dispute.[24]

The competence of the commission to establish responsibility

The Russian proposal regarding the establishment of responsibilities by the commission of inquiry was likewise rejected. In support of the proposal, Martens argued that by establishing responsibility, the commission of inquiry would not become a sort of tribunal, but it would be similar to an investigating magistrate (juge d'instruction) who presents

---

[20]See Scott, *Proceedings, 1907*, ii. 381.   [21]Ibid.   [22]Ibid., p. 223.   [23]Ibid., p. 35.
[24]The final English text of Art. 9 of the Convention of 1907 has been published in at least two versions. While the translation contained in Scott's *Proceedings, 1907* (i. 601) uses the phrase 'essential interests', the version appearing in a number of other sources (see below, App. I, p. 334 and footnote) employs, incorrectly it is believed, the phrase 'vital interests'.

the sum and substance of the affair, and from it makes clear, 'by the force of the things themselves', the responsibilities in the case. However, it is not for him to determine those responsibilities. That was the fundamental distinction to be established between a commission of inquiry and a court of arbitration, as between a report and a decision.[25] Faced with what was, in his view, unjustified misunderstanding, Martens reiterated at a later stage of the debate that the Russian delegation wished in no way to confuse the commissions of inquiry with arbitral jurisdiction. On the contrary, it wished to distinguish clearly between these two absolutely different institutions. If reference was made in the Russian text to the establishment of responsibilities, it was because these responsibilities must logically result from the impartial exposition of the circumstances of fact presented by the commissions of inquiry to the governments. Once more, these commissions were but examining judges. It was incumbent upon the governments to draw the conclusions from their reports.[26]

The president of the Committee of Examination said that, if he had properly understood Martens's ideas, the examination of the facts which the commission was to undertake should furnish the source of the responsibilities.[27] Other members of the committee were obviously not prepared to give such a limited interpretation to the Russian proposal. Sir Edward Fry insisted that the discussion should not end with confusing absolutely and necessarily distinct questions—the question of fact on the one hand, and the question of right or morality on the other hand.[28] Fromageot remarked that some conflicts might arise without there being any need to attempt to establish the responsibilities; and if no such responsibilities existed there was no reason to urge the commissioners to deal with them. Such action might become a source of new difficulties.[29] Sensing the growing opposition, Martens felt impelled to withdraw his proposal.[30]

[25]Ibid., p. 218. According to Dalloz (*Dict. pratique de droit*, 11th ed. (undated), p. 771) the competence of a juge d'instruction consists in his right to investigate certain facts, in relation to certain persons, in certain places. As juge d'instruction, he carries out or orders all the acts which constitute the preliminary or preparatory examination. As an official of the judicial police he has particularly the right of investigation and establishment of facts constituting offences. In the course of a visit to the scene of the crime the juge d'instruction can proceed to the ascertainment of the main evidence of the offence and the condition of the scene of the crime and, in addition, to the making of searches, to the hearing of witnesses, and to the arrest and interrogation of accused.

It is a fundamental principle that the prosecution and the inquiry ('l'instruction') must be separated. Except in the case of flagrant délit—when the law confers on the prosecutor certain of the powers of a juge d'instruction—the Public Prosecutor alone prosecutes, and the juge d'instruction alone makes the inquiry.

[26]Ibid., p. 384.　　　　　[27]Ibid.

[28]At the meeting of the First Sub-Commission on 9 July 1907, Sir Edward Fry opposed the establishment of responsibility since this implied, in his view, a decision upon questions of right or morality, whereas the inquiry ought to confine itself to the establishment of the facts (ibid., p. 220).

[29]Ibid.

[30]Bustamente notes (p. 116) that if the commission of inquiry were to extend its com-

Effect of the report

The Russian proposal that the parties were to be free, following the report of the commission, either to conclude a friendly settlement or to resort to the Permanent Court of Arbitration, did not meet with the approval of the conference. Martens argued that if two powers agreed to establish a commission of inquiry, they might go even further in the manifestation of their devotion for peace.[31] Moreover, the Russian delegation wished to see a link established between the commissions of inquiry and the Court.[33] While James Brown Scott (United States) supported the Russian proposal, many other delegates opposed it. Thus Fusinato (Italy) believed that its adoption would mean the acceptance of the principle of obligatory arbitration. This prospect did not 'frighten' him but, if this was the implication of the proposal, it should be clearly stated.[38] Fromageot thought that if the Committee of Examination wished to adopt the article embodying the proposal, it should place it in a conspicuous place, for the commission of inquiry would thus become the first cog in a wheel ending in obligatory arbitration.[34] Bourgeois expressed his fear that, if adopted, the stipulation would interfere with the frequent and successful use of commissions of inquiry. States might, at times when it was expedient to act with great prudence and without constraint, shrink from the obligation to have recourse to arbitration, even before the facts had been clearly set out.[35] Bourgeois was convinced that after the publication of the report, which should set forth the truth, the parties would find themselves forced to abandon their hostile attitudes and to settle their difference in a friendly manner.[36]

Following the intervention of the president, the Committee of Examination preserved the stipulation in Article 14 of the 1899 Convention (above, p. 33), which stated that the report leaves to the powers in dispute entire freedom as to the effect to be given to the finding of facts.[37]

---

petence to the establishment of responsibilities, its work would resemble a kind of 'instruction préparatoire'; there would be a confusion between the nature of the inquiry commission and that of an arbitral tribunal, and a hybrid institution would thereby be produced.

[31]See Scott, *Proceedings, 1907*, ii. 404.

[32]Ibid., p. 219. Martens spoke of a twofold link: (1) the possibility of a recourse to the Court following the report of the commission; and (2) the choice of the third commissioner from among the members of the Court.

[33]Ibid., p. 402.

[34]Ibid.

[35]See, to the same effect, the report of Baron Guillaume: ibid., i. 412-13.

[36]Ibid., ii. 402.

[37]See Art. 35 of the 1907 Convention. According to the English translation of this article in Scott's *Proceedings, 1907* (i. 605), the report of the commission 'is limited to a *finding of facts*' and leaves to the powers in dispute entire freedom as to the effect to be given 'to this *finding*'. According to another version of Art. 35 (see below, App. I, p. 338), the report of the commission 'is limited to a *statement of facts*' and leaves to the parties

Dead-line for setting up the commission

The conference likewise rejected the Russian proposals with regard to the period of two weeks within which the commission was to be constituted. Asser (The Netherlands) and Bourgeois believed that it would be difficult to lay down a time-limit; what would happen if two weeks elapsed and no action had yet been taken? Sir Edward Fry agreed to this view and observed that Article 9 recommended the constitution of a commission of inquiry only when diplomatic negotiations had failed; and was not the chancelleries' wise way of proceeding slowly proverbial?[38] The conference adopted instead an amendment to Article 10 of the Convention of 1899, according to which the inquiry convention would determine the time (and also the manner) in which the commission was to be formed.[39]

Composition of the commission

The conference had no difficulty in agreeing that the commission of inquiry should be composed—subject to any provisions to the contrary —of five members, three of whom were to be neutral (Art. 12, referring to Arts 45 & 57).[40] The notable change, in relation to the parallel provision of the 1899 Convention (above, p. 32) was that the neutral members—not nationals of the parties to the dispute—were to be in the majority. It will be recalled that at the First Hague Conference the US delegation favoured the strengthening of the neutral element (above, p. 22). Similarly, the draftsmen deemed it necessary to adopt the same provisions regarding death, retirement, or disability of a member of a commission of inquiry (Art. 13) as applied to members of an arbitral tribunal (Art. 59).

---

entire freedom as to the effect to be given 'to the *statement*' (emphasis added). It appears that the French 'constatation des faits' (see below, App. I, p. 333) is translated in the first instance as 'finding of facts', and in the second instance as 'statement of facts'.

[38]Ibid., p. 395. See to this effect the report of Baron Guillaume: ibid., i. 402.

[39]According to Bustamente (p. 118), the proposed 'fatal delay' seemed completely inconsistent with the voluntary character of the institution. It was less than desirable to deprive states of the right to make use of a peaceful method for solving their disputes because a certain number of days had passed, or to oblige them to hasten the conclusion of certain agreements on detail in order to avoid the expiry of the time-limit.

[40]Art. 45 enjoins that the members of arbitral tribunals must be chosen from the general list of members of the PCA. Failing direct agreement of the parties on the composition of the tribunal, each party is to appoint two arbitrators, of whom one only can be its national or chosen from among the persons selected by it as members of the Permanent Court, and these arbitrators together choose an umpire. If the votes are equally divided, the choice of the umpire is to be entrusted to a third power, selected by the parties by agreement. If they fail to agree on the choice of a third power, each party selects a different power, and the umpire is chosen in concert by the powers thus selected. If, within a period of two months, these two powers cannot reach agreement, each one of them presents two candidates from the list of members of the PCA, exclusive of the members selected by the parties and not being nationals of either of them. The umpire is determined by lot from the candidates thus presented. In accordance with Art. 57, the umpire is president of the tribunal ex officio; when there is no provision for an umpire, the tribunal appoints its own president.

As regards the qualifications of the commissioners, the convention laid down no rule. The delegates considered that the qualifications would depend on the object of the inquiry: if the facts to be clarified were not closely linked with questions of law, there would be an advantage in choosing experts.[41]

The value and extent of the functions of assessors claimed particular attention in the Committee of Examination. It was recognized that in certain cases assessors might be useful, but that their presence was not always indispensable. Consequently, the convention left it to the parties to decide in each case whether assessors should be appointed. As to the qualifications of the assessors, there was general agreement that if the commissioners were experts, the assessors should be jurists, and vice versa.[42]

Concerning the powers of the assessors, Lammasch (Austria-Hungary) observed[43] that when the commissioners are specialists, the assessor-jurists would exercise great influence on the decisions of the commission. Since this presented a certain danger, it would have been more logical, in such a case, to grant them not a deliberative but an effective voice, i.e. to appoint them members of the commission.[44] The Committee of Examination was not prepared to decide in advance on the question whether it would sometimes be expeditious to give them a vote. It proposed, instead, to stipulate that if the parties deemed it necessary to appoint assessors, the inquiry convention should determine the method of their designation and the extent of their powers.[45] This view was incorporated in Article 10 of the convention.

Representation of the parties

According to Article 14 of the Convention of 1907, the parties are entitled to be represented before the commission by agents, counsel, or advocates. Fromageot recalled in the Committee of Examination that in the Dogger Bank case there had been some uncertainty as to the role of the agents. He therefore suggested specifying that the agent was to be the representative of his country.[46] This suggestion, which was adopted by the committee, was apparently designed to enhance the position of the agents as compared with that of counsel and lawyers. Martens, similarly, insisted on the importance of the role of the agents. In his view, it was imperative to appoint agents, whereas the employment of counsel or advocates should be left to the parties.[47]

[41] See Politis, p. 179.
[42] See report of Baron Guillaume (Scott, *Proceedings, 1907*, i. 400).
[43] Ibid., ii. 386.
[44] Le Ray (p. 140) wonders on what basis Lammasch claimed that assessor-jurists would exercise great influence, since the example of 1905, from which Lammasch drew support, showed that the role of assessor-jurists was, on the contrary, of little importance.
[45] See report of Baron Guillaume (loc. cit., i. 400).
[46] Ibid., ii. 394.
[47] Ibid.

At the end of the discussions, the committee agreed on the optional appointment of agents, as well as of counsel and lawyers. Nevertheless, the greater importance attached to agents was stressed in the report of the First Commission, which stated that agents, being the representatives of their governments, had an essential and necessary place before the commission of inquiry. This was not the case with counsel or lawyers, whose employment was not indispensable and should be left to the decision of the parties.[48]

With regard to the role of counsel or advocates, the Russian draft spoke of the 'defence' of the interests of the parties, and the Franco-British draft of the 'defence of their rights or interests'. According to the report of Baron Guillaume,[49] care in preserving the distinction between the duties of arbitral tribunals and commissions of inquiry had led the Committee of Examination to modify the Franco-British formulation slightly. Instead of providing that the parties should be authorized to name counsel or lawyers to have charge of the defence of the rights or interests of the parties, the committee proposed—and the conference agreed—to provide that counsel or advocates be engaged to state the case of the parties and to uphold their interests before the commission (Art. 14).

Seat of the commission

The Russian proposal that the commission should sit, when possible, in the place where the incident had occurred, was not adopted. Instead, the conference approved a provision that if the inquiry convention did not determine where the commission should sit, it was to sit at The Hague.[50] The place of meeting, once fixed, could not be altered by the commission except with the assent of the parties (Art. 11).

The Committee of Examination was hesitant about giving undue encouragement to the parties to conduct the inquiry in the place where the incident had occurred. Most members of the committee considered

---

[48]See report of Baron Guillaume (ibid., i. 402). According to Le Ray (p. 114), the Conference of 1907 skilfully separated the agents from counsel and advocates. The agents usually combined the functions of agents, advocates and counsel, and their role of agents obliged them to set forth and uphold the interests of the parties. The advocates were, at the most, secretaries to the agents.

[49]Loc. cit., i. 401.

[50]Le Ray writes (p. 108) that the draftsmen designated The Hague because that city was the seat of the PCA. The setting-up of a commission of inquiry in The Hague constituted in effect an invitation to choose the commissioners from among the members of the Court. One could not, in his view, hope for a better choice; their high competence in matters of international disputes permitted them, better than anyone else, to conduct an inquiry and to draft a report.

Following their decision to establish, in principle, the seat of the commissions at The Hague, the draftsmen adopted a provision that the International Bureau of the PCA is to act as the registry for the commissions which sit at The Hague. The bureau is to place its offices and staff at the disposal of the commissions (Art. 15). If the commission meets elsewhere, its archives are to be transferred subsequently to the bureau of the Court (Art. 16).

that it might sometimes be dangerous for a commission of inquiry to go hastily to the very spot where a dispute had taken place a short time before. Tense feelings might exist for several weeks after the occurrence of the events which it was the duty of the commission to determine, and the appearance of the commissioners—who might only too easily be taken by the public for judges—might cause great excitement.[51] Therefore, the commission should change its meeting-place only with the consent of the parties in dispute. The state upon whose territory the disputed facts were to be established would generally be able to furnish useful suggestions as to the opportune time for changing the place of meeting.

The provisions of Article 20 enable the commission, subject to the permission of the state concerned, to move temporarily to any place or to send one or more of its members to any place, in order to conduct an inquiry. Every investigation and every examination on the spot must be made in the presence of the agents and counsel of the parties or after they have been duly summoned (Art. 21). The latter provision was designed to ensure the impartiality of the commission. It was feared that by going alone to the scene of the incident the commission might be influenced by external circumstances.[52]

Regarding the conduct of inquiries on the territory of a third state, it was decided that in order to obtain the necessary authorization the commission should apply directly to the government of that state, without being obliged to ask for the intercession of the states in dispute (Art. 24).[53]

The language of the commission

The Committee of Examination discussed the question whether the interested powers or the commission itself should determine the languages to be used. The adoption of the first solution would avoid the appearance of the commission showing partiality towards one of the parties in the event that it excluded or accepted, by a majority vote, a specific language. Moreover, the determination a posteriori of the language to be employed could render practically useless the nomination of certain agents, counsel, or advocates, and even of certain commissioners. To this the reply was made that the difficulty of the parties themselves in agreeing on a language was an additional obstacle in the way of the appointment of commissions of inquiry; even if this obstacle did not arise, the adoption of a definite language might cause difficulties in the nomination of certain competent commissioners who might not understand the language chosen or at least might not know it thoroughly. The first set of arguments, supported by the practical experience of

[51]See statement to that effect by the president of the committee, **Bourgeois**, in Scott, *Proceedings, 1907*, ii. 392.
[52]See Le Ray, p. 128.
[53]See report of Baron Guillaume (loc. cit., i. 405).

Lammasch and Martens, prevailed in the committee, and it was decided that the parties in dispute should determine the language to be used and that, in the absence of agreement, it was for the commission itself to decide on the language (Arts 10 & 11).[54]

Publicity of meetings

The leading consideration on this subject was that publicity sometimes causes difficulties and even harm. In some circumstances it might be embarrassing to witnesses called upon to testify before the commission. The question arose in the Committee of Examination whether to lay down that, as a rule, meetings should be held in public, leaving it to the commissioners and the parties to ask for secrecy. The prevailing opinion was that the public should not be allowed to attend, except on the decision of the commission and subject to the consent of the parties (Art. 31). It was believed that prudence demanded the adoption of the principle of secrecy. It would always be easier for a commission, when it deemed it possible, to declare that the discussions should be open to the public, rather than order the doors to be closed. The latter measure would run the risk of being misunderstood by the public.[55]

The process of inquiry: rules of procedure[56]

The process of inquiry, as envisaged in the convention, consists of all or some of the following elements: communication by the parties of statements of facts and documents useful for ascertaining the truth

[54]See Bustamente, p. 117, and report of Baron Guillaume (loc. cit., i. 400).

[55]See statement of Fromageot to that effect in Scott, *Proceedings, 1907*, ii. 402, and report of Baron Guillaume, ibid., i. 411.

[56]Art. 17 of the Convention of 1907 refers to the 'following rules which shall be applicable to the inquiry procedure', and Arts 18–36 provide, i.a., for such diverse matters as the hearing of both sides, change of meeting-place, supply of facilities by the parties, summoning and examination of witnesses, statements by agents, deliberations in private, decision by majority, publicity of meetings, signing of the report, effect of the report, and sharing of expenses.

The term 'procedure' is used in constitutional documents in a broad or in a narrow sense, or in both at the same time. In the first sense, it comprises rules regarding the constitution of the relevant body, its competence, the submission of documents, the conduct of hearings, the publicity of hearings, the publicity of sessions, the way decisions are adopted, the effect of the judgment, award, or report, and the costs involved. In the narrow sense, the term is used to cover only the rules relating to the acquisition of evidence.

The diversity of the use of the terms 'procedure' and 'rules of procedure' and the resulting confusion is revealed by a comparison of the following documents: the *Règlement* of the Dogger Bank Commission (see above, p. 61); the Model Rules on Arbitral Procedure adopted by the ILC in 1958 (see ILC Report covering the work of its 10th session, 28 Apr.–4 July 1958, UN Doc. A/3859); the ICJ Statute; the rules of the ICJ (see p. 4, n. 8).

Since it seems incorrect to designate as rules of procedure rules relating, e.g., to the appointment of commissioners or the effect of the judgment or the distribution of costs, the term is used in the present work in its narrow sense, as implying the rules by which the inquiry proper, i.e. the acquisition of information, is conducted. Cf. Art. 5 of the rules contained in the resolution of the League Assembly of 22 Sept. 1922 (below, p. 122), to the effect that the commission of conciliation shall establish 'rules of procedure for the obtaining of evidence'.

(Art. 19); examination of a locality (Art. 21); examination of witnesses and experts (Arts 26 & 27); and concluding written statements by the agents (Art. 29).

The rules of procedure governing the above stages were the subject of detailed discussion. The Committee of Examination was unanimous in regretting the almost complete absence of rules of procedure in the 1899 Convention, and in stressing the need to recommend such rules to future disputants. However, divergent views appeared as to the number of rules which it would be proper to embody in the new convention. Some members held that only a few general provisions should be laid down, while others were in favour of drawing up a list of precise and detailed rules. The supporters of both these divergent views were inspired by the same idea, that the resort to international commissions of inquiry should be simple and prompt. If states did not find in the convention a clear and practical guide to facilitate the preliminary steps and the immediate commencement of the investigation itself, it was to be feared that they would abandon the use of the inquiry method. The facts in dispute might have created a dangerous situation, and it was necessary to make available a simple and well-fashioned instrument which could be used without loss of time.[57]

Bearing in mind that a profusion of rules could arouse apprehension, the committee incorporated in the draft only those rules which it believed really useful to recommend to states. The committee took care to specify the purely voluntary character of the rules by providing that '. . . the Contracting Powers recommend the following rules, which shall be applicable to the inquiry procedure in so far as the parties do not adopt other rules' (Art. 17).[58]

With regard to the beginning of the proceedings, certain delegates wanted the statements of facts to be obligatory, while others wanted them to be voluntary. Fromageot caused the adoption of the latter view by convincing the Committee of Examination that statements of facts could often be detrimental to one of the parties. This could be so, for instance, if a state was obliged to produce a document bearing on national defence, or a paper whose divulgence would be prejudicial to it.[59] Article 19 provides, therefore, that at the dates fixed each party communicates to the commission and to the other party statements of facts, *if any*, and any other documents which it considers useful for ascertaining the truth.

[57]See report of Baron Guillaume (loc. cit., i. 403 f.). As stated by Fromageot at the meeting of the First Sub-Commission, on 9 July 1907, the absence of ready-made rules of procedure would be a serious drawback for the commissioners, whether jurists or not. If they were jurists, it would be a waste of time for them to have to formulate rules. If they were not jurists they might find it difficult to cope with matters of procedure (ibid., ii. 216).

[58]The relevant provision in the Franco-British proposal stated that the powers had agreed on the rules.

[59]See Scott, *Proceedings, 1907*, ii. 389, and Le Ray, p. 126.

The apprehensions of states in connection with the supply of information to the commission also became evident during the discussion of a Franco-British draft article which sought to grant the commission the right to ask the parties for necessary explanations or information, and stipulated that the commission should take note of a refusal to do so.[60] The Committee of Examination adopted the first part of the draft article, but considered it useless to provide for the case of a refusal. Apparently the committee thought that the implementation of such a provision might in certain instances offend a state which, for one reason or another, refused to give explanations on a certain point, and might hinder its co-operation with the commission.[61] Baron Guillaume relates that one of the committee's motives was to avoid any appearance of contradiction between this provision for a possible refusal and the terms of the article which follows and which provides for the parties to undertake to furnish the international commission of inquiry, as fully as they may deem possible, with all means and facilities necessary to enable it to become completely acquainted with the facts in question (Art. 23).[62]

Again, in the latter article, care was taken, by the reservation 'as fully as they may think possible' to relieve the parties in dispute of the obligation to furnish information which might be injurious to their security. As stated by the rapporteur, whatever might be the desire of the Committee of Examination to see litigant states shed full light on the inquiry, its members did not think that an absolute obligation should be imposed upon the governments to furnish all their means of proof. A commission might abuse this obligation and push its curiosity beyond the necessary limits—an abuse and a danger to be guarded against.[63]

During the discussion on the duty of states to assist the commission in its search for the truth, Lammasch raised the question whether the powers which had signed an inquiry convention were under an obligation to release their employees from professional secrecy. Such an obligation seemed to result, in his view, from the wording of paragraph 2 of Article 23, which laid down that the parties undertake to make use of the means at their disposal, under their municipal law, to ensure the appearance of witnesses or experts who are in their territory. Nevertheless, he believed that it would be more prudent not to provide for an obligation for release from professional secrecy. Bourgeois and Fromageot noted that paragraph 2 refers to the municipal legislation of states. They believed that, with regard to professional secrecy, governments must have the same freedom before international commissions of inquiry as before their own tribunals. The committee agreed that the

[60]A provision to that effect is contained in Art. 69 concerning the parallel competence of the arbitral tribunal.
[61]Cf. Le Ray, p. 130.
[62]See his report (loc. cit., i. 406).
[63]See ibid., and the statement by Fromageot to that effect (ibid., ii. 399).

silence of the convention on the matter should be interpreted in the sense conveyed by the French delegates.[64]

Witnesses or experts are summoned at the request of the parties or ex officio by the commission (Arts 23–5). However, not being a national authority, and not participating in the exercise of any sovereignty, the commission has no means of coercion or threat to ensure the appearance of a witness or an expert; it would always have to ask the state within whose territory the witness or expert is found, for his appearance (Art. 25, para. 1).[65] If that state is a party to the litigation, it assumes by the very fact of signing the inquiry convention the moral and legal obligation to use its sovereignty in order to ensure the appearance of resident witnesses or experts, whether nationals or aliens. This obligation is qualified by the proviso that states should use all the means at their disposal 'under their municipal law' (Art. 23, para. 2). They are not obliged to fill any lacunae which their laws might contain in this respect.[66] But if, as a result of a legal or material obstacle, the appearance of witnesses could not be obtained, the parties would arrange for the evidence to be taken before the qualified officials of the country concerned (Art. 23, para. 3).

The Committee of Examination agreed that those states signatory to the convention which were not parties to the dispute had certain obligations regarding the appearance of witnesses or experts.[67] According to Article 24, the requests of the commission to third contracting powers for steps to procure evidence are to be executed, so far as the means at the disposal of the power applied to under its municipal law allow; they cannot be rejected unless the power in question considers that they are likely to impair its sovereign rights or its safety.[68]

As regards the examination of witnesses (Art. 25, para. 2, and Arts 26–8), the rules of procedure of the Dogger Bank Commission have evidently served as a model, with the exception of two points. (1) It was not considered desirable, as envisaged in the Franco-British proposal, to enable several testimonies of a witness to be heard on the same fact; in the view of the Committee of Examination, a witness could be called again to give evidence only for the purpose of confronting him with another witness whose testimony contradicted his.[69] (2) The Anglo-American system of direct examination by advocates was abandoned in favour of the system, used in most states, whereby the interrogation is

[64]See ibid., p. 400.

[65]See report of Baron Guillaume, ibid., i, 406, and statement to that effect by Kriege (Germany), ibid., ii, 396.

[66]See Politis, p. 180.

[67]See report of Baron Guillaume (loc. cit., i. 407).

[68]The Committee of Examination believed that it might sometimes be advantageous to seek the assistance of third contracting powers through the intercession of the state upon whose territory the commission is sitting. A provision to that effect was inserted in the last para. of Art. 24.

[69]See Art. 25, para. 2, and report of Baron Guillaume (loc. cit., i. 409).

conducted by the president (Art. 26). The commissioners are permitted to ask questions directly, and the assessors would doubtless, if the case arose, enjoy the same right, by virtue of the inquiry convention; but the agents and counsellors must present their questions through the president (Art. 26). Baron Guillaume explained that the committee was not prepared to adopt the British system, which permits direct questioning of a witness by the agents and counsel themselves, because it was feared that this system would present difficulties to the subjects of countries where this method of questioning was not permitted and who would not be prepared for such 'cross-examination'.[70] It might discountenance the witness, and affect the clarity and even the accuracy of his testimony.[71]

Witnesses are to give their evidence without reading. However, they may be permitted by the president to consult notes or documents if the nature of the facts in question necessitates their use (Art. 27). A minute of the evidence of each witness is to be drawn up forthwith and read to the witness. He may make alterations, and is then asked to sign the whole statement (Art. 28). These provisions, asserts Baron Guillaume, were dictated by experience and agreed with wise judicial practice.[72]

The agents are authorized, in the course of or 'at the close of the inquiry', to present in writing statements, requisitions, or summaries of the facts (Art. 29). During a discussion in the Committee of Examination on the desirability of oral pleadings, Martens suggested emphasizing that such pleadings were not necessary. After an exchange of views, the committee accepted the present wording of Article 29, since its object was to emphasize 'the difference between the operation of the commission of inquiry, which does not necessarily include pleading, and arbitration'.[73] (In practice, the difference between inquiry and arbitration as regards pleadings might not exist, since in inquiry the pleadings are not necessary but are permitted, while in arbitration they are usual but are not obligatory.)[74] The committee was careful to draw a distinction between the inquiry process and that of arbitration, not only by the specific authorization of written statements but also by replacing

---

[70]For the opposing positions, see statements of the delegates of the UK and USA, on the one hand, and of Austria-Hungary and France, on the other (ibid., ii. 397–401).

[71]See report of Baron Guillaume, ibid., i. 410. According to Scott, exclusion of the method of cross-examination so familiar to British and American lawyers was justified, for the commission was appointed to ascertain the facts in controversy and was as desirous as the agents of the parties to elucidate the truth. The questions put by the president and commissioners were likely to be searching, and the method adopted had the advantage of vesting the examination of witnesses in impartial, though not disinterested, hands. As this procedure was well known in advance, agent and counsel might well conform to it, and, by the submission of necessary questions, the president would be able to meet their desires and make the examination as searching, thorough and profound as the interests of justice required (*Hague Peace Conferences*, p. 271).

[72]Loc. cit., i. 410.

[73]Scott, *Proceedings, 1907*, ii. 397.

[74]See Politis, p. 183, and Le Ray, p. 41.

the word 'conclusions' in the Franco-British draft by the expression 'summaries of fact'.[75]

In accordance with Article 32, after the parties have completed their presentations and all the witnesses have been heard, the president is to declare the inquiry terminated, and the commission is to adjourn in order to deliberate and draw up its report. The Committee of Examination inserted here the reference to the hearing of all the witnesses in order to indicate clearly that no testimony should be permitted after the closure of the inquiry.[76]

Dissenting opinions

Article 30 of the Convention of 1907 provides that all questions are to be decided by a majority of the members of the commission; if a member declines to vote, this fact must be recorded in the minutes. Similarly, in accordance with Article 33, if one of the members refuses to sign the report of the commission, this fact must be mentioned. These provisions differ from the corresponding provisions on arbitration which, unlike those of the Convention of 1899, no longer permit the revealing, in the award, of the opinion of the minority, and confine the signing of the report to the president and the registrar of the tribunal only (Art. 79).

The rule of Article 33 was adopted without discussion. Politis (p. 182) thinks that, in theory, the rule seemed to be justified by the difference between an arbitral award and the report of an inquiry commission. Being obligatory, the sentence must be definitive, in the sense that it should exclude any possibility of subsequent discussion. Mention of a minority opinion could only weaken the authority of the sentence. Likewise, the refusal of an arbitrator to sign has no effect and mention of it is, therefore, useless. On the other hand, the inquiry does not necessarily end the proceedings. It is confined to the clarification of facts, the final solution belonging to the parties. The refusal of a commissioner to sign, or the mentioning of dissents, by showing the parties that complete light has not been thrown on the matter, would furnish them with useful indications as to the steps to be taken regarding the effect of the report.

However, in the view of Politis this explanation is not completely satisfactory. Although not having the same force as a sentence, the report is none the less a decision which—as regards the findings of fact—binds the parties, and for this reason it is important to preserve it from any cause for discredit. Moreover, because the report is less effective than the sentence, it is in greater need of protection. The reasons which led to the deletion, in regard to arbitration, of mention of a minority

---

[75]The new expression was adopted, in the words of Baron Guillaume, 'to avoid the appearance of trespassing upon the field of arbitration by the commissions of inquiry' (loc. cit., i. 410).

[76]Scott, *Proceedings, 1907*, i. 411.

opinion became more pressing in the case of inquiry, since, if the dissent of arbitrators might cause a reopening of a closed discussion, the disagreement of inquiry commissioners risked compromising the achievement of an agreement which had yet to be reached. If, after all, the parties in dispute did not wish to follow the report with a peaceful solution, they could always find reasons to ignore it. It was unhelpful for the law of peace to provide them with a pretext.[77]

CONCLUSIONS

The work of the Second Hague Peace Conference of 1907 and its results reflect a tendency to make improvements in the institution of international inquiry by the adoption of those rules relating to arbitration which would improve the machinery of inquiry without impairing its basic nature as an independent method for the peaceful settlement of international disputes.

The organizational similarity of both institutions is expressed in the following phenomena: the need for a preliminary agreement (Arts 10 & 52); the seat of the commission, fixed, in principle, at The Hague, and its subsequent transfer only by agreement of the parties (Arts 11 & 60); the choice of language, made by the commission (tribunal) in the absence of a contrary provision in the preliminary agreement (Arts 11, para. 3, & 61); the composition of the commission (tribunal) which, subject to provisions to the contrary, must have five members, three of whom are to be neutral (Arts 12 & 45); the manner of filling vacancies (Arts 13 & 59); the registry of the commission, which is the Bureau of the Permanent Court of Arbitration when the inquiry is held at The Hague (Arts 15 & 43, para. 2); the nomination by the parties of special agents, counsel or advocates (Arts 14 & 62); the communication of statements of facts and documents by each party (Arts 19, para. 2, & 63, para. 2); requests by the commission (tribunal) for information (Arts 22 & 69); the obligations of the parties to enlighten the commissioners (arbitrators) (Arts 23 & 75); the relations of the commission (tribunal) with third states regarding procedural acts to be performed on their territory (Arts 24 & 76); the non-publicity of meetings (Arts 31 & 66, para. 2), and the secrecy of proceedings (Arts 30 & 78, para. 1); the closure of the proceedings (Arts 32 & 77); majority vote (Art. 30, para. 2, & 78, para. 2); the public reading of the decision (Arts 34 & 80); and the expenses incurred (Arts 36 & 85).

The tendency to preserve the independent nature of the inquiry method, as distinguished from arbitration, found expression in the following attitudes and provisions: The Russian proposal to empower the commissions of inquiry to establish responsibilities was rejected (above, p. 93); another Russian proposal, that following the report

[77]Cf. Le Ray, pp. 156–7.

the parties had the limited choice either to conclude a friendly settlement or to resort to the Permanent Court of Arbitration, was also rejected (above, pp. 95). Provisions in the Russian and Franco-British projects that counsel or advocates should be charged with the 'defence' of the interests, or rights or interests, of the parties, were excluded in favour of a stipulation authorizing counsel or advocates to state the cases of the parties and uphold their interests before the commission (above, p. 98); written statements and written conclusions were accorded preference to oral pleadings (above, p. 104); and finally, the commission of inquiry was not empowered formally to take note of the refusal of the parties to supply necessary information (above, p. 102).

Underlying the efforts of the delegates to maintain the distinctive character of inquiry was their conviction that in the Dogger Bank case the new institution had proved its raison d'être and that, after the improvements dictated by experience, its future contribution to the peace of the world would be assured. This optimism was shared by Bustamente, amongst other writers. In international law, he wrote, an institution of this kind has a precarious existence so long as it has not been proved in practice. The Dogger Bank incident put to the test the institution of 1899 and guaranteed the success of the improvements of 1907.[78]

Politis, on the other hand, was sceptical about the future of the institution. In his view (pp. 185–7), inquiry could no longer maintain its status as an independent method: it was bound either to become fused into arbitration or to become an instrument of diplomacy. At the time of his analysis—1912—Politis discerned tendencies in both these directions. The first was marked by the general treaties of arbitration of 3 August 1911 between the United States and France and the United States and Great Britain (below, pp. 113–14). By virtue of these treaties, the parties undertook to refer to a commission of inquiry all disputes of a specified nature before submitting them to arbitration. The report of the commission was not to be binding, except on the question whether or not a dispute was subject to arbitration. In practice, the commission could impose arbitration if it was not certain that the parties would accept its recommendations.

The tendency of inquiry to become a method of conciliation or mediation (Politis uses the terms interchangeably) was reflected in the

---

[78]See Bustamente, p. 123.

In their report to the secretary of state the US delegates to the Second Peace Conference said, i.a.: '. . . In 1907 the procedure actually adopted by the [Paris] commission of inquiry was presented to the Conference, studied, considered, and made the basis of the present rules and regulations. The nature of the commission of inquiry is, however, unchanged. It was and is an international commission charged with the duty of ascertaining the facts in an international dispute, and its duty is performed when the facts in controversy are found. It does not render a judgment, nor does it apply to the facts found a principle of law, for it is not a court (Article 35)' (see Hackworth, 6 *Digest of international law* (1943), 4).

recommendation of the fourteenth Universal Congress of Peace (Lucerne, 1905)[79] that the provisions of the Hague Convention concerning inquiry be revised so as to create a more complete institution, which would not only establish the facts but would also formulate opinions. Commenting on the latter suggestion, Politis points out that it would be more realistic to establish a college of conciliation, from which the parties would be free to choose their commissioners. Conceived in this way, inquiry would in his view be nothing but a variety of mediation.

Our subsequent examination will, it is believed, show to what extent inquiry has developed as an independent institution, distinguished from arbitration, on the one hand, and from mediation and conciliation, on the other.

[79]See text of the relevant resolution in 12 *RGDIP*, 656. (In the article of Politis reference is inadvertently made to the 15th, instead of the 14th, session of the Universal Congress of Peace.)

CHAPTER 5

Inquiry under Subsequent Treaties

INTRODUCTORY NOTE

The prominence given to the method of international inquiry in the Hague Conventions of 1899 and 1907, as well as the successful experience of the Dogger Bank Commission, stimulated states to provide for the use of inquiry in many treaties dealing with the pacific settlement of disputes. The great variety of treaties concluded by various states at different times reflects a number of approaches regarding the nature of the inquiry method and its place among other peaceful means of settlement. The purpose of the present chapter is to analyse these approaches. More specifically, the following questions will occupy our attention:

(1) Whether, or to what extent, the concept of inquiry as defined in the Hague Conventions has undergone any change. Inquiry as envisaged in the two conventions is equivalent to fact-finding. Subsequent treaties have enlarged the scope of inquiry beyond the mere facts in dispute, and it will be of interest to discover whether the substance of the method has not been changed thereby.

(2) Whether any change has occurred with regard to the kind of disputes subject to inquiry. We shall keep in mind, in this connection, the Hague reservations relating to honour and vital interests, and shall examine to what extent the confidence of states in the Hague method of inquiry, and in other schemes providing for inquiry, has prompted them to discard these reservations.

(3) To what extent it has been found expedient to entrust international commissions with the sole function of inquiry or, alternatively, to what extent such commissions employ inquiry in the framework of conciliation. In this connection it will be advisable to define the function, or functions, of various commissions on the basis of their terms of reference, and not necessarily on the basis of their name or the title of the relevant treaty. Thus if the task of the commission is to investigate and report on all aspects of the dispute, we may define this process as 'enlarged inquiry'. On the other hand, if the commission is empowered to recommend to the parties a scheme for the settlement of the dispute, or to endeavour to bring the parties to an agreement, then the process is one of conciliation.[1] Commissions of conciliation are, as a rule, called

---

[1]Cf. the classification of treaties adopted by Habicht, *Post-war treaties for the pacific settlement of international disputes* (1931), p. xx.

upon to investigate all aspects of the dispute prior to making recommendations. While this investigation is generally considered as part of the overall method of conciliation, for our purposes we may distinguish between conciliation proper, i.e. the efforts of the commission to bring the parties to an agreement, and the elucidation of the questions in dispute.

(4) To the extent that international commissions are competent to deal with one and the same dispute by using both inquiry and conciliation, what is the relevant importance of inquiry? As we shall see, in certain cases states have taken care to ensure, by appropriate provisions, that the inquiry should not be dispensed with, or, as the case may be, should not be overshadowed by the efforts to reconcile the parties.

(5) Whether, or in what way, the establishment of the League of Nations and the UN has affected the conclusion of treaties providing for the employment of inquiry outside the framework of these organizations. The question has been asked whether the centralization of political power in those organizations does not justify the increased employment of peaceful methods, including inquiry, independently of those organs of the League or the UN charged with the peaceful settlement of disputes. Since the establishment of the League gave impetus to the conclusion of treaties providing for inquiry and conciliation, we shall pay special attention to the reactions of states during and after the adoption of the Covenant.

(6) Finally, an attempt will be made to ascertain whether our examination of various treaties leads to a conclusion pointing to a definite trend of thought regarding resort to inquiry.

In order to make the presentation which follows as systematic as possible, it is proposed to combine chronological development with an analysis of particular types of treaties, in such a way that whenever a new type of treaty is concluded, other treaties belonging to the same type will be examined together with it, even if they were concluded later.

TREATY BETWEEN THE USA AND CANADA RELATING TO BOUNDARY WATERS, 1909[2]

The purpose of this treaty, as recited in its Preamble, is

to prevent disputes regarding the use of boundary waters, and to settle all questions which are now pending between the United States and the Dominion of Canada, involving the rights, obligations or interests of either, in relation to the other, along their common frontier, and to make provision for the adjustment and settlement of all such questions as may hereafter arise.

[2]Treaty between the United States and Great Britain relating to Boundary Waters between the United States and Canada, signed in Washington on 11 Jan. 1909, 36 Stat.

With a view to attaining this purpose, the parties agreed to establish an International Joint Commission composed of three Canadian and three American members.[3]

It appears from the analysis of the various tasks of the commission that, under Article VIII of the treaty the commission acts as an arbitral tribunal, under Article IX it assumes inquiry and conciliation functions, whereas by virtue of Article X it combines the powers of an arbitral tribunal and an organ of conciliation.[4]

The influence of the Hague model of inquiry commissions is reflected in the provisions of Article IX, whereby the parties agree that matters of difference, with respect to which the approval of the commission is not specifically required by virtue of the treaty, shall, upon the request of either party, be referred from time to time to the International Joint Commission for examination and report. The commission is authorized in each case so referred 'to examine into and report upon the facts and circumstances of the particular questions and matters referred, together with such conclusions and recommendations as may be appropriate'. The reports of the commission are not to be regarded as decisions either on the facts or the law and shall in no way have the character of an arbitral award. The commission shall make a joint report to both governments in all cases in which all or a majority of the commissioners agree, and in case of disagreement the minority may make a joint report to both governments, or separate reports to their respective governments. In case the commission is evenly divided, separate reports shall be made by the commissioners on each side to their own government. The commission's task of examining and reporting on the questions submitted to it was considered so basic at the time of the conclusion of the treaty, that contemporary authorities designated the International Joint Commission as a 'commission of inquiry' so far as its status under Article IX is concerned.[5]

According to the rules of procedure, adopted by the commission in December 1964,[6] the handling of a 'question or matter of difference'

2448. For text see 4 *AJIL* (1910), Official Documents, p. 239. For earlier analyses of the treaty see editorial comments, 'Boundary waters between the US and Canada', ibid., pp. 668–73, and 'The International Joint Commission between the US and Canada', ibid., 6 (1912), pp. 191–7.

[3]Two comprehensive studies of the law and practice of the International Joint Commission established in accordance with the treaty have been published: see Chacko, *The International Joint Commission between the USA and the Dominion of Canada* (1932), and Bloomfield & Fitzgerald, *Boundary water problems of Canada and the US* (1958). For a specific case, concerning the water level of the Great Lakes, see Piper, 'A significant docket for the International Joint Commission', in 59 *AJIL* (1965), 593–7. See also a selection of documents on the St Lawrence Seaway (ed. by Baxter), *ICLQ*, Spec. Suppl. (1960).

[4]See editorial comment, *AJIL* (1912), pp. 192–3.

[5]See editorial comment, ibid. (1910), p. 672.

[6]I am grateful to the Canadian embassy at Tel-Aviv for providing me with the text of the rules, as well as with other material concerning recent activities of the commission.

under Article IX begins with the submission of 'reference' by one or both governments. The commission may appoint a board of qualified persons to conduct on its behalf investigations and studies. Such a board ordinarily would have an equal number of members from each country. The commission may hold hearings at which governments and persons interested are entitled to present, in person or through counsel, oral and documentary evidence. Witnesses may be examined and cross-examined by the commissioners and by counsel for the governments and the commission. With the consent of the presiding chairman, counsel for any interested person may also examine or cross-examine witnesses.

The matters considered by the commission under Article IX include apportionment of waters, dams, drainage, diversion of upstream waters in trans-boundary rivers, irrigation, regulation of lake levels, navigation, power projects, pollution of the atmosphere, pollution of boundary waters, and water resources.

In recent years the investigatory functions of the commission have taken predominance over its judicial functions.[7] One of the most extensive and complex investigations being conducted in pursuance of a joint reference, dated 7 October 1964, concerns the pollution of Lake Erie, Lake Ontario, and the international section of the St Lawrence River.[8]

The achievements of the International Joint Commission, particularly in exercise of its investigatory competence, have been impressive.[9] The record would indicate that a treaty for the establishment of a commission of inquiry is more likely to be successfully implemented when the subject matter is technical, and when the parties involved have a tradition of neighbourly co-operation for the mutual benefit of their populations.[10]

[7]See MacCallum, 'The International Joint Commission', *Canad. Geog. J.*, Mar. 1966, pp. 76–87, and Heeney, 'Along the common frontier; the International Joint Commission', *Behind the headlines*, July 1967. Bloomfield & Fitzgerald note (at p. 61) that in recent years the number of lawyer-members has markedly decreased: 'This is a far cry from the early years when five of the Commission's six members belonged to the legal profession.'

[8]In order to make the necessary investigations and studies to form the basis of its report, the commission established two advisory boards: the International Lake Erie Water Pollution Board and the International Lake Ontario and St Lawrence River Water Pollution Board. In 1969 these boards submitted a comprehensive 3-volume report to the commission. Another example of the application of Art. IX is the investigation concerning the development of the Pembina River Basin, following a joint reference of 3 Apr. 1962. In its report of Oct. 1967 the commission recommended a plan for co-operative development of the water resources of the river.

[9]See Bloomfield & Fitzgerald, p. 39. The authors point out (at p. 60) that, as regards references under Art. IX, the record has been remarkable, although, owing to the complex nature of some of the recent references, progress towards the formulation of common recommendations has been difficult. Sixteen of the 23 references under this article have ended in joint recommendations to the two governments concerned; work on 6 out of the remaining 7 references had not yet been completed; while in the 7th reference (Waterton—Belly Rivers, 1951), the two sections of the commission disagreed, and each filed a separate report with its own government.

THE TAFT OR KNOX TREATIES OF ARBITRATION, 1911[11]

The institution of international inquiry first came into prominence after 1907, when President Taft of the United States and his secretary of state, Knox, negotiated arbitration treaties with France and Great Britain. The two identic texts signed on 3 August 1911 provided that all differences or controversies between the parties must be submitted either to an arbitral tribunal or to a Joint High Commission of Inquiry.

The parties agreed to submit to the Permanent Court of Arbitration, or to any other tribunal, all differences which it had not been possible to adjust by diplomacy and which had the following characteristics: (1) those relating to international matters; (2) those involving conflicting claims of right; and (3) those which were justiciable 'by reason of being susceptible of decision by the application of the principles of law or equity' (Art. I). At the request of either party, controversies belonging to the above category were to be referred first of all to a Joint High Commission of Inquiry 'for impartial and conscientious investigation'. All other controversies were also to be referred to a Joint High Commission of Inquiry. These included controversies whose arbitrable quality was disputed between the parties (Art. II). Whenever a question or matter of difference was to be referred to a Joint High Commission of Inquiry, each of the parties was to designate three of its nationals to act as members of the commission. However, the commission could be constituted otherwise in a particular case, if the parties so wished. The organization and procedure of the commission was to be governed by the provisions of Articles 9–36 of the Hague Convention of 1907, so far as applicable and unless inconsistent with the provisions of the treaty or modified by the terms of reference agreed upon in any particular case (ibid.).[12]

The Joint High Commission of Inquiry was authorized

to examine into and report upon the particular questions or matters referred to it, for the purpose of facilitating the solution of disputes by elucidating the facts, and to define the issues presented by such questions, and also to include in its report such recommendations and conclusions as may be appropriate.

In the Trail Smelter Investigation (1931), the commission proposed that Canada pay to the USA the sum of $350,000 to cover claims for damage caused by fumes from the smelter. The Canadian government accepted the recommendation and made the suggested payment (ibid., p. 137). See generally, ch. 4: The International Joint Commission as an investigative body.

[10]It will be noted that the commissioners act in their personal capacity, rather than as representatives of their countries. See statement of the American commissioner (Tawney) to that effect, in Annexes to editorial comment, *AJIL* (1912), p. 195.

[11]See text in TCIA, iii [*1910–13*] (1913).

[12]The treaty is silent on the manner in which decisions are taken. Art. 30 of the Hague Convention, it will be noted, provides that all questions are decided by a majority of the members of the commission.

The reports of the commission were not to be regarded as decisions either on the facts or on the law and were in no way to have the character of an arbitral award (Art. III). However, if the parties disagreed as to whether or not a dispute was subject to arbitration, and all, or all but one, of the commissioners reported that the dispute was arbitrable, their report was to be binding (ibid.).

The theoretical significance of the Taft (Knox) treaties, which never went into effect, consists in the wider application of inquiry and in its close connection with conciliation. To inquiry may be submitted purely legal disputes suitable for arbitration, and these disputes themselves, as well as all disputes subject to inquiry, are of a wide scope, since they might involve national honour or vital interests.

The power of the inquiry commission to give a binding decision on the arbitrability of a dispute is contrary to the basic nature of the Hague institution. It represents a marked departure from the freedom of action which the provisions of the Hague Convention of 1907 confer on the parties with regard to the report of the commission. By exercising this power the Joint High Commission of Inquiry would, in effect, have ceased to act as an inquiry commission and would have transformed itself into an arbitral tribunal without 'disguise'—to use the word favoured by Politis.

Another challenge to the genuineness of the Joint High Commission of Inquiry springs from its competence to make recommendations. Clearly, this competence has been considered throughout the century as characteristic of the conciliation method. The provisions of the Taft treaties show, in this respect, how conciliation had its origin in the inquiry. The parties thought that the inquiry would be more useful for the settlement of a dispute if it was carried a step further. If the facts had been elucidated and the commission had defined for itself the issues involved, the commission was in the best position to draw conclusions and make recommendations to the parties.

The composition of the inquiry commission, based as a rule on parity, would indicate the wish of the parties that the issues should be solved by way of reconciliation of divergent views rather than through the deciding votes of neutral commissioners. Nevertheless, the inquiry process is not, as in future developments (below, pp. 126 ff.), subordinated to that of conciliation. The emphasis in the treaties under consideration is on the Hague concept of inquiry, including its fact-finding element.

THE BRYAN TREATIES FOR THE ADVANCEMENT OF PEACE, 1913–40

These treaties put into effect the peace plan elaborated in the early part of this century by the eminent American statesman and pacifist William

Jennings Bryan.[13] Shortly after Wilson's inauguration as president in March 1913, Bryan was appointed secretary of state and was authorized to initiate the conclusion of bilateral treaties based on his plan. Many states responded favourably, and Bryan signed thirty treaties, officially called 'Treaties for the Advancement of Peace'. The United States remained faithful to the Bryan formula, and concluded a second series of Bryan treaties in 1928–31, and a third series, with the British Dominions, in 1939–40. The treaties signed between 1928 and 1931, as well as that with Liberia of 1934, are generally called treaties of con-ciliation, although they are practically identical with the original Bryan treaties and, like those treaties, do not empower the commissions of inquiry to recommend terms of settlement.[14] Most of the treaties have been ratified and are at present in force.[15]

By virtue of the Bryan treaties, the parties agree, as a rule, that all disputes between them, 'of every nature whatsoever', which are not subject to settlement by other treaties and which are not settled by diplomatic means, must be referred for investigation and report to a permanent international commission. The parties undertake not to declare war or begin hostilities before the report is submitted.[16] The composition of the commission follows the model of the Hague Con-vention of 1907. The various arrangements adopted seek to ensure that out of five members of the commission, only two would be nationals of the parties.[17] The United States, as we have seen, has always favoured the predominance of the neutral element, with a view to strengthening the authority and the impartiality of the commission.

Bryan attached great importance to the permanent character of the commission. He believed that the commissioners should be selected in an atmosphere of calm, before the occurrence of a dispute. In addition, permanency ensured that the commission had the necessary authority to enable it to accomplish its task more successfully.[18]

---

[13]See, generally, the Introduction by Scott in *Treaties for the Advancement of Peace between the United States and other powers negotiated by the Honorable William J. Bryan . . .* (1920). See also Bryan's editorials in the *Commoner* (17 & 24 Feb. 1905) and his speech at the 1906 Conference of the Inter-Parliamentary Union, *Official report of the 14th confer-ence held in the Royal Gallery of the House of Lords, London, July 23rd to 25th, 1906,* p. 125.

[14]In all, the USA concluded Bryan treaties with El Salvador, Guatemala, Honduras, Netherlands, Nicaragua, Panama (1913), Argentina, Bolivia, Brazil, Chile, China, Costa Rica, Denmark, Dominican Republic, Ecuador, France, Great Britain, Greece, Italy, Norway, Paraguay, Persia, Peru, Portugal, Russia, Spain, Sweden, Switzerland, Uruguay, Venezuela (1914), Albania, Austria, Czechoslovakia, Finland, Germany, Lithuania, Poland (1928), Belgium, Bulgaria, Egypt, Estonia, Ethiopia, Hungary, Kingdom of the Serbs, Croats and Slovenes, Luxemburg, Romania (1929), Greece (new treaty), Latvia (1930), Switzerland (new treaty) (1931), Liberia (1939), Australia, Canada, New Zealand, S. Africa (1940).

The texts of the first 30 treaties appear in Scott, *Treaties for the Advancement of Peace,* and of the remainder in UN *Survey.* See also TCIA iii & iv, and LNTS.

[15]See US State Dept, *Treaties in force* (1972).

[16]See, e.g. Art. I of the treaty with the Netherlands.

[17]e.g. ibid., Art. II.   [18]See Cot, p. 72.

Another characteristic feature of many Bryan treaties is the commission's initiative in offering its services to the parties in dispute.[19] Bryan felt that, at the time when investigation was most needed, the parties to the dispute might be restrained from asking for investigation by the fear that such a request might be construed as cowardice.

As regards the method of work, various treaties make general reference to the relevant provisions of the Hague Convention of 1907.[20] According to some treaties, the parties must furnish the international commission with all means and facilities required for its investigation and report.[21] Like the Hague Convention, the Bryan treaties leave the parties complete freedom of action regarding the report of the commission.[22]

To sum up, the Bryan system departed from the model of the Hague Conventions in the following respects: the international commissions are permanent; the investigation applies to questions of both fact and law; major disputes, involving the honour and vital interests of the parties, are subject to investigation; the commissions have very wide powers of initiative—a function which approximates the commissioners to mediators;[23] and finally, the principle of the moratorium is introduced.

The Bryan treaties have never been applied. Several commissions have been established, but resort has not been had to them.[24] Despite the failure of the parties to employ the machinery of the original Bryan treaties, the US government, convinced of their intrinsic value, has taken the initiative in concluding many more treaties for the advancement of peace. The US attachment to the Bryan principles had considerable influence on the future development of peaceful procedures. The Bryan treaties stimulated the Latin American countries to adopt the system in the so-called ABC and Gondra treaties, and had an important effect on the drafting of conciliation treaties after the First World War.

The ABC treaty concluded between Argentina, Brazil, and Chile on 25 May 1915[25] deviates from the Bryan model in the following respects: it fixes the seat of the commission; it lays down that it is sufficient for one party to request the convocation of the commission; it contains no stipulation that the commission may act on its own initiative; it provides for a commission of three instead of five members; it does not stipulate

[19]e.g. Art. III of the treaty with the Netherlands.
[20]e.g. the treaties with Denmark and Norway.
[21]e.g. Art. III of the treaty with the Netherlands. The treaty with Brazil provides in Art. III that the commission shall for preference sit in the country in which there are the greater facilities for the study of the question.
[22]e.g. Art. III of the treaty with the Netherlands.
[23]See Cot, pp. 72–3. In his view the concept of 'mediatory inquiry', dear to Max Huber, well describes the activity of the Bryan commission (p. 75).
[24]Quincy Wright stated at the 1961 session of the Institute of International Law that after the First World War the Bryan treaties had sunk into oblivion. In 1935, he said, he was asked to be a member of one of the commissions envisaged by these treaties, but he had heard nothing more (see *Annuaire, 1961*, p. 221).
[25]For text (in French) see 22 *RGDIP* (1915), 475.

as to the nationality of the commissioners; and it does not provide that the parties reserve their right to act independently on the subject-matter of the dispute after the submission of the report. This last omission is not to be interpreted as implying that the report was to have an obligatory character.[26]

Great Britain concluded Bryan-type agreements with Chile on 28 March 1919 (abrogated in 1922), and with Brazil on 4 April 1919.[27] The latter treaty lays down that, after the presentation of the report by the 'Peace Commission', the two governments shall have six months in which to negotiate an agreement in accordance with the commission's report, and if, at the end of this period, they do not succeed in coming to an understanding, they shall submit the dispute to arbitration (Art. 4).

The Treaty to Avoid or Prevent Conflicts between American States (the treaty of Gondra), concluded by sixteen American states on 3 May 1923,[28] provides for the constitution of a five-member 'Commission of inquiry' to investigate and report on controversies between two or more of the parties. The request for the convocation of the commission must be submitted to the other party or to one of two permanent commissions, sitting in Washington and Montevideo. These commissions are composed of the three American diplomatic agents longest accredited in the two capitals. The treaty incorporates the Bryan principles regarding the wide range of disputes, the moratorium on war, and the liberty of action of the parties subsequent to the receipt of the report. The main difference consists in the provision on the convocation of the commission, in case of emergency, even without an attempt to negotiate, and the provision extending the moratorium to mobilization, concentration of troops, hostile acts or preparations for hostilities. The prudence and foresight underlying such extension was amply demonstrated in June 1967, when war between the Arab states and Israel was precipitated by the very additional acts (mutatis mutandis) forbidden by the Gondra treaty.[29]

SOVIET TREATIES RELATING TO FRONTIER INCIDENTS, 1948–72

The Soviet Union has taken the initiative in concluding with her neighbours a series of bilateral agreements for the handling of frontier incidents by means of inquiries made by the frontier officials of the contracting parties. Other socialist countries have also concluded agreements on the same pattern.[30] The distinguishing characteristic of these

[26]See ibid., 'Chronique des faits internationaux', p. 478.
[27]See texts in Habicht, pp. 5 & 7, respectively.
[28]See text in TCIA, iv. 4691, and in LN *Survey*, p. 158.
[29]For the revision of the Gondra treaty by the General Convention of Inter-American Conciliation (1929), see below, p. 129.
[30]See agreements between the USSR and Poland (8 July 1948 & 15 Feb. 1961), Norway (29 Dec. 1949), Czechoslovakia (30 Nov. 1956), Iran (14 May 1957), Afghanistan (18 Jan. 1958), and Finland (23 June 1960). See also the agreements between Hungary and

E

treaties is the absence of any third-party element in the machinery for their implementation. In this respect the policy of the Soviet Union follows the principle embodied in her treaties of conciliation.[31]

The agreement between the Soviet Union and Poland of 15 February 1961,[32] which may be considered typical of the whole system, provides for the appointment by each party of 'Frontier Commissioners' and 'Deputy Frontier Commissioners' (Art. 35). Article 39 enumerates twelve examples of frontier 'disputes and incidents' which it is the duty of the frontier commissioners to investigate and, where appropriate, to settle. Article 13 extends this duty to other frontier questions 'which do not require settlement through the diplomatic channel', and to the examination and settlement of all questions relating to claims for damages.

Decisions taken jointly by the frontier commissioners in the settlement of any case of irregularity occurring at the frontier are binding and final and are to take effect upon signature of the protocol on the question examined. However, claims for damages in excess of a specified amount are to be submitted to the parties through the diplomatic channel (Art. 44). Under Article 43, frontier incidents of particular gravity, such as homicide or causing grievous bodily harm, must be submitted for settlement through the diplomatic channel. In all such instances the frontier commissioners must make the necessary investigation and record the result of the investigation in a protocol. Questions on which no agreement has been reached are to be referred for settlement through the diplomatic channel.

The agreement also establishes elaborate regulations for the conduct of investigations on the spot. By Article 49 a joint investigation on the ground is not to be regarded as a judicial examination or similar proceedings, for which competence vests in the judicial or administrative authorities of either party.[33]

The above arrangements remind us of the claim of the Romanian representative at the First Hague Conference that states could settle frontier incidents by means of bilateral commissions composed solely of representatives of the two states concerned; the participation of a third state was unwarranted since it would undermine the freedom of action of the states in dispute and might create political complications (above, p. 26). The reasoning of the Soviet Union and other socialist states probably follows analogous lines. The attachment of these states

---

Yugoslavia (13 Aug. 1949), Bulgaria and Yugoslavia (22 Apr. 1954), and Czechoslovakia and Hungary (13 Oct. 1956). For texts of all agreements see UN, *A survey of treaty provisions for the pacific settlement of international disputes, 1949–62* (1966).

[31]See, e.g. the treaties of conciliation with Germany (25 Jan. 1929), Poland (23 Nov. 1932), and France (29 Nov. 1932). For texts see UN *Survey*, pp. 520, 982, & 985 respectively.

[32]See ibid., p. 876 and 420 UNTS (1962), 234.

[33]A protocol attached to the agreement regulates, i.a., the establishment of sectors of operations of the frontier commissioners and the procedure for crossing the frontier.

to the system of bilateral settlement of frontier disputes can be understood in the light of their general reservations with regard to third-party settlement of international disputes.

It will be noted that, unlike the Hague system, the present network of treaties provides for the settlement of minor incidents by a local administrative procedure. Settlement at the diplomatic level would follow only if the local officials were unable to settle the dispute.[34]

TREATIES OF CONCILIATION, 1920-73

The examination which follows is confined to a number of typical treaties which provide for the conciliation[35] of the parties on the basis of an investigation.[36] As the emphasis on each of the two processes varies in different treaties, particular attention will be paid to those treaties which confer a relatively important role on 'investigation' or 'inquiry' (as the case may be).

In the course of the drafting of the League Covenant, Switzerland and some other small neutral states endeavoured to prevent the conferment on the League's Council of such wide powers as would hinder the initiative of states to resort to means of their own choice for the settlement of disputes between them. In a Memorandum of General Comments on the Draft Covenant of 14 February 1919, submitted in March 1919 to the League Commission of the Peace Conference, the Swiss government expressed its wish

that the principle of compulsory arbitration be assigned a field as wide as possible within the system of the League and that an intervention of the Executive Council or an appeal to that body be possible only in case a decision has been reached neither by a commission of conciliation nor by a tribunal of arbitration chosen by the parties.[37]

---

[34]See Rolin, 'Les pays de l'Est et le règlement pacifique des différends internationaux', 1 *RBDI* (1965), 385.

[35]Writing about the origin of the term 'conciliation' and the method of conciliation, Myers notes that the plans for a peace league elaborated during the First World War provided for the establishment of an international court, as well as a 'council of conciliation'. (The latter phrase was first used by the English group, headed by Lord Bryce, discussing peace plans in 1914–15.) In Myers's view, the draftsmen of these plans might have been guided by three considerations: (1) the 'extension of jurisdiction' of the Dogger Bank Commission which 'indicated a monetary settlement'; (2) the desire for simple and distinct language; and (3) by a definite intention to improve the system of peaceful settlement. The combination of court and council imparted a sense of completeness to the scheme likely to attract public support. In the wartime discussions, 'conciliation' acquired an identity of its own, but never disowned its parent, the commission of inquiry. Conciliation was not new, however, in the nomenclature of pacific settlement, having been used since 1822 in Latin America as a distinct form in treaty stipulations ('The modern system of pacific settlement of international disputes', *Pol. Sci. Q.*, 46 (1931), p. 560. Cf. below, p. 198).

[36]For an instance in which a commission could possibly dispense with the process of investigation, see below, p. 129.

[37]For the text of the memorandum, see Miller, *The drafting of the Covenant* (1928), i. 303. For the text of the draft Covenant of 14 Feb. 1919 see ibid., ii, Doc. 19, p. 327.

Accordingly, the Swiss government presented the following amendment to draft Article XII of the Covenant:

The High Contracting Parties agree that whenever disputes shall arise between
them, which can be settled neither by the ordinary means of diplomacy *nor
by a commission of conciliation and inquiry chosen by the parties*, they will in
no case resort to war without having previously submitted the question and
matters involved either to arbitration or to inquiry by the Executive Council
(emphasis in original).[38]

The precedence given to 'conciliation and inquiry' was also expressed
in a Swiss amendment to draft Article XIII, which read:

The High Contracting Parties agree that whenever any disputes or difficulty
shall arise between them which they recognize to be suitable for submission
to arbitration and which can be settled neither by the ordinary means of
diplomacy nor by a commission of conciliation and inquiry chosen by the
parties, they will, at the request of one of the parties, submit the whole
subject-matter to arbitration.[39]

Amendments to the same or similar effect were also submitted by
other neutral states.[40] The great powers preferred, however, that the
procedures for conciliation and inquiry should be concentrated in the
hands of the proposed Executive Council which would be competent
to appoint commissions of conciliation.[41] At the conclusion of the
deliberations it was decided to confer the power of 'inquiry' on the
Council and the Assembly.

Under the Covenant, the members of the League agreed that if there
should arise between them any dispute likely to lead to a rupture, they
would submit the matter either to arbitration or to judicial settlement or
to inquiry by the Council, and they further agreed (apparently under the
influence of Bryan's moratorium) not to resort to war until three months
after the award by the arbitrators or the judicial decision or the report
of the Council was rendered (Art. 12). In the exercise of its competence
of inquiry, the Council was to endeavour to effect a settlement of the
dispute, and if such effort was successful a public statement was to be
made, giving such facts and explanations regarding the dispute and the
terms of settlement as the Council deemed appropriate (Art. 15).[42]

The Commission on the League consisted of 15 members—2 members representing
each of the five great powers and 5 members elected to represent 'all the Powers with
special interests'. The 5 elected members were the delegates of Belgium, Brazil, China,
Portugal and Serbia (ibid., i. 229).

[38]Ibid., ii. 638.

[39]Ibid.

[40]Ibid.

[41]See Lord Cecil's proposal and President Wilson's statement, ibid., p. 351.

[42]If the dispute were not thus settled, the Council either unanimously or by a majority
vote was to publish a report containing a statement of the facts of the dispute and the
recommendations which were deemed just and proper regarding the dispute. Any member

The adoption of the Covenant's provisions on the settlement of international disputes by the organs of the League prompted Switzerland and the Scandinavian countries to conclude a series of bilateral treaties of conciliation with a large number of countries;[43] in addition, the Scandinavian countries took the lead in the League to promote, under its auspices, a system of conciliation to be effected outside the League.

In July 1920 the Norwegian and Swedish governments proposed amendments to Articles 12 and 15 of the Covenant to the effect that the consideration of international disputes should be referred, before any other action is taken, to previously appointed commissions consisting of a neutral chairman and an equal number of members appointed by each party to the dispute.[44] The main difference between the two proposals was that the Swedish proposal confined the role of the commissions to inquiry and conciliation, while the Norwegian proposal conferred on them, in addition, powers of arbitration.

In an Explanatory Statement accompanying the Swedish draft amendments to the Covenant, the Swedish government stated that objection might reasonably be taken to the relevant provisions in the Covenant on the grounds that the Council was a body of a too definitely political character and that the Assembly was too large to assume satisfactorily in the first instance the duties of a board of conciliation. In the opinion of the Swedish government, a commission whose composition is left to the choice of the parties concerned and whose members would therefore enjoy their full confidence, would be better qualified from the outset to apply a procedure of conciliation. Another advantage of the pro-

---

of the League represented on the Council had the right to publish a statement of the facts of the dispute and of its conclusions. The Council was empowered to refer the dispute under consideration to the Assembly of its own motion, or at the request of either party. The Assembly was to enjoy the powers of the Council with regard to a dispute so referred (Art. 15).

Art. 17 of the Covenant empowered the Council to 'institute an enquiry' into the circumstances of disputes involving non-members. The Council was to 'recommend such action as may seem best and most effectual in the circumstances' with regard to such disputes.

[43]The motives underlying Swiss policy in the matter, as well as the importance attached to the use of inquiry, are revealed in 'Rapport du Conseil fédéral à l'Assemblée fédérale concernant les traités internationaux d'arbitrage (du 11 décembre 1919)', *Feuille fédérale suisse, 1919*, v. 816–21. The author of the report (probably Max Huber) stated, i.a., that the Council and the Assembly were essentially political organs, whose composition did not offer all the necessary guarantees for an impartial examination of the dispute. Therefore an intermediary procedure by 'commissions of inquiry and conciliation', such as those provided for in the Hague Conventions, the Taft and the Bryan treaties, could usefully be employed. (The commissions referred to could hardly be regarded as commissions of conciliation, since they are not empowered to make recommendations.)

[44]See LN *Records of the First Assembly, meetings of the committees* (1920), *Minutes of the First Committee (Constitutional Questions)*, Annexes 3a & 3b, pp. 73 & 82 respectively. The Norwegian draft amendments were drawn up by a committee appointed by the Norwegian government in collaboration with two committees appointed respectively by the Swedish and Danish governments.

posed method was that the dispute would be submitted to the Council after it had been the subject of a thorough investigation.

The ensuing debates were dominated by apprehension lest the Scandinavian proposals would lead to the creation of a complex and rigid system of compulsory settlement of international disputes. Moreover, fear was expressed that the position of the Council would be undermined. At the same time, the resort to inquiry and conciliation was held to be very useful.[45] As a result, the Assembly adopted on 22 September 1922 a resolution,[46] in which it recommended the members of the League, 'subject to the rights and obligations mentioned in Article 15 of the Covenant', to conclude agreements with the object of submitting their disputes to conciliation commissions formed by themselves. With regard to the organization, competence, and procedure to be followed by these commissions, the parties were recommended to look for guidance to the provisions of the Hague Convention of 1907. In the view of the Assembly, the League Council was entitled to invite the parties to bring their disputes before a conciliation commission, and also to refer to such a commission any dispute submitted to it.

By virtue of Article 5 of the attached model rules, the parties were to furnish the commission with all the information which might be useful 'for the enquiry and the drawing up of the report'. Article 7 of the rules stipulated that 'in proper cases', the report was to include a proposal for the settlement of the dispute.

The states which first conceived the idea of promoting the establishment of 'commissions of conciliation and inquiry' or the 'procedure of inquiry and conciliation' by means of bilateral treaties did not wait for the outcome of the Scandinavian initiative within the League. On 26 March 1920 Sweden and Chile signed a treaty which was referred to as the first conciliation treaty,[47] although the inquiry function of the commission was predominant.[48] Article 1 provides that 'any dispute of any description' which it might not have been possible to settle through diplomatic channels, or which has not been submitted for judicial decision either to a court of arbitration or to the Permanent Court of International Justice to be established by the League, must be submitted 'for investigation' by a permanent commission. Thereafter, the article

[45]See report of the Council, *Records of the Second Assembly, plenary meetings, annex to the 6th meeting of 8 September 1921*, p. 137; report of the First Committee of the Assembly, ibid., *Annexes to the 28th meeting, 2 October 1921, Annex B*, p. 695; Committee for the Consideration of the Procedure of Conciliation, 'Report submitted to the Council on July 18th, 1922', *LNOJ*, Aug. 1922, *Minutes of the 19th session of the Council*, 17–24 July 1922, Annex 376, p. 903; additional report of the First Committee of the Assembly, *Records of the Third Assembly, plenary meetings*, vol. II, *Annexes*, Annex 14.

[46]For text see *Records of the Third Assembly, text of the debates (meetings held from September 4 to 30)*, p. 199.

[47]Text in 4 LNTS (1921), p. 273, and in LN *Survey* (p. 145), under the title 'Convention between Chile and Sweden, concerning the Establishment of a Permanent Enquiry and Conciliation Commission'.

[48]See Cot, p. 83.

embodies one of the main Swiss and Scandinavian ideas, that until recourse has been had to investigation (or inquiry) and conciliation, the parties are precluded from submitting the dispute to the League Council. The commission is to be composed of five members, each state appointing two, only one of whom may be a national. The fifth member, who is the president, is selected by agreement of the parties or, failing that, by the Permanent Court (Art. 2). The commissioners are appointed for three years (Art. 3).

In accordance with Article 6, the commission could offer its services on its own initiative, 'with a view to the opening of proceedings of inquiry'. Article 7 empowers the commission to conduct a 'visit to the spot', if it considers such a visit 'likely to assist the enquiry'. In Article 8, the parties undertake to supply the commission with all information which might be of value to it 'in connection with the enquiry and the drawing up of its report . . .'. By virtue of Article 12, the commission is bound to render a report, whereas it is to submit a scheme for the settlement of the dispute only 'if necessary'. After the receipt of the report, the parties reserve, subject to the provisions of the Covenant, full freedom of action 'as far as concerns the dispute submitted to the Commission for enquiry'.

The above treaty is typical of the first treaties providing for inquiry and conciliation concluded after the First World War. It follows the Bryan pattern very closely. The emphasis on the inquiry function is obvious throughout, while the conciliation function is confined to the optional provision in Article 12.

The Treaty of Arbitration and Conciliation between Switzerland and Germany, of 3 December 1921,[49] lays down that any dispute which, under the terms of the treaty, could not be referred to arbitration, must, at the request of one of the parties, be submitted 'to the procedure of conciliation' (Art. 13). If in a dispute falling into one of the categories of arbitrable disputes a party pleads that the issue affects its independence, territorial integrity, or other 'vital interests of the highest importance', and if the opposing party admits that the plea is well founded, the dispute must not be submitted to arbitration but to conciliation (Art. 4). A 'Permanent Board of Conciliation' is charged with drawing up a report which must determine 'the facts of the case',[50] and must contain

---

[49] 12 LNTS (1922), 281; LN *Survey*, p. 201.

[50] According to Habicht (p. 1023), the phrase should be 'state of things'. He notes that unfortunately the translations of the German-Swiss treaty have used the terms 'état de fait' and 'facts of the case' in the French and English texts, respectively, and that the expression 'questions de fait' was used for the German 'Sachverhalt', for instance, in Art. 6 of the treaty between Hungary and Switzerland of 28 Oct. 1924. For our purposes it is relevant that the competent Swiss authorities have not only constantly used the expression 'questions de fait', but have been fully aware of its implications.

Art. 5 of the Swiss-Italian treaty of 20 Sept. 1924, as published in the official *Feuille fédérale suisse, 1924*, iii. 702, reads: 'La Commission permanente de conciliation aura pour tâche de faciliter la solution du différend en éclaircissant, par un examen impartial

proposals for settling the dispute. The report is not, either as regards 'statement of facts'[51] or as regards legal considerations, in the nature of a final judgment binding upon the parties. Each of the parties must, however, state within a time-limit to be laid down in the report, whether and to what extent it recognizes the accuracy of the facts noted in the report and accepts the proposals which it contains (Art. 15).

In this treaty the two functions of inquiry and conciliation are more balanced. Both the inquiry into the facts and the submission of proposals for settlement are mandatory, and the parties are required to adopt a stand on the proposals of the commission as well as on its statement of facts. With regard to the range of the inquiry, the provisions clearly indicate that both law and facts are subject to investigation. The characteristic provision to the effect that the report must determine the facts of the case has been taken over by many subsequent treaties.[52]

The adoption of the Assembly resolution of 22 September 1922 stimulated countries in the American continent to adapt the conciliation method to previous arrangements for the pacific settlement of international disputes. On 7 February 1923 Guatemala, El Salvador, Honduras, Nicaragua, Costa Rica, and the United States, 'desiring to unify and recast in one single convention' the Bryan treaties of 1913 and 1914 between the United States and each of these countries, concluded the Convention for the Establishment of International Commissions of Inquiry.[53] The convention lays down that when two or more parties fail to adjust through diplomatic channels a controversy originating in some divergence or difference of opinion regarding questions of fact, relative to failure to comply with a treaty, and which affect neither the sovereignty and independence of the parties, nor their honour or vital interests, the parties are bound to institute a commission of inquiry with the object of facilitating the settlement of the dispute 'by means of impartial inquiry into the facts' (Art. 1). This obligation is to cease if the parties agree to submit the question to arbitration (ibid.). A commission of inquiry is not to be formed except

---

et consciencieux, *les questions de fait* et en formulant des propositions en vue du règlement de la contestation' (emphasis added).

[51]Unlike the expression 'facts of the case' (see previous footnote), there are no different versions of this phrase.

[52]See e.g. the following treaties: Switzerland–Netherlands, 12 Dec. 1925 (LN *Survey*, p. 192); Germany–Sweden, 29 Aug. 1924 (p. 219); Germany–Netherlands, 20 May 1926 (p. 291); Spain–Switzerland, 20 Apr. 1926 (p. 257); Finland–Netherlands, 9 June 1928 (UN *Survey*, p. 390); Italy–Turkey, 30 May 1928 (p. 377); Austria–Italy, 6 Feb. 1930 (p. 755); Czechoslovakia–Turkey, 17 Mar. 1931 (p. 879).

Some treaties, while not obliging the commission to conduct an inquiry into the facts or to include in its report findings on fact, contain, mutatis mutandis, the following provision, which expresses the strong expectation that the commission would deal with the facts of the dispute: 'The Commission's report shall not be in the nature of a compulsory final award as regards either the statement of facts, or the legal considerations.' See e.g. Greece–Roumania, 21 Mar. 1928 (LN *Survey*, p. 359); and Germany–Turkey, 16 May 1929 (p. 567).

[53]See TCIA, iv. 4677.

at the request of one of the parties 'directly interested in the investigation of the facts which it sought to elucidate' (ibid.). Within 30 days of ratification, each party is to nominate five nationals with the purpose of forming a permanent list of commissioners (Art. 3). Each of the parties directly interested in the dispute is to be 'represented' on the commission by one of its nationals selected from the permanent list. The commissioners selected by the parties must, by common accord, choose a president from persons on the list designated by a government which has no interest in the dispute.

The commission is empowered to examine all the facts, antecedents, and circumstances relating to the question or questions which might be the object of investigation, 'and when it renders its report it shall elucidate said facts, antecedents and circumstances and shall have the right to recommend any solutions or adjustments which, in its opinion may be pertinent, just and advisable' (Art. 5). The reports of the commission shall not have the force of judicial decisions or arbitral awards (Art. 6). However, in case of arbitration or complaint before the Tribunal created by the convention signed by representatives of the five Central American States on the same day as the convention under discussion, the reports of the Commission of Inquiry may be presented as evidence by any of the litigant parties (Art. 7).

Although the commissions established by the convention are called International Commissions of Inquiry, it is clear that, by virtue of their power to propose a settlement, they may be regarded as commissions of conciliation.[54] However, the constant references to the fact-finding task of the commission would suggest the prominence of the inquiry function as envisaged in the Hague Conventions and the Bryan treaties.

The Hague system of inquiry had a considerable influence on the authors of the conciliation treaties concluded in 1924 between Switzerland and Sweden, Switzerland and Denmark, and Switzerland and Hungary.[55] The formula contained in the treaties between Sweden and Switzerland and Hungary and Switzerland stating that

The task of the Permanent Conciliation Commission [in the latter treaty, the commissioner] shall be to further [promote] the settlement of disputes by an impartial and conscientious examination of the facts and by formulating [submitting] proposals with a view to settling the case

has been used in many other treaties for the pacific settlement of international disputes.[56]

[54]Hill writes (at p. 99) that while it might have been the intention of the contracting states to copy the Bryan treaties in many respects, 'the so-called "commissions of inquiry" are actually conciliation agencies'.

[55]This was explicitly revealed in two Messages of the Swiss Federal Council to the Federal Assembly, dated 28 Oct. 1924: *Feuille fédérale suisse, 1924*, iii. 640 & 655 (see Bibliography, below, p. 354). For texts of treaties see LN *Survey*, pp. 171, 176, & 210.

[56]See e.g. the following treaties: Denmark–Switzerland, 6 June 1924 (LN *Survey*, p. 176); Czechoslovakia–Poland, 23 Apr. 1925 (p. 236); Finland–Italy, 21 Aug. 1928

Until 1925 the drawing up of a report—which was expected to include an appraisal of the facts underlying the dispute—was always regarded as the principal task of the commissions of conciliation. The treaty between France and Switzerland concluded on 6 April 1925[57] introduced an innovation, which had the effect of diminishing the fact-finding task and elevating the task of conciliation to a predominant position.[58] By virtue of that treaty, the presentation of conclusions and proposals in a report is no longer essential, and can even be dispensed with. Article 6, defining the functions of the Permanent Conciliation Commission,[59] reads as follows:

The duty of the Permanent Conciliation Commission shall be to elucidate the questions in dispute, to collect with that object all useful information by inquiry or otherwise, and to endeavour to bring the Parties to an agreement. It may, after examining the case, intimate [proposer] to the Parties the terms of settlement which seem to it suitable, and lay down a time-limit within which they are to reach their decision.

At the close of its proceedings the Commission shall draw up a report [procès-verbal] stating, as the case may be, either that the Parties have come to an agreement and, if need be, the terms of the agreement, or that it has proved impossible to effect a settlement.

The Commission's proceedings must, unless the Parties otherwise agree, be concluded within six months of the day on which the dispute was laid before the Commission.

As pointed out by Habicht (pp. 1027–8), once the commission established by the Franco-Swiss treaty has been resorted to, it will not end its activities until the parties are reconciled or have clearly demonstrated that a reconciliation is impossible. The main task of the commission is to bring the parties to an amicable settlement of the dispute or, in the words of Article 5, 'to take all steps calculated to lead to a conciliation'. By virtue of Article 6, the submission of a report with proposals to that end is one possible means. The commission might, however, prefer the method of conference, by which the problem is informally discussed with the parties. The suggestions of the commissioners might be rejected, and they might make new proposals. The commission might not always be able to bring the parties to agreement simply by expressing an opinion

---

(UN *Survey*, p. 424); Italy–Panama, 14 Dec. 1932 (p. 992); Brazil–Poland, 27 Jan. 1933 (p. 1002).

[57]See French text in *Feuille fédérale suisse, 1925*, ii. 455, and both the French and English texts in Habicht, p. 226.

[58]See 'Message du Conseil fédéral à l'Assemblée fédérale concernant l'approbation du traité de conciliation et d'arbitrage obligatoires conclu, le 6 avril 1925, entre la Suisse et la France (du 15 mai 1925)', *Feuille fédéral suisse, 1925*, ii. 450–3.

[59]The commission is composed of five members, two of whom are appointed respectively by the parties from among their nationals, and three designated by agreement from among the nationals of three foreign states. The president is chosen by the parties from among the foreign commissioners (Art. 3).

on the facts of the case and the rights of the parties. In many instances it might find it necessary to reconcile conflicting interests and, in so doing, to go beyond the realm of law.[60]

This elasticity is reflected in the provisions of Article 7, on the procedure of the commission. It is there stipulated that, subject to any provisions to the contrary, the commission shall itself regulate its procedure, which must in all cases include the hearing of both sides. With regard to inquiries (presumably into the facts of the dispute, as distinguished from other issues), the commission is to conform to the provisions of Part III of the Hague Convention of 1907, unless it unanimously decides otherwise.

In the treaties examined so far, the reference to Part III was made in connection with the work of the commission in general, and not only with regard to 'inquiries'.[61]

The foregoing observations are also valid with regard to the Locarno treaties of 16 October 1925. The powers of the Permanent Conciliation Commissions established respectively by the Arbitration Conventions between Germany and Belgium and Germany and France, and by the Arbitration Treaties between Germany and Czechoslovakia and Germany and Poland,[62] were defined in almost the same terms as Article 6 of the Franco-Swiss treaty.[63] Analysing the Locarno treaties, Hyde expresses the opinion that the attempt to bring the parties to an

[60]In the event of failure of the conciliation effort, the dispute is to be referred either to the PCIJ or to an arbitral tribunal (Art. 14). Thus no dispute, whatever its nature, could escape judicial or arbitral settlement, after failure of the conciliation commission (see Message of the Federal Council of 15 May 1925, referred to at p. 126, n. 58 above).

[61]According to Art. 10 of the Franco-Swiss treaty, the commission is entitled to ask for oral explanations from the agents, counsel, and experts of the two parties and from any other persons whom it may think fit to summon with the consent of their governments; and in Art. 12 the parties undertake, i.a., to enable the commission to summon and hear witnesses or experts in their territory and to visit the localities in question. These provisions make no reference to relevant 'procedures' with regard to examination of witnesses and visits on the spot in the Hague Convention.

In the opinion of Baron van Asbeck, former president of the Permanent Franco-Swiss Conciliation Commission, the provisions on the 'inquiry' to be instituted by the commission are devoid of any real significance, especially in view of the wide scope of Arts 10 & 12 and the great freedom of procedure enjoyed by the vast majority of conciliation commissions (see van Asbeck, 'La procédure suivie par la commission permanente de conciliation franco-suisse', in 3 *Ned. tijd. int. recht* (1956), 218).

[62]For the text of the Locarno treaties see LN *Survey*, pp. 408–24.

[63]Art. 8 of all four treaties reads:

'The task of the Permanent Conciliation Commission shall be to elucidate questions in dispute, to collect with that object all necessary information by means of inquiry or otherwise, and to endeavour to bring the parties to an agreement. It may, after the case has been examined, inform the parties of the terms of settlement which seem suitable to it and lay down a period within which they are to make their decision.

'At the close of its labours the Commission shall draw up a report stating, as the case may be, either that the parties have come to an agreement and, if need arises, the terms of the agreement, or that it has been impossible to effect a settlement.

'The labours of the commission must, unless the parties otherwise agree, be terminated within six months from the day on which the commission shall have been notified of the dispute.'

agreement is 'the undertaking of the mediator whose good offices are tendered to States at variance'. The significant fact, he writes in another context, is that the commission of conciliation, with its broad powers and its freedom of action and potentialities as a quasi-mediator, is deemed by the parties to be a powerful agency of amicable adjustment.[64]

The Locarno treaties confirmed a growing tendency to relegate the inquiry function of conciliation commissions to a position of secondary importance. This tendency reached world-wide dimensions when the League Assembly formally endorsed the principles of the Locarno treaties regarding conciliation, and embodied them in the General Act for the Pacific Settlement of International Disputes, adopted on 26 September 1928.[65] On 28 April 1949 the UN General Assembly adopted certain amendments to the General Act, and instructed the Secretary-General to prepare a revised text under the title 'Revised General Act for the Pacific Settlement of International Disputes',[66] and to hold it open for accession by states.[67] The crucial Article 15, which defines the task of the conciliation commission, is an almost textual reproduction of Article 8 of the Locarno treaties, which, as we have seen, is practically identical with Article 6 of the Franco-Swiss treaty of 6 April 1925.

This definition has been used in over 150 treaties on the pacific settlement of international disputes.[68] The lasting influence of the theory underlying the definition is demonstrated, in particular, by the inclusion of the Locarno-General Act text in Article 15 of the European Convention for the Peaceful Settlement of Disputes, signed on 29 April 1957 by thirteen of the fifteen members of the Council of Europe,[69] and in the Treaty of Conciliation, Judicial Settlement and Arbitration of 7 July 1965 between Switzerland and the United Kingdom (below, p. 137).

[64]See Hyde, 'Commission of conciliation and the Locarno Treaties', 20 *AJIL* (1926), 103–8. The author points out that the commissions deal with disputes, however grave in character, for the solution of which adjustment by a judicial decision is not obligatory because the parties are not in conflict as to their respective rights.

[65]See text in LN *Monthly Summary*, Oct. 1928, 'Resolutions of the Assembly', Annex II, p. 305; 93 LNTS (1929), 343–63. Twenty-two members of the League were parties to the General Act.

[66]See res. 268 (III), GAOR, 3rd sess., pt II, Resolutions, 5 Apr.–18 May 1949, pp. 10–11. For the text of ch. I (Conciliation) of the Revised General Act see below, App. II, pp. 340–3.

[67]By the end of 1971 the following states had acceded to the Revised General Act: Belgium, Denmark, Luxembourg, Netherlands (part of the Act only), Norway, Sweden (part only), and Upper Volta (see UN, *Multilateral treaties in respect of which the Secretary-General performs depositary functions; list of signatories, ratifications, accessions, etc., as at 31st December 1971*, ST/LEG/SER.D/5, p. 31).

[68]See, e.g.: Sweden–Czechoslovakia, 2 Jan. 1926 (LN *Survey*, p. 232); Roumania–Switzerland, 3 Feb. 1926 (p. 249); Austria–Poland, 16 Apr. 1926 (p. 280); Hungary–Italy, 5 Apr. 1927 (p. 317); Belgium–Switzerland, 5 Feb. 1927 (p. 320); France–Sweden, 3 Mar. 1928 (UN *Survey*, p. 343).

[69]320 UNTS (1959), no. 4646, p. 244. The two members which have not signed are Austria and Turkey. In his analysis of the treaty, J. Salmon emphasizes the importance of the establishment of the materiality of facts ('La convention européene pour le règlement pacifique des différends', 63 *RGDIP* (1959), 35).

The conclusion of a series of treaties of conciliation by European countries in the years following the First World War, and the universal promotion of conciliation treaties by the League of Nations, stimulated the sixteen American states parties to the Gondra treaty of 3 May 1923 (above, p. 117) to revise the machinery set up by that treaty by the introduction of the conciliation method. On 5 January 1929, at the close of the International Conference of American States on Conciliation and Arbitration, these states signed the General Convention of Inter-American Conciliation[70] with the aim of 'giving additional prestige and strength to the action' (see Preamble) of the commissions established by the Gondra treaty. Article 2 of the General Convention provides that the 'Commission of Inquiry' to be established pursuant to the Gondra treaty shall likewise have the character of a 'Commission of Conciliation'. Moreover, the two permanent commissions, at Washington and Montevideo, are 'bound to exercise conciliatory functions' either of their own motion or at the request of a party to the dispute, until the commission of investigation and conciliation is established (Art. 3). According to Article 4, the commission of investigation and conciliation shall be at liberty to begin its work by attempting to reconcile the differences submitted to its examination with a view to arriving at a settlement between the parties. Similarly, the commission shall be free to try to effect a reconciliation between the parties at any time during the course of the investigation which the commission may consider favourable.

Article 6 lays down that the function of the commission 'as an organ of conciliation' is to procure the reconciliation of the differences it is examining by trying to effect a settlement between the parties. The commission must undertake a conscientious and impartial examination of the questions which are the subject of the controversy, it must set forth in a report the results of its proceedings, and it must propose to the parties 'the bases of a settlement for the equitable solution of the controversy'.

The prominent role of inquiry in the work of the commission established by virtue of the combined effect of the two treaties is clearly brought to the fore in the following passage of the report of Mr Varela of Uruguay, made on behalf of the Conciliation Committee of the conference:

The accompanying draft convention constitutes, then, essentially an amplified complement of the Gondra Treaty, and in such sense it should be clearly understood that it is not admissible for the Convention of Conciliation to be ratified by a state unless the Gondra Treaty be previously or simultaneously ratified. As a general rule, and whenever this is proper, investigation precedes conciliation and the commissions organized in accordance with Article 4 of the Gondra Treaty are first and foremost commissions of investigation. It is

[70]See text in TCIA, iv. 1763, and UN *Survey*, p. 505.

well understood that this does not preclude the commissions making use of the right to try conciliation which is authoritatively conferred upon them by paragraphs 1 and 2 of Article 4 of the draft convention, but, we again repeat, the process of pacific settlement normally begins with investigation and is continued with conciliation.[71]

The expressions 'as a general rule', 'whenever this is proper', and 'normally' which qualify the precedence of investigation show that the commission is at liberty, in circumstances which in the view of the rapporteur are exceptional, to begin its work with an attempt at conciliation, or may attempt conciliation at any opportune time during the investigation into the facts of a controversy. It is conceivable that instances may occur in which the likelihood of reconciling the parties will be greatly enhanced by dispensing with an investigation into the facts.[72]

The provisions of the General Convention of 1929 are generally considered to reflect a doctrine of conciliation which differs from that held by the European states. Hyde defines in the following way the difference between the European and American approach to conciliation as expressed in the 1929 Convention: according to European opinion, the recommendations of a conciliation commission should be the product of an investigation, elucidating the questions at issue and observing a procedure calculated to develop and disclose the contentions of the opposing states. In America it is held that the conciliation commission should be encouraged to investigate everything, but it should not be obliged to do so before pressing its recommendations. Moreover, under certain conditions, its labours for accord may well be supplemented, or rather preceded, by the unfettered endeavour of a body of diplomats.[73]

This view regarding the American approach to investigation and conciliation was vindicated by the settlement of the dispute between Bolivia and Paraguay (first phase, 1929–30) relating to sovereignty over the Chaco area, and of the dispute between the Dominican Republic

[71]See Murdock, 'Arbitration and conciliation in Pan America', 23 *AJIL* (1929), 279.

[72]Ibid., p. 281. According to Hyde (p. 1575), by rejecting the efforts of the commission to bring about an accord prior to investigation, either party may decline to consider any conciliatory endeavours until they have proved to be the product of the fullest investigation. Nevertheless, neither party can prevent itself from being subjected to proposals for settlement recommended by the commission at any stage of its work. By virtue of an Additional Protocol of 26 Dec. 1933 (TIAS, iv. 4798), the 'Commissions of Investigation and Conciliation' became permanent.

[73]See Hyde, 'The place of commissions of inquiry and conciliation treaties in the peaceful settlement of international disputes', 10 *BYIL* (1929), 108. Numerous European treaties prior to 1929, he writes (p. 101), prevent the commissioners from lapsing 'into the easy ways of mediators' by envisaging that the recommendations must be the consequence of prior investigation.

Cot states (at p. 219), with regard to the Convention of 1929, that the placing of conciliation before investigation signifies a deviation from current theory. Conciliation unquestionably glides into mediation. The agreement of the parties is secured as the result of the intervention of the commission, but one essential element of the notion of conciliation is missing: the settlement of the controversy is not based on an impartial opinion. The intervention of a third party brings the parties closer, but it does not elucidate the elements of the dispute.

and Haiti (1937–8) relating to the massacre in Haiti of Dominican migratory labourers. In the first dispute conciliation was effected on the basis of the principles embodied in the General Convention of 1929 without a thorough investigation of the basic issues (below, p. 199); the second dispute was settled by one of the two permanent diplomatic commissions established under the Gondra treaty and charged with conciliation functions in pursuance of the Convention of 1929.[74]

Two other treaties—the Anti War Treaty of Non-Aggression and Conciliation of 10 October 1933[75] and the American Treaty on Pacific Settlement of 30 April 1948 (known as the Pact of Bogotá)[76]—would indicate, at least in theory, that the General Convention of 1929 did not reveal any tendency on the American continent to limit to the minimum the elucidation of the questions at issue. The first treaty, which is in force among nineteen American and six European States, lays considerable stress on the duty to procure a conciliatory settlement, but it also indicates the expectation of the parties that the settlement will be reached after an inquiry into the facts (Art. X).

The Pact of Bogotá unites all the different procedures established by inter-American treaties: good offices, mediation, investigation and conciliation, arbitration, and judicial settlement. Chapter 3 of the pact, entitled 'Procedure of Investigation and Conciliation', lays down in Article XV that 'The procedure of investigation and conciliation consists in the submission of the controversy to a Commission of Investigation and Conciliation.' The duty of the commission is to clarify the points in dispute between the parties and to endeavour to bring about an agreement between them upon mutually acceptable terms. The commission shall institute such investigations of the facts involved in the controversy as it may deem necessary for the purpose of proposing acceptable bases of settlement (Art. XXII). If, in the opinion of the parties, the controversy relates exclusively to questions of fact, the commission shall limit itself to investigating such questions, and shall conclude its activities with an appropriate report (Art. XXVI).

Should an agreement be reached by conciliation, the final report of the commission is to be limited to the text of such agreement. If no

[74]On 14 Dec. 1937 the Haitian government requested that the dispute should be submitted for study and investigation to a 'commission of inquiry' under the Gondra treaty of 1923. The Dominican government considered this step unwarranted since the dispute was about to be settled by virtue of a direct understanding between the two countries. Eventually both sides requested the permanent commission in Washington to exercise the functions of conciliation granted to it under Art. 3 of the 1929 Convention. Two delegations, appointed by the Haitian and Dominican governments respectively, undertook negotiations under the auspices of the permanent commission, and on 31 Jan. 1938 signed an agreement for the final settlement of the dispute. (See the account on the 'Settlement of the Dominican–Haitian controversy', including the text of the agreement, in *Bull.* of the Pan American Union, 72 (1938), pp. 153 ff.) I am grateful to Mr Roberto E. Quirós, Deputy Director of the Dept of Legal Affairs of the OAS, for providing me with photocopies of the relevant diplomatic documents.

[75]See TCIA, iv. 4793; UN *Survey*, p. 1038.

[76]See text in 30 UNTS (1949), 55; UN *Survey*, p. 1161.

agreement is reached, the final report shall contain a summary of the work of the commission (Art. XXVII).

The somewhat isolated Article XXVI is of special significance for our study since it shows that, in the opinion of many states, the Hague method, which is confined to the examination of facts, still has its place among the increasing number of more sophisticated means for the peaceful settlement of disputes. The disputes envisaged in the article, like those contemplated in the Hague Conventions, relate exclusively to questions of fact. Therefore, the commission must limit itself to ascertaining the facts involved, and it may be assumed that, following Article 35 of the Hague Convention of 1907, the 'appropriate report' will be confined to a statement of facts and will not be binding.

It would appear that the Pact of Bogotá is in line with those treaties which enhance the employment of what may be called 'unrestricted' conciliation, while at the same time preserving, or rather reviving, as an alternative, the original and genuine method of inquiry.

THE UN CHARTER, 1945

Those who drafted the Charter were conscious of the need to clarify the distinction between the settlement of international disputes by the organs of the proposed organization on the one hand, and by means chosen by the parties to a dispute outside the organization on the other hand. The records of the San Francisco Conference do not reveal any apprehensions or differences of opinion similar to those which accompanied the discussions of the same problem in the Commission on the League of Nations (above, pp. 119 ff.).

The Dumbarton Oaks Proposals contained in Section A of Chapter VIII the following provisions on the subject:

3. The parties to any dispute the continuance of which is likely to endanger the maintenance of international peace and security should obligate themselves, first of all, to seek a solution by negotiation, mediation, conciliation, arbitration or judicial settlement, or other peaceful means of their own choice. The Security Council should call upon the parties to settle their disputes by such means.

4. If, nevertheless, the parties to a dispute of the nature referred to in paragraph 3 above fail to settle it by the means indicated in that paragraph, they should obligate themselves to refer it to the Security Council. The Security Council should in each case decide whether or not the continuance of the particular dispute is in fact likely to endanger the maintenance of international peace and security, and, accordingly, whether the Security Council should deal with the dispute, and, if so, whether it should take action under paragraph 5.[77]

[77]See UNCIO, iii. 13, Doc. G-1. According to para. 5, the Security Council should be empowered, at any stage of a dispute of the nature referred to in para. 3, to recommend appropriate procedures or methods of adjustment.

Against the background of the discussions in the League (above, p. 121), it seems somewhat paradoxical that at San Francisco a representative of a small state expressed the fear that the above formulation might prevent the Security Council from acting effectively in a dispute, and a representative of a great power had to reassure him that in case of need the Security Council would intervene.

The delegation of Ethiopia submitted a revised draft of paragraph 3 which omitted the words 'first of all'. In the accompanying comment the delegation expressed its belief that this modification was necessary in order to avoid the creation of a situation in which the Security Council would be required to withhold consideration of a dispute likely to endanger international peace and security until direct negotiations, mediation, conciliation, arbitration, judicial settlement, or other means had failed.[78]

At the meeting on 15 May 1945 of the committee charged with the drafting of the relevant section,[79] the Ethiopian delegate explained that the purpose of his delegation's amendment was

to allow the Security Council to intervene in or to be seised of a dispute even before recourse to other means of settlement were exhausted, if it appeared likely that the continued employment of such means would not result in a peaceful solution.[80]

The US delegate replied that the Ethiopian amendment would entail an undesirable modification of the purpose of the paragraph, and gave his interpretation of the provisions under discussion as follows: it was very desirable that the parties to a dispute should endeavour to settle the dispute by the use of conciliation or other ordinary methods of peaceful settlement. If, however, those methods were not successful and a threat to the peace or an act of aggression occurred, the Security Council should not delay but should act immediately, as provided in Chapter VIII, Section B, of the Dumbarton Oaks Proposals (subsequently Chapter VII of the Charter). He considered that the Security Council should and must intervene in any dispute which threatened world peace, but that it should not possess such power with regard to all disputes, since its competence would then be unduly and unnecessarily expanded. He assured the Ethiopian delegate that, if a serious situation arose, the Security Council acting under Section B need not wait for the completion of preliminary procedures; it was in fact obliged to act, and a country which was a victim of aggression could call on it for immediate assistance.

The Ethiopian delegate stated that in view of this clarification he would withdraw the amendment proposed by his delegation, it being

[78]UNCIO, Doc. 2, G-14 (n), iii. 559–60.
[79]Committee 2 (Peaceful Settlement) of Commission III (Security Council).
[80]UNCIO, Doc. 356, 111/2/II, xii. 32.

understood that any party to a dispute had the right to request the Security Council to intervene during the course of preliminary peaceful negotiations.[81]

The final text of Article 33 of the Charter reads as follows:

1. The parties to any dispute, the continuance of which is likely to endanger the maintenance of international peace and security, shall, first of all, seek a solution by negotiation, enquiry, mediation, conciliation, arbitration, judicial settlement, resort to regional agencies or arrangements, or other peaceful means of their own choice.

2. The Security Council shall, when it deems necessary, call upon the parties to settle their dispute by such means.

These provisions are supplemented by paragraph 1 of Article 37, which reads: 'Should the parties to a dispute of the nature referred to in Article 33 fail to settle it by the means indicated in that Article, they shall refer it to the Security Council.' It follows that the relevant provisions of the Charter entail not only an unequivocal legitimation of the initial use of the various methods of peaceful settlement, including inquiry, but also an obligation to resort to such methods according to the particular circumstances.

As to the meaning of the term 'inquiry' in Article 33, Goodrich, Hambro, and Simons (pp. 261 f.) are of the opinion that the reference is to the ascertainment of 'facts'[82] by an impartial body. As examples of numerous treaties providing for commissions of inquiry they cite the Hague Conventions of 1899 and 1907, thus confirming, it would seem, the restricted meaning of the term as opposed to the wider meaning given in those treaties which provide for inquiry or investigation of all aspects of the dispute.

CONCLUSIONS

Any comparative analysis of the treaties bearing on our subject must be based on a clear understanding of the terms used. And if various meanings have been given by different draftsmen to the same term, we must define our own conceptual framework in order to distinguish between the different peaceful methods envisaged in different treaties.

Two basic questions arise in this connection. First, is there a difference in substance between the process of 'inquiry' and the process of 'investigation'? Secondly, is there a difference in substance between 'inquiry' or 'investigation' on the one hand, and 'conciliation' on the other?

It is convenient to take up the second question first. Nineteen Bryan treaties, concluded in 1928 and subsequently, are entitled Treaties of

---

[81]Ibid., p. 3.   [82]Quotation marks are in the original.

Conciliation, while the treaty with Switzerland of 1931, incorporating the Bryan clauses, is called Treaty of Arbitration and Conciliation. The previously signed Bryan treaties are entitled Treaties for the Advancement of Peace. The text of all the Bryan treaties is virtually the same. In particular, the task of all the international commissions provided for in the treaties is formulated identically in terms of 'investigation and report'. This holds true of the commission envisaged in the treaty with Switzerland, which is the only commission named Conciliation Commission, the others being 'International' or 'Permanent International' commissions. With the notable exception of the treaty with Switzerland, which provides that the dispute shall be submitted 'to arbitration or to conciliation' (Art. II), the term 'conciliation' is not used in the text of any of the Bryan treaties. The treaties drafted on the Bryan model, e.g. the Gondra treaty of 1923, which also define the task of the commission as 'investigation and report', are not entitled conciliation treaties and do not employ the term 'conciliation'.

Prima facie the only justification for designating the twenty Bryan treaties as treaties of conciliation may be that, by the time the first treaty bearing this name was signed, there had been an international consensus, or at least international initiative, to the effect that the process of investigation and report by an international commission should be defined as a process of conciliation. However, there is no evidence to support the existence of such a consensus or initiative. On the contrary, by 1928 the discussions in the League of Nations concerning the application of the Locarno principles had clearly given expression to the universal view that the task of the conciliation commission consists in the exercise of two distinct functions: investigation and the submission of proposals for terms of settlement.[83] The conceptual difference inherent in the 'investigation' method of the Bryan treaties and the 'conciliation' method of other treaties was demonstrated in the modification of the Gondra treaty of 1923 by the General Convention of Inter-American Conciliation of 1929. The change of the terms of reference, to the effect that the international commission has a 'conciliatory function' in addition to that of investigation, brought about a corresponding change in the name of the commission from Commission of Inquiry to Commission of Inquiry and Conciliation.

It appears, therefore, that the denomination of many Bryan treaties as treaties of conciliation was not justified in view of the generally accepted concepts employed in the drafting of treaties for the peaceful settlement of international disputes. The choice of titles given to these Bryan treaties must have been made under the impact of the movement in favour of conciliation, without going into an analysis of the intrinsic differences between the various methods involved. For the above

[83]According to the LN *Survey* (p. 70), the role of the conciliation commission consists essentially of two parts: (1) to elucidate the question, and (2) to propose a solution.

reasons we prefer not to include the Bryan treaties in the category of conciliation treaties. The alternative would be to include them in the category of treaties of inquiry or treaties of investigation. And this brings us to the question of the possible differences of meaning between the terms 'inquiry' and 'investigation'.

The commission provided for in the Hague Convention of 1907 is an 'international commission of inquiry' charged to elucidate the facts of the dispute by means of 'investigation'. The convention speaks of 'inquiry procedure', it lays down that 'on the inquiry' both sides must be heard, it refers to a particular 'means of inquiry' on the spot, to the 'close of the inquiry', and to minutes and documents connected with the 'inquiry'. It follows from the terminology used that the process of investigation is meant to be that of inquiry, i.e. that the two words have the same meaning.

The Bryan treaties do not employ the word 'inquiry' at all. As we have just noted, they speak of 'investigation and report', and the commissions envisaged in them are simply called 'international commissions'. The term 'investigation' is often used to describe the work of these commissions. It may be thought that, having in mind the Hague model, the draftsmen of the Bryan treaties were conscious of an essential difference between an examination for the purpose of elucidating the facts only—defined in the Hague Conventions as inquiry—and an examination of all aspects of the dispute. Perhaps they wished to give terminological expression to this difference by reserving the term 'investigation' for their own scheme. If this was their reasoning, and if it were accepted by their followers, we could have clearly discerned two categories of treaties: those of inquiry, empowering the commission to elucidate facts only, and those of investigation, empowering the commission to elucidate all aspects of the dispute.

However, other draftsmen did not make such a distinction. The Taft treaties, whose formulation was influenced by Bryan's ideas, entrust the investigation of all aspects of the dispute to a Joint High Commission of Inquiry, while the Gondra treaty provides that disputes of a broad nature must be submitted for investigation to a Commission of Inquiry. Similarly, under the convention between Chile and Sweden, disputes of whatever description are to be submitted 'for investigation' to a permanent commission, and the work of this commission is repeatedly referred to as 'inquiry'. It follows that in these instances no distinction is made between inquiry and investigation.

On the other hand, the draftsmen of the Locarno-General Act type of treaties seem to have been more discriminative, by laying down that the task of the Conciliation Commission shall be to elucidate the questions in dispute and to collect with that object all necessary information 'by means of inquiry or otherwise'. In this case the elucidation of the questions in dispute—or, we might say, the examination of all aspects of the dispute—is not necessarily identical with inquiry, which is confined to facts.

However, this is only one line of interpretation. The other possible approach is to conceive the whole process of elucidation as an 'inquiry', and the 'inquiry' mentioned in the phrase 'by means of inquiry or otherwise' as a specific but unidentified means of acquiring information. Such an approach seems to have been adopted by the author of the UN *Systematic survey of treaties for the pacific settlement of international disputes, 1928–48*. He points out that the main task of a conciliation commission is to bring the parties to an agreement. As this object can best be attained by a clarification of the issues involved and of the facts which gave rise to the dispute, the commission is usually directed to elucidate the questions in dispute and hence to collect all necessary information by means of inquiry or otherwise, thus becoming, in addition, a commission of inquiry.[84] In other words, according to the writer, the commission is held to be a commission of inquiry even if it does not apply the particular type of 'inquiry' envisaged in the Locarno-General Act formulation.

The same approach is reflected in the Treaty for Conciliation, Judicial Settlement and Arbitration of 1965 between Switzerland and the United Kingdom.[85] Article 13 of the treaty defines the task of the conciliation commission in Locarno-General Act terms (the expression 'enquiries or otherwise', not 'inquiry or otherwise' is here used). Article 7 of the attached Rules of Procedure stipulates that after the parties have presented their explanations and evidence, and the witnesses have been heard, 'the President shall declare the inquiry terminated . . .'.[86] It appears that on the one hand the commission is given discretion to make or not to make inquiries, while on the other hand it is expected, *per definitionem*, as it were, to make an inquiry into the dispute—whether it collects all necessary information by 'inquiries' or 'otherwise'. There are obviously two meanings attached to the term 'inquiry' in the same Rules. The one is in the nature of a comprehensive method of elucidation of the manifold aspects of the dispute, while the other is a fact-finding device (cf. above, p. 127, n. 61).

A distinction between 'inquiry or investigation' confined to facts and the larger function of the commission has been clearly brought out in the Protocol of the Commission of Mediation, Conciliation and Arbitration which is part of the Charter of the Organization of African Unity of 25 May 1963.[87] Article XVIII of the Protocol provides that where in the course of mediation, conciliation, and arbitration it is deemed

---

[84]See UN *Survey*, p. 143.   [85]605 UNTS (1967), 206.

[86]See to the same effect Arts 9 & 13 of the Rules of Arbitration and Conciliation for settlement of international disputes between two parties of which only one is a state, elaborated by the International Bureau of the Permanent Court of Arbitration in 1962. The text of the Rules appears in 57 *AJIL* (1963), 500–12.

[87]See text in UN, *A survey of treaty provisions for the pacific settlement of international disputes, 1949-62*, p. 74.

necessary to conduct an investigation or inquiry for the purpose of elucidating facts or circumstances relating to a matter in dispute, the parties concerned and all other member states shall extend fullest co-operation in the conduct of such investigation or inquiry. The Board of Conciliators whose duty it is to clarify the issues in dispute and to endeavour to bring about an agreement between the parties upon mutually acceptable terms (Art. XXIV), may undertake 'any inquiry', or hear any person capable of giving relevant information (Art. XXV).

Amidst the varying terminology of numerous treaties two types of inquiry are to be distinguished: that confined to the elucidation of facts (Hague Conventions of 1899 and 1907, as well as Article XXVI of the Pact of Bogotá of 1948), and the enlarged inquiry comprising the elucidation of all aspects of the dispute (Taft treaties (1911), Bryan treaties (1913–40) and Gondra treaty (1923)).

Another dichotomy which emerges from our analysis of the treaties relates to the use of inquiry on its own or in conjunction with conciliation. In the latter case the treaties reflect three basic approaches:

(1) inquiry has a predominant place in relation to conciliation, e.g. the convention between Chile and Sweden (1920) and the convention signed by six American states in 1923;

(2) inquiry and conciliation are more or less balanced, e.g. the treaty between Switzerland and Germany (1921) and that between Sweden and Switzerland (1924);

(3) conciliation is given a predominant position in relation to inquiry, e.g. the treaty between France and Switzerland (1925), Locarno Treaties (1925), the General Act (1928–49), Convention of Inter-American Conciliation (1929), Pact of Bogotá (1948), European Convention for the Peaceful Settlement of International Disputes (1957), and the treaty between Switzerland and the United Kingdom (1965).

Our examination reveals a definite tendency to submerge inquiry into the facts in favour of the enlarged inquiry, and subsequently to submerge the enlarged inquiry in the process of conciliation. Soon after the Second Hague Conference, states were inclined to engulf the inquiry confined to facts in wider processes, until by 1925 the general opinion had emerged that fact-finding should not be used on its own.

As far as enlarged inquiry is concerned, the treaties for the peaceful settlement of disputes do not display any tendency to develop or reaffirm it as an independent method. The US government extended its network of Bryan treaties in the late 1930s out of pure inertia. At that time most states had put on record their preference for the method of conciliation. Within that method the enlarged inquiry had preserved its raison d'être.[88]

---

[88]By way of exception, the Convention of Inter-American Conciliation of 1929 enables the commission to start proceedings with an effort to conciliate. However, as our examination has shown, the theory underlying this approach has not been supported in subsequent treaties.

Regarding the place of inquiry in the wider framework of the pacific settlement of disputes, the general trend in recent years has been to conclude treaties providing simultaneously for conciliation (including inquiry), arbitration, and judicial settlement, although a large number of treaties provide for only one or two of these methods.[89] Only a few among the treaties are devoted exclusively to conciliation, while—to the best of our knowledge—none of the treaties concluded after the Treaties for the Advancement of Peace of 1940[90] deals exclusively with inquiry either into all aspects of the dispute or fact-finding alone.

As to the nature of the disputes submitted to conciliation, three main possibilities are envisaged: (1) all disputes; (2) non-legal disputes; (3) legal disputes if the parties agree thereto. In the event of failure of conciliation, some treaties provide no further method of settlement, others refer them to an arbitral tribunal or—in a limited number of cases—to the International Court of Justice.[91]

During the League period, the proponents of conciliation emphasized the desirability of settling disputes by conciliation before any reference to the League Council. The provision of the treaty between Chile and Sweden that neither party may submit a dispute to the League Council until investigation by a permanent commission, is significant in this respect.

Our examination has brought out the tension created between the promoters of bilateral conciliation, who feared the undue political influence of the Council, and the representatives of states who were anxious lest the status of the Council should be undermined if states preferred to settle their differences by means of conciliation commissions outside the League. A balance between these opposing views was struck in the General Act of 1928, which was silent over any connection between the submission of the dispute to a conciliation commission and its submission to the Council. Similarly, no reference was made to the rights and duties of states under the Covenant.[92] This silence was maintained, mutatis mutandi, in the Revised Act of 1949. The draftsmen of the General Act of 1928 had probably come to the conclusion that any stipulation on the subject might create the impression of legitimizing conflicting obligations. On the other hand, the silence may be interpreted as encouragement of the recourse to conciliation in the first instance, while maintaining the overriding obligations under the Covenant if the situation deteriorated.

The founders of the UN tried to resolve the problem in explicit terms.

[89]See UN *Survey*, p. 3.
[90]Between the USA and S. Africa, Australia, Canada, and New Zealand, respectively.
[91]See UN *Survey*, p. 130.
[92]The clause in the 'General Provisions' that disputes for the settlement of which a special procedure is laid down in other conventions in force between the parties shall be settled in conformity with those conventions (Art. 29), does not seem to refer to the Covenant. The provisions immediately following show that the reference is to other, special treaties for the pacific settlement of international disputes.

Article 33, paragraph 1, of the Charter lays down that the parties to any dispute the continuance of which is likely to endanger the maintenance of international peace and security shall, first of all, seek a solution by negotiation, inquiry, mediation, conciliation, arbitration, judicial settlement, resort to regional agencies or arrangements, or other peaceful means of their own choice. By Article 37, paragraph 1, should the parties to a dispute of the nature referred to in Article 33 fail to settle it by the means indicated in that article, they shall refer it to the Security Council.

The interpretation of these articles (above, p. 134) follows closely the prevailing opinion of the members of the League on the same issue. For the purposes of our discussion, this means that the recourse to the method of bilateral inquiry is limited not only by the alternative choice of other bilateral methods, but also by the primary responsibility of the League and the UN for the maintenance of peace. The restrictive impact of the UN in this respect will be the subject of our attention in Chapter 8.

CHAPTER 6

Disputes Handled by Commissions of Inquiry

INTRODUCTORY NOTE

The present chapter and Chapter 7 deal with the practical application
of the system established by the Hague Convention of 1907 on the one
hand, and that established by numerous treaties of conciliation on the
other. In this chapter we shall analyse four cases which have been
brought before commissions of inquiry by virtue, either explicitly or
implicitly, of the provisions of Part III of the Convention of 1907.[1] It
will be recalled that the only application of the Convention of 1899—
with regard to the Dogger Bank incident—had raised doubts as to the
viability of the regime of genuine inquiry. Nevertheless, the delegates to
the Second Peace Conference expressed their faith in the 1899 institution
by reaffirming and elaborating its structure. Subsequent theoretical
developments cast their shadow on the 1907 version of genuine inquiry.
We shall now attempt to evaluate to what extent the Hague institution
has been preserved in practice. It will be of special interest to ascertain
whether states which found it useful to resort to the services of inquiry
commissions accepted the powers of the commissions as envisaged in the
Convention of 1907, or introduced changes to suit their particular aims
in the circumstances. Another problem to which attention will necessarily be paid is whether states sought to achieve, by means of commissions of inquiry, a final settlement of their dispute, or saw in the
process of inquiry a transition between negotiation and judicial or
arbitral settlement. In this connection it is pertinent to ascertain to what
extent a finding on fact implied an unequivocal answer to the legal
questions underlying the various disputes.

As in Chapter 3, it is proposed to examine here the nature of the
disputes submitted to inquiry commissions. We shall thereby be able to
estimate whether the 1907 reservation relating to honour or essential
interests was regarded as a *conditio sine qua non* of the method of inquiry.
Finally, the organization and procedure of the commissions will be

---

[1]Attention may be drawn to two additional cases handled by international commissions of inquiry: (1) a dispute between Germany and the Netherlands (1917) concerning the German submarines UB30 and UB6 which were stranded in Netherlands territorial
waters and their crews interned (Hackworth, vii (1943), p. 462); and (2) a dispute between
Germany and Denmark (1918) concerning the Spanish steamer *Igotz Mendi* which was
taken prize by a German cruiser, was subsequently stranded in Danish territorial waters
and the prize crew interned (ibid., pp. 582–3).

examined, with a view to determining whether there was a tendency to use a unified or similar pattern throughout.

THE 'TAVIGNANO' CASE: FRANCE–ITALY, 1912

Like the Dogger Bank case, the *Tavignano* case[2] arose out of incidents involving vessels of a belligerent and of a neutral power. On 25 January 1912, during the Turco-Italian war, the Italian torpedo-boat *Fulmine* seized the French mail steamer *Tavignano* off the coast of Tunis—then a French protectorate—and conducted it to Tripoli under suspicion of carrying contraband of war. Since no contraband was found, the vessel was released.

On the same day and in the same waters, the Italian torpedo-boat *Canopo* fired on the Tunisian mahones (flat-bottomed sailing vessels formerly used by the Turks) *Camouna* and *Gaulois* which were suspected of co-operating with the *Tavignano* in the carriage of contraband. No significant damage was done to the mahones.

The French government maintained that the *Tavignano*, *Camouna*, and *Gaulois* were in Tunisian territorial waters when challenged by the Italian warships, and that, consequently, Italy had violated international law and was liable to pay damages. The Italian government claimed, on the other hand, that the three suspected vessels were at the time of the incidents on the high seas, and that no rule of international law was therefore violated.

The political circumstances surrounding the incidents were not of a nature to provoke extreme attitudes, as happened in the Dogger Bank case. Indeed, in the European balance of power France and Italy were formally in opposing camps. France belonged to the Triple Entente with England and Russia, while Italy was united with Germany and Austria-Hungary in the Triple Alliance. However, Italy was an uncertain ally, regarded with some suspicion by her two partners. In 1882, when the Triple Alliance was signed, Italy had declared that the treaty was in no case to be directed against England; and in June 1902 Italy announced—in return for a secret French undertaking of 1900 to give her a free hand in Tripoli—that the Triple Alliance was not directed against France. In November 1902 France and Italy entered into a

[2]See Commission internationale d'enquête constituée à Malte en vertu de la convention d'enquête signée à Rome entre la France et l'Italie le 20 mai 1912, *Incidents du vapeur français 'Tavignano' et des mahonnes 'Camouna' et 'Gaulois' arrêtés et visités par les contre-torpilleurs 'Fulmine' et 'Canopo' de la marine royale italienne, documents et procès-verbaux* (n.d.) (hereinafter referred to as *Procès-verbaux*).

For the original French text of the commission's report see ibid., p. 177, and Scott, *Hague Court reports* (1916), p. 616. For an English translation see ibid., p. 413; 16 *AJIL* (1922), pt II, Official Documents, p. 485.

The French text of the agreement for inquiry is published in *Procès-verbaux*, p. 7, and in Scott, *Hague Court reports* (1916), pp. 6, 7. The English translation appears at p. 417.

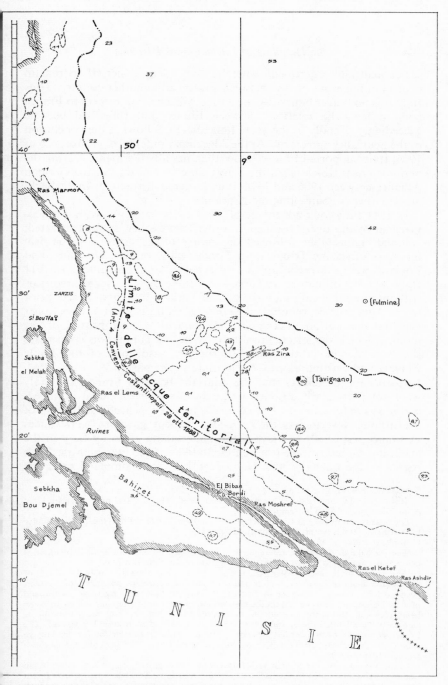

Italian version of the *Tavignano incident*

⊙ Point at which the *Fulmine* saw the steamship *Tavignano*
• Point at which the *Tavignano* was anchored

(Reproduced from the *Procès-verbaux* of the commission.)

secret neutrality agreement whereby Italy pledged herself to remain neutral in the event of war between France and another country. Thus Italy was no longer bound by the Triple Alliance with respect to France and, in fact, the relations between France and Italy had become exceedingly friendly in the years immediately following the conclusion of the neutrality agreement. At the Algeciras Conference on Morocco of 1906, Italy supported France rather than her ally Germany. During the periodic crises which faced the Triple Entente and the Austro-German Alliance between 1906 and 1914, Italy fluttered distractedly in the background always counselling moderation.[3]

In 1911 Italy took advantage of the Agadir crisis, involving Franco-German rivalry over Morocco, in order to press her, so far frustrated, colonial claims.[4] She followed the course of the crisis with the firm intention of seizing Tripoli from Turkey while France, Germany, and England were too preoccupied to prevent her. On 26 September 1911 Italy sent an ultimatum to Turkey and three days later declared war, without any provocation on the part of Turkey. Italy had indeed, prior to the Agadir crisis, obtained the consent of all the great powers to her eventual occupation of Tripoli, but none of them approved of the moment which she selected to do so.[5] As far as Turkey was concerned, she had become at that time thoroughly suspicious of the Triple Entente and was more pro-German than in the past.

It appears, therefore, that the relations between France and Italy were not particularly strained when the *Tavignano* incident occurred, and it was natural for the two countries to seek a peaceful settlement of the dispute. Nevertheless, the *Tavignano* incident[6] gave rise to grievances in France, especially in view of the undertaking given by Italy in the arbitral *compromis* signed by representatives of the two countries with regard to the *Carthage* and *Manouba* cases,[7] to recommend prudence

[3]See Grant & Temperley, pp. 335, 336, 341, & 347.
[4]Italy's colonial ambitions with regard to Tunis had been checked by France in 1881. Abyssinia repulsed Italy's assault in 1896.
The resentment of Italy at the French seizure of Tunis drove her into the Triple Alliance with Austria-Hungary and Germany (ibid., p. 317).
[5]Ibid., p. 372.
[6]For the sake of simplicity, reference will occasionally be made to a single incident, it being understood that it also comprises the action against the two mahones.
[7]The first of these cases involved the seizure by an Italian warship, on 16 Jan. 1912, of the French steamer *Carthage*, which had on board an aeroplane and parts of another, destined for a private consignee in Tunis. Italy claimed that this cargo was contraband of war. The seizure was effected on the high seas in the course of a regular voyage between Marseilles and Tunis; the *Carthage* was conveyed to Cagliari in Sardinia; the aeroplane and parts were landed there, and the *Carthage* was allowed to resume her voyage. The French government was awarded the sum of 160,000 francs in satisfaction for the damage suffered by the private parties concerned. See award of 6 May 1913 in Scott, *Hague Court reports* (1916), p. 330.
In the second case, the French vessel *Manouba* was captured, on 18 Jan. 1912, by an Italian warship and taken to Cagliari on suspicion that some Turkish passengers on board belonged to the Ottoman army. As in the first incident, the capture took place on the high seas, during a regular voyage between Marseilles and Tunis. The tribunal awarded the

and moderation to her navy. The French government, which had just announced in the Chamber of Deputies the successful conclusion of the *compromis*, was anxious to settle the new controversy immediately.[8]

Shortly after the incident, on 27 January 1912, the Italian government advised the French ambassador in Rome that the *Tavignano* had long been suspected of carrying contraband, that she had been arrested on the high seas, that she had refused to be visited, and that she had been conducted to Tripoli in order that visit could be made. In reply, the French Ministry for Foreign Affairs instructed the French ambassador in Rome immediately to express strong reservations with regard to the Italian allegations concerning the place of arrest and the presumption of contraband. The ambassador was to add that Tripoli was not 'recognized by Europe as an Italian port', and that it had no prize court.[9] Three days later the ambassador was requested to reiterate his reservations in view of the report of the captain of the *Tavignano*, which stated that the arrest of the vessel had taken place in territorial waters.

On 3 February 1912 the French Ministry for Foreign Affairs instructed the embassy in Rome to propose the submission to an international commission of inquiry of the questions of fact regarding the seizure of the *Tavignano* and the cannon shots fired at the two mahones. If the commission should recognize that these events took place in Tunisian territorial waters, the Italian government was to express its regrets. The Italian government did not accept the proposal. It suggested instead that the questions of fact should first be clarified by means of negotiation, and that recourse be had afterwards to arbitration. As a first step, it proposed transmitting a report drawn up by the Italian minister of the navy, with a map.

The legal adviser to the French Ministry for Foreign Affairs, Louis Renault, expressed disappointment at the Italian attitude. In a note dated 5 February, he asserted that the matter in dispute could be regarded as a most suitable subject for investigation by an international commission of inquiry. It concerned the ascertainment of a point of fact, which could be better done by sailors on the spot than by arbitrators acting on the basis of memorials submitted by the parties. He added that the procedure could be very quick, and that the circumstances would be better clarified if the scene of the encounter were reconstructed promptly, while the memories of the witnesses were still fresh. In his view, inspection of the place would be more instructive than examining maps.[10]

French government the sum of 4,000 francs for losses and damage sustained by the private parties concerned. See award of 6 May 1913: ibid., p. 342.

[8] See Gros, 'Observations sur une enquête internationale: L'affaire du "Tavignano" ', in *Mélanges offerts a Juraj Andrassy* (1968), p. 99.

[9] Ibid., p. 100.

[10] Ibid., p. 101.

Following further exchanges of views, in which it became apparent that each government adhered to its own version regarding the place of the incident, the Italian minister for foreign affairs and the French ambassador signed, on 15 April 1912, a preliminary agreement[11] for the submission of the case to an international commission of inquiry. By the agreement the commission was to deal with 'the questions of fact' raised by the seizure of the *Tavignano* and by the cannon shots fired by the torpedo-boat *Canopo* upon the two mahones. After the commission had concluded its investigation the result was to be transmitted, if it were deemed necessary, to the arbitral tribunal charged with the settling of the *Carthage* and *Manouba* affairs, for it to decide the questions of law, fix responsibility, and determine the moral and material reparation which was due.[12]

The agreement for inquiry was signed on 20 May 1912. It read as follows:[13]

The Government of the French Republic and the Royal Italian Government, equally desirous of settling the dispute caused by the capture and temporary detention of the French mail steamer *Tavignano*, on January 25, 1912, by the Royal Italian naval vessel *Fulmine*, as well as the firing upon the mahones *Camouna* and *Gaulois*, on January 25, 1912, by the Italian torpedo boat *Canopo*;

Have resolved, conformably to Part III of the Hague Convention of October 18, 1907, for the pacific settlement of international disputes, to confide to an international commission of inquiry the task of clearing up the actual circumstances under which the said capture and detention, and the said firing took place;

And have, to this end, agreed upon the following provisions:

Article 1

An international commission of inquiry, composed as hereinafter stipulated, is entrusted:

I. To investigate, mark and determine the exact geographic point where occurred: (1) the capture of the French mail steamer *Tavignano* by the Royal Italian naval vessel *Fulmine*, on January 25, 1912; (2) the pursuit of the mahones *Camouna* and *Gaulois* by the same vessel and also by the Royal Italian naval vessel *Canopo*, and the firing by the latter upon the said mahones;

II. To determine exactly the hydrography, configuration and nature of the coast and of the neighbouring banks, the distance between any points which one or the other of the commissioners might deem useful to mark, and the distance from these points to those where the above-mentioned deeds occurred.

III. To make a written report of the result of its investigation.

---

[11]See text in Scott, *Hague Court reports* (1916), p. 419.

[12]It was agreed during the preceding diplomatic negotiations that the tribunal would be charge d with determining at the same time questions of law, such as the point of departure of the three-mile limit and the delimitation of bays at the place of the incident, as well as the eventual reparation to be made (see Gros, *Mélanges . . .*, p. 102).

[13]See reference at p. 142, n. 2, above.

Article 2

The international commission of inquiry shall be composed of three commissioners, of which two shall be national naval officers of France and Italy, of a rank at least equal to that of captain. The Government of His Britannic Majesty shall be asked to choose the third commissioner from among his naval officers, of a higher or the highest rank. The latter shall assume the office of president.

Two secretaries shall be appointed, one by the Government of the French Republic and the other by the Royal Italian Government, as registrars of the commission, and they shall assist it in its operations.

Article 3

The international commission of inquiry shall be qualified to secure all information, interrogate and hear all witnesses, to examine all papers on board either of the said ships, vessels and mahones, to proceed, if necessary, with sounding, and, in general, to resort to all sources of information calculated to bring out the truth.

The two Governments agree in this respect to furnish the commission with all possible means and facilities, particularly those of transportation, to enable it to accomplish its task.

Article 4

The international commission of inquiry shall meet at Malta as soon as possible and shall have the power to change its place of meeting conformably to Article 20 of the Hague Convention of October 18, 1907, for the pacific settlement of international disputes.

Article 5

The French language shall be used by the international commission of inquiry; however, in their deliberations the commissioners may use their respective languages.

Article 6

Within a period not to exceed fifteen days from the date of its first meeting the international commission of inquiry shall arrive at the conclusions of its report and shall communicate them to each of the two Governments.

Article 7

Each party shall pay its own expenses and an equal share of the expenses of the commission.

Article 8

All points not covered by the present convention of inquiry, especially those relating to the procedure of inquiry, shall be regulated by the provisions of the Hague Convention of October 18, 1907, for the pacific settlement of international disputes.

The commission of inquiry which was established in pursuance of the above agreement was composed of Captain Th. Somborn (French commissioner), Captain G. Genoese Zerbi (Italian commissioner), and Captain J. R. Segrave, of the British Royal Navy (president). The two French and Italian secretaries were also naval officers.[14] The commission met between 1 and 23 July 1912:[15] the first fourteen meetings took place at Malta, the next on the way to Zarzis (Tunis), the following three at Zarzis, the next on the way back to Malta, and the last two at Malta.

During the first meeting the French and Italian commissioners exchanged lists of witnesses whom they wished to be heard. The commission decided to hear all Italian witnesses at Malta, and the French witnesses partly at Malta and partly at Zarzis. The dates of the hearings were fixed, and it was agreed that the French and Italian commissioners should take the necessary steps to ensure the appearance of the witnesses on their respective sides. In order to comply with the provisions of Article 1 of the inquiry agreement, the commission considered it necessary to conduct an inquiry in the waters of Zarzis and decided to hire a yacht for that purpose.

At its second meeting the commission proceeded to an examination of the documents submitted by the French and Italian commissioners. During the third meeting the Italian commissioner asked for the report on the incident from the *Gaulois*, and also requested that her owner be added to the list of witnesses. The French commissioner expressed no objection, and it was so agreed. At the same meeting the French commissioner submitted a file of an inquiry conducted by the Tunisian authorities with a view to examining the allegations of the commander of the *Fulmine*, as stated in his report of the incident, that the *Tavignano* was carrying, if not contraband of war, at least ordinary contraband. The Italian commissioner, considering that the file did not bear directly on the facts subject to the inquiry, requested that the file should be withdrawn, and the French commissioner agreed.

The fourth to nineteenth meetings were devoted mainly to the examination of witnesses. At the twentieth meeting the president asked the other two commissioners whether they wished to submit more documents or to have more witnesses heard. Having received negative answers, he declared the inquiry closed and the commission adjourned to deliberate and to draft its report. The two secretaries were not present during the deliberations, and did not participate in the drafting of the report. At its twenty-first meeting, held on 23 July 1912, the commissioners adopted and signed their report.

While in the waters of Zarzis the commission observed the scene of the incident, paying particular attention to the configuration of the banks, the depth of the waters, and the visibility of the beacon of Ras-Zira, which was a crucial point of reference in the course of the inquiry.

[14]In the course of its work the commission decided to appoint an Englishman to keep the official file, and an Italian (nominated by the French commissioner) to act as typist-interpreter.

[15]For the minutes, see *Procès-verbaux*.

As the parties did not employ agents, counsel, or advocates, there were no oral statements of facts, summaries, or conclusions. The written evidence submitted by the French and Italian commissioners was supplemented by the examination of witnesses, which was conducted in a spirit of fullest co-operation. The conflicting arguments of the parties emerged mainly from the reports of the captain of the *Tavignano* and the owners of the mahones on the one hand, and the captains of the *Fulmine* and the *Canopo* on the other hand. In addition to these reports, the commission examined, i.a., the log-books and engine journals of the *Fulmine*, the *Canopo*, and the *Tavignano*, as well as several documents concerning the hour of departure of the *Tavignano* from Zarzis.

On the basis of the written evidence, the commissioners conducted an examination of witnesses likely to throw more light on the relevant facts. Among those examined were the commanders of the *Fulmine*, the *Canopo*, and the *Tavignano*, the seconds-in-command and helmsmen of the *Fulmine* and the *Tavignano*, the *Fulmine*'s chief signalman and her signalman in charge of sounding, the boatswain's mate in charge of inspecting the depth of the water in front of her, the gunner in charge of her telemeter, the chief and second mechanics and the boatswain of the *Tavignano*, the owners of the *Camouna* and the *Gaulois*, and a gunner from the *Canopo*. Technical information on the probable mistake in observation of 6,900 metres on the telemeter was given by a British officer. Several persons working in Zarzis testified to the hour of departure of the *Tavignano*.

During the examination, the captain of the *Fulmine* and his second-in-command were asked to explain why they did not determine, together with the captain of the *Tavignano*, the exact point at which the encounter took place. The president of the commission asked the *Fulmine*'s second-in-command whether he himself could have fixed the position of the *Tavignano* when he was on board the vessel. The officer replied that since he went on board amicably, he did not think this was necessary. The president then asked whether he had suggested to the officers of the *Tavignano* that they should fix their position more exactly. The answer was 'no'. The French commissioner pressed further by asking why, at the time of the departure of the *Fulmine* to chase the mahones, he did not request the *Tavignano* to anchor in order to determine the position of the vessel. The second-in-command replied that he was unable to do that because his commander had signalled him to follow.[16] On the same problem, the French commissioner asked the commander of the *Fulmine* whether he knew that the commander of the *Tavignano* claimed to be in Tunisian territorial waters at the time of the visit. Having received a positive answer, he inquired why the commander of the *Fulmine* did not himself determine, in the presence of the commander of the *Tavignano*, the point where the visit took place.

[16]Ibid., pp. 163–4.

The commander answered that he did not know of the difficulties raised by the *Tavignano* until he returned from the pursuit of the mahones.

Another central issue during the examination was the depth of water at the spot where the visit took place. The captain of the *Tavignano* reported, as proof of his being in territorial waters, that the sounding, made in the presence of an Italian officer, showed 5·50 metres. The report of the commander of the *Fulmine* was silent on this question. The president of the commission asked the *Fulmine*'s second-in-command whether the question of sounding was raised on board the *Tavignano*. The witness answered that, after having steamed ahead to follow the *Fulmine*, the commander of the *Tavignano* requested a sounding; the report of the sounding was brought to the bridge and he remembered that somebody said 'quinze mètres', and that the second-in-command of the *Tavignano*, he thought, said 'quindici metri'.[17]

During the examination of the commander of the *Tavignano*, the French commissioner asked whether he had shown the sounding-machine to the Italian officer. The commander said that he had given the order to the boatswain: 'Sound!' The boatswain shouted very loudly 'five metres, five metres fifty'. The second-in-command of the *Tavignano* was on the bridge and the commander told him to go and check the sounding-machine; he found the same depth. The Italian commissioner then asked whether the sounding was made in the presence of the Italian officer. The commander answered that the Italian officer was next to him on the bridge, which was very low and from which everything that was taking place on the deck could be seen. In the same connection, the witness quoted the Italian officer as saying: 'I shall report to the commander and I think he will let you continue on your way.'[18]

Other questions addressed to various witnesses related, i.a., to speeds, visibility, distances, directions of voyage, state of the sea, force of the wind, colour of the water, and nature of the seabed. Occasionally, certain omissions or inconsistencies in the records were revealed. Thus the French commissioner asked the *Fulmine*'s chief signalman whether it did not seem to him to be the duty, as well as the habit, of a chief signalman to note the hour at which he sees, all at the same time, one ship, two mahones, and one beacon. The answer was that, needing to warn the commander, to call the men to their positions of manoeuvre, and being busy with the observation, he did not have the time to do so, especially as the commander arrived immediately.[19]

The Italian commissioner pointed out to the *Tavignano*'s commander that in her engine journal the speed of the engine was noted as 100 turns. Why then, he asked, did the log-book indicate the speed of the vessel

---

[17]Ibid., p. 77. An Italian corporal testified that the second-in-command of the *Tavignano* made the sounding, and came to report in French to his captain; afterwards he came to talk to the corporal in Italian; the corporal asked him what depth he had measured and he answered 'quindici metri'.

[18]Ibid., p. 116.   [19]Ibid., p. 94.

as eight knots? The commander answered that this was a mistake and that the speed was nine knots.[20]

In its report of 23 July 1912,[21] adopted unanimously, the commission stated that the evidence presented was not of a nature to permit the determination of the exact geographical points where the various acts submitted to inquiry had occurred. It was possible only to determine the zones in which these acts took place. Regarding the point where the *Tavignano* stopped, the commission found that it was within the area of a rectilinear quadrilateral set off by four apexes, specified in latitudes and longitudes. While the commission did not make any reference to territorial waters in the whole report—it was not requested to do so in the terms of reference—in fact part of the zone lay in territorial waters and part on the high seas.[22] The crucial question thus remained undecided.

With regard to the pursuit of the mahones, the commission determined in latitudes and longitudes three points, which were the centres of inexact circles of half-mile radii. According to the report, the pursued mahones *Camouna* and *Gaulois* were located at the first two points, respectively, and the *Gaulois* was at the second point, when fired on by the *Canopo*. The third point shows the position of the *Canopo*, as indicated in her log-book, when it fired on the *Gaulois*. The commission further determined, in degrees of latitude and longitude, two points at which the visit of the two mahones by the *Canopo* had taken place.[23] It follows from these findings that the incident involving the mahones took place in Tunisian territorial waters.[24]

The report lacks clarity in certain respects. Although the commission stated at the beginning that it was impossible to determine the exact geographical points where the various acts occurred, it definitely ascertained two geographical points indicating the location of the pursued mahones. and two geographical points at which the visit of the mahones took place. With regard to the location of the mahones, it is not clear at what stage of the pursuit they were at the respective points, except that the *Gaulois* was at one of the points indicated when it was fired on by the *Canopo*. Finally, the commission did not clarify the meaning of the three circles relating to the pursuit of the mahones. No map was attached to the report; the only map accompanying the *procès-verbaux* was one depicting the Italian version of the incident.[25]

Following the report, the French government held that the Italian government must express its regrets with regard to the *Tavignano*, and

[20]Ibid., p. 109.
[21]See Scott, *Hague Court reports* (1916), p. 413.
[22]See Gros, *Mélanges . . .*, p. 104.
[23]The passage in the report which contains this last finding does not appear in the English version.
[24]See Gros, *Mélanges . . . .*, p. 104.
[25]See reproduction of the map on p. 143, above.

must pay a small reparation for the mahones which, 'although un-
damaged', had undergone severe stress. Failing that, France would have
recourse to the arbitral tribunal charged with the *Carthage* and *Manouba*
cases.[26] Since the Italian government refused to satisfy the French
demands, on 8 November 1912 the two governments signed a *compromis*
of arbitration[27] authorizing the above-mentioned tribunal, on the basis
of the inquiry agreement of 15 April 1912 (above, p. 146) 'to pronounce
upon the incidents concerning the seizure of the French steamer
Tavignano and the cannon shots fired upon the Tunisian mahones, as
well as to decide the question of law, fix the responsibility and determine the moral and material reparation which is due' (Art. 1). In all
that concerns the questions of fact raised by the two incidents, the
tribunal was to make use of the report of the commission of inquiry,
as well as its *procès-verbaux* (Art. 2). The parties undertook to deposit
with the Bureau of the Permanent Court of Arbitration by 25 January
1913 their respective memorials and documents. On 1 March 1913 each
party was to deposit its counter-memorial with the papers appertaining
thereto, and its final conclusions (Art. 3).

When the arbitral tribunal finished, in effect, dealing with the
Carthage and *Manouba* cases (above, p. 144, n. 7 & below, p. 154,
n. 32) and was about to take up the *Tavignano* dispute, the two governments settled the latter out of court. In an agreement signed on 2 May
1913,[28] they declared that as the two affairs of the *Carthage* and the
Manouba were about to be settled by an arbitral award, a direct settlement of the affair concerning the *Tavignano* and the two mahones was
particularly desirable. To this end they agreed that 'it will be equitable
to indemnify the individuals for the losses sustained by them'. Since the
Italian government declared itself willing to pay the sum of 5,000 francs
for this purpose, the French government declared that it would accept
this sum 'and consider this affair thus definitely settled'.

The agreement implies that, by the payment of indemnities, the
Italian government accepted responsibility for the incidents involving
the *Tavignano* and the mahones. Nevertheless, the government was not
prepared to express its regrets. It would seem that the French government renounced its request for an apology in order not to compromise
'the spirit of cordial friendship' which animated the two governments.[29]

Conclusions. The above case illustrates perfectly the employment of the
method of genuine inquiry, i.e. fact-finding, 'conformably'[30] to the
Hague Convention of 1907. Unlike the Dogger Bank Commission,

---

[26]Gros, *Mélanges* . . ., p. 104.
[27]See text in Scott, *Hague Court reports* (1916), p. 419.
[28]See text, ibid., p. 421.
[29]See Gros, *Mélanges* . . ., pp. 104 f.
[30]See Preamble of the inquiry agreement at p. 146 above.

which was charged with the additional task of establishing responsibility and guilt, and unlike the commissions provided for in numerous treaties, which are empowered to examine all aspects of the dispute, the task of the *Tavignano* Commission was confined to the simple ascertainment of the exact location of particular incidents. The authorization of the commission to proceed to the vicinity of the incidents, and its actual visit to the waters, fully demonstrated its fact-finding function.

The agreement of 15 April 1912 which preceded the inquiry agreement of 20 May distinguished clearly between the task of the inquiry commission to deal with 'the questions of fact' and the task of the arbitral tribunal to decide on questions of law, to fix responsibility, and to determine the moral and material reparation due.

The case under consideration is also an outstanding example of fact-finding with clear legal implications. Although the function of the commission was not judicial, the very ascertainment of the facts indicated prima facie whether there was a violation of international law. Conscious of its narrow terms of reference, the commission did not enter into the question whether the incidents took place within or outside Tunisian territorial waters. However, the approximate determination of the geographical locations of the incidents provided, to a certain extent, an answer to the questions of law. It is possible, of course, that complicated legal problems relating to the exact extent of the territorial waters could have been dealt with by an arbitral tribunal. But, in principle, the juridical significance of the findings of fact is indisputable, especially in view of the provision in the arbitral *compromis* of 8 November 1912 that

in all that concerns questions of fact raised by the two incidents, the arbitral tribunal must make use of the report presented by the international commission of inquiry of July 13, 1912, as well as the *procès-verbaux* of the said commission (Art. 2).

To 'make use of the report' does not mean that the tribunal was bound to accept the findings of fact contained in the report. It is unlikely, however, that in the circumstances the tribunal would have disregarded the findings of the inquiry commission and would have conducted an inquiry of its own. The intention of the parties, as shown in the agreement of 15 April 1912, was that there should be a division of labour between the two organs. And the views expressed during the Hague Conferences tend to support the premise that the arbitration tribunal was not going to perform a fact-finding function in a dispute already dealt with by an inquiry commission.[31]

The above observations are connected with the question, raised during our examination of the Hague discussions and various treaty provisions, whether inquiry is to be regarded as an independent method or as a

[31]See e.g., above, p. 27.

part of the arbitration process. The present case suggests that inquiry can be used independently in two senses: as an exclusive method for the settlement of a dispute, and as a preliminary (also independent) stage of a settlement, to be followed by the stage of arbitration.

The agreement of 15 April 1912 provided that the result of the inquiry should be submitted to the arbitral tribunal only 'if it is deemed necessary'. This suggests that in the view of the parties the commission of inquiry was likely to provide the basis for a settlement. It was conceivable that there would be no need to solve legal questions, such as the exact location of the limits of Tunisian territorial waters. And the amount of possible reparations could perhaps be agreed upon by means of diplomatic negotiations (above, p. 70).[32] As it turned out, after having referred the case to the tribunal the parties decided to settle out of court.

As regards the nature of the dispute, the present case is amply covered by the Hague Convention of 1907, not only because the dispute arose from a difference of opinion on points of fact, but because it involved neither the honour nor the essential interests of the parties (Art. 9 of the convention). However, this observation must be qualified so far as honour is concerned. It is difficult to imagine an international dispute in which the honour of the parties, or at least of one of the parties, is not involved to a certain degree. The intention of the Hague draftsmen was, it is believed, that disputes are not suitable for an international inquiry only if a *serious* attack on the honour of one or both parties has occurred, just as an attack on 'vital' or 'essential' interests only can prevent the submission of the dispute to a commission of inquiry. In the *Tavignano* case the French government asked for apologies and the Italian government refused to comply with the request. Obviously, the issue was one of prestige and honour, but it was not so grave as to impute to the dispute a character which would prevent, in principle,[33] its submission to inquiry.

The organization and procedure of the *Tavignano* Commission was, similarly, in conformity with the Hague Convention of 1907. The parties took advantage of the latitude of the relevant provisions of that convention to make the arrangements most suitable, in their view, to the particular case.

[32]Mr Justice Gros relates that the arbitral tribunal in the *Carthage* case found it impossible to agree on the amount of reparations. The French agent asked for 200,000 francs while the Italian agent was prepared to agree to no more than 125,000 francs. It would have been an enormous task for the tribunal to open the individual files of claims in order to fix the amount. It was then decided that the two national arbitrators, Renault and Fusinato, would consult their respective Ministries for Foreign Affairs, in the utmost secrecy, with a view to reaching a compromise. As a result, the French government accepted, on 25 Apr. 1913, the sum of 160,000 francs proposed jointly by the two arbitrators (see Gros, *Mélanges* . . ., p. 104 n. 1, and above p. 146 n. 12).

[33]It is generally held that the parties can submit to inquiry disputes involving honour or essential interests if they so wish (cf. above, pp. 71 & 93).

The choice of a commission of three members instead of five would suggest that the parties regarded the case as relatively simple and therefore capable of being dealt with by a small commission, under the direction of a tactful president. As it happened the president did not seem to need the assistance of other, neutral, commissioners. The French and Italian commissioners, in the words of the president, worked in 'parfaite courtoisie' and with 'grand esprit de conciliation'.[34]

Regarding the qualifications of the commissioners, it seemed natural to choose naval officers to perform a narrowly technical task suited to their knowledge and experience. Even the two secretaries were naval officers, required at times to make certain technical calculations. There was no need for legal assessors as no legal points were at issue.

The parties chose not to appoint agents, probably guided by the same considerations which governed the size of the commission. The absence of agents was, as pointed out by Gros, a drawback, since the national commissioners played the role of agents in the examination of witnesses. The impartiality of a commission is better ensured, states Gros, if the examination of witnesses is conducted by the agents, with the commissioners, except for the president, intervening only in a supplementary way. (We have noticed an obvious bias in the formulation of some of the questions posed by national commissioners (above, pp. 149–51).) The agents maintain in the course of the proceedings the arguments of their government, rectifying from time to time the effect of evidence by recalling written statements or previous oral evidence, or by pointing out contradictions on the basis of documents produced. They ensure that all possible information is collected and that all obscure points are clarified before the deliberations of the commission. They present at the end of the oral debate a summary of the facts, which also facilitates the deliberations of the commissioners.[35]

The inquiry agreement did not lay down any rules concerning the presentation of written and oral evidence, except with regard to the general power of the commission to secure all information, interrogate witnesses, and examine papers on board ship. According to Article 8, all points not covered by the agreement, especially those relating to the procedure of inquiry, were to be regulated by the provisions of the Hague Convention of 1907. That convention contains only general rules on procedure, and recommends that the commission of inquiry itself shall supplement these rules and the rules formulated in the special inquiry convention (above, pp. 100 ff. & below, App. I, p. 330).

Although the *Tavignano* Commission did not find it necessary to draft rules of procedure, as did the Dogger Bank Commission, its work does not suggest any rigidity of form. No statement of facts, no memorials or counter-memorials, and no conclusions were presented. The commission relied heavily on a variety of documents presented to it at the

[34]See *Procès-verbaux*, p. 181.   [35]See Gros, *Mélanges . . .*, p. 105.

beginning of its work, and the examination of witnesses was confined to clarifying certain moot points. In the face of obviously conflicting oral evidence, as in the case of the sounding of 5·50 or 15 metres, no attempt was made to put pressure on the witnesses.

The consecutive presentation of questions by the president and the national commissioners was preserved throughout, and there was no inclination on the part of any commissioner to correct the evidence obtained by his colleagues.

Generally, the first implementation of the inquiry method after 1907 must be regarded as successful. The *Tavignano* Commission contributed, within a relatively short period, to the settlement of a controversy which disturbed the relations between France and Italy. It appears that the method of inquiry, in preference to arbitration, was chosen with a view to the 'immediate' settlement of the dispute (above, p. 145). The commission was requested to report within a period of fifteen days from its first meeting, and it accomplished its task almost on time.

The case of the *Tavignano* proved the value of the inquiry method employed independently as a basis for the amicable settlement of international disputes.

THE 'TIGER' CASE: GERMANY–SPAIN, 1918

This case concerns an incident which took place on 7 May 1917—during the First World War—off the northern coast of Spain. A German submarine pursued, arrested, and sank the Norwegian vessel *Tiger* on the grounds that she was carrying contraband of war destined for Germany's enemies. Both Spain and Norway were neutral in the war. Spain claimed that the incident took place in her territorial waters, while Germany denied the charge.

Diplomatic negotiations.[36] The evidence acquired by the Spanish government immediately after the incident[37] served as a basis for its diplomatic steps vis-à-vis the German government with a view to obtaining adequate satisfaction.

On 15 May 1917 the Spanish ambassador in Berlin, Polo de Bernabé, informed the German secretary of state for foreign affairs, Zimmermann, that on 7 May, shortly before noon, the Norwegian vessel *Tiger* was attacked by a German submarine at a distance of just over a mile from the Spanish coast opposite the roadstead of Baquio and approximately three miles from Cape Machichaco (see chart, p. 158). The submarine fired some six cannon shells and rifle shots, and four shells hit the vessel. The crew of the *Tiger* took refuge in a lifeboat. Five sailors from

---

[36]The following account is based on copies of the diplomatic correspondence included in Annexes IV & X of the commission's procès-verbaux (see Bibliography, p. 349). I am grateful to the Director-Librarian, Drs J. B. van Hall, and to the staff of the library of the Peace Palace at The Hague for their courtesy and assistance.

[37]The file of the Spanish inquiry is included, ibid., Annex III.

the submarine boarded the *Tiger*, placed bombs on her, set her engines in motion and, after having sailed beyond the three-mile limit, sank the vessel on the high seas.

These facts, wrote the ambassador, were proved not only by the depositions of the captain and the first officer of the *Tiger*, but also by the evidence of many Spanish fishermen who had seen the act of aggression and the arrest of the *Tiger* in Spanish sovereign waters, as well as her being conducted to the high seas in order to be sunk. 'This very grave violation of Spanish sovereign waters', which had vividly impressed public opinion, was in contrast with the assurances given by the German government that its naval forces were under orders scrupulously to respect Spanish sovereignty.

The Spanish ambassador protested most energetically and demanded the severe punishment of the commander and crew of the submarine 'guilty of aggression', whose victim was a neutral vessel sailing under Spanish protection. Furthermore, he demanded reparation for the damage caused, in conformity with Article 3 of Hague Convention No. XIII,[38] apologies for the abuse of Spanish sovereignty, as well as the most formal promise that acts contrary to the first and second articles of the above convention[39] would not be repeated in future. The Spanish government, warned the ambassador, was ready to use the most forceful means to ensure respect for its neutrality and its sovereignty.

On 26 May 1917 Zimmermann informed the Spanish ambassador that, according to the report of the commander of the submarine, the *Tiger* had been arrested and sunk outside Spanish territorial waters. When the submarine had met the *Tiger* and requested it to stop, the captain of the *Tiger* tried to reach territorial waters but was prevented from doing so by several shots fired from the submarine. The commander of the submarine had then fixed by bearings the position of the *Tiger*. These bearings had permitted him to determine with the utmost certainty that the *Tiger* was a distance of more than three sea-miles from the shore. The commander did not doubt the accuracy of the result obtained, especially as clear weather facilitated observation. The German government, Zimmermann went on, was ready to submit 'les divergences d'appréciation qui pourraient surgir sur les faits' to an impartial international examination.

On 7 June 1917 Zimmermann conveyed to the Spanish ambassador the findings of an inquiry ordered by the German naval authorities. It was established that the *Tiger* was arrested at a distance of 3·8 sea-miles from land and, in order to prevent the vessel from being carried closer to land by the current, the commander ordered the prize crew to conduct

---

[38]Convention concerning the Rights and Duties of Neutral Powers in Naval War (1907).
[39]These articles provide for the duty of belligerents to abstain from violating neutral territory for military or naval purposes of the war.

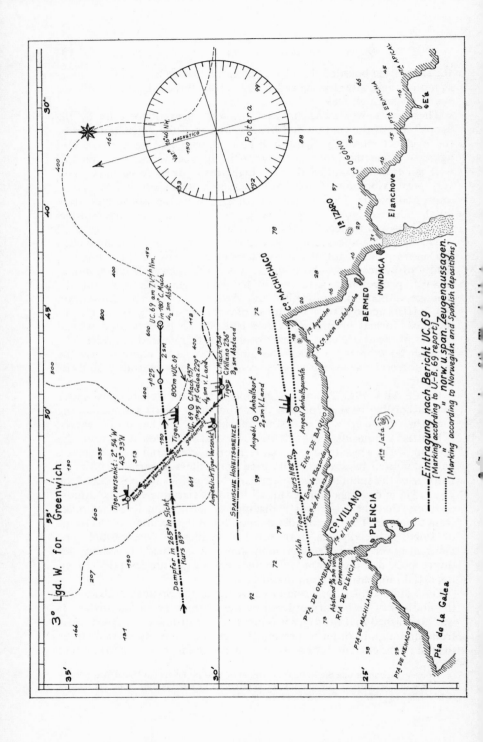

Eintragung nach Bericht UC.69.
[Marking according to U-B. 69 report.]
"   "   "   norw. u. span. Zeugenaussagen.
[Marking according to Norwegian and Spanish depositions.]

the vessel farther out to sea, where she was subsequently sunk at 43° 33″ north latitude and 2° 54″ west longitude.

In these circumstances, wrote Zimmermann, the German government believed that the Spanish government would not maintain its protest. If, on the other hand, the Spanish government still considered the information at its disposal to be accurate, the German government again declared itself ready to submit to impartial examination by an international commission the question of ascertaining whether the *Tiger* was pursued, arrested, and sunk within or outside the zone of three sea-miles from the Spanish coast. The German government undertook to recognize in advance the decision of such a commission as absolute and binding.

On 29 April 1918, following repeated assertions of the original positions of both governments, the Spanish ambassador informed the German Ministry for Foreign Affairs that the Spanish government thought the time suitable to apply the method proposed in the German notes of 26 May and 7 June 1917. Consequently, with a view to settling 'les différences d'appréciation' on the question of ascertaining whether the *Tiger* was or was not attacked and captured in Spanish territorial waters, the Spanish government proposed submitting the question to the examination and decision of an international commission, whose composition and functions would form the object of subsequent negotiations.

In a note dated 20 May 1918 the German Ministry for Foreign Affairs assured the Spanish embassy that the German government was still ready to submit the question to the impartial examination of an international commission. This examination was to be based on Article 9 of the Hague Convention for the Pacific Settlement of International Disputes of 1899. Consequently, the German government proposed that the commission be composed of two naval officers, one German and one Spanish, and a neutral naval officer as president, the latter to be nominated by the king of Denmark. It was desirable that the commission sit in Berlin, since the commander of the submarine was not able to travel to Spain. The German ministry suggested further that, in view of the usual useful practice in similar cases, each of the two governments should name a special agent who, following the instructions of his government, would formulate the allegations and the necessary requests. In all other respects, 'les négotiations de la commission' must take place in complete liberty and without being hampered by any formality. The German government, the note went on, named Captain Vanselow as the German member of the commission and asked the Spanish government to name the Spanish member. As for the president of the commission, the German and Spanish ministers in Denmark could jointly take steps to obtain his nomination.

The Spanish government wished to clarify two questions prior to appointing the Spanish member. The first question related to the legal basis of the inquiry, and the second to the seat of the commission. On 23 July 1918 the Spanish embassy conveyed to the German Ministry for Foreign Affairs the understanding of the Spanish government that, since the two governments accepted in advance the decision of the international commission as absolute and binding, they were prevented from subsequently invoking the application of Article 14 of the Hague Convention of 1899, i.e. the parties had waived the freedom of action affirmed in that article.[40] As to the seat of the commission, the Spanish government considered it more natural that the commission should meet in Copenhagen, since its president would most probably be a Danish officer.

On 9 August 1918 the German ministry replied that the German government was in complete agreement with the Spanish government on the binding effect of the commission's report. Consequently, if the commission ascertained that the *Tiger* was sunk outside Spanish territorial waters (this fact was not in dispute), the Spanish government must formally withdraw its protest relative to the sinking. If, however, the commission found that the sinking took place within Spanish territorial waters, the German government must give to the Spanish government all satisfaction due to it according to the law of nations, and must also accept the consequences as regards other interested parties.

Further, the German government proposed basing the arrangements for the holding of the inquiry not on the Hague Convention of 1899, but on that of 1907 (Arts 9–36). With regard to the seat of the commission, the German government, in a spirit of conciliation, agreed to the choice of Copenhagen, in spite of the difficulties which that would involve in the examination of the submarine's crew.

The apprehensions of the Spanish government being thus allayed, it named Commander Joaquin Montague y Miro as its member of the commission.[41] The German government named, on its part, Captain Horn as successor to the German member previously chosen, and also named the attorney Dr Scheurer as its agent.[42] This was followed by the designation of the special auditor of the Spanish navy, José Tapia, as the agent of the Spanish government,[43] and the designation, by the king of Denmark, of Rear-Admiral Thomas Vilhelm Garde as president of the commission.

The work of the commission. The international commission of inquiry held six meetings between 1 and 8 November 1919. During the first

[40]See text of Art. 14 at p. 33, above.
[41]See letter of 29 Aug. 1918 from the Spanish ambassador in Berlin to the German secretary of state for foreign affairs, von Hintze.
[42]See note of 8 Sept. 1918 from the German Ministry for Foreign Affairs to the Spanish embassy.
[43]See note of 1 Oct. 1918 from the Spanish embassy to the German Ministry for Foreign Affairs.

meeting the commissioners agreed on the appointment of two secretaries and two stenographers. The secretaries held, respectively, the positions of head of section at the Danish Ministry for Foreign Affairs and archivist of the Danish parliament.

At the same meeting the president stated that, following the agreement reached between the two governments, the task of the commission was to examine and decide the question of ascertaining whether the Norwegian vessel *Tiger* was pursued, arrested, and sunk by a German submarine within or outside the zone of three miles from the Spanish coast. This examination was to be based on Article 9 of the First Hague Convention of 1907. He expressed the opinion that the commission should apply the formal rules indicated in Part III of the convention except for Article 34, the parties having agreed that the report of the commission would not be read at a public meeting. There is no mention in the record of the meeting of any statement of the president that the parties had waived their freedom of action by accepting in advance the decision of the commission, i.e. that they had agreed not to apply Article 14 of the Convention of 1899 corresponding to Article 35 of the Convention of 1907.

The president stated further that, in accordance with a communication addressed to him by the two parties, the French language would be adopted for the work of the commission.[44] He proposed thereupon that the minutes of the meetings, as in previous analogous cases, should not be verbatim but summary. Nevertheless, the exposés of the agents, the special declarations and the depositions of the witnesses were to be recorded verbatim. The commission adopted this proposal.

Finally, the president proposed that one copy of the commission's protocol be given to the king of Denmark, and another copy be deposited at the International Bureau of the Permanent Court of Arbitration, in conformity with Article 16 of the Hague Convention. This proposal was likewise adopted.

Afterwards, the commission accepted a suggestion made by the German commissioner that the essential contents of the oral deliberations be subsequently translated into German. The commission also accepted a proposal of the German agent that, in order to avoid misunderstandings, the exposés of the agents should, so far as possible, be based on written projects which could be submitted, after having been read, to the commission and to the agent of the adverse party.

During the same first meeting, the two agents read their exposés and submitted pertinent documents, including nautical maps.[45]

[44]The German government delegated the counsellor of the German embassy in Copenhagen to assist the German agent in any difficulties he might have in the use of the French language.
[45]While the map submitted by the Spanish agent (Annex IV of the *Procès-verbaux*) did not indicate the positions of the *Tiger* and the submarine, the chart submitted by the German agent (Annex VIII) indicated the German version of the incident, and also the

The Spanish agent summed up the results of the inquiry conducted by the Spanish naval authorities and submitted to the commission the original file of the inquiry together with a French translation. He then recalled the protest of his government to the German government, and presented copies of the relevant notes.

A large part of the exposé of the German agent consisted in the quotation of a report written by the commander of the submarine on 28 October 1918 especially for the purposes of the international inquiry. This report, based on a deposition dated 25 May 1917 by the commander to the chief of staff of the German navy, gave essentially the same version of the incident as that transmitted by the German government to the Spanish government on 7 June 1917. One important correction was made, however: the position of the *Tiger* at the time of seizure was indicated as being 3·2, not 3·8, sea-miles from the Spanish coast. The commander also added, in his report of 28 October 1918, that the log-book of the submarine as well as the nautical map of the *Tiger* had been destroyed when the submarine was lost (see n. 46).

The German agent supplemented the information contained in the commander's report by quoting a telegram, dated 23 May 1917, from the chief of staff of the German navy to the German Admiralty, sent after his interview with the commander of the submarine. In this telegram the chief of staff stated that the *Tiger* was sunk outside Spanish territorial waters and added that he saw no inconvenience in submitting the case to arbitration, if necessary.

Upon the completion of his exposé the German agent informed the commissioners that the commander of the submarine had on numerous occasions been ordered to appear before the commission, but last-minute military duties had always made it impossible for him to do so.[46] The Spanish agent stated that the Spanish witnesses could be called to appear before the commission, if it so wished. The commission did not consider that the personal presence of these witnesses was necessary.

In the course of the second meeting, the Spanish agent asked the German agent to explain how the submarine's log-book—a document so important for the settlement of the disagreement between the two governments—had been left on board, thus exposing it to the risk of loss or

---

Spanish version as understood by Germany. For a reproduction of the latter chart see above, p. 158.

[46]During the second meeting, on 4 Nov. 1918, the president pointed out to the German agent that, in a note of the German government of 16 Sept. 1918, reference was made to the whole crew of the submarine as possible witnesses (cf. above, p. 160), while the agent declared that only the commander was prevented from appearing before the commission. The agent answered that the whole crew, with the exception of the commander, had perished with the loss of the submarine. The German Ministry for Foreign Affairs was not aware of this fact at the time of the dispatch of the note, since communications of that nature were not published.

At the third meeting the German agent informed the commission that the submarine UB69 was considered lost as of 7 Dec. 1917.

alteration. The German agent conceded that it was a mistake on the part of the German Admiralty not to have obtained the log-book, but it was important for the subsequent navigation of the submarine in the same waters. Moreover, the chief of staff of the German navy had examined the log-book.

With regard to further proceedings, the president asked the Spanish agent whether he was ready to answer the exposé of the German agent, made at the previous session. The Spanish agent answered that he was not ready, whereupon the Spanish commissioner explained that the representatives of Spain had not been aware of the need to present a written reply. The president then drew attention to the terms of Article 19 of the Hague Convention, which provided that both sides must be heard. Moreover, it had already been decided that the exposés of the agents should, so far as possible, be based on written texts.

In those circumstances, the German agent was given the opportunity to present his second exposé. He made a detailed analysis of the evidence given by the crew of the *Tiger* and the Spanish fishermen, alleging contradictions between various statements and emphasizing the lack of measurement by proper instruments. Nevertheless, he drew attention to the fact that some of the fishermen had estimated the crucial distance as 2–3 miles, an estimate close to the accurate measurement of 3·2 miles.

During the reading of the exposé the president observed, i.a., that the director of the Spanish Royal Hydrographic Institute had informed him that on the photograph of the map presented by the German agent, Cape Machichaco projected into the sea some 0·2 miles farther than it actually does. This was due to the fact that the photographic process caused the light from the lighthouse to be reproduced on the map as part of the land.

At the third meeting, held on 6 November 1918, the president stated that he had inquired whether the log-book of the *Tiger* could be shown to the commission and whether the captain of the *Tiger* could come to Copenhagen and give evidence. He was informed that the captain was in New York and that the owners of the *Tiger* were to be approached with regard to the log-book.

The Spanish agent then delivered his second exposé. He recalled that the incident had taken place at the beginning of fierce submarine warfare, when any intentional violation of the rights of neutral powers would have caused grave international complications for Germany. In such exceptional circumstances, the commander of the submarine was not only justified in distorting the truth, but he also had the duty to do so. Quoting from the report of the commander that the submarine changed course 'at full speed' towards the coast in order to approach the *Tiger*, the Spanish agent asked who could sincerely believe that the submarine would stop promptly just outside the limit of territorial waters? He further maintained that the commander of the submarine should have determined the position of the *Tiger* in the presence of the Norwegian captain. The necessary calculations would have taken only a few minutes. If the commander had chosen instead to conduct the *Tiger* away from the coast for three-quarters of an hour, it was because he knew that the *Tiger* was well within the three-mile zone.

In what seemed to be a crucial argument, the Spanish agent alleged that the limits of the territorial waters as indicated on the map submitted by the German agent were not exact; and that it was possible to prove on the 'original map' that, even on the basis of the data given by the German commander, the *Tiger* had been in Spanish territorial waters. In effect, he said, bearings are always taken with reference to well-determined points. Therefore, the commander must have taken bearings, not from the beach of Machichaco and the cliff of Villano, but from the lighthouse of the cape and the heights of Villano.[47] He could not have done otherwise since, owing to the narrow view obtainable from the submarine, he would not have been able to see the low-lying land. It followed that if one marked on the map the bearings alleged by the German commander, starting from the lighthouse of Machichaco and the mount of Cape Villano, one would arrive at a point within Spanish territorial waters.

After the exposé of the Spanish agent, the German agent observed that the truthfulness of the German commander, whose report was made under his oath of service, should not be doubted. In the event of the commission not having faith in the German commander's declaration, the agent would feel obliged to ask for the postponement of the deliberations to enable the commander to appear as a witness before the commission or before a competent tribunal in Germany. In response, the Spanish agent noted that in all lawsuits it was usual to believe in the sincerity of witnesses to a greater or lesser extent according to their interest in the case. One should not forget that 'the war also had its politics'. The Spanish commissioner added that, if the declaration of the commander were to be believed without any reservation, the reference of the case to an international commission would be superfluous.

In the course of the same meeting, the president referred to the delimitation of the territorial waters on the map produced by the German agent. In his view, the line was not accurately drawn. It appeared that no account was taken of the small islands of Aqueche and Gastelugache situated west of Cape Machichaco. A discussion then followed on the question of determining the limit of the territorial

[47]The relevant passage in the report of the commander included in the first exposé of the German agent reads: 'Le point de navire fut, à cet instant, par relèvement, fixé ø Machichaco 134° ø Villano 236°, c'est-à-dire: à 3.2 mm de la côte . . .' The Spanish agent pointed out that in most cases the commander fixed points by bearings taken from heights ('hauteurs').

waters, taking these two islands into consideration. After a confidential exchange of views without the agents, the president drew the attention of the German agent to the opinion of the Spanish agent on the question of the bearings, namely, that the bearings were taken from the lighthouse and not from the coast itself. The president pointed out, in addition, that the position of the lighthouse on the map did not correspond to that indicated in the official list of lighthouses. The German agent's reply to the last comment was that the map submitted by him was only a sketch.

At the fourth meeting, on 7 November 1918, the German agent read a formal declaration concerning some of the questions raised at the previous meeting. In his view, the report of the commander clearly stated that the bearings were taken from the capes of Machichaco and Galea, and not from the lighthouses thereof.[48] If the bearings were taken from the lighthouses, this would have been explicitly recorded. The presence of the island of Aqueche, he continued, brought the point of arrest of the *Tiger* closer to the limit of the territorial waters than the German government had originally thought. That is why a distance of 100 metres might, perhaps, play an important role in the decision of the commission. It was necessary, therefore, to fix the limit of the territorial waters absolutely exactly.

The German agent emphasized that should the decision of the commission be unfavourable to his government, the latter would always be under the burden of a grave reproach for having committed a violation of neutrality, not to mention the resulting obligation to pay compensation. Therefore he requested, in the name of his government, that if the commission were inclined to think that the place of arrest was on, or even within, the territorial limit, it should not pronounce a final verdict until the exact position by latitude and longitude of the low-tide mark of the island had been fixed. On the basis of this position, the commission could fix the exact spot at which the arrest had taken place. He added that, in maps of such small scale as those submitted, small islands could easily appear enlarged. Moreover, they were often not accurately indicated. The agent also drew attention to the fact that the relevant bearings referred to the position of the submarine and not to that of the *Tiger*, which was located farther away from the coast at the time of arrest.

The Spanish agent stated that the maps which he had submitted to the commission were the only documents that could be used for a decision in the case (above, p. 161, n. 45).

The president then invited the agents to retire, and the commission

---

[48]The German agent referred, apparently, to the following passage in the commander's report: 'Sur cette route le point du navire fut, à plusieurs reprises, contrôlé par un relèvement de deux points et il fut fixé, à 1.55 h. à ø Machichaco 137° et ø Galea Pt. 228°, c'est-à-dire à 4.5 mm de la côte.' It is not clear why he did not refer to the passage which the Spanish agent had in mind. Cf. previous footnote.

continued its deliberations in private. When the agents were recalled, the president announced the provisional closure of the inquiry.

The fifth meeting of the commission, on 8 November 1918, was held in private; the sixth meeting, on the same day, was devoted to the reading of the commission's report and of the opinion of the German commissioner which was attached under the heading 'special vote of the German member of the inquiry commission'.

The report of the commission[49] consists of three parts: (1) a short introduction noting the composition and powers of the commission; (2) a statement of the reasons underlying the arguments of the parties and the deliberations of the commission; and (3) the 'judgment' of the commission ('sentence de la commission').

The commission pointed out, in the part dealing with its own deliberations, that on the maps deposited by the German agent the small islands of Aqueche and Gastelugache were not taken into account. It followed that, at the spot where the arrest took place according to German indications, the limit of territorial waters was marked on the maps at least 0·2 sea-miles closer to land than it should have been. Moreover, if the bearings taken by the German commander referred to the lighthouse—which in the opinion of the commission was the most probable assumption—then the place of the arrest was exactly on, or even within, the limit of territorial waters. If the bearings were taken from the most outlying points of the cape, the point arrived at would be a little distance outside the limit. It was not possible to determine, on the basis of the data presented to the commission, whether the bearing was taken from the lighthouse or from the extreme visible point of Cape Machichaco. Assuming that the bearing was taken from the extreme point of the cape, as declared by the German agent, this was not, in the commission's view, the proper way to proceed in circumstances which required the utmost accuracy, perhaps to within 50 or 100 metres. The commission considered that a bearing from the farthermost point of a cape was an uncertain method, especially as the German manual for the northern and western shores of Spain noted that it was very difficult to recognize Cape Machichaco from the geographical point at which the submarine was located. Moreover, on the day of the incident the swell was so strong that the commander of the submarine was afraid lest, aided by the current, it might carry the *Tiger* closer to land.

In the opinion of the commission, even a very small concession in favour of the estimates of distances made by the Spanish and Norwegian witnesses would lead to the result that the place of arrest was within the limit of territorial waters. Similarly, if the point of arrest marked on the maps submitted by the German agent was accepted and the limit of territorial waters—taking into account the island of Aqueche —was rectified, then the place of arrest lay within Spanish territorial

[49]See *Procès-verbaux*, pp. 33–47.

waters. As to the place of sinking of the *Tiger* by the submarine, there was no doubt whatsoever that it was located outside Spanish territorial waters.

The commission did not find it necessary in these circumstances, the report goes on, to adjourn its meetings in order to seek more information concerning the points raised by the German agent. Nevertheless, the commission ascertained that no other nautical maps of the northern coast of Spain were more accurate than the official Spanish map deposited with the commission.

In its 'sentence' the commission expressed the opinion that the *Tiger* was pursued and arrested by a German submarine on 7 May 1917, within the zone of three sea-miles off the Spanish coast, whereas the said vessel was sunk outside that zone. All three commissioners signed the report, although the German commissioner also attached a separate opinion.[50]

Conclusions. The *Tiger* case is significant in two main respects: (1) It illustrates the true nature of the Hague method of inquiry, as distinguished from inquiry into all aspects of the dispute, and (2) it confirms the possibility of a definitive settlement of a dispute by means of fact-finding, without reference of legal questions of responsibility to an arbitral tribunal.

The purely fact-finding role emerges from the function of the commission as defined in the diplomatic exchanges (above, pp. 157 & 159), together with the agreement of the parties to base the arrangement concerning the inquiry on Part III of the Convention of 1907 (above p. 160). The task of the commission was, as in the *Tavignano* case, to ascertain the place of the incident. The specific invocation of Article 9 of the Convention of 1899 in the course of the diplomatic correspondence (above, p. 159), as well as the invocation of Article 9 of the Convention of 1907 in the opening address of the president of the commission, show that the dispute was regarded by the parties as arising from a difference of opinion on points of fact.

What distinguishes the present case from that of the *Tavignano* was the wish of the parties to regard the report of the commission as finally settling not only the question of fact but also, by implication, the legal question of responsibility. The two governments undertook in advance

[50]Most of his arguments were intended to refute the evidence of the Spanish and Norwegian witnesses. The commissioner made no reference to the islands. His main contention, it seems, was as follows: if the commission was inclined to think that the submarine was not capable of determining her position with an accuracy of close to one-tenth of a sea-mile, it must take into consideration a possible mistake in both directions, i.e. towards the territorial waters and away from them. It followed that the position of the submarine in relation to the territorial waters was doubtful and, consequently, no proof of violation of neutrality was given. It was not the German but the Spanish government which must produce the proof, since it was the Spanish government which had asserted the violation of its neutrality. Therefore, the submarine must be acquitted of the accusation of having violated the territorial zone.

to accept the report as binding and, consistently, they agreed that Article 35 of the Convention of 1907, according to which the report has in no way the character of an award and leaves the parties entire freedom as to the effect to be given to the findings contained therein, should not be applied (above, pp. 160 & 161) The theoretical significance of this approach is great. It shows that in certain circumstances decisions on fact cannot be separated from decisions in law. Since the two parties had agreed in advance that the pursuit and seizure of the *Tiger* in Spanish territorial waters, if proved, would entail a violation of international law by Germany, a decision of the commission that the incident did in fact take place in Spanish territorial waters, settled both the factual and the legal questions.

The commission itself went to the extreme in this respect by entitling its final finding 'sentence de la commission', while the German commissioner concluded his opinion with the phrase: 'Ceci c'est mon jugement'.[51]

We may consider the above approach of the two governments and the international commission of inquiry as more realistic than that of the Hague draftsmen. If the inquiry per se does not involve legal issues, and if the questions of fact can only be determined by an expert finding and the parties, acting in good faith, agree to seek such expert finding, then there is no reason for them to be entirely free with regard to the legal consequences of the report. Our study has shown that the promoters of the inquiry method at the Hague Conferences stressed the voluntary character of recourse to international commissions of inquiry and the non-binding character of the report in order to allay the apprehensions of many delegations who were opposed to compulsory arbitration. However, the *Tiger* incident shows that the emphasis on the non-binding character of the report obscured the true nature of the fact-finding method. In effect, in disputes of this kind the report has the character of an arbitral award, and there seems to be nothing objectionable in that so long as the parties have *voluntarily* agreed in advance to reach a definitive settlement of their dispute by means of an international commission of inquiry.

The *Tiger* case also raises certain doubts about the realism of the Hague draftsmen with regard to the qualification on honour or essential interests. It will be recalled that in the present case the German agent stressed the importance of the commission's finding for the honour of Germany, and the honour of the German navy in particular (above, pp. 164 & 165). The Spanish agent, for his part, did not fail to note that it was particularly important for Germany, at the beginning of the fierce submarine warfare, not to be found guilty of violating neutral rights. So far as Spain was concerned, it could hardly be denied that her firm attitude, including her readiness to employ the most forceful means

[51] *Procès-verbaux*, p. 47.

(above, p. 157), signified her wish to defend what were, in her view, her essential rights and interests as a neutral power. Moreover, both parties recognized that Germany must offer apologies if violation by her was proved, i.e. she had to give compensation in this way for her attack on the honour of Spain.

Despite considerations of honour and essential interests, the present dispute could not be considered as grave. There was no danger of hostilities between the two countries as a result of its continuance. The parties themselves chose to define it in mild terms as 'divergences d'appréciation qui pourraient surgir sur les faits' (above, pp. 157 & 159).[52] Bearing in mind the similar non-dangerous nature of the *Tavignano* dispute, there seems to be sufficient ground for the view that genuine inquiry may be particularly suitable for disputes of a moderate character. (It will be recalled that the serious *Maine* dispute was not submitted to an international commission of inquiry (above, pp. 33–5.)

Regarding the establishment of the commission, its composition, and its procedure, it is noteworthy that the parties did not sign a preliminary inquiry agreement. All questions concerning the legal basis of the resort to a commission, its composition, its seat, and the effect of its report were settled during the continuous exchange of notes. It appears that the parties purposely refrained from defining rules of procedure, relying on the general framework of the 1907 Convention, and being of the view that the nature of the inquiry was not likely to raise complicated procedural problems.

The reasoning of the parties in favour of a commission composed of three naval officers without legal assessors was probably the same as in the *Tavignano* case. The issue was relatively simple, and called only for expert non-legal knowledge.

In contrast to the *Tavignano* case, both Germany and Spain appointed agents. In the present case, the participation of the agents in the work of the commission was fully justified. They defended the interests of their respective countries with vigour. Their confrontation was at times very sharp. If the national commissioners had acted in their place, either the issues would have been blurred or the friendly atmosphere of the proceedings as well as the impartiality of the commissioners would have been undermined. In addition, the formal declaration submitted by the German agent towards the end of the deliberations clearly justified his function, namely, following the instructions of his government to produce the allegations and formulate the necessary requests (above, pp. 159 & 164–5).

While both governments agreed that the deliberations of the commission must take place in complete freedom, without being hampered by any formality, the commission displayed an overall inclination to

---

[52]The term 'désaccord' was used in the introductory part of the commission's report.

follow the provisions of the 1907 Convention regarding the method of work of commissions of inquiry. Thus the president declared that, subject to the application of Article 14 (above, p. 160), the formal rules of Part III of the convention should be applied (above, p. 161). And in the course of the proceedings he requested, on the basis of Article 19 of the convention, that the Spanish agent should give a formal answer to the first exposé of the German agent (above, p. 163). Again, reference to Article 19 of the convention was made by the Spanish agent when he requested the commission to accept several documents.[53]

The decisions with regard to the appointment of secretaries and stenographers, as well as those relating to the working language, the written statements, and the form of the minutes, were reached without difficulty (above, pp. 160–1). This shows that a formal preliminary agreement with regard to such matters is not always necessary.

Unlike the *Tavignano* Commission, the commission charged with the *Tiger* case did not examine witnesses. This was due to the promptness and thoroughness of the preliminary inquiries, especially on the Spanish side. The commission saw no advantage in again examining the Spanish fishermen. Moreover, the inquiries made by the president as to the possible appearances of the captain of the *Tiger* and the commander of the submarine did not indicate any great eagerness to put them in the witness box. The commission obviously considered that the written statements relating to the respective versions of the two officers contained the maximum evidence to be obtained from them. Otherwise the commission would have adjusted the dates of its meetings so as to enable the officers to appear.

In spite of the usefulness of preliminary inquiries, the case under review shows the drawbacks of delay in establishing the commission over a year after the incident occurred. As it happened, the crew of the submarine (with the exception of the commander) had perished in the meantime, together with very important documents. Because of the delay, the German agent had to rely to a considerable extent on a report by the commander of the submarine written seventeen months after the event with the special purpose of being submitted to the commission.

With regard to the main point at issue, attention should be paid to the fact that, as in the case of the *Tavignano*, the commander of the capturing vessel failed to determine, in the presence of the captain of the captured vessel, the place where the seizure had occurred. It would appear that many difficulties could have been avoided if both officers had been bound jointly to proceed with the necessary measurements in order to establish the crucial fact of their exact position.

---

[53]At the first meeting of the commission. For the text of Art. 19 see below, App. I, p. 335.

THE 'TUBANTIA' CASE: GERMANY–NETHERLANDS, 1922

This case, like that of the *Tiger*, involved the sinking of a neutral merchant vessel by a German submarine during the First World War.[54]

On 16 March 1916 the Dutch steamer *Tubantia* was sunk by a torpedo on the high seas, a few hours out from Amsterdam. The Netherlands contended that the *Tubantia* was torpedoed by the German U-boat 13. Germany maintained, on the other hand, that the *Tubantia* struck a floating torpedo which had been launched by the U-boat at a British vessel ten days earlier and which had missed its target.

In September 1916 the German government accepted the proposal of the Dutch government to submit the case to an international commission of inquiry in accordance with the provisions of the 1907 Hague Convention for the Pacific Settlement of International Disputes; the commission was to be constituted after the war.[55] Consequently, the following agreement for inquiry was signed in Berlin on 30 March 1921:[56]

The Royal Government of the Netherlands and the German Government having agreed to submit to an international commission of inquiry the dispute as to the cause of the sinking of the Dutch steamer *Tubantia* on March 16, 1916, have appointed the undersigned, namely:

For the Government of the Netherlands, Baron W. A. F. Gevers, Ambassador Extraordinary and Minister Plenipotentiary of Her Majesty the Queen of the Netherlands at Berlin;

For the German Government: Dr. Ernst von Simson, Counsellor of Legation and Director in the Foreign Office;

Who, being duly authorized therefor, have agreed upon the following convention of inquiry:

Article 1

The task of the international commission of inquiry shall be to ascertain the cause of the sinking of the Dutch steamer *Tubantia* on March 16, 1916.

Article 2

The commission of inquiry shall consist of five members. Each of the parties shall choose one member, and the Danish and Swedish Governments shall be requested to appoint one naval officer each as additional members.

[54]The following account of the facts of the case is based on the report of the commission of inquiry as published in English translation in Scott, *Hague Court reports* (1932), pp. 135–43. The original French text of the report was published separately by the PCA under the title *Rapport de la commission internationale d'enquête concernant la perte du vapeur néerlandais 'Tubantia'* (1922). The French text appears also in *Grotius Annuaire international, 1921–2* (1922), pp. 263–72, and Scott, *Hague Court reports* (1932), pp. 211–17. For the English text of the inquiry agreement between Germany and the Netherlands of 30 Mar. 1921, see ibid., pp. 143–5.

[55]See 'Aperçu de faits internationaux juridiques', *Grotius Annuaire international pour 1916* (1917), p. 106.

[56]See reference in n. 54 above.

The Swiss Government shall be requested to designate a jurist as chairman of the commission.

Article 3
Each party shall be represented by a special agent who will serve as an intermediary between it and the commission. The agents shall furnish such explanations as the commission may require of the parties; they are authorized during or at the close of the investigation, to submit in writing to the commission and to the opposite party such evidence, proofs or statements of fact as are considered necessary for establishing the truth.

The parties shall also be entitled to appoint technical assistants or counsel to be charged with stating and protecting their interests before the commission.

Article 4
The commission shall meet at The Hague.

Article 5
The memorials of the parties may be presented in French, German or Dutch. If they are submitted in the German or Dutch language, a French translation shall be attached. The commission shall decide what language it will employ, and what language may be used in the proceedings.

The first exchange of memorials shall take place four months after the signing of this protocol, and the exchange of the counter-memorials within two months thereafter. The chairman of the commission may extend this period, or require a further exchange of memorials.

The memorials shall be deposited in fourteen copies with the Bureau of the Permanent Court of Arbitration at The Hague. The Bureau will immediately transmit three copies to the opposite party and two copies to each commissioner. One copy shall remain in the archives of the Bureau.

Article 6
The period for oral proceedings shall be determined by the chairman.

Article 7
The meetings of the commission shall not be public nor shall the protocols and documents of the commission be published. The final report of the commission, however, shall be read in a public session and shall be published.

Article 8
The provisions of the third chapter of the Hague Convention for the Pacific Settlement of International Disputes, October 18, 1907, in so far as they are not at variance with the provisions of this convention, shall be applicable to the procedure of the commission, especially as regards the production of evidence and the form and effect of the report to be made by the commission.

In witness whereof the plenipotentiaries have signed this convention of inquiry and have affixed their seals thereto.

The commission of inquiry set up in accordance with the above agreement was composed of the following members: Hoffmann, a Swiss jurist, formerly a member of the Swiss Federal Council, as president; Rear-Admiral (Reserve) Surie, of the Dutch navy; Captain Ravn, director of the Hydrographic Service of the Danish navy; Commander Unger, of the Swedish navy; and Lt-Commander Gayer, of the German navy.

The German government named as its agent Captain (Reserve) Karl von Mueller; the government of the Netherlands named Professor A. A. H. Struycken, member of the Permanent Court of Arbitration, as its agent, and Captain Canters, director of the torpedo factory, as counsel.

The meetings of the commission took place in the palace of the Permanent Court of Arbitration at The Hague from 18 January to 27 February 1922. In pursuance of Article 5 of the agreement for inquiry, the Dutch and German memorials were deposited in the International Bureau of the Permanent Court of Arbitration on 27 and 29 July 1921 respectively, while the counter-memorials were deposited on 23 September and 14 October 1921 respectively.

After the presentation of all the explanations and proofs on behalf of the parties, and after the hearing of witnesses and experts, the president of the commission pronounced the inquiry closed. At its last session, on 27 February 1922, the commission delivered its report, which contained the following statements of facts, contentions of the parties, and findings of the commission:

On 15 March 1916 the *Tubantia* left Amsterdam on her way to South America. At 6.15 p.m. she was in the open sea. The vessel was sufficiently illuminated; besides the prescribed lights of position, two arc lamps illuminated the name 'Tubantia—Amsterdam' on the planking, and two other arc lamps illuminated the name on the plate.

At 9.59 p.m. the weather was indicated in the *Tubantia*'s records as follows: misty horizon, visibility from four to five sea-miles, gentle east-north-east wind, choppy sea. At 2.00 a.m. the captain ordered everything to be made ready for casting anchor near the lightship *Nord-Hinder*. At 2.20 a.m. the fourth officer suddenly observed a streak in the water, approaching the vessel in a straight line at about six points. He thought that it was the wake of a torpedo and a moment before the explosion he cried 'Look there!'.

The same observation of a thin white streak moving at great speed in the direction of the vessel was made by the look-out man. He claimed before the commission that he immediately recognized it as the wake of a torpedo—a phenomenon which he had seen repeatedly during practice launchings of torpedoes. He announced to the first officer immediately after the explosion that the vessel had been hit by a torpedo whose wake he had seen moving towards the ship. The exclamation 'Look there!' was heard by the first officer and the third officer, as well as by the captain.

It must be conceded to the agent of the German government, stated the commission, that the depositions of the witnesses did not agree on all points, and also that in the different examinations of the same witnesses a certain amplification might be noted in the addition of details. But neither these discrepancies, which were common in similar circumstances, nor the general consideration that in observations of this kind examples of autosuggestion are easily found, could detract from the value of the evidence. The depositions of the witnesses were clear and positive; they did not contradict each other, and what some said they saw was confirmed in a manner worthy of belief by what others heard immediately after the disaster.

In several of the lifeboats of the *Tubantia*, the report went on, fragments of metal were found which were recognized as being parts of a torpedo. In two boats there were found two scraps of copper on which the number 2033 was impressed. As appeared from the declaration of the chief of the German Admiralty, made on 11 May 1916, these scraps were recognized as being fragments of the bronze torpedo C 45/91 No. 2033, which was part of the armament of the submarine UB13.

From the depositions of the officers and sailors of the *Tubantia*, according to which they saw the wake of the torpedo immediately before the explosion, and from the fact that the fragments of torpedo No. 2033 belonging to the armament of the UB13 were found in the boats of the *Tubantia*, it resulted,[57] in the view of the commission, that UB13 launched the torpedo which caused the explosion.

The commission referred thereupon to the claim of the German agent that submarine UB13 was during the critical night, at 3.55 a.m., at 51° 52' north latitude and 2° 23' east longitude, i.e. a distance of twelve sea-miles from the position of the lightship *Nord-Hinder* at the time, and that from that position the submarine launched a torpedo against a ship which bore no light except at the head of the mast. After pointing out that the German assertion was based on an unauthenticated copy of the submarine's log-book,[58] the commission held that the difference in time between the entry in the copy of the log-book and the actual time of the sinking (2.20 a.m.) was not considerable[59] and might be ascribed to errors, on one side or the other, in observations or annotations. The difference between the indications of the location of the *Tubantia*, on the one hand, and the location of the UB13, on the other

---

[57]The original report uses the expression 'il résulte', while the translation employs the rather vague term 'it appears'.

[58]The original of the commander's report was destroyed with the majority of the documents relative to the submarine war, in part during the retreat from Flanders and in part during the revolution.

[59]The clocks of the *Tubantia* were regulated according to astronomical time, while the entry in the copy of the log-book was based on Central European time.

hand, was more considerable. The *Tubantia* was sunk at 51° 48′ 40″ north latitude and 2° 50′ 15″ east longitude. This calculation, made at the time of the examination of the wreck, could not be subject to any doubt, stated the commission. On the other hand, the copy of the submarine's log-book might have been erroneous. Apart from certain difficulties inherent in a determination of location demanding such great precision, the experiences of the war showed that the possibility of errors in navigation could by no means be excluded.

Having thus considered that the evidence produced by the German side with regard to the time and place of the incident did not refute the Dutch argument, the commission took up the additional German assertion that the torpedo launched about the time of the incident was directed against a vessel which bore no lights save for one on her mast, and therefore could not have been the *Tubantia*. Here again the commission examined the possibility of error. It recalled that the captain of the *Tubantia* estimated visibility at four sea-miles. Nevertheless, it was not absolutely excluded, in the commission's view, that perhaps the lower part of the vessel might have been hidden by one of those intermittent fogs so frequent in the North Sea.

Admitting that an error on the part of the captain of the UB13 in this respect was not impossible,[60] the commission did not consider 'this fact' as 'decisive proof' that the *Tubantia*, recognized as such, was not torpedoed intentionally. The commission stated that the commander of the UB13 might have acted in violation of the instructions and orders of his superiors and against the intentions and decisions of the German government. It is true, the commission said, that a witness, one Dehmel, on board the UB13 testified that on the night in question a vessel of medium size and entirely without lights was torpedoed, and that, while he was a sailor on that submarine, a large vessel sufficiently lighted had never been torpedoed. But the manner in which this witness had ventured to offer his testimony in favour of a foreign government was not likely to inspire confidence in his words. Moreover, his credibility was weakened by the fact that he had served a term of imprisonment.[61]

The commission then took up what seemed to be the main argument in the German memorial, namely that the torpedo C 45/91 No. 2033 had already been launched by the UB13 on 6 March 1916, at 4.43 p.m., against a British destroyer, about three miles north-east of the lightship *Nord-Hinder*, and having missed its target it had continued to float until it was struck by the *Tubantia*. A Dutch expert refuted this claim, estimating, on the basis of periodical tidal currents, that the torpedo would have reached a distance of at least nineteen sea-miles from the point of the disaster. A German expert claimed, on the other hand, that

---

[60] By 'error' the intention apparently was to convey that the captain of the submarine was mistaken *in fact* by thinking that the boat was suspect because it was, so far as he could see, unilluminated.

[61] Apparently the witness was not German.

floating bodies moved in a direction against the progressive current and that the method applied by the Dutch expert was not as accurate as the methods of modern oceanographical science. Moreover, account should have been taken of the wind.

The commission expressed its belief that, in spite of the most minute observations of currents and winds, it would not be possible to find a torpedo which had been launched and had remained afloat for ten days, at the point where it ought to be according to the calculations. Consequently, the commission could not decide that it was impossible that a floating torpedo struck the *Tubantia* at the point where this vessel sank.[62]

On the same issue, the commission considered the implications of the damage done to the *Tubantia* as a result of the impact. The Dutch agent contended that the *Tubantia* was not struck by a floating torpedo since, in view of the size and shape of the hole, the vessel was not hit at the water-line but two or three metres below it. The expert of the German government claimed that a torpedo floating at a slight depth could have only insignificant effects above the water-line. He believed that the explosion took place about a metre below the water-line. The commission stated that it did not consider it possible to fix the point where the explosion of the torpedo took place by judging only from the size and shape of the hole. Nevertheless, in view of the size of the hole and the considerable damage within the ship, it seemed more likely that the explosion had taken place several metres below the water-line.

Again with regard to the 'floating-torpedo' argument, the commission referred to the claim of the Dutch agent that there might have been an error in the registration of the number of the torpedo launched by the submarine ten days before the sinking of the *Tubantia*. The commission admitted that such an error could easily be made, given the fact that the number of the torpedo had to be transcribed several times. The supposition that the error would have been found during the inspection of the torpedoes at Kiel, and that a claim would then have been made upon the commander of the UB13, was hardly compatible with the difficulties and exigencies of war. However that may be, the commission said, the fact that the same torpedo number was found in the list of torpedoes launched and on the torpedo fragments found in the boats of the *Tubantia* was not of sufficient importance to invalidate the depositions made by the officers and crew of that vessel.

The last possibility considered by the commission was that the *Tubantia* was torpedoed by a vessel belonging to a power hostile to Germany. In default of any proof, the commission rejected this hypothesis.

[62] The commission apparently meant that it was only with regard to the considerations under discussion that it was not in a position so to decide. It will be recalled that previously the commission accepted the version of the *Tubantia* witnesses, according to which the torpedo was not floating. See also the subsequent findings to the same effect.

At the end of its report the commission stated that, after weighing all the evidence, it was convinced that the *Tubantia* had been sunk on 16 March 1916 by the explosion of a torpedo launched by a German submarine. The question of determining whether the torpedoing took place knowingly or as the result of an error on the part of the commander of the submarine must remain in abeyance. It was not possible to determine that the loss of the *Tubantia* was caused by her striking a torpedo that had remained afloat. Although it could not be denied that a certain number of indications militated in favour of the latter possibility, the commission, after examining them conscientiously and comparing them with the other evidence, could not recognize that these indications were conclusive and had the force of proof. No indication permitting the assumption of any other cause for the loss of the *Tubantia* could be produced.

The German government accepted the conclusions of the report and paid an indemnity in the amount of $6\frac{1}{2}$ million Dutch florins.[63]

Conclusions. This is an additional case of genuine inquiry, or fact-finding, handled on the basis of the 1907 Hague Convention. As stated in the introduction to the commission's report, the two governments

respectively signatories of the Hague Convention of 18 October 1907 for the Pacific Settlement of International Disputes, have agreed to submit to an international commission of inquiry constituted in accordance with the provisions of Chapter III of the said convention, the question of ascertaining what was the cause of the loss of the Dutch steamer *Tubantia* which occurred on March 16, 1916.

The dispute concerned a question of fact, and the commission was not called upon to decide whether the legal responsibility of one or the other party was involved. Nevertheless, it is obvious that its decision had clear legal implications, namely that Germany was responsible for violating international law since her submarine had torpedoed the *Tubantia* without legitimate cause.

Unlike the commissions in the *Tavignano* and *Tiger* cases, but like the Dogger Bank Commission, the present commission interpreted its task as including an examination of the question whether the German commander acted wilfully or in error. It would seem that the commission was justified in doing so, since its terms of reference provided for the ascertainment of the 'cause' of the sinking. The powers were not narrowly defined as determining whether or not the *Tubantia* was torpedoed by a German submarine.

This approach of the commission has theoretical significance since it shows that, in its view and perhaps also in the view of the governments concerned, genuine fact-finding in accordance with the Hague Con-

---

[63]See François, *Handboek van het Volkenrecht*, ii, 2nd edn (1950), p. 99.

ventions need not necessarily be confined to a search for 'what happened', in the sense of physical action, but may—and perhaps must, depending on the case—ascertain the intentions and motives of the parties concerned.

We came across this problem in connection with the Dogger Bank incident. Our analysis there was hampered by the fact that the states involved decided to confer upon the commission the power to determine responsibilities. In the present case, on the other hand, the question of motive was dealt with—though not as a central issue—within the framework of the unequivocal fact-finding task.

Unlike the Dogger Bank Commission, the *Tubantia* Commission was not anxious to avoid making any statement which might cast doubts on the military integrity and the humanity of the naval commander involved. On the contrary, it insinuated that the German commander might have consciously and purposely torpedoed the neutral merchant vessel. (There was no mention in the report of the possibility that the *Tubantia* was carrying contraband.) Nevertheless, the commission was careful to note that, if the commander had acted in such a way, he would have disobeyed the orders of his government.

The composition of the commission in the *Tubantia* case differed from that of the Dogger Bank, *Tavignano*, and *Tiger* Commissions. Unlike the last two, it was composed of five, not three, members; and unlike all three, not all the commissioners were naval officers, the president being a well-known jurist. The difference may be explained by the seriousness of the charge and the complicated issues involving the evidence of experts. In the Dogger Bank case there was a strong presumption that Admiral Rojdestvensky believed he had been attacked by Japanese torpedo-boats and that the English fishing-boats were, at the most, accidental targets. In the *Tavignano* case the seizure, not sinking, of a vessel was involved; while in the *Tiger* case the contest was, as it were, between the country of the attacking submarine and a third country anxious to preserve her territorial sovereignty. The *Tubantia* case, on the other hand, involved the charge of a merciless night attack on an unarmed, illuminated, and unsuspicious neutral vessel.

The choice of a prominent lawyer as president can be explained, in particular, by reference to the problems of obtaining and analysing abundant evidence of various kinds. There is here an express recognition of the fact that international inquiry has many features in common with arbitration. The proceedings in a case like the present one have all the characteristics of a lawsuit. A glance at the inquiry agreement shows that in matters of procedure for acquiring evidence the parties went beyond the general terms of Part III of the Convention of 1907. Provision was made for the exchange of memorials and counter-memorials before the sittings of the commission, and 'oral proceedings' were especially envisaged. The English version of the report of the commission (para. 2) speaks of the 'cross-examination' of witnesses, and the French of several examinations of the same witnesses. This would suggest an involved procedure which an experienced jurist-president could handle more efficiently.

The report of the *Tubantia* Commission was signed by all five commissioners, although Article 33 of the 1907 Convention envisages the possibility of refusal to sign (below, App. I, p. 337). Unlike the report of the *Tiger* Commission, no dissenting opinion was attached.

Another notable difference between the *Tiger* and *Tubantia* cases is that, while in the former case the parties expressly accepted in advance the report of the commission as binding, the parties in the latter case 'especially' undertook to apply the provisions of the 1907 Convention with regard to the effect of the report, i.e. they explicitly reserved their 'entire freedom' of action as to the effect to be given to the findings of the report. It may well be asked why, after five years of negotiations, the parties should decide to undertake elaborate proceedings designed in effect to establish authoritatively whether one of them had committed a gross violation of international law as against the other, if the guilty party was to be free to disregard the eventual findings. There is, indeed, some merit in such an arrangement, inasmuch as one of the parties is likely at least to be morally vindicated. But if recourse to commissions of inquiry is to be conceived as a method for the settlement of disputes, the parties in the *Tiger* case would seem to be on stronger ground, as regards both the theoretical and the practical implications of the inquiry.

THE 'RED CRUSADER' CASE: DENMARK–UNITED KINGDOM, 1962

An interval of some forty years passed before the international community again witnessed the establishment of a commission of inquiry charged with fact-finding functions in accordance—though not expressly—with the Hague Convention of 1907. As in the cases analysed so far, the dispute between Denmark and the United Kingdom concerned an incident at sea, but unlike the earlier cases neither of the disputing countries was involved in a war. Moreover, the two opposing sides in the *Red Crusader* case belonged at the time of the incident (and still do) to the same military alliance—the North Atlantic Treaty Organization. This fact considerably influenced their respective attitudes in handling the dispute.

On 29 May 1961 the Scottish trawler *Red Crusader* was arrested by the Danish frigate *Niels Ebbesen* off the coast of the Faroe Islands, on a charge of fishing in an area from which British fishermen were excluded by virtue of an agreement of 27 April 1959 between the two countries.[64]

---

[64]For the development of the incident see PCA, *Report of the commission of enquiry established by the government of the United Kingdom of Great Britain and Northern Ireland*

The skipper of the *Red Crusader* was ordered to follow the *Niels Ebbesen* and go to Thorshavn in order to be tried by a Faroese court. A lieutenant and a corporal from the *Niels Ebbesen* were put on board the *Red Crusader* to effect the arrest. After following the Danish vessel for some time, the *Red Crusader* changed course with a view to escaping from her captor. The *Niels Ebbesen* pursued her and opened fire. The prow, masts, wireless aerials, and radar installation of the *Red Crusader* were damaged. After having communicated by radio with the Danish Admiralty, the frigate stopped firing but continued pursuit. Meanwhile, the British Royal Navy frigate *Troubridge* and the fishing protection cruiser *Wootton* were directed to the area with instructions 'to find out both sides of the case'.[65] The British ships met the pursued and pursuing vessels midway between the Faroe Islands and the Orkney Islands situated off the north coast of Scotland. Five officers from the *Wootton* went on board the *Niels Ebbesen* and a conference took place between the Danish and British officers. Agreement was reached that the *Red Crusader* should not be forced to proceed to the Faroes (below, p. 190, n. 82).

When the outcome of the negotiations on the high seas became known in Copenhagen, consultations took place between the Admiralty and the government and it was decided that the *Niels Ebbesen* should stop pursuit at the three-mile limit off the Scottish coast but should stay there for the time being as a symbolic upholding of the arrest of the Scottish trawler.[66] This decision of the Danish authorities expressed the grave view which they had taken of the incident. The ill feeling on the Danish side was reinforced by the fact that the abducted prize crew from the *Niels Ebbesen* was unarmed, in pursuance of a previous request of the United Kingdom made with a view to avoiding tension between

---

and the government of the Kingdom of Denmark on November 15, 1961; *investigation of certain incidents affecting the British trawler 'Red Crusader'* (the '*Red Crusader*' incident) (March 1962). See also 35 *International law reports* (1967), 485–501; E. Lauterpacht in *The contemporary practice of the UK in the field of international law, 1962*, i (*January 1– June 30*) (1962), pp. 50–3; 'Chronique des faits internationaux', 65 *RGDIP* (1961), 824–7, and 66 *RGDIP* (1962), 597–601. For the text of the agreement of 27 Apr. 1959 (Cmnd 776), see 55 UKTS (1959), 337 UNTS (1959), 417.

In para. 1 of the agreement of 1959 the UK government undertook to raise no objection to the exclusion, by the competent Danish or Faroese authorities, of vessels registered in the UK from fishing in the area between the coast of the Faroe Islands and 'the blue line' shown on the map annexed to the agreement (see below, p. 182). This 'blue line' is approximately 6 miles from the coast, with the exception of a small section where it extends to 12 miles.

On its part, the government of Denmark agreed, in para. II, to raise no objection to such vessels continuing to fish in the area between 'the blue line' and a line 12 miles from the low-water mark along the coast of the Faroe Islands drawn as shown by the red dotted line on the same map.

In view of the exceptional dependence of the Faroese economy on fisheries, the fishing by British vessels in three areas lying within the area mentioned in para. II was to be limited to fishing with long line and hand line between specified dates (para. III).

[65]*The Times*, 31 May 1961.
[66]Ibid.

3 The *Red Crusader* incident (general area)

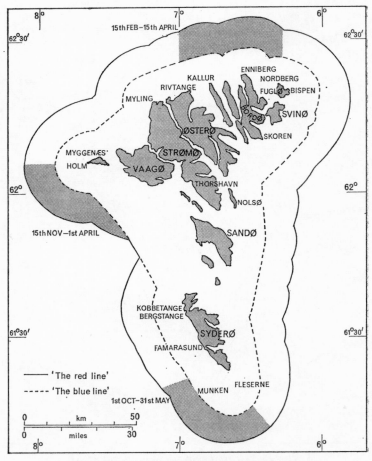

4 The *Red Crusader* incident (fishing zones)

(Reproduced from 337 *UNTS*, 1959.)

Faroese coastguards and British fishermen. It was not surprising, there-fore, that on the day after the incident the Danish Admiralty decided to re-arm the Danish marines in charge of fishery inspection 'who are sent on board law-breaking foreign ships'.[67]

The statements of Skipper Wood of the *Red Crusader* did nothing to alleviate the misgivings of the Danish authorities. He declared on 31 May that he had eluded the Danes before and he would do so again. 'They are now trying to chase us off the sea, and if somebody doesn't do something about it, then we will starve', he said. Asked by journalists if he had been inside the six-mile limit, he replied: 'Would you expect me to answer that question?'[68]

On the diplomatic and parliamentary scene the following develop-ments took place: On 30 May the Danish ambassador in London presented to the Foreign Office a request that the *Red Crusader* should proceed to Thorshavn to face charges of trawling within the six-mile limit and abducting the Danish prize crew. While waiting for a reply to this démarche, the Danish authorities made it clear that the order of the Danish Admiralty to stop further shooting at the *Red Crusader* did not mean that Denmark was giving up her demand for the trial of the skipper in a Danish court.[69]

In the House of Commons, Mr Hector Hughes, Labour member for Aberdeen, declared, on 31 May 1961, that the civilized world would deplore 'this resort to violence by a nation which belongs to NATO and to the United Nations'. The Lord Privy Seal, Mr Heath, was careful, on the other hand, not to pass judgment on the rights and wrongs of this 'most unhappy incident', pending receipt of a full report. At the same time, he agreed with the leader of the Labour opposition, Mr Gaitskell, who had said that there should be some sensible way of settling disputes of this kind without resorting to force. Mr Heath pointed out that there was machinery for dealing with such disputes, and assured the House of his anxiety that relations between the two countries should not be impaired.[70]

On 7 June 1961 the Foreign Office sent an aide-mémoire to the Danish embassy, in reply to the Danish démarche of 30 May. The British govern-ment deplored the incident, which in its view was not characteristic of the good relations between the two countries. It did not question Denmark's right to control fishing within the Faroe fishery limits, but as there appeared to be doubts as to the facts of the case, it was unable to take a decision. At that stage the government was conducting discussions with the *Red Crusader*'s owners and with the fishermen's organizations concerned. Pending the conclusion of these discussions, it was unable to put forward any proposal for a solution of the dispute. However, it wished to emphasize that neither the government nor its representatives

[67]Ibid., 2 June 1961.   [68]Ibid., 1 June 1961.
[69]Ibid.   [70]641 HC Deb., 257–9.

had cast any doubts on the impartiality and independence of Faroese or other Danish courts.[71]

The Danish minister for foreign affairs, Mr Krag, told the Danish parliament on 8 June 1961 that this reply was unsatisfactory. After careful investigation, he said, the Danish government had no doubt that the *Red Crusader* had fished in forbidden waters, and it would consider it advantageous to submit its proof to an impartial body. Accordingly, the Danish ambassador in London would be instructed to propose the investigation of the case by a special commission. In a reference to the shots fired at the *Red Crusader*, Mr Krag said: 'If we are to protect the interests of the Faroes it is necessary that the existing treaties be enforced.' He added that the means used by Denmark might seem violent for such a peaceful country, but enforcement was necessary since the Faroese had little to live off except fish.[72]

On 12 June 1961 Mr Hector Hughes asked the Lord Privy Seal what decision he had reached about claiming compensation from Denmark for the damage that the owners, officers and crew of the *Red Crusader* had suffered. Mr Heath replied that he could not reach any conclusion as regards the claim against the Danish government for compensation until the facts had been established. From a report on the incident received by the secretary of state for Scotland and from the information given by the Danish government it was clear that there were differences of opinion as to the facts of the case. The Danish government had meanwhile proposed that a commission of inquiry be appointed to ascertain the facts. The British government agreed that an impartial inquiry into the facts was desirable, but the terms of reference, the composition of the commission, and other matters had still to be agreed.[73]

The British government officially accepted the Danish proposal on 23 June 1961. The next day the London *Times* commented in an editorial that whatever the law of the sea about pursuit, it was lamentable that a fishery incident should involve shooting between ships of Britain and Denmark. Britain had suffered more than most countries from the extension of fishing limits, and had conceded more. The Aberdeen trawlermen had always had a large stake in the Faroese fisheries, but the Faroes had in May 1961 asked that the limited right of British vessels to fish up to six miles from the shore be ended.[74] If the *Red*

---

[71]*The Times*, 8 June 1961. On 29 Sept. 1961 the skippers of two Scottish trawlers from Aberdeen were acquitted by the High Court of Copenhagen on charges of illegally fishing inside Faroese territorial waters. They had appealed against fines of £2,000 and £1,000, respectively, imposed in 1960 by the District Court of Thorshavn, which also had ordered the tackle and catch to be confiscated (ibid., 30 Sept. 1961).

[72]Ibid., 9 & 12 June 1961.

[73]642 HC Deb., 29–30.

[74]At the beginning of May 1961 Mr Krag informed the UK government of the intention of Denmark to conclude a new fishing agreement, similar to the agreement between the UK and Iceland of 11 Mar. 1961 which excluded British ships from a 12-mile belt, with certain exceptions, for a period of three years (*The Times*, 9 June 1961). For subsequent developments, see p. 191, n. 86.

Crusader had trespassed in the area banned to her by treaty, there was nothing heroic in what she did. But the continual restriction of fishing grounds was a bitter thing for British fishermen. What was needed was not only international agreement on fishery limits, but a co-operative system of conservation and control based on ascertained facts and common courtesy among friends.

On 28 October, when the negotiations for the establishment of the inquiry commission were considerably advanced, the diplomatic correspondent of *The Times* commented: 'In effect both Governments have evidently decided that the lively interest taken in the incident at the time should be allowed to die a slow, and, if possible, painless death.'

The international commission of inquiry charged with the investigation of the incident was established in accordance with the following exchange of notes of 15 November 1961:[75]

I

*The Danish Ambassador at London to the Secretary of State
for Foreign Affairs*

I have the honour to refer to the recent communications between representatives of the Government of the Kingdom of Denmark and the Government of the United Kingdom of Great Britain and Northern Ireland about certain incidents affecting the British trawler *Red Crusader* which occurred in the period of the 29th to the 31st of May, 1961. I now have to propose on behalf of the Danish Government that a Commission of Enquiry shall be established to investigate those incidents and that an Agreement for this purpose shall be concluded in the following terms:

(*a*)—(i) The Commission of Enquiry (hereinafter called 'the Commission') shall be composed of the following members:

1. Professor Charles de Visscher.
2. Professor André Gros.
3. Captain C. Moolenburgh.

(ii) The President of the Commission shall be Professor Charles de Visscher.

(iii) Should any member of the Commission die or become unable to act, the vacancy shall be filled by a new member appointed by agreement between the two Governments.

(*b*) The Commission is requested to investigate and report to the two Governments:

(i) the facts leading up to the arrest of the British trawler *Red Crusader* on the night of the 29th of May, 1961, including the question whether the *Red Crusader* was fishing, or with her fishing gear not stowed, inside the blue line on the map annexed to the Agreement between the two Governments concerning the regulation of fishing around the Faroe Islands constituted by the Exchange of Notes of the 27th of April, 1959;

(ii) the circumstances of the arrest, and

(iii) the facts and incidents that occurred thereafter before the *Red Crusader* reached Aberdeen.

[75]420 UNTS (1962), 67.

(*c*)—(i) The Commission shall, subject to the provisions of the Agreement, determine its own procedure and all questions affecting the conduct of the investigation.

(ii) In the absence of unanimity, the decisions of the Commission on all questions, whether of substance or procedure, shall be given by a majority vote of its members, including all questions relating to the competence of the Commission, the interpretation of the Agreement and the determination of the matters specified in sub-paragraph (*b*) above.

(*d*)—(i) Each Government shall, within fourteen days of to-day's date, appoint an Agent for the purposes of the investigation and shall communicate the name and address of its Agent to the other Government and to the President of the Commission.

(ii) Each Government shall have the right to be represented before the Commission by the Agent and such counsel and advisers as it may appoint.

(*e*)—(i) The proceedings shall be written and oral.

(ii) Written Memorials shall be submitted to the Commission on behalf of each Government within such time limits as the Commission shall determine.

(iii) The oral proceedings shall follow the written proceedings and shall, subject to the provisions of subparagraph (*f*) (i) below, be held in private where and when the Commission, after consultation with the two Agents, shall determine.

(iv) Each Government shall have the right to present oral evidence to the Commission and to question any witnesses called by the other Government to give evidence before the Commission.

(*f*)—(i) The Commission shall select its own seat and inform the two Governments of the address to which written communications to the Commission may be sent. In addition to the place selected as its seat it may carry out its functions in Denmark, including the area of the Faroe Islands, and in the United Kingdom.

(ii) Each Government shall co-operate in making available the facilities necessary for the conduct of the investigation.

(*g*)—(i) The Commission shall terminate its investigation as rapidly as possible, shall deliver its report in writing and shall transmit one signed copy to each Agent.

(ii) Any question of subsequent publication of the proceedings shall be decided by agreement between the two Governments.

(*h*) The two Governments shall accept as final the findings of the Commission.

(*i*)—(i) The remuneration of members of the Commission shall be borne equally by the two Governments.

(ii) The general expenses of the investigation shall be borne equally by the two Governments, but each Government shall bear its own expenses incurred in, or for, the preparation and presentation of its case.

2. If the foregoing proposals are acceptable to the Government of Great Britain and Northern Ireland, I have the honour to suggest that this Note and Your Lordship's reply in that sense shall constitute an Agreement between the two Governments in this matter, which shall enter into force on this day's date.

II
The Secretary of State for Foreign Affairs to the Danish Ambassador at London

I have the honour to acknowledge receipt of Your Excellency's Note No. 641/61 of today's date. . . .

2. I have to inform Your Excellency that the foregoing proposals are acceptable to the Government of the United Kingdom of Great Britain and Northern Ireland, who therefore agree that your Note and the present reply shall constitute an Agreement between the two Governments, which shall enter into force on this day's date.

The commission was constituted on 21 November 1961. None of its members was a national of the United Kingdom or Denmark. They were, respectively, a Belgian, a French, and a Dutch national. At the time of their appointment they held the following positions: Charles De Visscher was professor at the University of Louvain and Honorary President of the Institute of International Law; Professor André Gros was legal adviser to the French Ministry for Foreign Affairs; Captain Moolenburgh was the Netherlands Inspector-General of Shipping.

The government of Denmark was represented by Mr Bent Jacobsen, agent, assisted by Professor Max Sørensen, LL.D., legal adviser to the Ministry for Foreign Affairs, Mr Otto Borch, head of department at the same ministry, Captain E. J. Saabye, Lt Cdr. Harald Rossing of the Ministry of Defence, and Mr Hans Sørensen. The government of the United Kingdom was represented by Mr F. A. Vallat, CMG, QC, legal adviser to the Foreign Office, agent, assisted by the Rt Hon. Sir Reginald Manningham-Buller, Bart., QC, MP, Attorney-General, as counsel, Mr Eustace Roskill, QC, Mr B Sheen, Mr N. H. Marshall, Mr C. Sim, and Lt Cdr. J. C. E. White, RN.

At the first meeting of the commission, on 21 November 1961, it was agreed, in the presence of the agents, that memorials would be exchanged in London and deposited in The Hague on 5 December, with one copy to each member of the commission and to the Registry of the Permanent Court of Arbitration. Counter-memorials were to be exchanged and deposited in the same manner on 16 January 1962. It was then decided that oral proceedings would begin on 5 March in the following order: Danish evidence, British evidence, Danish oral statements, British oral statements—followed by Danish and British replies, if required. Each witness was to be examined, cross-examined and, if necessary, re-examined. The statements were to be made upon an 'engagement of honour', no oath being administered. The written procedure was to be in English and additional documents were to be admitted upon reasonable notice. The Danish witnesses and experts were to have the possibility of expressing themselves in Danish, provision being made for simultaneous and, if necessary, consecutive translation.[76]

[76]See report of the commission, p. 3.

Following consultations between the president of the commission and the Secretary-General of the Permanent Court of Arbitration, Mr Malcolm Eliot Long was appointed registrar and acted as such during the oral proceedings and the deliberations of the commission.

On 3 March 1962 the commission met in private and settled with the agents of the parties questions of internal procedure and material arrangements. The oral proceedings lasted from 5 to 16 March 1961. The commission heard nine Danish witnesses and two Danish experts at the meetings held from 5 to 9 March. Eight of the witnesses were from the crew of the *Niels Ebbesen*, and included her commanding officer; the remaining witness was the skipper of a Danish fishing-vessel. The experts were a member of the service department of the telecommunications division of the Danish navy, and the chief engineer of the electronics department of the Danish navy. After examination by the Danish agent, the witnesses were cross-examined by British counsel and, in some cases, re-examined.[77]

From 10 March three witnesses and one expert called by the British side were heard. The witnesses were the skipper of the *Red Crusader*, the commanding officer of HMS *Troubridge*, and another officer from the same ship. The expert was the technical manager of the Marconi International Marine Communication Company Ltd. After examination by British counsel and Mr Roskill, the witnesses and the expert were cross-examined by the Danish agent and, in some cases, re-examined.[78] The oral statements and replies were heard from 14 to 16 March 1962.

The report of the commission, delivered at The Hague on 23 March 1962, is divided into three chapters, under the following headings: (a) facts leading up to the arrest of the *Red Crusader* and circumstances of the arrest; (b) events between the arrest of the *Red Crusader* and the meeting with the British naval vessels; (c) events after the meeting with the British naval vessels.

In Chapter One the commission relates that, having studied written material about the Faroes and having seen a number of photographs of the rocks, cliffs, and headlands on which double-angle measurements and radar distances-and-bearings were taken, it did not think it necessary to visit the scene where the arrest of the *Red Crusader* had taken place. The commission later analysed the results of the measurements taken by the crew of the *Niels Ebbesen* with regard to the positions of the *Red Crusader* and the Danish frigate at the time of the incident. A detailed examination was made of the accuracy of the different methods employed: double-angle measurements on landmarks, radar readings, and observations by a range-finder. The impression given by this part of the report is that the officers of the *Niels Ebbesen* were careful to

[77]Ibid., p. 5.
[78]Ibid.

keep the most detailed records of the positions of the two ships in order to be able eventually to justify their actions.[79]

As a result of its investigation of the facts leading up to the arrest of the *Red Crusader*, the commission found as follows:

(1) that no proof of fishing inside the blue line has been established, in spite of the fact that the trawl was in the water inside the blue line from about 21.00 hours until 21.14 hours on May 29, 1961;

(2) that the 'Red Crusader' was with her gear not stowed inside the blue line from about 21.00 hours until 21.14 hours on May 29, 1961;

(3) that the first signal to stop was given by 'Niels Ebbesen' at 21.39 hours and that this signal and the later stop-signals were all given outside the blue line.[80]

In Chapter Two, dealing with the events which occurred between the arrest of the *Red Crusader* and the meeting with the British naval vessels, the commission first described the visit of a fishery officer and a signalman from the Danish frigate to the *Red Crusader*. During the visit the fishery officer and Skipper Wood took radar measurements with a view to establishing the position of the trawler at the time of the arrest. The commission then described the discussions which took place on board the *Niels Ebbesen* between her commander, Captain Sølling, and Skipper Wood. During that conference, Captain Sølling informed the skipper that his trawler was under arrest and 'gave the reasons which, in his view, justified such arrest'. Skipper Wood denied that he had ever been fishing inside the blue line. The commission then noted the return of Skipper Wood, accompanied by the same fishery officer and signalman, and described the attempt of the *Red Crusader* to escape, as well as the treatment of the Danish officer and rating who were on board the trawler. There followed a detailed description of the shooting which, it is stated, took place in Danish territorial waters. (Denmark claims a three-mile zone of territorial waters.)

The findings of the commission on the events examined in Chapter Two were as follows:

(1) that the 'Red Crusader' was arrested. This conclusion is established by Captain Sølling's declarations as well as by the evidence given by Skipper

[79]Exhibit 16 presented by the Danish delegation was described as 'Sworn translation of tape-recording made on board *Niels Ebbesen* during pursuit of trawler, arrest and subsequent events on May 29 and 30, 1961, from approximately 20.53 hours on May 29' (35 *International law reports*, 489, n. 1).

Exhibits 3, 5, 6, & 8 presented to the commission by the Danish government comprised, respectively, 'Original notes concerning 7 double-angle measurements', 'Certified copy of form containing radar distances and bearings from *Niels Ebbesen to Red Crusader*', 'Chart No. 81 with positions plotted during action' and 'Radar plot made during action' (ibid., p. 491).

The commission does not refer in Ch. One of its report to any records on board the *Red Crusader*. In Ch. Two, it is stated that at the time when two members of the Danish crew first visited the *Red Crusader*, no positions or indications relevant to the incident of 29 May were plotted on the skipper's chart.

[80]For the legal significance of the third finding, see E. Lauterpacht, p. 51.

Wood. Even if the Skipper formally denied his guilt, his answers clearly implied that he considered at the time that he had been duly arrested for illegal fishing. Notes made in the Skipper's red pocket-book (Annex 12 to the British Counter-Memorial) and the 'Red Crusader's' log-book also leave no doubt on that point.

(2) that Skipper Wood, after having obeyed for a certain time the order given him by Captain Sølling, changed his mind during the trip to Thorshavn and put into effect a plan concerted with his crew, whereby he attempted to escape and to evade the jurisdiction of an authority which he had at first rightly, accepted.

(3) that, during this attempt to escape, the Skipper of the 'Red Crusader' took steps to seclude Lieutenant Bech and Corporal Kropp during a certain period and had the intention to take them to Aberdeen.

(4) that, in opening fire at 03.22 hours up to 03.53 hours, the Commanding Officer of the 'Niels Ebbesen' exceeded legitimate use of armed force on two counts: (*a*) firing without warning of solid gun-shot;[81] (*b*) creating danger to human life on board the 'Red Crusader' without proved necessity, by the effective firing at the 'Red Crusader' after 03.40 hours.

The escape of the 'Red Crusader' in flagrant violation of the order received and obeyed, the seclusion on board the trawler of an officer and rating of the crew of 'Niels Ebbesen', and Skipper Wood's refusal to stop may explain some resentment on the part of Captain Sølling. Those circumstances, however, cannot justify such a violent action.

The Commission is of the opinion that other means should have been attempted, which, if duly persisted in, might have finally persuaded Skipper Wood to stop and revert to the normal procedure which he himself had previously followed.

(5) that the cost of the repair of the damage caused by the firing at and hitting of the 'Red Crusader' submitted by the British Government has been considered reasonable by the Danish Agent.

In Chapter Three, dealing with the events after the meeting with the British naval vessels, the commission stated that in an aide-mémoire of the Danish government of 2 June 1961, as well as in the Danish counter-memorial, certain officers of the British navy were criticized for interfering with the lawful authority exercised by the *Niels Ebbesen* over a trawler which she had legitimately arrested. The criticisms related first to the circumstances of the return to the *Niels Ebbesen* of the boarding party put on the *Red Crusader*, and secondly to the question of interference by HMS *Troubridge* with an attempt by the *Niels Ebbesen* to return the boarding party to the *Red Crusader*. In the course of the proceedings the Danish delegation withdrew all the allegations on both points.[82]

[81]This solid gun-shot did not hit the *Red Crusader*. The commission notes in Ch. Three of its report that the first two gun shots, as well as the first two machine-gun shots, were intended to be warning shots to stop, and were not aimed at hitting the *Red Crusader*. It was from 03.40 hours only that fire was aimed directly at the *Red Crusader*.

[82]The correspondent of *The Times* in Copenhagen reported on 31 May 1961 that, according to the Danish authorities, the prize crew left the *Red Crusader* against the wish of the *Niels Ebbesen*'s commander, and allegedly under false pretences (*The Times*, 1 June 1961). On that point, the commission notes that some misunderstanding arose on

The finding of the commission with regard to the events involving the British naval vessels was 'that Commander Griffiths and the other Officers of the British Royal Navy made every effort to avoid any recourse to violence between 'Niels Ebbesen' and 'Red Crusader'. Such an attitude and conduct were impeccable.'

The commission's report was published simultaneously in London and Copenhagen on 30 March 1962. The rapidity and simultaneity of publication have been considered as showing that both governments were equally satisfied with the commission's findings.[83]

On the day following the publication of the report, the diplomatic correspondent of *The Times* wrote, under the title 'Both Sides in the Wrong', that neither of the two governments was prepared to say what further steps would be taken by them on the report. Since the incident, however, both governments had done their best to 'take the heat out of an incident which could yet arouse emotional overtones on both sides'.[84]

Soon afterwards, on 4 April 1962, the Lord Privy Seal said in the House of Commons: 'In accordance with the agreement for reference to the commission, Her Majesty's Government accept its findings as final.'[85] Nevertheless, it took nearly a year for the United Kingdom and Danish governments to reach agreement on the final settlement of the incident—by a mutual waiver of all claims. This agreement was summed up on 23 January 1963 by the British joint under-secretary of state for foreign affairs as follows:

Her Majesty's Government and the Danish Government have now completed their consultation about the report of the commission of inquiry into the incidents affecting the Scottish trawler *Red Crusader* at the end of May 1961. In their desire to remove a source of disagreement between them, the two Governments have decided that the incident should be settled by a mutual waiver of all claims and charges arising out of the incident. These waivers enter into effect forthwith. The owners of the trawler have concurred in this settlement.

As a result, Skipper Wood and the *Red Crusader* are free to enter Danish waters without fear of arrest in relation to the events of May 1961, and the owners' claim for compensation has been dropped. The two Governments consider that the incident can now be considered closed, though without prejudice to the view on points of law maintained by each Government.[86]

board the *Red Crusader* at the moment of embarking in HMS *Troubridge*'s boat. Whatever its cause, the commission felt that the return of the boarding party to the Danish frigate was in fact the best solution: nothing would have been gained by the taking to Aberdeen of a Danish naval officer and a Danish rating on board a British trawler which had escaped from the jurisdiction of the Danish and Faroese authorities (see report of the commission, p. 23).

[83]See 'Chronique des faits internationaux', 66 *RGDIP* (1962), 598.

[84]*The Times*, 31 Mar. 1962.

[85]657 HC Deb., Written Answers, col. 43; 35 *International law reports*, 500.

[86]670 HC Deb., Written Answers, cols 77–8; 35 *International law reports*, 500.
On 28 Apr. 1962, shortly after the publication of the commission's report, the Danish

Conclusions. The most remarkable feature of the *Red Crusader* case is the judicial character of the inquiry, as reflected in the composition of the commission, its procedure, and its findings. While we had no hesitation in describing the *Tavignano*, *Tiger*, and *Tubantia* cases as examples of the application of genuine inquiry, because the examination and findings of the respective commissions were confined to the facts in dispute,[87] the same cannot be said of the present case. Although the commission was charged with investigating and reporting the 'facts', 'circumstances', and 'incidents' (above, pp. 185–6), it chose to give findings not only on facts but also in law. Thus, as pointed out by E. Lauterpacht (p. 53), Skipper Wood's action in accepting arrest was described by the adverb 'rightly' (above, p. 190)—which could carry with it the implication that even if the arrest were ultimately to be wrongful in terms of international law, the skipper was bound to accept the assertion of Danish jurisdiction involved in his arrest.

More explicitly, the commission held that, in opening fire at a certain time, the commanding officer of the *Niels Ebbesen* 'exceeded legitimate use of armed force' on two counts: firing without warning of solid gunshot, and creating danger to human life on board the *Red Crusader* without proven necessity. These findings express the view of the commissioners that the commander committed an unlawful act, i.e. violated international law. In this sense one should also interpret the commission's statement that the escape of the *Red Crusader* and the seclusion of the Danish officer and rating 'cannot justify such a violent action' (above, p. 190). It will be recalled that in our analysis of the Dogger Bank case we envisaged that the term 'justified' as employed by an inquiry commission may not necessarily have a legal meaning, in the sense of compliance with international law. In the present case and in the above context, the expression 'cannot justify' is certainly used in terms of a violation of international law. The same considerations are valid with regard to the finding that the attitude and conduct of the British officers involved 'were impeccable' (above, p. 191).

We have the authoritative evidence of Professor Charles De Visscher, the president of the commission, that he and his colleagues made findings on legal questions. The terms of reference themselves, he

government gave notice to the UK government of its termination of the agreement of 1959 (*The Times*, 30 Apr. 1962). The Faroese authorities insisted that the exclusion of British fishermen from the 12-mile zone would take effect from 28 Apr. 1963, i.e. one year after the termination of the agreement, while the Danish government, being anxious to reduce the difficulties vis-à-vis the UK, preferred the exclusion to take effect from 12 Mar. 1964, the date of expiry of the transitional period of three years laid down in the agreement between the UK and Iceland of 11 Mar. 1961 (see above, p. 184, n. 74). Negotiations on the subject between the UK and Danish governments took place in Feb. 1963, without result. On 5 Apr. 1963 the Danish government communicated to the UK government its decision to put the 12-mile rule into effect as from 12 Mar. 1964. The new regime was accordingly introduced on that date (see 'Chronique des faits internationaux', 67 *RGDIP* (1963), 621–2, & 68 *RGDIP* (1964), 729).

[87]These facts undoubtedly entailed legal implications.

writes,[88] implied that the commission could not confine itself to the ascertainment of facts. From the depositions of written documents and during the oral procedure, which took place in authentically judicial forms, the parties were seeking, through the facts, a decision in law. It was a clarification of the juridical nature of the facts that the two governments expected from the commission. The questions put by the parties, especially with regard to the facts and incidents after the arrest of the *Red Crusader*, evidently related to 'la correction ou l'incorrection' of the conduct of the skipper on the one hand, and the commander of the Danish frigate on the other. Not only, states De Visscher, was there no objection by the parties to this broad conception of the powers of the commission, but it was at their instigation that the commission placed itself on a plane which led it from mere ascertainment of facts to an appreciation of their lawful or unlawful nature. The conclusions of the report, which revealed that both sides had committed offences, furnished the two governments with the basis of a satisfactory final settlement.

The composition of the *Red Crusader* Commission represents an innovation as regards both the qualifications of the commissioners and their countries of origin. Of the five cases concerning naval incidents analysed in this study, the *Red Crusader* case is the first in which the majority of the commissioners were jurists. The choice of commissioners, none of whom was a national of a party to the dispute, was made to ensure to the greatest possible extent an 'impartial and conscientious investigation'.[89] It is significant that in a dispute which involved, i.a. the propriety of the behaviour of naval units on both sides, Denmark and the United Kingdom—unlike the parties in the earlier cases—put their trust in a quasi-judicial inquiry commission composed entirely of non-nationals. It would seem that, as suggested by Timsit, the two countries had taken note of the frequent criticism that national commissioners vote uniformly in favour of their own countries rather than on the basis of the merits of the case.[90]

The proceedings of the commission were clearly divided into written and oral. The written proceedings consisted of the simultaneous exchange of written memorials and, at a later date, counter-memorials. Additional documents were to be admitted 'upon reasonable notice'.[91]

The oral proceedings consisted in the successive examination of Danish witnesses and experts and British witnesses and an expert, followed by oral statements and replies by the representatives of the parties. Contrary to Article 26 of the Hague Convention of 1907, the

---

[88]*Aspects récents du droit procédural de la Cour Internationale de Justice* (1966), pp. 215–16. See also, by the same author, *Théories et réalités en droit international public*, 4th edn (1970), pp. 372–3.

[89]Art. 9 of the Hague Convention of 1907.

[90]'Le fonctionnement de la procédure d'enquête dans l'affaire du "Red Crusader" ', *AFDI, 1963*, pp. 464–5.

[91]See report of the commission, p. 3.

examination of the witnesses was not conducted by the president, but mainly by the representatives of the parties. The members of the commission confined themselves to examining some of the witnesses, and this only on certain points.[92] The commission adopted the Anglo-American system of cross-examination.[93] In this connection, it will be recalled that questions of internal procedure were discussed by the commission with the agents of the parties.

The parties decided to deviate from the provisions of Article 34 of the 1907 Convention, which stipulates that the report of the commission be read at a public sitting. Instead, they laid down in paragraph (*g*) (ii) of the exchange of notes of 15 November 1961 that the question of the subsequent publication of the proceedings should be decided by agreement between the two governments (above, p. 186). This provision is relevant in particular to the publication of the report. As *The Times* of 19 March 1962 put it: '[The report] will be submitted to the British and Danish Governments, who will decide whether to publish it.' We have noted earlier that the prompt publication of the report has been regarded as signifying the satisfaction of both governments with the findings of the commission. Presumably, if the commissioners had held that the conduct of the British officers was not above reproach, the United Kingdom would have been reluctant to agree to the publication of the report. The Danish consent to publication may be explained by the fact that the fault of the commander of the *Niels Ebbesen* was balanced, as it were, by the unequivocal violations of Danish jurisdiction on the part of the skipper of the *Red Crusader*.

As regards the effect of the report, the exchange of notes provided, in paragraph (*h*) that 'The two Governments shall accept as final the findings of the commission.' Here again, the agreement for inquiry does not follow the parallel Article 35 of the Hague Convention which lays down that the report of the commission is limited to a statement of facts, that it has in no way the character of an award, and that it leaves the parties entire freedom as to the effect to be given to the statement.[94] The parties did not go as far as their predecessors in the *Tiger* case, who accepted in advance the findings of the report as binding (above, p. 160). Nevertheless, the effect in both cases is the same, in the sense that the United Kingdom and Denmark accepted in advance the conclusions of the commission. (This would mean that the two governments undertook not to challenge these conclusions in the event of future judicial proceedings connected with the same case.) They thus confirmed the

---

[92]See Timsit, p. 468.

[93]See report of the commission, p. 5.

[94]A comparative analysis of the 1907 Convention and the exchange of notes of 1961 shows that the draftsmen of the latter formulated the various provisions on the basis of the convention, deciding in each case whether or not to adopt the relevant rule of the convention. For instance, provisions (*g*) (ii), (*h*) and (*i*) of the exchange of notes deal respectively with the same matters as Arts 34, 35, & 36 of the convention.

theoretical postulate that in bilateral inquiry the findings on the facts are final.[95]

However, the findings in the *Red Crusader* report do not have the character of an award, which constrains the parties to a definite line of action. Thus, it did not follow from the finding concerning the fishing in forbidden waters that legal action had to be taken against the skipper of the *Red Crusader*, or that the United Kingdom had to compensate Denmark for the unlawful act committed by her national. In fact, the two governments agreed, through diplomatic negotiations, that Skipper Wood and the *Red Crusader* were free to enter Danish waters without fear of arrest in connection with the events of May 1961 (above, p. 191). In this sense, although accepting the findings as final the parties were free—to use the language of Article 35 of the Convention of 1907—'as to the effect to be given' to the findings.

The freedom of action of the parties was also expressed in the matter of the possible payment of compensation. The commission confined itself to stating that the Danish agent considered reasonable the estimate submitted by the British government for the repair of the damage caused to the *Red Crusader*. This statement might be regarded as a hint on the part of the commission that compensation for the damage ought to be made,[96] or as an appraisal intended to enable the parties to evaluate the degree of seriousness of the various acts committed on both sides. However that may be, the parties, being free as to the effect to be given to the conclusions of the commission, agreed, with the concurrence of the owners, that the claim for compensation would be waived (above, p. 191).

Our final observation relates to the suitability of employing commissions of inquiry in disputes which, though causing considerable tension, do not endanger peaceful relations between the parties. In our comments on the *Tiger* case we expressed the view that the Hague method of inquiry might be particularly appropriate in such circumstances. The *Red Crusader* case seems to confirm this postulate. Two traditionally friendly countries, members of the same military alliance, searching for a speedy way to settle their dispute (above, pp. 179 & 183), found that the setting up of a commission of inquiry would be the most suitable method of meeting the exigencies of the situation. The commission lived up to their expectations by providing them with the basis for a satisfactory settlement.

---

[95]Cf. above, pp. 42–3 and 179. It is conceivable that, in agreeing that the findings of the commission should be final, the parties were influenced by their expectation that a commission composed of jurists would authoritatively settle any legal issues which might arise (cf. above, pp. 192–3).

[96]See to this effect Timsit, p. 471.

CONCLUSIONS

In the cumulative observations which follow the presentation of each individual case we have discussed most of the main issues arising from the application of the 1907 system of inquiry. By way of overall review it may be pointed out that, despite the limited resort to commissions of inquiry, the system proved its value and its potentialities. The Hague method of inquiry was found particularly appropriate in the solution of disputes arising from incidents at sea, when the governments involved were in possession of conflicting information. The same method can also be employed in connection with incidents which take place in remote border areas, or in the air.

Like the single resort to an inquiry commission in conformity with the 1899 Convention (the Dogger Bank case), the four cases analysed in the present chapter show that the parties concerned made certain departures from the letter of the 1907 Convention. However, they did not go so far as to charge the respective commissions explicitly with the establishment of responsibilities. It is nevertheless significant that in the last case examined—that of the *Red Crusader*—the commission went beyond the task of mere fact-finding by adopting certain supplementary findings in law. This extension of powers should not lead to the conclusion that the method of fact-finding cannot be applied independently of other methods. The analysis of the three preceding cases would not support such a conclusion. And even the *Red Crusader* case provides ample evidence of the beneficent possibilities of the exclusive use of fact-finding. In that case the main preoccupation of the commission was to determine a 'material' fact. Had the dispute been confined to a difference of opinion on the question whether the *Red Crusader* was fishing in forbidden waters, the commission would have performed a purely fact-finding task, and its thorough and conscientious examination would certainly have assisted the parties in reaching a final settlement.

It is submitted that the *Red Crusader* Commission could have accomplished its additional task of investigating the conduct of the Danish commander without reference to the legality or illegality of his actions, i.e. without going beyond the terms of reference of a genuine inquiry commission. Apparently, the commissioners had no qualms in this regard. Led by a prominent jurist, they did not consider that the formulation of supplementary legal findings was inconsistent with the nature of a commission established on the Hague model.

The practice of the five international commissions of inquiry analysed in this study indicates the following variations as regards their competence and the nature of their reports:

(1) Explicit competence to ascertain the facts, coupled with the power to make findings in law; report on facts formulated in non-legal terms with clear legal implications (Dogger Bank).

(2) Explicit competence confined to the ascertainment of facts; report on facts whose legal implication is clear (*Tavignano, Tiger, Tubantia*).

(3) Explicit competence confined to the ascertainment of facts; report containing findings on facts whose legal implication is clear, coupled with findings in law (*Red Crusader*).

A fourth possibility may be postulated, i.e. explicit competence to ascertain the facts coupled with the power to make findings in law; report containing findings on facts whose legal implication is clear and findings in law. This model, which is a combination of the first and third variations, would signify that neither the commission nor the parties had any reason to conceal their wish to clarify certain legal points.

It follows that the commissions of inquiry established so far by the parties to a dispute can be divided into two main categories: first, genuine commissions of inquiry with exclusively fact-finding powers, as envisaged in the Convention of 1907; and secondly, commissions with dual fact-finding and judicial powers. Our examination has shown that the practice adopted in different instances has depended on the particular circumstances of the case. From the theoretical point of view it would seem that the only justification for designating the second category of commissions as commissions of inquiry would be their predominantly fact-finding task. The parties to an essentially legal dispute who do not wish to have recourse to judicial proceedings may find it expedient to resort to a commission of conciliation rather than a commission of inquiry.

CHAPTER 7

Inquiry in the Work of
Commissions of Conciliation

INTRODUCTORY NOTE

In an article published in 1957, Professor Henri Rolin drew the attention of the governments and national assemblies of the Council of Europe to 'une procédure un peu oubliée des hommes d'Etat, à savoir l'enquête et la conciliation'.[1] The procedure of conciliation, he went on, constitutes the synthesis of two distinct procedures mentioned in the Hague Convention of 1899: mediation[2] and inquiry. The synthesis was effected in 1920 when the commissions which the Hague Convention had envisaged for inquiry were given the task of mediation. From that time onwards the task of mediation took the name of conciliation, while inquiry came to be mentioned only occasionally and in a subordinate capacity.

In the course of our examination of treaties of conciliation, we have attempted to discover how various draftsmen conceived the above synthesis of inquiry and conciliation. It emerged that, while the first treaties were based on the conception of a two-stage process, i.e. inquiry into all aspects of the dispute (enlarged inquiry) followed by efforts to reconcile the parties, later treaties did not envisage inquiry as a necessary preliminary stage to conciliation. We have noted, in addition, that when inquiry and conciliation were envisaged in different treaties, the relative importance given to each varied according to the intentions of the contracting parties.

The purpose of the present chapter is to ascertain, in the light of the practice of conciliation commissions and the theoretical discussions following that practice, what is the present conception of the function of inquiry in the process of conciliation. We shall first analyse, by way of example, the work of one 'commission of inquiry and conciliation' and three 'commissions of conciliation'. Thereafter it is proposed to examine the doctrine on the subject, as expressed primarily in the discussions of the Institute of International Law in the years 1959–61.

---

[1]See 'L'heure de la conciliation comme mode de règlement pacifique des litiges', in *Ann. européen*, iii (1957), p. 3.

[2]Rolin defines mediation as the interposition of a third party who takes part in the negotiations between the states in conflict, directs them, and suggests bases of agreement which the parties are free to accept or reject (ibid., p. 4).

THE CHACO COMMISSION, 1929

This commission (to be distinguished from the Chaco Commission set up by the League of Nations in 1933) dealt with frontier incidents of a nature particularly suitable for settlement by a commission of inquiry. The incidents took place in the Chaco Boreal, over whose sovereignty Bolivia and Paraguay had a long-standing dispute. According to Bolivia, the main incident developed in the following manner.[3]

On 5 December 1928 a large force of Paraguayan soldiers proceeded towards the Bolivian Fortin[4] Vanguardia. A cavalryman, bearing a white flag, entered the fort and was conducted before the two officers in charge. Since the Paraguayan troops continued to close in on the fort and isolated shots were heard, the Bolivian officer in command warned them to stop with the conventional cry of 'halt'. The call went unheeded by the Paraguayan forces, who continued their advance. The officer repeated his order to halt, this time followed by a shot, and again it went unheeded. The invading troops opened intensive rifle fire on the garrison of the fort, which returned the fire, despite its clear numerical inferiority. After a short fight, the Paraguayan troops, who had meanwhile surrounded the Bolivian garrison, captured the fort. Five Bolivian soldiers were killed, and the two officers as well as nineteen soldiers were taken prisoner. The Paraguayan troops demolished the barracks and houses of the fort and abandoned the place. The manner in which the attack was carried out showed, in the view of the Bolivian government, that it was the result of a premeditated plan made by the Paraguayan General Staff.

According to Paraguay,[5] a Paraguayan military detachment stationed in Fortin Galpón discovered one day that a Bolivian fort, called Vanguardia, had been set up in the vicinity.[6] A courier was dispatched shortly afterwards to request the garrison to evacuate the post. Far from heeding the message conveyed by him, the Bolivians took him prisoner. In view of this attitude, the troops of Fortin Galpón advanced towards Fortin Vanguardia for the purpose of reiterating the demand that the garrison withdraw. This time they were received with a volley of fire by the Bolivians, and a battle ensued. Finally, the intruders fled from

---

[3]See Preliminary Statement of Bolivia in *Proceedings of the Commission of Inquiry and Conciliation, Bolivia and Paraguay, March 13, 1929–September 13, 1929* (1929) (hereinafter referred to as *Proceedings*), pp. 190 ff.

[4]A *fortin* was described in the Bolivian preliminary statement as 'an observation post which colonizing troops occupy for the purpose of protecting civilized men against the dreadful invasions of savages or the depredations of cattle thieves'. It is far from being a fortification in the military and proper sense of the word. On the contrary, it is virtually a skeleton post the garrison of which, always scant, is hardly sufficient for defence against acts of aggression by regular troops (*Proceedings*, p. 192).

[5]See Memorial of Paraguay (ibid., pp. 516 ff.).

[6]Bolivia claimed that Fortin Vanguardia had been in existence for a long time (ibid., p. 442).

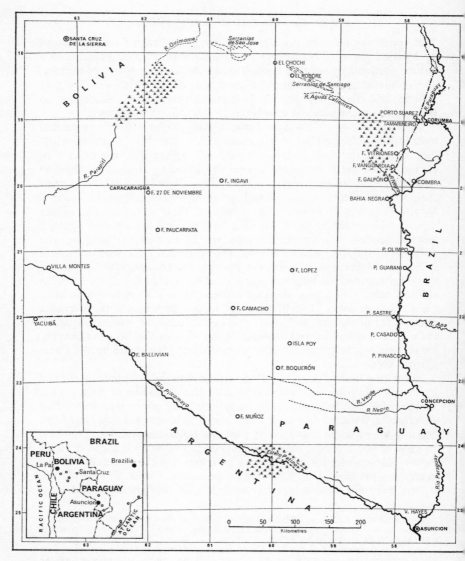

5 The Chaco Boreal

(Based on the maps appended to the report of the League of Nations Chaco Commission (LN Doc. C. 154. M. 64. 1934. VII). The small inset map has been added.)

Vanguardia, leaving some soldiers lying dead in the entrenchments and taking others prisoner.

Each of the parties claimed that Fortin Vanguardia was situated in its own territory (below, p. 206).

Two days after the incident, on 7 December 1928, the government of Paraguay invoked the Gondra treaty of 1923. On the same day the Paraguayan minister for foreign affairs wrote to his Bolivian opposite number as follows:

In view of the bloody conflict which has taken place between Paraguayan and Bolivian forces in the neighborhood of Fortin Galpón, provoked by the latter, and of other recent events which reveal the existence on the part of Bolivia of an aggressive purpose against Paraguay, my Government being desirous of placing beyond any doubt the correctness of its conduct and its always conciliatory aims and, at the same time, of showing its respectful and loyal deference to international duties entered into, has instructed me to inform Your Excellency's Government that under this date it has addressed the Foreign Office of Uruguay with the purpose of causing the meeting of the Commission of Inquiry, provided for in Article 2 of the Treaty to avoid or prevent conflicts between the American States, signed at Santiago, on May 3, 1923, and which has been ratified by Paraguay and Bolivia.[7]

Bolivia's reaction was immediate and abrupt: next day she severed diplomatic relations with Paraguay. In a circular dated 9 December 1928[8] to Bolivian legations, the Ministry for Foreign Affairs explained that the procedure proposed by Paraguay was useless and ill timed. It was not possible that 'the very country which was the aggressor should invoke the intervention of a court of conciliation intended to prevent the conflict and not to remedy it'. No country could submit, even to the highest tribunal in the world, the sacred attributes of sovereignty, and the nation's dignity. For these reasons, it was stated, Bolivia was forced to suspend diplomatic relations with Paraguay until 'the reparation for the outrage and the apologies to which she is entitled are forthcoming'.

On 7 December 1928 the president of the Montevideo permanent commission, operating under the Gondra treaty, invited the government of Bolivia to designate the persons 'who shall make her share' of the membership of the commission of inquiry.[9] In its answer of 11 December, the government declared, i.a., that

the notoriously uncalled-for, surprising and violent aggression on the Bolivian Fortin Vanguardia, by the regular forces of the Paraguayan army, has brought about a *de facto* situation which jeopardizes the sovereignty, the honor and the dignity of Bolivia and which renders indispensable and justifies an absolute apology of the aggressor nation prior to any suggestions.[10]

[7]Ibid., p. 444.   [8]See text, ibid., p. 448.
[9]Ibid., pp. 447, 448.   [10]Ibid., p. 453.

On 12 December the president of the permanent commission wrote to the Bolivian legation in Montevideo as follows:

... We are in total ignorance as to the way in which [the events] may have come about, whether they occurred in the part of the disputed territory occupied by Bolivians or in that held by the Paraguayans, as well as the form which the aggression took and with whom it may have originated. Only the operation of the Commission of Inquiry provided for in the Gondra convention, and the report rendered by individuals of honorable and unblemished character who would no doubt constitute it, would allow us to know with accuracy where the responsibilities for the events belong.[11]

During the next few days Bolivian forces attacked Paraguayan forts and dropped bombs without detonators on the Paraguayan town of Bahia Negra. On 16 December they occupied Fortin Lopez, and on 18 December Fortin Boquerón, taking some prisoners. Fortin Lopez was subsequently abandoned, but the Bolivian troops remained in Fortin Boquerón. The Paraguayan forts were occupied, according to the Bolivian government, with the object of frustrating the aggressive plans of Paraguay and of exercising a legitimate act of reprisal for the aggression committed at Vanguardia. The dropping of bombs on Bahia Negra was merely a demonstration.[12]

The above events took place at the time when the Conference of American States which supplemented the Gondra treaty with the General Convention of Inter-American Conciliation, was meeting in Washington. It was natural for the conference to offer its good offices to the disputing parties, with a view to reaching a settlement. A special committee of the conference was charged on 10 December 1928 with the duty of promoting conciliation. The Bolivian and Paraguayan governments accepted the good offices of the conference and, on 3 January 1929, the representatives of the two countries signed, in the presence of the chairman of the conference, Mr Frank Kellogg, secretary of state, a protocol for the establishment of a commission of inquiry and conciliation.[13]

In the Preamble the signatories expressed their wish that 'a commission of investigation and conciliation establish the facts which have caused the recent conflicts which have unfortunately occurred'. There is no mention of any conciliatory function of the commission. In the operative part of the protocol the two governments agreed as follows:

[11]Ibid., p. 457.
[12]Ibid., pp. 930–2.
[13]For the text of the protocol see, ibid., p. 1, and 23 *AJIL* (1929), 98. According to the US minister in Paraguay, in view of the threatening Bolivian advances the government of Paraguay authorized its representatives in Washington to sign the protocol although it was certain that investigation of the incidents would not lead to conciliation and lasting peace. The government felt that until the entire Chaco question was solved, Paraguay would be insecure and peace would be undermined. See two telegrams of 30 Dec. 1928 from the US minister in Paraguay to the secretary of state (*FRUS, 1929*, i (1943), pp. 826–7).

First. To organize a commission of investigation and conciliation which shall be composed as follows:

(*a*) Two delegates each from the Governments of Bolivia and Paraguay, and

(*b*) One delegate appointed by the Governments of each of the following five American Republics: United States of America, Mexico, Colombia, Uruguay and Cuba.

All the said delegates, once they have entered upon the discharge of their duties, shall remain in office until the procedure contemplated in this protocol is carried out, except in the case of proven illness. In case of said illness or because of any other reason of *force majeure*, the incapacitated delegate shall be replaced, as soon as possible, by the government of his nation.

Second. The commission of investigation and conciliation shall undertake to investigate, by hearing both sides, what has taken place, taking into consideration the allegations set forth by both parties, and determining in the end, which of the parties has brought about a change in the peaceful relations between the two countries.

Third. The commission shall fulfill its mission within the period of six months from the date of its organization.

Fourth. The procedure of the investigation shall be that agreed upon by the commission itself.

Fifth. Once the investigation has been carried out, the commission shall submit proposals and shall endeavour to settle the incident amicably under conditions which will satisfy both parties.

If this should not be possible, the commission shall render its report setting forth the result of its investigation and the efforts made to settle the incident.

Sixth. The commission is empowered, in case it should not be able to effect conciliation, to establish both the truth of the matter investigated and the responsibilities which, in accordance with international law, may appear as a result of its investigation.

Seventh. The commission shall begin its labours in Washington.

Eighth. The Governments of Bolivia and Paraguay bind themselves to suspend all hostilities and to stop all concentration of troops at the points of contact of the military outposts of both countries, until the commission renders its findings; the commission of investigation and conciliation shall be empowered to advise the parties concerning measures designed to prevent a recurrence of hostilities.

Ninth. It is understood that the procedure contained in this protocol does not include nor affect the territorial question, as contended by Bolivia, and the boundaries, as contended by Paraguay, which exists between both countries, nor does it include or affect the agreements in force between them.

Tenth. The high contracting parties reiterate their firm purpose of having said controversy settled, in any event, by juridical means and in perfect peace and friendship between the two countries.

The protocol envisaged two clearly distinguished stages in the work of the commission. In the first stage the commission was bound to ('shall') investigate the facts and to determine, in effect, which of the parties was responsible for the armed incidents. During the second stage, i.e. after 'the investigation has been carried out', the commission was to submit proposals and endeavour to settle the dispute amicably. (The word 'incident' seems to have been used in the protocol in the sense of 'dispute').

If the attempt at conciliation should fail, the commission had to render a report setting forth the results of its investigation and the efforts made to settle the dispute. This provision was mandatory. In the same contingency the commission might, in addition, establish the truth of the matter investigated and the legal responsibilities which the investigation had revealed.

It appears that the intention of the parties was that independently of any efforts at conciliation, the commission must investigate the facts. If, on the basis of the investigation, a conciliation was effected, it would not be necessary to make a report on the facts. If, however, conciliation was not achieved, such a report would be necessary. In the latter case the commission might, if it deemed it expedient, act in a quasi-judicial capacity[14] by reporting both on the facts and on the legal issues involved.

The powers of the commission were limited to ascertaining the causes and consequences of the recent armed incidents. The broad territorial dispute over the Chaco Boreal, which had been the subject of a centuries-long controversy and numerous agreements, was specifically excluded from the competence of the commission.[15]

The commission established in pursuance of the protocol of 3 January 1929 was composed of 9 members, 2 of whom were chosen by the government of Bolivia, 2 by the government of Paraguay, and the remaining 5, generally known as the neutral commissioners, by the governments of 5 other American states. The Bolivian 'delegation' consisted of the two commissioners, a legal adviser, a military attaché, and an attaché, while the Paraguayan 'delegation' comprised the two commissioners, a secretary, and a counsellor. Mr Walter Bruce Howe acted as counsellor to the commission. Neither of the parties appointed an agent. The role of agents was assumed by the national commissioners, who presented orally and in writing the arguments of their respective governments and conducted, on their behalf, negotiations with the neutral commissioners.

The secretariat-general consisted of a secretary-general, two secretaries holding the rank of captain, a Spanish secretary, special legal assistant, press liaison officer, editor, translator, fiscal and distributing officer, an archivist and three stenographers.[16]

Between 20 March and 13 September 1929 the commission held ten

[14]See Hyde, 10 *BYIL*, 107 f.

[15]For the background to the Chaco dispute and for the activities of the League inquiry commission in 1933 and 1934 see LN, *Dispute between Bolivia and Paraguay; report of the Chaco Commission*, LN Doc. C. 154. M. 64. 1934. VII.

[16]For the composition of the commission and of the secretariat-general see *Proceedings* pp. 5–7.

'formal' and a number of 'informal' meetings.[17] At its first meeting, chaired by Mr Kellogg, the commission elected the US commissioner, Brigadier General Frank Ross McCoy, as permanent chairman of the commission. At the same meeting the US Chief Justice administered the 'Oath of Office'.[18] During its second meeting the commission approved a series of rules for the functioning of the secretariat-general[19] and discussed other organizational matters. It was decided that formal meetings of the commission would be public except when the commissioners decided otherwise, and that such sub-committees as might be appointed would meet privately. It was also decided that the informal meetings of the commission would not be held in public, and that whenever the commission might deem it advisable communiqués would be issued to the press on its activities and decisions.[20]

The third meeting of the commission was devoted to additional organizational matters. At its fourth meeting, held on 13 May 1929, the commission resolved to take over the negotiations for the repatriation of the Bolivian and Paraguayan soldiers captured by the two countries as a consequence of the events of December 1928. The chairman appointed a sub-commission on repatriation. During the same meeting the commission discussed the further armed clashes which had occurred in the zone of the destroyed Fortín Vanguardia. (According to the Bolivian government, a Bolivian detachment located in the zone was attacked on 4 May and a sentry was wounded.) The commission adopted a resolution stating that the governments of Bolivia and Paraguay should ensure that completely effective measures be taken to prevent any friction between their respective forces, and that they should issue categorical orders to that effect. The commission urged, in particular, that measures should be taken to preclude the possibility that subordinate commanders in the more inaccessible regions of the Chaco 'jeopardize the successful and pacific settlement of the matters now pending between the said Governments'. After the unanimous adoption of the resolution the incident of 4 May was 'by tacit assent' considered closed.[21] This action of the commission was taken, it would seem, in accordance with point eight of the protocol of 3 January 1929, which laid down that the commission was to be empowered to advise the

[17]See summary records of the meetings, in *Proceedings*.

[18]The text of the oath ran as follows: 'You and each of you do solemnly swear or affirm that you will duly and faithfully perform the duties of your office as members of the Commission of Inquiry and Conciliation provided for by the Protocol between Bolivia and Paraguay of January 3, 1929. So help you God.' The commissioners answered: 'Juro', 'Prometo', or 'I do' (ibid., p. 15).

[19]See text ibid., pp. 17 f.

[20]As regards the attendance of secretaries and advisers at the meetings, it was decided that any commissioner desiring to be accompanied by them to private meetings should first secure the consent of the commission (or the sub-committee, as the case might be) (ibid., pp. 18 f.).

[21]Ibid., pp. 29–31.

parties concerning measures designed to prevent a recurrence of hostilities.

The delegations of Bolivia and Paraguay delivered their memorials on 4 April, and their replies on 16 May. At several meetings of the neutral commissioners with the two delegations separately, the delegations furnished such additional information as was requested for the purpose of elucidating various points in their respective memorials.[22]

In its memorial the Bolivian delegation expressed the hope that the case submitted to the study of 'this Commission of Inquiry' would be resolved in a manner which would not only satisfy Bolivia's 'outraged national honor' with reparation for damage suffered, but also in a way that would contribute to foster in the two countries a state of mind leading to the peaceful and final settlement of the Chaco problem.[23]

In the view of the Bolivian delegation it was indispensable, in order to ascertain the facts, to make an investigation on the spot. For that purpose, it proposed that a sub-committee inspect the territory of Fortin Vanguardia, verify its true geographical location, and hear the statements of the Bolivian officers and soldiers involved.[24]

The Paraguayan memorial contained, in addition to a description of the Vanguardia incident, general charges of secret penetration by Bolivian military forces in the Chaco Boreal 'populated by and in the possession of Paraguay under a just title'.

An interesting 'difference of opinion on points of fact'—to use the language of Article 9 of the 1907 Hague Convention—was revealed in the respective memorials and replies of the two delegations. Bolivia claimed that Fortin Vanguardia was not situated in the Chaco, but in territory never disputed by Paraguay. It lay to the north of the parallel of Bahia Negra and the course of the Otuquis River or Rio Negro— which marked the 'farthest limits of the Paraguayan claims to Bolivian territory'.[25] The Paraguayan delegation claimed, on its part, that Fortin Vanguardia lay south of the Otuquis River 'and therefore in territory under full Paraguayan jurisdiction'.[26] Both delegations asserted that a field survey could confirm their respective claims. However, the commission concentrated on other problems, preferring not to conduct an investigation on the spot.

At its fifth meeting, on 23 May, the commission worked out technical arrangements for the repatriation of the prisoners held by both parties.

During an informal meeting on 31 May, the chairman suggested, on behalf of the neutral commissioners, that the delegations of Bolivia and Paraguay, duly authorized by their respective governments, should empower the neutral commissioners to prepare and submit to them

[22]See report of the chairman of the commission to the US secretary of state in his capacity as successor to the chairman of the International Conference of American States on Conciliation and Arbitration (ibid., App. 5, pp. 176–81).

[23]Ibid., pp. 196–9.   [24]Ibid., pp. 196–7.   [25]Ibid., p. 961.   [26]Ibid., p. 1157.

such plans for a settlement of 'the fundamental question' as they might deem suitable. This procedure, he explained, did not imply the abandonment of the 'process of investigation' which was being conducted by the commission in pursuance of the protocol of 3 January 1929.[27] The two delegations undertook to consult their governments on the matter. (It will be recalled that under the protocol of 1929 the commission's task of submitting proposals was specifically confined to the incidents of December 1928. Moreover, the protocol expressly excluded the territorial question from the competence of the commission.)

At its sixth meeting, held on 17 June 1929, the commission exercised a purely fact-finding function by formulating, for its own information, a questionnaire for the examination of the detained officers and soldiers. Each of the persons to be repatriated was to be asked, i.a.: 'Why were you detained?'; 'How did the events which caused your detention occur?'; 'What part did you take in said occurrences?'; 'How do you happen to know what you have testified?'[28]

The examination of the prisoners was conducted in Argentina and Brazil under the supervision of 'neutral committees'[29] appointed by the commission. One Paraguayan officer and 12 soldiers were repatriated on 29 June 1929 from Formosa (Argentina), while 2 Bolivian officers and 19 soldiers were repatriated on 8 July 1929 from Corumbá (Brazil).[30]

At the seventh meeting, on 2 July 1929, the commission was informed of the answers given by the disputing governments to the suggestion regarding the settlement of the fundamental question. Both Bolivia and Paraguay agreed to the course proposed. In accepting the proposal that the neutral commissioners should 'offer suggestions . . . for the purpose of defining the territorial question', the Bolivian government expressed its understanding that the activities of investigation under the protocol of 3 January 1929 would proceed uninterruptedly, and that the proposals of the neutral commissioners bearing on the fundamental question would have an unofficial and informal character only and would be conducted outside the scope of the protocol.[31] The Paraguayan government, for its part, took the opportunity to assert that previous

[27]Ibid., pp. 62 & 178.

[28]Ibid., p. 53.

[29]The committees consisted of the military attaché of the US embassy in Argentina and a representative of the Argentine government on the one hand, and the military attaché of the US embassy in Brazil and a representative of the Brazilian government on the other.

On 25 May 1929 Secretary of State Stimson informed his representatives in Argentina and Brazil that the two governments would be asked to arrange for the taking of depositions in accordance with their respective civil procedures and under the supervision of the neutral committees. The duly designated representatives of Bolivia and Paraguay could be present at this time only as observers of the proceedings. Pending the handing of the repatriates to the representatives of their own governments and prior to the taking of their depositions, no unauthorized person was to be permitted access to them (see *FRUS, 1929* (1943), i. 855.

[30]*Proceedings*, pp. 130, 148–73, & 177.

[31]Ibid., p. 63.

governments of Paraguay had always made efforts definitively to determine the dividing line between the respective sovereignties of the two republics.[32] Acknowledging the receipt of these replies, the chairman of the commission affirmed that the task of the neutral commissioners with regard to the settlement of the fundamental question at issue was distinct from the work to be performed by the commission as a whole.[33]

From then on the commissioners operated within two frameworks. On the one hand the commission as a whole proceeded with its task as defined by the protocol of 3 January 1929; on the other hand the neutral commissioners endeavoured to deal with the root of the controversy.

At the eighth meeting, on 18 July 1929,[34] the Colombian commissioner was charged with studying and preparing the bases for the report which the commission might be called upon to render in pursuance of point five of the protocol, i.e. should the commission fail to settle the incident amicably, it must submit a report on the results of its investigation and the efforts to settle the incident. But this contingency did not arise, for at the ninth meeting, on 12 September 1929, the commission unanimously adopted a Resolution of Conciliation[35] which was entirely satisfactory to both parties. The Preamble of the resolution stated that, whereas the historical account of the facts revealed that the incident at Vanguardia preceded the events which took place in the Boquerón sector, and whereas the employment of coercive measures on the part of Paraguay in the Vanguardia incident caused the reaction of Bolivia, the governments of Bolivia and of Paraguay, at the unanimous suggestion of the neutral commissioners, had agreed upon the following:

1. Mutual forgiveness of the offenses and injuries caused by each of the Republics to the other;
2. Re-establishment of the state of things in the Chaco on the same footing as prior to December 5, 1928, though this does not signify in any way prejudgment of the pending territorial or boundary question; and
3. Renewal of their diplomatic relations.

It was also stated in the Preamble that the two governments had agreed to proceed to the re-establishment of the state of things which existed prior to 5 December 1928 through the restoration of Fortin Vanguardia by Paraguay to Bolivia and the evacuation of Fortin Boquerón by Bolivian troops.

The operative part of the resolution set out the decisions of the commission as follows:

1. To consider that conciliation of the Parties has been effected in the terms stipulated by the Protocol of January 3, 1929;

[32]Ibid., pp. 64–5.   [33]Letter of 2 July 1929 (ibid., p. 66).
[34]Ibid., p. 77.   [35]Ibid., pp. 79–81.

2. Likewise to acknowledge that the Parties being conciliated, the Commission, in accordance with the provisions of Article 6 of the said Protocol, has not established responsibilities;

3. To record its satisfaction at the lofty spirit of concord which has been shown by the Governments of Bolivia and Paraguay in removing the difficulty which arose from the incidents of the month of December, 1928;

4. To recommend earnestly to the Governments of Bolivia and of Paraguay that they carry out the conciliatory measures above set forth without delay; and

5. To ask the Government of Uruguay to be so kind as to designate two officers of its Army to proceed, with the consent of the Governments of Bolivia and of Paraguay, to Fortin Vanguardia and Fortin Boquerón, respectively, and to be present at the execution of the measures designed to restore the state of things which existed prior to December 5, 1928.

The return to the status quo ante was effected by virtue of an Act of 4 April 1930, signed by representatives of Bolivia, Paraguay, and Uruguay. On 23 July 1930 Forts Boquerón and Vanguardia were returned in the presence of Uruguayan officers.[36]

The efforts of the neutral commissioners to bring about a settlement of the fundamental territorial or boundary question were not successful. They made a careful study of the different aspects of the problem, with the unofficial advice of geographical, economic, and other experts, and suggested a plan for the direct settlement of the boundary dispute.[37] The plan was not accepted and the neutral commissioners concluded that it was not possible, for the time being, to reconcile the divergent views.[38]

Conclusions. The above examination of the activities of the Chaco Commission may enable us to assess the extent to which that commission exercised inquiry functions. Let us take as a basis the following passage of the chairman's report to the US secretary of state:

Under the provisions of the Protocol of January 3, the Commission was (1) *to investigate, by hearing both sides, what had taken place, taking into consideration the allegations set forth by both parties, and determining in the end which of the parties brought about a change in the peaceful relations between*

[36]See *FRUS, 1929*, i. 326–7. See also below, p. 211, n. 40.

[37]The commission's records do not reveal the nature of the plan.

[38]See report of the chairman to the secretary of state (*Proceedings*, pp. 179–80).

On 31 Aug. the chairman delivered to the delegations of Bolivia and Paraguay a draft Convention on Arbitration (ibid., App. 7), which did not meet with the approval of the parties. At the final meeting of the commission on 13 Sept., the neutral commissioners put on record their unanimous agreement to recommend their respective governments to proffer their friendly good offices to the parties in the event that these might be of service to them (ibid.).

For the attitude of the parties on the question of arbitration at that time see Woolsey, 'The Bolivia–Paraguay dispute', 24 *AJIL* (1930), 124–6. For a summary of subsequent developments and the settlement of the dispute by arbitration in 1938 see Hackworth, vi. 43–51.

the two countries; and (2) to submit proposals and to endeavour to settle the incident amicably under conditions which would satisfy both parties; (3) if this should not be possible, the Commission was to render its report setting forth the result of the investigation and the efforts made to settle the incident, and (4) the Commission was empowered, in case it should not be able to effect conciliation, to establish both the truth of the matter investigated and the responsibilities which, in accordance with International Law, might appear as a result of its investigation.

Having fulfilled the first duty, the Neutral Commissioners made all the efforts necessary to discharge the second, that is, to conciliate the parties. While the conversations to this end were under way, the Commission directed the drafting of the bases for the report it might be called upon to render in the eventuality contemplated by its third duty. The Delegations of Colombia and Uruguay each submitted drafts for that purpose.

Fortunately, the conciliatory action met with full success and in the Plenary Meeting of September 12, the Commission unanimously adopted a Resolution of Conciliation entirely satisfactory to both parties.

Conciliation, the second function of the Commission under the Protocol of January 3, having been effected, it became unnecessary to render the report and to establish the truth of the matter investigated and the responsibilities.

Thus was fulfilled the desire expressed during the International Conference of American States on Conciliation and Arbitration that, *whenever possible, conciliation be undertaken rather than proceeding to the investigation.* (Emphasis added.)[39]

This account is significant since, on the one hand it is stated that the investigation was completed while on the other hand, it is inferred that, in deference to a wish expressed during the Conference of American States, the commission did not proceed with an investigation (cf. above, pp. 129–30). How is this inconsistency to be explained?

According to the protocol of 3 January 1929, the commission was bound to investigate and to determine, as a result, which of the parties had brought about a change in their peaceful relations. With a view to arriving at its conclusions on the matter, the commission undoubtedly examined the voluminous material setting out the conflicting versions of the parties, as well as the evidence supplied by the prisoners. It appears that it reached the conclusion that Paraguay was responsible for the change in the peaceful relations. The commission, it seems, wished to avoid recording this conclusion in a categorical statement, since such action would have compromised its twofold effort at conciliation: a mutually acceptable settlement of the dispute arising from the military clashes and the overall territorial dispute. Instead, the commission expressed its findings on the incidents in a disguised form: it stated in the Preamble of the Resolution on Conciliation that the Vanguardia incident preceded the events which took place in the

[39]*Proceedings*, pp. 177 f.

Boquerón sector and that the 'employment of coercive measures' by Paraguay in the Vanguardia incident caused the reaction of Bolivia.

These findings of fact amounted to a vindication of the Bolivian case and were probably included in the resolution in order to assuage Bolivian 'outraged national honor' and to persuade Bolivia to waive her claim for reparations, to abandon Fortin Boquerón, and to agree to the renewal of diplomatic relations. On the other hand, it would seem that on the basis of its findings the commission exercised pressure on Paraguay to agree to what was in fact a formal, though mild, condemnation of her attack on Fortin Vanguardia.[40]

In this way the fact-finding function assisted the effort at conciliation. To achieve this complementary role, fact-finding was not carried out strictly in accordance with the 1907 Hague Convention. In particular, the commission found it expedient not to deliver a special report containing the results of its 'elucidation of the facts'. It is also conceivable that the commission did not conduct its investigation of the facts in the thorough manner envisaged by the Hague Convention. It was sufficient for the neutral commissioners to form such a general opinion on the responsibilities involved as would enable them to proceed with their conciliatory task.

THE FRANCO-SIAMESE COMMISSION, 1947

The dispute handled by this commission was of a purely political character. Siam requested the revision of its frontier with French Indo-China on ethnical, geographical, and economic grounds. France saw no reason for any changes in the frontier.

On 17 November 1946 the two countries signed an agreement for the submission of their dispute to a special conciliation commission. The composition, powers, and procedure of the commission were set out in Article 3 of the agreement, which reads as follows:

---

[40]The susceptibilities involved appear from the following: Paraguay agreed to rebuild Fortin Vanguardia, provided that this undertaking was not stipulated in the agreement of conciliation. The president of Paraguay told the US minister in Asunción that he regarded this condition as absolutely essential because of the danger of violent reactions against his government. See the telegram of 11 Sept. 1929 from the US minister in Paraguay to the US secretary of state: *FRUS, 1929*, i. 859.

During the protracted negotiations on the implementation of the conciliation agreement, Bolivia insisted that the terms of the agreement should be carried out in the order in which they were set forth, namely re-establishment of the status quo ante in the Chaco before the renewal of diplomatic relations, and restoration of the buildings of Fortin Vanguardia by Paraguay before the abandonment of Fortin Boquerón by Bolivia. In the view of Paraguay, on the other hand, there was nothing in the conciliation resolution from which it could logically be inferred that one obligation took preference over another. 'It is desired unduly to transform a resolution of purely conciliatory character into a penal resolution.' See the letter of 12 Dec. 1929 from the US chargé d'affaires in Uruguay to the secretary of state (ibid., *1930*, 1 (1945), p. 309), and the telegram of 8 Jan. 1930 from the US minister in Paraguay to the acting secretary of state (ibid., p. 312).

Aussitôt après la signature du présent accord, la France et le Siam constitueront, par application de l'article 21 du traité franco-siamois du 7 décembre 1937, une commission de conciliation composée de deux représentants des parties et de trois neutres conformément à l'Acte Général de Genève du 26 septembre 1928 pour le règlement pacifique des différends internationaux qui règle la constitution et le fonctionnement de la Commission. La Commission commencera ses travaux aussitôt que possible après que le transfert des territoires visés au deuxième paragraphe de l'article 1 aura été effectué. Elle sera chargée d'examiner les arguments ethniques, géographiques et économiques des parties en faveur de la révision ou de la confirmation des clauses du traité du 3 octobre 1893, de la convention du 13 février 1904 et du traité du 23 mars 1907 maintenues en vigueur par l'article 22 du traité du 7 décembre 1937.[41]

The powers ('les attributions') of the commission were defined in accordance with the provisions of the above article and the provisions of Chapter I of the General Act for the Pacific Settlement of International Disputes of 1928.[42]

The commission thus established consisted of the following members: Víctor Andrés Belaúnde (Mexico), ambassador, member of the Consultative Committee of Foreign Relations of Peru, president of the Catholic University of Lima and member of the Permanent Court of Arbitration; William Phillips (United States), formerly US ambassador to Italy and former under-secretary of state; Sir Horace Seymour (United Kingdom), formerly UK ambassador to China; Prince Wan Waithayakon (Siam), Siamese ambassador to the United States; and Paul Emile Naggiar (France), French ambassador *en mission*, formerly French ambassador to China and the Soviet Union.

France appointed Francis Lacoste, minister plenipotentiary, counsellor at the French embassy at Washington, as agent, and Jean Burnay, state counsellor, as counsel and deputy agent. Siam, on her part, appointed Prince Sakol Varavarn, former counsellor at the Ministry of the Interior, as agent, and Nai Tieng Sirikhanda, member of the Siamese National Assembly, as deputy agent.

The parties agreed that William Phillips should be president of the commission and that its seat should be in Washington.

Between 5 May and 27 June 1947 the commission held numerous 'plenary sessions' in the presence of the agents and experts of the parties. The first two meetings were devoted to organizational matters. M. Belaúnde was designated as rapporteur. French and English were

[41]This text is from the report of the commission of 27 June 1947, published in *La documentation française, notes documentaires et études*, No. 811, 23 Jan. 1948 (at p. 2).

In the course of the diplomatic negotiations, France proposed that the commission should examine the arguments and rule ('statuer') on the revision or maintenance of the treaty of 23 March 1907. The text adopted leaves each of the parties free with regard to the consequences of the commission's examination. See Bastid, 'La commission de conciliation franco-siamoise', in *Etudes en l'honneur de Georges Scelle*, i (1950), p. 8.

[42]See report of the commission, p. 1. Cf. below, App. II, p. 340.

adopted as the working languages of the commission. In accordance with Article 10 of the General Act, it was decided that the work of the commission would not be conducted in public. Minutes taken at meetings attended by the agents could be transmitted to the parties, but the deliberations of the commissioners among themselves were to remain strictly secret.[43]

On 12 May the Siamese agent deposited his application, as well as a map, and the commission began the examination of the questions submitted to it. The French agent replied with a memorial on 22 May. The commissioners asked the two agents for additional information with regard to the subjects treated in the Siamese application and the French memorial. The neutral commissioners then prepared a draft questionnaire relating to various points which the commission wished to examine. The draft was submitted to the full commission and to the agents, who were invited to suggest modifications. 'Le plan des investigations' of the commission was thus established by common agreement.[44] The agents of Siam and France answered the questions formulated in the questionnaire in replies dated 29 May and 7 June respectively.

In this manner, observes Professor Bastid, the commission 'elucidated the questions in dispute' according to the wording of Article 15 of the General Act, and proceeded with the second part of its task, i.e. 'to endeavour to bring the parties to an agreement'.[45] Prior to drafting its recommendations the commission arranged a meeting of the two agents in the hope that they would reach an agreement, either on the subject of the controversy or on discussions to be pursued within a different framework. Since the divergence of views was very wide and the agents were subject to strict instructions, the meeting had no result. Consequently, the commission prepared its report,[46] which contained a summary of the main arguments of the parties, the conclusions of the commission with respect to those arguments, as well as certain specific recommendations.

In effect, the commission rejected the Siamese claim for a revision of the frontier which would entail the transfer of over a third of Indo-China to Siam. The commission held, in particular, that it had no competence to consider the Siamese request for the transfer of the whole of Laos to Siam. In the view of the commission, a request for revision of the treaty of 3 October 1893 could validly be brought before it if it referred to adjustments or changes in the delimitation of the frontier itself and so far as these adjustments affected only territories which were not 'organized in a political unit'.[47]

With regard to the sector of Luang Prabang, the commission was of

---

[43]See report of the commission, p. 1, and Bastid, *Etudes . . . Scelle*, p. 10.
[44]See Bastid, *Etudes . . . Scelle*, p. 11.
[45]Ibid.
[46]See reference at p. 212, n. 41, above.
[47]The commission here referred to the Franco-Laotian modus vivendi of 27 Aug. 1946.

H

the opinion that the ethnical arguments advanced by the agent of Siam were not sufficient, in themselves, to justify a modification of this frontier in favour of Siam. Its examination of the economic situation did not lead the commission to recommend such a modification, since the two banks of the Mekong River in fact constituted an economic unit involving constant inter-communal exchanges. From the geographical point of view, the commission considered that the watershed between Mekong and Menam was 'une frontière appropriée et naturelle, bien établie et clairement définie'. Thick forests extended on both sides of the summits of the mountain range which was passable only by means of two cart tracks. In conclusion, the commission could not, on any of the ethnic, economic, or geographical grounds put forward, support the Siamese claims to the territory of Luang Prabang west bank (Lanchang), and Siam's request for the revision of that part of the frontier.[48]

The commission similarly refuted the Siamese arguments with regard to the rest of the territories claimed by Siam—the Mekong frontier area, the territory of Bassac right bank (Champasak), and the province of Battambang. It pointed out, for instance, that while the economic ties of the province of Battambang could be developed, it was none the less true that the 'natural flow of commerce' of Battambang in fact followed the existing waterways, roads, and railways towards the south and east. In these circumstances, the commission was of the opinion that the separation of this province from Cambodia would be disadvantageous for its inhabitants and for other inhabitants of the state, without offering compensating advantages.[49]

While the commission did not uphold the Siamese claims, it made several suggestions intended to 'devaluate' the existing frontier.[50] These included the establishment of a permanent international advisory commission to study technical questions of common interest, the extension of the competence and functions of the Mekong Commission to additional areas, a small modification of the river frontier, and an arrangement to ensure to Siam an adequate supply of fish from the Great Lake Tonlé Sap.

The commission's report was submitted to the agents of the parties at its meeting on 27 June 1947. On 25 July the French agent informed the president of the commission that his government accepted the report. On 1 November the Siamese agent communicated the rejection of the report by his government on the grounds that it was not based on UN principles of justice and of freedom and self-determination of peoples. He criticized, in particular, the failure of the commission to consult the interested peoples.[51]

[48]See report of the commission, p. 4.
[49]Ibid., p. 6.
[50]See Bastid, *Etudes . . . Scelle*, p. 18.
[51]Ibid., pp. 18–19.

Soon afterwards a change of regime took place in Siam and the new government considered the territorial dispute with France as closed.

Conclusions. This dispute involved a conflict of interests based on differing appreciations of the facts.

The conciliation agreement, in conjunction with the General Act of 1928, charged the commission to examine the ethnic, geographical, and economic arguments of the parties and to endeavour to effect a settlement. The 'examination' under the conciliation agreement is to be understood as identical with the 'elucidation of the questions in dispute' under Article 15 of the General Act (the article providing that the elucidation is to be achieved by the collection of all necessary information 'by means of inquiry or otherwise').

The examination conducted by the Franco-Siamese commission was threefold: ascertainment of facts relating to the ethnical structure of the population and to the geography and economy of the area; ascertainment of the parties' interpretation of these facts; and the commission's own analysis of the facts.

Ascertainment of the facts was particularly indispensable in this case since, in the words of Professor Bastid, the commissioners 'devaient, *en la motivant fortement,* donner leur opinion sur le moyen de régler de façon raisonnable l'opposition d'intérêts . . .' (emphasis added).[52] We have noted that, before preparing its recommendations, the commission tried to achieve conciliation by arranging a meeting between the agents. If that meeting had borne fruit the commission would have dispensed with the reasoned report and would have confined itself to recording the agreement reached. Compelled, as it were, to voice its opinion, the commission had to make a complete and thorough examination of the facts.

In sum, we can assert that in so far as the commission ascertained the relevant facts, it functioned as a commission of inquiry as envisaged in the Hague Conventions. The question arises whether—by interpreting the facts, as distinguished from simply ascertaining them—the commission also acted as a genuine inquiry commission on the Hague model. The theory and practice of the Hague commissions showed that they were intended to limit their activity to the ascertainment of alleged facts. The very ascertainment of the facts—for instance the establishment of the exact location of an incident at sea—would enable the parties to draw the necessary conclusions for the solution of the dispute.

The interpretation of facts effected by the present commission seems to be more appropriate to an inquiry commission of the Bryan type, charged with elucidating all aspects of the dispute.

[52] Ibid., p. 13. The words 'leur opinion' are italicized in the original text, the author intending to emphasize that the parties were interested in the opinion of individuals of great experience, who should not seek the role of 'censors' appealing to the public opinion of States which are reluctant to abandon their claims.

The various types of functions carried out by the Franco-Siamese commission may be illustrated by the following findings with regard to the watershed between Mekong and Menam:

(1) Thick forests extend on both sides of the summits of the mountain range which is passable only by means of two cart tracks. This description reflects the fact-finding function as envisaged in the Hague Conventions.

(2) The above watershed is an appropriate and natural frontier, well established and clearly defined. This conclusion reflects an extended inquiry function on the Bryan model.

(3) There is no need to change the status quo as regards this section of the frontier. Expression is here given to the conciliatory task of the commission to submit recommendations for a settlement.

As regards the method of work, the commission obtained its information 'otherwise' than by 'inquiry' if, by 'inquiry' under Article 15 of the General Act, the examination of witnesses and visits on the spot are meant. On the other hand, the commission conducted an 'inquiry' in the sense of the larger function conferred on inquiry commissions under the Hague Conventions, by obtaining written evidence, by formulating a questionnaire, and by asking the agents and experts for oral explanations. These means seemed sufficient to the commission for the accomplishment of its first task of examining the questions submitted to it.

The foregoing analysis leads to the conclusion that the Franco-Siamese Commission was in effect a commission of inquiry and conciliation. It will be noted that commissions with similar functions established by international organizations, such as the League of Nations' Chaco, Mosul, and Lytton Commissions, as well as UNSCOP, were generally called 'commissions of inquiry'.

THE BELGIAN-DANISH COMMISSION, 1952

This commission dealt with a case involving two Danish merchant ships, the *Gorm* and the *Svava*. The ships were in the Belgian port of Antwerp at the beginning of May 1940, when both Belgium and Denmark were occupied by German forces.[53] On 10 May the two Danish captains received written notification from the Belgian authorities that their vessels had been seized ('saisis') and that, consequently, they could not depart. An armed guard was placed on them. Two days later, a general evacuation of the port took place. The two vessels were conducted towards Ostend (Belgium). In the course of the voyage the *Gorm* struck a mine, probably German, and sank. Her cargo and the personal effects

---

[53]See 'Exposé des faits' included in a verbal communication made by the president of the commission on 12 Sept. 1952 (Rolin, 'Une conciliation belgo-danoise', 57 *RGDIP* (1953), Annex II, pp. 363–8).

of the crew were lost, but the crew were safely transferred to the *Svava*. On 14 May the captains and crews of both vessels were taken off the *Svava* and, after being harshly treated, were transferred to France. They were interned there until 16 August 1940, when they were repatriated to Denmark.

The *Svava*, manned by a Dutch crew with a Belgian captain, was directed towards England. On arrival, she was seized by the British authorities and her cargo taken off and stored. During a German bombardment of London warehouses the cargo was damaged and was later sold at approximately a quarter of the list price. Denmark claimed compensation from Belgium for the damage suffered by her nationals, and on 29 January 1952 the two governments requested the Permanent Conciliation Commission, established in accordance with the Belgian-Danish treaty of 3 March 1927,[54] to proceed with any measure likely to lead to a reconciliation. By Article 7 of the treaty the commission was charged with submitting to the parties the terms of settlement which it deemed most suitable ('convenable'), and with fixing a period within which the parties were to make their decision on the matter. At the end of its work the commission was to draw up a procès-verbal indicating whether or not a settlement had been effected.

The members of the commission were: Judge Sandström (Sweden) president, Mr M. C. T. Le Quesne, QC, Barrister-at-law (United Kingdom), Professor J. P. A. François (The Netherlands), Dr G. Cohn, Minister Plenipotentiary (Denmark), and Professor H. Rolin, Belgian senator. The Danish government was represented before the commission by its ambassador at Stockholm, by a lawyer, and by a counsellor at the Danish Ministry for Foreign Affairs. Four persons accompanied the Danish representatives for the purpose of supplying information. The Belgian government was represented by its minister at Stockholm, by a lawyer, and by the assistant-director of the Belgian Ministry for Foreign Affairs.[55]

The commission held meetings in Stockholm from 8 to 12 May 1952. The written proceedings consisted of the 'traditional exchange of memorials, replies and rejoinders in use in arbitral procedure'. The oral proceedings were confined to 'pleadings' by the representatives of the parties.[56] At the final session the president presented the agents with the terms of settlement proposed by the commission.

In order to determine if and to what extent the Belgian government must pay compensation, the commission considered it essential, first of all, to determine the juridical nature of the measures taken by the Belgian authorities with regard to the two vessels.[57] According to one view, the vessels were seized as prize. The commission did not accept

---

[54]See LN *Survey*, p. 305. [55]See Rolin, 57 *RGDIP*, 360. [56]Ibid., p. 356.
[57]The present account of the views expressed by various commissioners is based on Section B ('Discussion') of the verbal communication made by the president (ibid., p. 363).

this view, since the Belgian government had made formal declarations that it had never intended to treat Danish ships as enemy vessels.

Another opinion expressed was that the vessels had been requisitioned by Belgium to prevent their falling into German hands. The majority of the commission held that the measure taken on 10 May 1940 did not have this character, seeing that requisition was in no way compatible with the terms of the Belgian communication to the Danish captains. In the view of the majority, the Belgian government was exclusively concerned with the notified prohibition to depart. Some members of the commission, however, were of the opinion that the character of the seizure on 10 May might have changed at the moment when, without a new written communication, the vessels received orders to sail and were conducted towards Ostend. This new measure could be regarded as similar to a requisition or as an act of the government taken in the national interest. However legitimate this measure might have been, it seemed in the view of these members to entail the duty of Belgium to 'assume any supplementary risks' resulting from her decision. This opinion was challenged by other members of the commission, who claimed that the transfer to Ostend, as well as the original seizure, were measures which, like an act of state, would not, in the absence of fault, entail the responsibility of the state which resorted to them.

After the various opinions were put forward, relates Professor Rolin,[58] the commissioners realized that, in order to accomplish their mission, it was not necessary for each of them to opt unequivocally for the acceptance or rejection of the different Danish claims. Neither was it necessary for the commission to count votes. The commission agreed to see its task as being not that of a judge, but that of a lawyer who is asked by his client whether to go to court or to settle his dispute by a compromise ('transaction'). In accordance with this approach, the commission had to take into consideration the doubts and differences of opinion expressed by its members. The elaboration of a proposal for a settlement thus became a juridical operation and not a psychological speculation intended to discover, behind the official positions, what were 'the last points of retreat' of the parties. Professor Rolin states that the adoption of this approach enabled the commissioners to reach, relatively quickly, unanimity on the terms of settlement to be submitted to the parties.

The next problem was in what form to convey the proposals to the parties. The final provision of Article 7 of the treaty of 3 March 1927 seemed to forbid the commission to give its opinion on the different points of fact and of law with regard to which the parties were in disagreement. The intention of the draftsmen apparently was to prevent the use of the commission's opinion in case of possible resort to judicial proceedings.[59] But, asks Rolin, what kind of arguments could the commission offer in order to have its proposals accepted by the parties? The solution found was to authorize the president to deliver a verbal commentary when presenting the terms of settlement to the agents and counsel of the parties. The agents were to be allowed to take notes during the reading of the commentary.

Accordingly, on 12 September 1952, the president made 'une communication verbale'[60] consisting of two parts: 'Exposé des faits' and 'Discussions'. The first part described the 'succession of the facts of the case' as they appeared after the 'supplementary information' received by the representatives of the parties. The 'discussions' consisted of the presentation of the views expressed by the commissioners on the juridical nature of the measures taken by the Belgian authorities with regard to the two vessels, and the reasoning which led the commission to recommend several 'principles' relating to the payment or nonpayment of compensation for the various heads of damage suffered. Under a previous agreement between the parties, the commission was not authorized to fix the amounts to be paid.

The president pointed out in the verbal communication that, taking into account the differences of opinion and the doubts of certain members as to the legal merits of the dispute, the commission was unanimous in considering that it would be 'in conformity with the interests of the two parties' to accept the proposed terms of settlement. At the end of his verbal communication the president announced that the commission had fixed a period of one month within which the parties were to accept or reject these terms.

On 4 and 9 October 1952, respectively, the two governments informed the president of the commission of their acceptance of the proposed settlement. As a result, on 10 October 1952 the president signed a procès-verbal[61] in which he recorded the agreement obtained, defined once again the principles of settlement, and invited the parties to agree within three months on the amount of compensation. He added that if no agreement were reached at the end of that period, each of the parties was entitled to request the commission to render its conciliatory services in the matter. The procès-verbal was confirmed by the signatures of the other commissioners. The parties agreed on the amount of compensation to be paid by Belgium to Denmark, and the dispute was thus finally settled.

Conclusions. In the case under review the conciliation commission conducted a substantial investigation into both the factual and the legal aspects of the dispute. In view of the essentially legal character of the conflicting claims, the commission took special care to analyse the legal implications of the facts. Nevertheless, it also exercised an important fact-finding function by obtaining documentary evidence of the attitude of the Belgian authorities, by ascertaining the manner in which the

[60]See text ibid., Annex II, pp. 363–8.   [61]See text ibid., Annex III, pp. 369–71.

Danish crews were treated, and by investigating in detail the events which occurred after the arrival of the *Svava* in England. Professor Rolin testifies that the commissioners discussed, like arbitrators, the respective merits of the arguments regarding different *points of fact* and of law on which the parties were in disagreement.[62] Moreover, the procès-verbal of the sessions of the commission[63] records that it decided at its first meeting to ask the parties various questions 'pour élucider les faits'. These questions were answered by the representatives of the parties in the course of the pleadings. The importance of fact-finding in the eyes of the commissioners also found expression in the detailed 'Exposé des faits' which was an essential part of the verbal communication of the president.

The emphasis on the inquiry task of the commission, in the wide sense of the Bryan treaties, clearly emerges from the basic attitude of the commission. Once the commission conceived its task as determining the prospects of success or failure in possible judicial proceedings, it had to analyse seriously questions both of fact and of law. Moreover, it had to convince the parties that it was 'fitting' and 'in conformity with their interests' to accept a 'compromise' rather than go to court. The conciliatory effort did not start at the beginning or in the course of the investigation, but only after the questions in dispute had been extensively elucidated.

In sum, the Belgian-Danish commission acted to a limited extent as an inquiry commission on the Hague model and to a large extent as an inquiry commission on the Bryan model. Given the basic approach of the commission, if the issue involved a difference of opinion about facts then the commission would have assumed predominantly the character of a commission of inquiry as envisaged in the Hague Conventions.

THE FRANCO-SWISS COMMISSION, 1955

While the minutes and the report of this commission have not been published, a most valuable analysis of its work is contained in two articles written by its president, Baron F. M. van Asbeck, in *Nederlands tijdschrift voor internationaal recht*.[64] The observations of Baron van Asbeck are of special relevance to our study since they describe the relative roles played by the processes of examination and conciliation.

The Permanent Franco-Swiss Conciliation Commission was called upon to deal with two disputes of a legal character. The first concerned the alleged obligation of France to reimburse the expenses of the intern-

---

[62]Rolin, 57 *RGDIP*, 357.
[63]See text ibid., Annex I, pp. 359–62.
[64]'La tâche et l'action d'une commission de conciliation', in vol. iii (1956), pp. 1–9 (henceforth cited as 'van Asbeck,1st article'), and 'La procédure suivie par la commission permanente de conciliation franco-suisse' (henceforth cited as 'van Asbeck, 2nd article'), ibid., pp. 209–19.

ment in Switzerland, during the war years 1940-5, of the second Polish division which had fought under French command. The division was part of the 45th French corps which crossed into Switzerland in June 1940, and which was disarmed and interned in accordance with Hague Convention No. V.[65] France maintained that she was not responsible for paying these expenses, and that it was incumbent upon the Polish government to deal with questions pertaining to the Polish internees. Switzerland, on the other hand, held that the responsibility of France was involved since the Polish division was a French military unit.

The second dispute concerned the Swiss allegation that French officials charged with the repression of customs frauds had violated Swiss territorial sovereignty by inciting Swiss bankers to make private compensation, which was forbidden under Swiss law. The French government denied that its officials had transgressed the limits of permissible action.

On 20 August 1954 Switzerland seised the Permanent Conciliation Commission by means of two unilateral applications addressed to its president. The commission was composed of the following members: Baron van Asbeck, Professor of International Law (Netherlands); Charles Corbin, French ambassador; André Ponchaud, Swiss Federal judge; Luis de Zulueta, formerly Spanish minister for foreign affairs; and Lord McNair, formerly president of the International Court of Justice (United Kingdom). The Swiss position was 'defended' by Professor G. Sauser Hall, of Geneva, and the French by Professor André Gros, of Paris.[66] The sessions of the commission were held on the premises of the Permanent Court of Arbitration between 29 September and 24 October 1955. The then secretary-general of the International Bureau of the Court, Professor J. P. A. François, acted as secretary of the commission.

Baron van Asbeck was careful to point out in his opening address[67] that conciliation should not be effected at the expense of a thorough investigation of the issues involved. In his opinion, conciliation was not to be conceived as a simple compromise ('transaction') based on the principle of 'split the difference' or on practical equity. Such an attitude would limit the commission to acting as an 'amiable compositeur', whereas the two disputes laid before it required first of all the elucidation of the conflicting legal positions in order to enable the commission to provide the parties with an objective opinion. Any settlement of the two disputes which did not take into consideration the law involved would be ineffective.

So far as the facts underlying the disputes were concerned, the president of the commission urged his colleagues to keep constantly in

[65]For particulars of the disputes see ibid., and Bastid, 'La commission de conciliation franco-suisse', *AFDI, 1956*, pp. 436–40.

[66]See communiqué referred to at p. 224, below.

[67]The main part of the address is reproduced in van Asbeck, 1st article.

H 2

mind any doubts that there might be with regard to the facts alleged by one party or the other or, even more important, with regard to the legal implications of the facts.[68]

The above observations notwithstanding, Baron van Asbeck struck a balance in the concluding part of his address between the conciliatory and the investigatory functions of the commission. The commission, he said, must accomplish its task by obeying the juridical norms, since conciliation had its own place in the juridical organization of the world. Nevertheless, the commission would fail in its duty if it did not reserve the right to make 'une appréciation de faits et de prétentions plus libre que celle dont un juge peut faire usage'. The commission was faced with the eternal problem of determining the relationship between justice and peace, without sacrificing one to the other.

In line with the above theoretical framework, the commission proceeded with the 'customary succession' of examination ('instruction') and 'oral debates'. The parties submitted memoranda—a French memorial, a Swiss reply, and a French rejoinder—which shed light both on the facts which were at the origin of the disputes and on the legal questions involved.[69]

At the beginning of the oral proceedings, on 28 October 1955, the commissioners agreed upon the necessity of emphasizing the confidential, informal, and friendly character of their work. The commission's proceedings were in no way to resemble those of a tribunal. Whenever the agents were in attendance, they were to sit round the same table with the commissioners, so that all of them together could study the questions in dispute. No gowns were to be worn. In accordance with the same basic approach, it was decided that no minutes should be taken except for short notes intended to indicate the general course of the work.

With regard to the first case, the commission saw advantage in condensing its initial deliberations concerning the historical facts and the legal interpretation which should be given to them, into a series of 'provisional conclusions'. These were presented to the agents of the parties for their observations.[70]

Baron van Asbeck states that, in the view of the commission, neither of the cases provided for 'inquiry' as envisaged in Articles 6 (1) and 7 of the treaty of 1925, or for the summoning of witnesses (Art. 10), or for a visit on the spot (Art. 12).[71] The detailed documentation submitted by

[68]In another context van Asbeck characterized conciliation as the younger sister of inquiry—a successful sister who had surpassed the elder, since the work of conciliation does not stop once the facts of the dispute are clarified.

[69]See van Asbeck, 2nd article, pp. 211, 212.

[70]Ibid., p. 213.

[71]For the text of Art. 6 and the content of Art. 7 of the treaty of 1925 see above, pp. 126 and 127, respectively. Van Asbeck here puts the term 'inquiry' in inverted commas. As pointed out above (p. 127, n. 61), he reached the conclusion that the term as used in the Franco-Swiss treaty and in the General Act is devoid of any real significance.

both parties and the services rendered by the agents in the course of the commission's deliberations enabled the commission to obtain all the information needed for the 'elucidation of the questions in dispute' (Art. 6).

One of the important methodological questions which the commission considered in the course of its work was whether it could attempt to reconcile the parties before the completion of its examination of the disputes. In the view of Baron van Asbeck, Article 6 (1) of the Franco-Swiss treaty (corresponding to Article 15 (1) of the General Act (below, App. II, p. 340)) seemed to indicate that at any time, even during the study of the questions in dispute, the commission could try to effect a reconciliation between the parties. He notes, however, that the commission recognized from the very beginning that the wide gap between the points of view and the conclusions of the parties in both cases rendered fruitless any thought of conciliation 'en cours de route'.[72]

In accordance with Article 6 of the treaty of 1925, after the commission had completed the examination of the cases it embarked on an elaboration of the solutions to be proposed to the parties. With a view to ensuring that its proposals had the greatest possible persuasive force, the commission kept in mind that it was essential to obtain unanimity among its members.[73] Like their colleagues who examined the Belgian–Danish dispute, the commissioners also considered that for their conclusions to be accepted they must present the parties with a statement of reasons. Again, like their predecessors, they were faced with the problem of how to present the reasons without making their use possible in the event of judicial proceedings. It was decided that in each of the two cases the president would deliver an oral statement containing the reasons, which would include the following sentence: 'The proposal of the commission being inspired exclusively by the wish to effect a conciliation of the parties, the present statement does not prejudice the legal position of the parties and must not be invoked in the event of subsequent judicial proceedings'. With this safeguard,[74] the full text of the statement was submitted to the agents of the parties, together with the proposed terms of settlement.[75]

On 24 October 1955, at the final session of the commission, the president read, in each of the two cases, first the statement of reasons and then the proposals for terms of settlement. The two statements of reasons summed up the respective positions of the parties on the

---

[72]See van Asbeck, 2nd article, pp. 213 f.
[73]Ibid.
[74]Professor Bastid (*AFDI, 1956*, p. 439) observes that the above-quoted proviso could hardly be implemented. It was easy to imagine that a party would not hesitate to use the statement of reasons to support its position and that, in fact, the statement would play the role of a decision of an inferior court.
[75]See van Asbeck, 2nd article, p. 215.

questions of fact and of law, described the efforts of the commission—in co-operation with the two governments and their agents—to 'elucidate the questions in dispute'', and presented the conclusions that the commission had drawn from the information at its disposal.

According to a communiqué issued by the two governments on 24 November 1955,[76] 'Après s'être livrée à un examen très approfondi des éléments de fait et de droit de ce différend', the commission proposed that France should pay the expenses of the internment of the Polish soldiers up to February 1941—the date when the interned French soldiers were freed. As for the rest of the period, extending to 1945, 'for reasons of equity' France was to pay Switzerland a substantial sum in compensation. With regard to the second case, the commission was not able, according to the above communiqué, to establish in an unequivocal manner that a violation of Swiss territorial sovereignty had occurred, and in these circumstances it confined itself to formulating certain recommendations of a general character.

On 18 November 1955 the two agents communicated to the commission the decision of their governments to accept the proposed terms of settlement and, on 24 November, the president and the secretary of the commission signed a procès-verbal confirming that the parties had come to an agreement.[77]

Conclusions. We may infer from the activities and basic approach of the Franco-Swiss conciliation commission that the conciliatory function did not prevent the extensive exercise of the function of examination, or enlarged inquiry. Any attempt at conciliation before the end of the elucidation of the questions in dispute seemed useless to the commission. Moreover, the examination had to be as complete as possible in order to enable the commission to present convincing reasons for its recommended solutions.

The disputes being primarily legal, the fact-finding function of the commission appeared to be limited, especially in the first case. The commission's conclusions in the second case, as contained in the communiqué of the two governments, suggest that, in its opinion the alleged facts constituting a violation of Swiss territorial sovereignty did not exist. To reach this finding the commission had obviously undertaken a fact-finding task.[78]

The success of the Franco-Swiss conciliation commission has been attributed by its president to the informal and confidential character of the proceedings. This character reflected, in his view, the mixed nature of conciliation. On the one hand, conciliation is a prolongation of the

[76] I am grateful to the Swiss Ministry for Foreign Affairs for sending me the text of the communiqué.
[77] See van Asbeck, 2nd article, p. 216.
[78] Cf. Nguyen-Quoc-Dinh, 'Les commissions de conciliation sont-elles aussi des commissions d'enquête?', 71 *RGDIP* (1967), 620.

diplomatic negotiations which preceded it, with the help of independent and impartial commissioners chosen from among the nationals of third powers. (He points out that the designation of three such commissioners, instead of one, is important in this respect.) On the other hand, conciliation is close to judicial settlement and to arbitration. In effect, states Baron van Asbeck, the institution of conciliation represents a transition from diplomatic negotiations to judicial or arbitral settlement—a transition permitting, if the commission accomplishes its mission, at least an impartial opinion to be obtained.[79] The same dual character, he continues, is reflected in the procedure followed by the commission and in the terms of settlement proposed by the commission to the French and Swiss governments.[80]

It follows that the role attributed by van Asbeck to the national commissioner is self-explanatory: although not sitting as a representative of his government, the national commissioner is nevertheless not independent of it. He is in a position to convince his government that its point of view has been duly taken into account by the commission. Moreover, the national commissioner can also explain to his government the reasons underlying the proposals of the commission and perhaps recommend the making of any sacrifices which may be necessary for the solution of the dispute.[81]

The observations relating to the prominence of the diplomatic aspect of the work of the commission, coupled with the attempt, or at least the idea of the commissioners to effect conciliation before the completion of the elucidation of the questions in dispute, would suggest that the extent of the enlarged inquiry conducted by conciliation commissions depends on the particular circumstances of each dispute. The fact that Article 6 (1) of the Franco-Swiss treaty, following the Locarno-General Act formulation, conferred on the commission wide powers of investigation or elucidation, did not in itself invest the conciliation commission with the character of a commission of inquiry in the Bryan sense of the term.

THE ROLE OF INQUIRY IN THE CONCEPT OF CONCILIATION

The recourse by states to the process of conciliation in recent years has given impetus to theoretical research on the concept of conciliation. Efforts have been made to define anew the task of conciliation commissions and to formulate rules on the procedure to be followed by them. The Institute of International Law considered it necessary to replace the Regulations on the Procedure of Conciliation which it had

---

[79]The author here refers to the report of the Swiss Federal Council of 11 Dec. 1919 (see above, p. 121, n. 43).
[80]Van Asbeck, 2nd article, pp. 218–19.
[81]Ibid., p. 5.

adopted on 2 September 1927,[82] with new Regulations, adopted on 11 September 1961.[83] Several members of the Institute who had taken part in the work of various conciliation commissions were able to make a concrete contribution to the discussions on the subject.

For our purposes it is of special relevance to examine what are the conceptions of different scholars with regard to the role of enlarged inquiry—and fact-finding in particular—in the process of conciliation. As will be seen, these conceptions are reflected in the opinions of writers and in discussions concerning both the general task of the commissions and their method of work.

The question which interests us especially is whether the process of conciliation is conceived as necessarily consisting of two distinct and successive stages—examination of the dispute and the effort to conciliate. In so far as the examination is believed to be an integral part of the process, the question arises to what extent this examination is complete, in the sense of the thorough inquiry envisaged in the Hague Convention of 1907. We shall be concerned to discover, in addition, what is the role attributed to fact-finding in the general process of examination of a dispute. The answer to these questions will enable us to ascertain whether conciliation commissions are regarded as inquiry commissions, either on the Hague or on the Bryan model, whose task is extended to include the effort to conciliate the parties.

For our frame of reference it is proposed to take the opinions of Professor André Gros and Professor Henri Rolin, each of whom has stimulated a detailed academic discussion on the method of conciliation.

Professor Gros has expressed his views, i.a., in his article 'Remarques sur la conciliation internationale' written in 1956.[84] His reflections are generally based on the experience of the Franco-Siamese and Franco-Swiss commissions. (He acted as agent in both the cases dealt with by the latter commission.)

The main argument of Professor Gros is that the process of conciliation is and should be clearly distinguished from that of arbitration or judicial settlement. Conciliation is not, in his view, a judicial instance but a preliminary to such an instance. In effect, conciliation is the resumption of negotiations between two states. What they have not succeeded in settling by means of diplomacy, they wish to settle by way of conciliation.

However, writes Gros, commissions of conciliation are often composed of jurists, and the agents are legal advisers or practising lawyers who are generally employed by their governments for contentious cases. The natural tendency of these men to imitate the judicial process

---

[82]See 33(iii) *Annuaire, 1927*, 339–42. The Regulations are reproduced in 48(i) *Annuaire, 1959*, 112–14.

[83]See 49(ii) *Annuaire, 1961*, pp. 374–80. For the English text of the resolution see ibid., pp. 385–91.

[84]In *L'évolution du droit public; études offertes à Achille Mestre* (1956), pp. 279–83.

impedes the normal course of conciliation. Gros believes that one of the reasons for not employing conciliation more often may be found in the inclination of conciliators to assume the position of judges. States are not interested in having recourse to two degrees of jurisdiction. It is sufficient for them to have accepted international jurisdiction in the event of the failure of conciliation. What they expect of the commission is not a sentence of first instance, but the renewal of negotiations by a different method. Any attempt to bring conciliation nearer to judicial settlement is doomed to failure, since the parties, believing that they are pleading before a court of first instance, reinforce their legal argumentation, without opening the way for a friendly accommodation of their points of view.

It follows, states Gros, that conciliation would always be difficult in disputes where the question of responsibility has not yet been decided. On the other hand, when the conciliators are called upon to measure the extent of the responsibility of a state, their role becomes easier. Their object then is to effect a compromise.

As far as the method of work of the conciliation commissions is concerned, Gros approves entirely of the principle followed by the Belgian-Danish commission, to the effect that conciliation is a confidential operation which does not in any way prejudice eventual recourse to a judicial organ. The commission should, in his view, inform the parties of its reasons, without providing them with arguments; it should lead them towards conciliation, without appearing to condemn the one or the other; it should regulate, without judging. As in the Belgian-Danish case, the feeling ('sentiment') of the commission should not be expressed in a decision, either on the facts or in law.

The method whereby the president of the commission informs the agents of the reasons underlying the proposed terms of settlement could be combined, in his view, with the system followed by the Franco-Siamese commission, where the agents participated actively in the work of the commission. If the agents confine themselves to the delivery of statements and the commission thereafter continues its deliberations without them, the parties are likely sometimes to be confronted with a proposal which neither of them can accept. The principle of conciliation requires the fullest participation of the agents in the preparation of the proposal for a settlement, due allowance being made for certain restricted sessions at which the conciliators draft their questions and requests for clarification.

When the first phase of the work of the commission is finished, at the moment when the facts are elucidated and the law defined, a real dialogue between the commission and the agents must start for the purpose of establishing the framework of the agreement sought.

Assembled around the same table, the commissioners and the agents can define the questions to be resolved, study them, form an opinion, and produce a plan for conciliation.

In conclusion, Professor Gros takes exception to the view that between the conciliatory and the arbitral or judicial settlement, there is less difference in the method than in the result.[85] In his opinion, the progress of conciliation—'négotiation qui si poursuit et non pas opération juridictionnelle'—could be achieved by reform of its procedures.

The above views clearly endorse the two-stage inquiry-conciliation sequence, in spite of the extreme emphasis placed on the informal nature of negotiation. The function of the elucidation of the problems in dispute is not blurred by the exigencies of the diplomatic technique.

Professor Rolin elaborated his views on the subject, i.a., in a preliminary report which he wrote in his capacity as rapporteur of the commission of the Institute of International Law dealing with international conciliation. The report was submitted to the commission on 9 May 1958.[86]

In the section entitled 'The tasks of conciliation commissions', Rolin expresses approval for the view of Gros to the effect that conciliation is the renewal of negotiations between two states, but he disagrees with the recommendations of Gros that the commission should dispense with the formalities of a lawsuit. In Rolin's view, this should be done only in certain cases. Thus, when there is a simple conflict of interests, without any contest of rights, the task of the conciliators would not be to elucidate points of fact and of law but to explore the wishes or real needs of the parties, to search for meeting points or possible accommodations. In such a case, it would probably be advisable to dispense altogether with the contentious procedure, to avoid the written and oral repetition of arguments publicly expounded, to meet the agents separately, to learn their unofficial views, and even to obtain from them confidential material. The national commissioners could be used as intermediaries to facilitate the work of the commission to that end.

However, the services that the parties expect of the commission are more often of a different nature. The disputes which arise between them spring less from opposition of interests than from divergences between the information which they each have received with regard to certain facts, or between the opinions which have been given to them on certain points of law. What the parties require of the commissioners in such cases is to complete their information on the facts with data obtained in the course of a 'contradictory' procedure, to state objectively the 'for' and the 'against' with regard to the opposing legal theses, and on

---

[85]The author is here quoting from p. 656 of the Message of the Swiss Federal Council to the Federal Assembly dated 28 Oct. 1924, concerning the approval of the conciliation treaties between Switzerland and Sweden and Switzerland and Denmark (see below, p. 354). Inadvertently he makes reference to the treaties between Switzerland on the one hand, and Sweden and Norway (instead of Denmark) on the other.

[86]See text in 48(i) *Annuaire, 1959*, 30–42.

the basis of these to propose a reasonable compromise. This process, states Rolin, is entirely different from that described by Gros. This time one is not concerned with an essentially psychological operation. The opinion given by the commission springs much less from the aims of the parties than from the relative merits of the arguments put forward.

According to Rolin, the procedure of conciliation follows that of arbitration or judicial settlement only as far as the end of the 'contradictory' hearings (above, p. 29, n. 23). Unlike judges or arbitrators, the conciliators charged with elucidating a dispute are not called upon to pronounce their opinion on the respective claims of the parties. Such a collective opinion, even of an advisory nature, would risk putting an end to the conciliatory action, since neither of the parties would be prepared to renounce rights recognized by the commission. Therefore the commission must limit itself to producing an objective analysis of the dispute, comprising an account of the depositions or findings made in the course of the inquiry on the contested facts, and a statement of the questions of law which would mention the arguments and the authorities in support of or against the respective claims. No doubt, states Rolin, this work would lead the conciliators to conclusions more or less favourable to one or the other of the contentions put forward. But none of the commissioners would be obliged to pronounce himself for or against any of these arguments, and in any case the commission would abstain from taking a stand itself.

In Rolin's view, the task of the conciliation commission consists of two parts: elucidation and conciliation. When the case has been elucidated, 'the commission embarks on the second part of its task—the conciliation proper'. This usually comprises the elaboration of the compromise solution to be recommended. At this stage the conciliation commission often finds itself in the position of a lawyer who is consulted by a client on the question of whether to go to court or to agree to a compromise. A conscientious lawyer will almost always advise a compromise, but its nature must vary according to the prospects of success in court. Therefore, the solution proposed by the commission would not, as a rule, be identical with the solution which the majority of the commissioners would have adopted if they had had the responsibilities of judges or arbitrators. It would reflect the differences of opinion expressed during the deliberations and the degree of hesitation which had marked certain opinions.

The second section of Rolin's preliminary report is devoted to the procedure to be followed in the case of inquiry ('enquête'). After reference to relevant provisions of the Hague Convention of 1907 and the General Act, the author suggests that the procès-verbaux of the examination of witnesses and of material findings should be remitted to the parties. Thus a party would not be deprived of the possibility of producing evidence in subsequent proceedings if witnesses die, or if documents are lost.

In the third section, Rolin considers whether the provisions of the Hague Convention of 1907, which provide for the submission of a report on the facts, should be applied. In his view 'the transfer to the procedure of conciliation' of the report to be given by a commission of inquiry, as envisaged in the Hague Convention, is open to objection. To ascertain the facts, after having collected the evidence, means to express an opinion on their respective value; this amounts in numerous cases to the imposition of a final solution; to impose a final solution is not in the spirit of conciliation. On the other hand, it would be useful to include the 'elucidation of facts' in an objective written statement, consisting of the description and analysis of the dispute as it appears to the commission after the examination of witnesses and evidence and after the exchange of views among the commissioners.[87] This statement, in the opinion of the rapporteur, should be submitted to the parties. However, the parties should not be given a written statement of the proposed terms of settlement and the accompanying comments of the president, in order to prevent their use in eventual judicial or arbitral proceedings.[88]

The members of the Commission on International Conciliation contributed to the clarification of the concept of conciliation in their comments on the above report, as well as in their answers to twelve questions which Professor Rolin addressed to them.

Baron van Asbeck challenged the rapporteur's view that, after the stage of examination, the procedure of conciliation necessarily departs from that of arbitral or judicial settlement. Similarly, he did not agree that the aim of the conciliatory effort is, as a rule, the achievement of a compromise.[89] In his opinion the task of the conciliation commission depends on the nature of the dispute and on the attitude and intentions of the parties. Thus, the charge of violation of territorial sovereignty in one of the Franco-Swiss cases did not leave the conciliators any latitude in their search for a solution. The commission had to give a quasi-judicial answer of 'yes' or 'no', which excludes any idea of a compromise. In the other Franco-Swiss case, the parties presented their case in a purely judicial form, with no intention of effecting a compromise, and the commission adapted itself by proceeding on a legal basis.

However, it was conceivable, wrote Baron van Asbeck, that in some cases the parties would wish non-judicial considerations to be taken into

[87]In his article in *Ann. européen* (referred to at p. 198, above), Rolin expressed the view that if the dispute submitted to a conciliation commission is about facts, the commission should not formally declare that certain facts have or have not been ascertained. In particular, if the inquiry is coupled with a mission to conciliate, it would often seem expedient to make use of the subsisting doubts in order to obtain some concession on the part of the state in whose favour the balance lies. (At p. 11.)

[88]The fourth and last section of the report deals with the question of publicity.

[89]See 48(i) *Annuaire, 1959*, pp. 47–59.

account. In other cases the parties might regard conciliation as a transitional stage between negotiations and other means of settlement. It was also possible that parties who were willing to reach an amicable agreement without the intervention of a judge or an arbitrator, would regard the process of conciliation as a prolongation of their diplomatic negotiations. Depending on the circumstances in each particular case, conciliation should be effected either on a strictly legal basis, or on judicial considerations tempered by equity, or on considerations of pure utility and expediency.

Baron van Asbeck also disagreed with Rolin's view that, in principle, conciliators do not have to pronounce on the contentions of the parties. Silence may mislead a party whose juridical position is weak. Moreover, a government may use an impartial decision given against it to justify, before its national assembly and before public opinion, its manner of handling the dispute.

According to Professor Bastid,[90] conciliation must be distinguished from consultative arbitration designed to provide a non-binding judicial opinion. The object of conciliation, in her view, is the search for a compromise between the claims of the parties. The aim of states which resort to conciliation is to find a settlement. In such conditions the task of the commission must be less to formulate its own opinion on the contested points than to seek an acceptable solution in active collaboration with the agents of the parties and the national commissioners. The commission must, as a rule, start its effort of conciliation as soon as it is informed of the dispute. The opinion of the commission on a suitable solution of the dispute should be formulated only if the direct discussions with the parties have failed. In such a case, a 'consultation' of the commission on the whole of the dispute may enable it to give detailed information to the governments concerned, and this may lead to fresh negotiations.

Professor Bastid recognized that in certain disputes, notably those in which the main or preliminary question is legal, a procedure resembling consultative arbitration may be more rational. The opinion of the commission would then be the second stage of the procedure, the first stage consisting of the statement of the contentions of the parties and the examination ('instruction') of the dispute by the commission. However, the Institute should not recommend the generalization of this system. She noted that the proceedings of the commission in two consecutive stages is envisaged in the General Act and in the European Convention for the Peaceful Settlement of Disputes as a simple option open to the commission.

The comments of Professor François[91] were based on the premise that, in practice, commissions of conciliation always deal with disputes on legal points. In his opinion the commission should first examine the

---

[90]Ibid., pp. 60–5.   [91]Ibid., pp. 66–72.

soundness of the legal claims. After the study of the legal position has been completed, the commission must find out on what point there is room for mitigating the strictness of the law, in order to reconcile the opposing views in a spirit of mutual understanding. However, it is not necessary for the commission always to proceed in this manner. In one recent case, Professor François stated, one of the parties was not prepared to accept under any conditions certain legal submissions, not because of the consequences which they entailed in the specific case, but in view of the repercussions which their acceptance could have in similar cases. As it was important to avoid the creation of a legal precedent, the commission which examined the case had to base its recommendations on reasons of equity, valid in the dispute, without making an attempt to submit to the parties a report dealing with the juridical issues involved.[92]

In principle, Professor François was in favour of the inclusion in the commission's report of the legal or other considerations which served as a basis for the proposed solution. The inclusion of such considerations would not, in his view, prejudice the position of the parties in subsequent judicial proceedings. The court or arbitral tribunal would examine the arguments with the same objectivity and independence with which a court of appeal examines the legal reasoning of a court of first instance. In the opinion of Professor François, the commission's report should also include the conclusions reached by the commission with regard to the inquiries which it has conducted.

Professor Guggenheim also confined his remarks to legal disputes.[93] In his view, the commission of conciliation should pronounce its opinion on the legal questions involved if the parties so wish. He stated that in three disputes which Switzerland brought before conciliation commissions,[94] the Swiss government wished to know the opinions of the conciliators on the legal arguments propounded by the agents of both parties. The reasoned opinion of the majority, and eventually also of the minority, permitted the Swiss government to evaluate its chances of success in the event of the disputes being brought before a judicial

[92]In pursuance of the treaty of 23 Sept. 1928 the Greek and Italian governments submitted to a conciliation commission a dispute relating to the torpedoing of the Greek boat *Roula* by an Italian submarine off the coast of Crete in Aug. 1940. (Greece was still neutral at that time.) The commission was presided over by Professor François (Netherlands), the other members being Professor Monaco (Italy) and Professor Spiropoulos (Greece). It held nine meetings between 12 and 20 Mar. 1956. After taking a position on the legal problems, and basing itself on principles of equity, the commission proposed that the Italian government pay an indemnity to the Greek government. The two parties accepted the proposal and agreed on the amount of reparation. They did not authorize the publication of the report. See François, 'Le Palais de la Paix en 1956', 4 *Ned. tijd. int. recht* (1957), 71.

[93]48(i) *Annuaire, 1959*, pp. 73–9.

[94]In addition to the two Franco-Swiss cases examined in this chapter, he refers to the case concerning the subjection of Swiss citizens to payment of the Italian extraordinary property tax. The dispute was considered by the Swiss-Italian conciliation commission in 1956 (see Nguyen-Quoc-Dinh, pp. 624–7).

or arbitral organ. The statement of motives enabled it to define its position on the concessions proposed by the commissions. Finally, the compromise solution repeatedly proposed by the commissions could be defended more easily by the Swiss government before the parliamentary commissions concerned and in other interested quarters.

Professor Hambro elaborated, i.a., on the question of including the results of an inquiry in the report of the commission.[95] He thought that, in principle, such results should not be included. However, there was a possibility that the parties might request the commission to transform itself into a commission of inquiry 'pure and simple', if the commissioners considered that they could not succeed in their task within the framework of a commission of conciliation. In such a case, even a finding on facts might be useful as a basis for subsequent negotiations.

Professor Jessup suggested, by way of general comment, that the conciliation procedure should have a minimum of formality and as little rigidity as possible.[96] Procedural devices which experience had proved to be useful should be recommended, but not required. The parties should always be free to change, by mutual agreement, any predetermined rule. The greater the simplicity and flexibility, the greater the political probability of acceptance of an obligation to resort to conciliation.

A similar opinion opposed to rigid rules was expressed by Lord McNair.[97] In his view, the main object must always be to settle the particular dispute referred to the conciliation commission, unlike the case of a lawsuit ('affaire'), where a tribunal must also bear in mind the development of the law. Lord McNair had no objection to the discussions of the conciliators resulting in the revelation of the opinion of the majority, but he did not think that this should be their main objective. Where, as usually happens, the commission includes representatives of the parties, it may be useful for them to learn what the view of the majority of the commission is, or is likely to be, because they can infer from this opinion what the prospects of the parties will be if the conciliation fails and the question is referred to judicial or arbitral settlement.

Professor Stone questioned the conception of the rapporteur that conciliation is like a preliminary conference at which a client and learned counsel discuss what the prospects of success are in the event of judicial proceedings.[98] In many instances the purpose of the resort to conciliation is to remove the controversy from the plane of legal argument altogether, either because the law is considered by one or both sides to be unsatisfactory, or because the claimant state recognizes the difficulty of effectively vindicating its rights under the law. In these circumstances the conciliator's position is nearer to that of an *amicus*

---

[95]See 48(i) *Annuaire, 1959,* pp. 79–82. [96]Ibid., pp. 82–5.
[97]Ibid., pp. 85–8. [98]Ibid., pp. 88–105.

of both parties in a 'social' dispute, than to that of legal counsel of the parties in a dispute concerning legal rights. It follows that clarification of the legal position by the conciliators should rarely rise above a secondary role. Basically, the conciliator is concerned with the legal position only so far as it is relevant in estimating the likely resistance of the parties to various proposed solutions. His main function is to reduce this resistance through properly exercised suggestion and mediation. Conciliation does not depend for success on decisions, or even on recommendations made on the authority of the conciliator, but on bringing the minds of the disputants to a meeting point on the issue in conflict. While Professor Stone objected, in principle, to the submission of proposals in writing, he agreed to the submission of a carefully written analysis of the opposing positions and the arguments in support of each.

In answer to a question with regard to the conduct of inquiry by the commission, Professor Stone observed that fact-finding must inevitably involve some degree of drawing conclusions from the evidence available, and in some cases these implicit conclusions may give vital indications to the parties. He agreed with the rapporteur, however, that the ascertainment of facts can and should stop short of any *explicit* (emphasis in the original) conclusions and, *a fortiori*, of evaluation of the facts in terms of the final overall merits of the respective cases. While it is not the conciliator's role to pass judgement on either the facts or the law, the clarification of the facts is one of the paths, and a very important one, towards the goal of mediation.

Professor F. de Visscher was of the view that it is not necessary to define the notion of conciliation.[99] The task of the conciliators, and the methods which they may adopt, vary considerably according to the character of the dispute and the attitudes of the parties. Thus, it can happen that, in the course of a procedure of conciliation, the commission invites the representatives of the parties themselves to deduce the elements of a solution which can subsequently be proposed by the commission.

Having received the comments of the members of the Commission on International Conciliation, Professor Rolin wrote and submitted his final report to the commission, accompanied by a draft resolution on the subject.[100] The commission formulated a new draft resolution for consideration by the whole body of members.[101] The provisions of the new draft were debated at the plenary session of the Institute held in 1961. On 11 September 1961 the Institute adopted, by a vote of 54 to 0, with 7 abstentions, a resolution[102] which reflected the common wish of its members that the rules governing the procedure of conciliation should

[9911]See ibid., pp. 107–11.   [100]Ibid., pp. 5–29.
[101]See text in 49(ii) *Annuaire, 1961*, 198–204.
[102]See text ibid., pp. 374–80. For an English translation by Professor Briggs see ibid., pp. 385–91.

be flexible enough to allow their application in disputes of any nature. The Institute recommended in its resolution that states wishing either to conclude a bilateral conciliation convention or to submit a dispute to an ad hoc conciliation commission, should adopt or be guided by the rules contained in the Regulations annexed to the resolution. The proposed Regulations are neither the expression of *lex lata* nor recommendations *de lege ferenda*, but comprise a series of opinions and advice.[103]

The following articles of the Regulations on the Procedure of International Conciliation are of special relevance to our study:

[Section 1. Definition of Conciliation]

Article 1

For the purpose of the present provisions, 'conciliation' means a method for the settlement of international disputes of any nature according to which a Commission set up by the Parties, either on a permanent basis or on an *ad hoc* basis to deal with a dispute, proceeds to the impartial examination of the dispute and attempts to define the terms of a settlement susceptible of being accepted by them, or of affording the Parties, with a view to its settlement, such aid as they may have requested.

[Section 2. Procedure for Conciliation]

Article 4

At its first meeting the Commission will name its secretary and, taking account of such circumstances, among others, as the time which may have been granted to it for the completion of its task, will determine the method for proceeding to the examination of the affair, whether, in particular, the Parties should be invited to present written pleadings, and in what order and within what time-limits such pleadings must be presented, as well as the time and the place where the agents and counsel will, should occasion arise, be heard.

Article 5

If the Commission establishes that the Parties are in disagreement on a question of fact, it may proceed, either at their request or *ex officio*, to the consultation of experts, to investigations on the spot, or to the interrogation of witnesses. In such case ['*Dans ce dernier cas*'], the provisions of Part III of the Hague Convention of 18 October 1907 on the Pacific Settlement of International Disputes are applicable, except for article 35 which requires the Commission to set forth in a report the facts resulting from the investigation.

[Section 3. Conclusion of the Commission's Work]

Article 7

At the conclusion of its examination, the Commission will attempt to define the terms of a settlement susceptible of being accepted by the Parties.

[103]See statement of the rapporteur to that effect: ibid, p. 217.

In this connection, it may proceed to an exchange of views with the agents of the Parties, who may be heard either together or separately.

Once decided upon, the terms of the proposed settlement will be communicated by the President to the agents of the Parties with a request to inform him within a stated period whether or not the governments accept the proposed settlement. The President of the Commission will[104] accompany his communication with a statement, either orally, or in writing, of the principal reasons which, in the opinion of the Commission, appear likely to persuade the Parties to accept the settlement. He will refrain in this statement from setting forth definitive conclusions with reference to disputed facts or from formally deciding questions of law involved, unless the Commission has been requested to do so by the Parties.[105]

[Section 4. Secrecy of the Proceedings]

Article 11

No declaration or communication of the agents or members of the Commission made with regard to the merits of the affair will be entered in the *procès-verbaux* of the meetings except with the permission of the agent or member of the Commission making it. On the other hand, written or oral reports of experts, the reports of investigations on the spot and depositions of witnesses will be annexed to the *procès-verbaux* of the meetings, unless, in a particular case, the Commission decides otherwise.

Article 12

Certified copies of the *procès-verbaux* of the meetings and copies of the annexes will be delivered to the agents through the secretary of the Commission unless, in a particular case, the Commission decides otherwise.

Article 13

Except for evidential material which may be derived from reports of experts, investigations on the spot or interrogations of witnesses, of which the agents will have received the *procès-verbaux*, the obligation to respect the secrecy of the proceedings and deliberations continues for the Parties as well as for the members of the Commission after the closure of the proceedings and even includes the terms of settlement in case the Commission has succeeded in its task of conciliation, unless, by common agreement, the Parties authorize a total or partial publication of the documents. When the Commission has completed its task, the Parties will consider whether or not to authorize the total or partial publication of the documents. The Commission may address recommendations to them on the subject.[106]

---

[104]The English translation erroneously employs the word 'may'. The French original reads: 'Le Président de la Commission accompagne . . .'. Elsewhere in the resolution the translator has affixed the auxiliary 'will' to the present tense of the French original, e.g. 'He will refrain . . .' for 'Il évite . . .' (in the same article).

[105]Art. 8 provides that if the parties accept the proposed settlement, a procès-verbal will be drawn up setting forth its terms. In accordance with Art. 9, if any of the parties do not accept the settlement, and if the commission decides that no purpose will be served by attempting to reach an agreement on the terms of a different settlement, a procès-verbal will be drawn up stating, without setting out the terms of the proposed settlement, that the parties have been unable to accept the conciliation proposal.

[106]The last section (5) deals with the expenses of the commission.

Article 1, which defines the concept of conciliation, does not include the customary treaty provision concerning the task of the commission to collect all necessary information 'by means of inquiry or otherwise' (e.g. Art. 15 of the General Act). The omission was intended, according to the rapporteur, to distinguish the method of conciliation from that of inquiry. Whereas the commission of conciliation can proceed to 'an inquiry and also to the ascertainment of facts' if it deems it useful, the aims of the inquiry procedure as envisaged in the Hague Convention of 1907 remain essentially different from those of the conciliation procedure: the commission of inquiry would ascertain the facts as they appeared to it, even if it knew that such an ascertainment would encounter objection from one of the parties; the commission of conciliation, on the contrary, would abstain from ascertaining the facts in similar circumstances.[107]

The definition includes 'the impartial examination' of the dispute as one of the main functions of the commission. During the plenary debate on draft article 1, Professor Rolin asserted that the essence of conciliation is a thorough examination ('examen au fond')—which distinguishes it from good offices—followed by a non-binding recommendation—which distinguishes it from arbitration.[108]

The last proviso of the article enables the commission to be seised of a request for an advisory opinion on legal questions. This was not stated explicitly, perhaps in order to avoid any resemblance to judicial proceedings. The present formulation does not, it would seem, exclude initiatives of a purely diplomatic character.

Article 4 confirms the importance attached to the process of examination. What is certain is that the examination must be carried out, and that the commission is expected to obtain the necessary information. How this is to be done must depend on the nature of the case. The Institute was careful, again, not to tie the procedure of conciliation to that of arbitration or judicial settlement.

Draft Article 4 ended with the expression '. . . where the agents and counsel will, should occasion arise, be heard either separately or contradictorily'. In plenary session Sir Humphrey Waldock observed that it was not advisable to allow the commission to choose at any stage of its work whether the agents should be heard together or separately. In his view, when the commission is at the first stage, i.e. when it proceeds with the examination of the facts, the agents must be heard together. The parties would not, at this stage, be likely to agree that one of them should give information to the commission in the absence of the other.

---

[107]This observation was made in the final report of Professor Rolin (48(i) *Annuaire, 1959*, p. 7). The ascertainment of facts is here meant in the sense of a formal finding submitted in writing to the parties. In the course of subsequent discussions, to be examined shortly, Professor Rolin adopted the view that the commission of conciliation should make an ascertainment of facts, in the above sense, only if authorized by the parties.

[108]See 49(ii) *Annuaire, 1961*, pp. 226 f.

On the other hand, at the end of this examination, when the commission is seeking the basis of an eventual solution, it would find it essential in many instances to address the parties separately, in order to find out their respective views on the terms of a compromise.[109] The rapporteur agreed with the above comment. There are two phases in the procedure of conciliation, he said—that of the examination, and that of the search for a solution. The examination must be 'contradictory'. The information furnished by one party must be checked by the other. On the other hand, in the search for a solution, the agents should be heard and should discuss matters with the commission separately.[110] As a result of the discussions, the provision with regard to separate or joint hearings of the agents and counsel was transferred to Article 7, dealing with the conclusion of the commission's work.

Article 5 avoids the ambiguity of Article 15 of the General Act with regard to the recourse to 'inquiry'. Instead of using the term 'inquiry' in a general way, Article 5 enumerates consultation of experts, investigations on the spot, and interrogation of witnesses. It is thus made clear that the 'examination' does not relate to the whole process of inquiry as envisaged in the Hague Convention of 1907. Another improvement on Article 15 of the General Act is the definition of the proper circumstances in which 'inquiry' should be applied, namely when the parties are in disagreement on a question of fact. Keeping in mind the basic principle that the rules of procedure to be followed by conciliation commissions should be as flexible as possible, the members of the Institute stipulated that the commission 'may' proceed to the consultation of experts, to investigations on the spot, or to the interrogation of witnesses.

The derogation in the final proviso of Article 5 is intended to underline one of the main differences between the method of inquiry and conciliation, namely that the commission of conciliation is not called upon to prepare a special report on the results of its fact-finding efforts. It will be noted that this proviso is not qualified to allow for the submission of a report on the facts even if the commission has been requested by the parties to present such a report. The general approach of the Institute in favour of flexibility would have justified a qualification to that effect. Professor Hambro's observation that the parties may ask the conciliation commission to transform itself into a commission of inquiry is pertinent in this respect (above, p. 233).

The question of conveying to the parties the conclusions of the commission on the issues of fact or law was the subject of a heated discussion which ended in the adoption of Article 7 of the Regulations by a majority. According to the relevant draft provision submitted to the plenary session of the Institute, a commission of conciliation which chose to conduct an inquiry would abstain, unless authorized by the parties, from stating the facts ('constater les faits') which emerged from

---

[109]Ibid., p. 234.　　　　　[110]Ibid., p. 235.

the inquiry, since such statement ('constatation') could render the commission's task more difficult. Similarly, the commission was to abstain, in the absence of a contrary authorization by the parties, from expressing an opinion which would decide ('tranche') the questions of law involved.[111]

Professor François asked in plenary session what was the purpose of an examination of facts from which no conclusions were to be drawn? Moreover, it having been agreed that the commission may convey to the parties the reasons for its proposal for a settlement, how can this be done if the commission is not allowed to draw conclusions from its inquiry? He maintained that if the terms of settlement are not accompanied by an opinion of the commission on the points of law and of fact, the proposal for settlement will have no influence on the parties. According to Professor François, there was no reason to fear that the findings or opinion of the commission would be of such a nature as to prejudice the legal position of the parties. The relevant provision in the Preamble of the resolution,[112] and the provisions on the secrecy of the proceedings, were sufficient guarantees.[113]

Professor Rolin, on the other hand, maintained that, unless authorized by the parties, the commission is precluded, at the ultimate stage of the presentation of the terms of settlement, from setting forth and conveying to the parties a formal opinion on the questions of fact and law involved. Before that stage, he said, the commission could unofficially inform the agent of each party of the opinion that seemed to predominate among its members. The commission would certainly take into account in its decision the results of its examination into questions of fact and of law. But if it announced these results officially, it could compromise the chances of adoption of its proposal.[114]

[111]See ibid., p. 201.

[112]This provision reads as follows: '*Declares* that no admission or proposal formulated during the course of the conciliation procedure, either by one of the Parties or by the Commission, can be considered as prejudicing or affecting in any manner the rights or the contentions of either Party in the event of the failure of the procedure; and, similarly, the acceptance by one Party of a proposal of settlement in no way implies any admission by it of the considerations of law or of fact which may have inspired the proposal of settlement . . .'.

[113]See 49(ii) *Annuaire, 1961,* 237, 251, 252. Professor Guggenheim supported that view, stating that the parties would always wish to know the results of an inquiry (ibid., p. 239). Sir Humphrey Waldock asserted that in certain categories of cases a party is not in a position to discuss a compromise without first knowing what the opinion of the commission is. He suggested that the commission would ascertain the facts and state the law to the extent that it considered this necessary for the fulfilment of its task (ibid., pp. 239 f.). In the same line of thought, Professor Charles De Visscher proposed a formula according to which the commission would abstain from ascertaining the facts or setting forth an opinion in law if such action would compromise its mission (ibid., p. 241).

[114]Ibid., pp. 241, 249 f. Professor Bastid and Professor Gros supported the position of Professor Rolin. Professor Bastid was apprehensive that, if conciliation failed, the rendering of an opinion in law would prejudice the legal position of the parties (ibid., pp. 253 f.). Professor Gros pointed out that the agents could be informed of the opinion of the commissioners when the parties were heard separately. What was dangerous, in his view, was to record this opinion in a form which would ultimately be regarded as a kind of judgment (ibid., p. 256).

At the conclusion of the debate, Professor François submitted an amendment whereby the commission would refrain in its statement from setting out definitive conclusions with reference to disputed facts or from formally deciding questions of law involved, unless it considered that the setting out of findings of fact or of an opinion in law would facilitate its mission, and provided that this was not contrary to its mandate.[115] This amendment was rejected by 44 votes to 13, while the whole draft Article 7, slightly amended in the meantime, was adopted by 48 votes in favour, 7 against, with 2 abstentions.

As for the meaning of the controversial part of Article 7, Professor Rolin explained that to exclude 'definitive conclusions' meant that the commission could not make a final finding on the existence of a fact. Similarly, although the commission was forbidden to decide formally on the legal contentions of the parties, it was given the possibility of bringing out the weaknesses of this or that argument without, however, expressly rejecting it.[116]

Articles 11, 12, and 13 regulate, i.a. the procedure to be followed in the case of fact-finding *stricto sensu*. While the commission is precluded, by Article 5, from setting forth in its report the facts resulting from its investigation, the above articles provide for the keeping of complete records of the reports of the experts, the reports of investigations on the spot, and the depositions of witnesses. Moreover, these reports and depositions are to be delivered to the agents of the parties, and the evidential material which may be derived from them is not subject to the general rule of secrecy. As stated by the rapporteur, a party should not be forbidden to use the procès-verbaux of the examination of witnesses or the findings reached in a 'contradictory' procedure ('constats auxquels la Commission aurait procédé contradictoirement'). These are elements of proof which belong to the parties. It is inconceivable to impose on the parties the burden of collecting the same evidence outside the framework of the commission. Moreover, in the absence of suitable precautions, the parties would be exposed to the risk of losing the evidence obtained in the course of the inquiry.[117]

---

[115]Ibid., p. 264.

[116]Ibid., p. 261. According to the rapporteur, one of the differences between Art. 15 of the General Act and the present Art. 7 is that the latter does not leave the commission the latitude of finishing its work with a 'procès-verbal de carence' if it does not see the possibility of formulating proposals having a chance of being accepted. In the view of the rapporteur, even if the attitude of the parties, or of one of them, left no hope of seeing them subscribe to what the majority of the commission would consider reasonable, the commission has the duty to formulate its attitude in a precise text. It is conceivable that a text which has been rejected may have a certain effect in future negotiations or in a future settlement. See final report in 48(i) *Annuaire, 1959*, p. 18.

It will be noted that the presentation of a statement of reasons is also considered mandatory. The relevant provision submitted by the rapporteur read: 'Elle peut, si elle le juge utile, accompagner sa proposition d'un rapport verbal ou écrit indiquant les raisons . . .', while the provision actually adopted reads: 'Le Président de la Commission accompagne sa communication oralement ou par écrit de l'exposé des principales raisons. . .'.

[117]Ibid., p. 22.

The provisions of Articles 11, 12, and 13 confirm the general opinion that fact-finding is or may often be an essential task of conciliation commissions.

CONCLUSIONS

The present examination has had the object of determining whether, and to what extent, commissions of conciliation perform functions of inquiry—either on the Hague model, or on the Bryan model, or both. It emerged that conciliation commissions perform both fact-finding and wider inquiry functions. While the extent of the fact-finding task depends on the circumstances of each individual case, the enlarged inquiry or 'impartial examination' of the dispute in all its aspects is carried out to a considerable extent and, in some cases, in a most thorough and complete manner.

Contrary to the relative uniformity which was characteristic of the nature of the disputes submitted to commissions of inquiry established in conformity with the Hague Conventions, and contrary to the similarity of the procedure followed by these commissions, we encountered in the present chapter a great diversity, both as regards the kinds of disputes submitted, or likely to be submitted, to conciliation, and as regards the character of the proceedings. Sometimes disputes submitted to conciliation would have at their origin mainly a difference of opinion on a point of fact—as in the Chaco case. In other instances, differences would centre on a point of law—as in the Franco-Swiss case concerning the Polish division interned in Switzerland. It is also possible that, far from any legal contest, a dispute would involve a conflict of interests—as in the Franco-Siamese case.

So far as the intentions of the parties are concerned, sometimes the parties may wish to obtain an advisory opinion on legal questions. The Institute of International Law allowed for this contingency in Article 1 of its Regulations. Alternatively, the states in dispute may wish the commission to enlighten them on the arguments which can be advanced for or against the existing claims. Professor Guggenheim had in mind such a function when he mentioned that the Swiss government was interested to know the opinion of the conciliation commissions which had handled the disputes to which Switzerland was a party. In other instances, the parties might ask the commission to propose a suitable compromise, likely to be accepted by them.[118]

Whatever the nature of the dispute or the intention of the parties, our analysis seems to confirm that the conciliation commission is always called upon to conduct a serious examination of the dispute. The observation of Professor Bastid to the effect that the commission must, as a rule, start its effort of conciliation as soon as it is informed of the

[118]Cf. ibid., p. 7.

dispute, i.e. before it proceeds to its examination, does not seem to reflect the predominant theory and practice. None of the jurists who, like Professor Bastid, emphasized the mediatory function of the conciliation commission, felt that in the early stages of its work the commission could dispense with the examination of the dispute.[119] The Regulations adopted by the Institute of International Law confirm the traditional concept of conciliation as a two-stage process: examination of the dispute, and conciliation proper. Under the terms of Article 1, the commission proceeds to the impartial examination of the dispute and attempts to define the terms of settlement. Article 7 of the Regulations provides expressly that 'at the conclusion of its examination' the commission will attempt to formulate the terms of settlement. Moreover, according to the same article, the proposal for settlement should be accompanied by a statement of reasons. These reasons cannot be defined without a considerable preliminary examination of all aspects of the dispute, in the sense of the Bryan treaties.

Our analysis of the four cases submitted to conciliation commissions has shown that in all of them the commission did not find it possible to accomplish its task successfully without elucidating the conflicting claims. This was so not only with regard to the juridical and 'factual' disputes, but also with regard to the purely political Franco-Siamese dispute.

As far as the role of fact-finding alone is concerned, it will have been observed first of all that the name 'Commission of Inquiry and Conciliation' does not indicate any particular emphasis on fact-finding in the actual work of the commission concerned. Thus the Chaco Commission did not devote more efforts to fact-finding than certain other commissions which were called simply 'Commissions of Conciliation'. It will be recalled that the Chaco Commission attached primary importance to the conciliation effort.

The position is similar with regard to the Franco-Moroccan 'Commission of Inquiry and Conciliation' which, in 1957-8, examined the dispute concerning the diversion of an aeroplane carrying the Algerian revolutionary leader Ben Bella and some of his colleagues. According to the president of the commission, Charles De Visscher, the questions of fact, on which the powers of inquiry could have been exercised, were of only secondary importance and most of them were not even contested. The commission had a strongly judicial character.[120]

---

[119]Professor Bastid agreed that in cases where the main or the preliminary question is legal, the first stage of the commission's work should consist of the examination of the dispute. She objected to the generalization of the system (see above, p. 231). However, as she herself pointed out, the obviously non-legal Franco-Siamese dispute was handled in two successive stages: elucidation of the questions in dispute, and an endeavour to bring the parties to an agreement (see above, p. 213).

[120]See Ch. De Visscher, *Aspects récents . . .*, p. 214.

On 22 October 1956 an aeroplane carrying Ben Bella and four other leaders of the Algerian revolt from Morocco to Tunis was ordered by the French authorities to land in

The extent of the fact-finding functions of a conciliation commission vary from the bare minimum to an almost exclusive preoccupation with matters of fact. The Franco-Swiss conciliation commission did not have to make an elaborate examination in order to verify the facts relating to the internment of Polish and French soldiers in Switzerland. It may happen, on the other hand, that in the first stage of its work the conciliation commission would act virtually as a commission of inquiry on the Hague model. This would be the case where the dispute is about alleged facts and the parties have requested the commission to set forth 'definitive conclusions' with reference to these facts (Art. 7 of the Institute's Regulations).[121] Between these two extremes a series of variations, involving a greater or lesser emphasis on fact-finding, is possible. Certainly, when the dispute relates exclusively to alleged facts, the emphasis on the fact-finding function will be considerable. However, a commission of conciliation is distinguished from a commission of inquiry in two main ways: (1) it is not called upon to conduct a minute examination into every detail of the facts involved; (2) it is not bound to issue a report on its findings of fact.

The commission of conciliation must constantly keep in mind that its inquiry into the facts must serve the purposes of conciliation. It must judge whether the extension of its inquiry into certain alleged facts would not be likely to produce tension prejudicial to its conciliatory effort.[122] It is submitted that if the alleged fact is central to the immediate issue of the dispute, the commission should not avoid examining it even if one party should be proved completely in the wrong as a result. However, if the alleged fact is not so crucial, the commission may find it expedient not to deal with it or not to make a thorough examination of the circumstances connected with it. The example of the Chaco Commission comes to mind here.

The absence of a duty to submit a report on the facts of the dispute also enables the commission of conciliation, if it considers it expedient, to abstain from a thorough investigation of certain claims. The commission is not called upon to present in writing an analysis of the facts

---

Algiers. The incident caused a dispute between France and Morocco. The Commission of Inquiry and Conciliation which dealt with the dispute was composed of Charles De Visscher (Belgian), R. Ago (Italian), J. Mekkaoui (Lebanese), R. Massigli (French), and A. Filalli (Moroccan). The task of the commission was twofold: (1) to determine whether the Moroccan government was correct in claiming that the diversion of the aeroplane was contrary to the rules of public international law; and (2) to effect a conciliation of the parties. During the oral proceedings the commission decided by three votes to two not to call Ben Bella and his colleagues as witnesses. In consequence, the Moroccan commissioner withdrew from the commission, and its work came to an end. See 'L'affaire du F. OABV', *AFDI*, *1958*, pp. 282–95.

[121]The case there envisaged must be distinguished from that mentioned by Professor Hambro (above, p. 233). He had in mind the complete abandonment of conciliatory functions. In that event, it seems, the conciliation commission would cease to exist as such and would be transformed into an inquiry commission 'pure and simple'.

[122]Cf. Cot, p. 205.

'in their logical sequence'—to use the opening phrase of the Dogger Bank report (above, p. 75). Not being bound to submit a report intended to announce publicly 'the whole truth', the commissioners need not fear that a gap in their investigation would be disclosed.

It is conceivable that, in view of the primary aim of conciliation, the parties themselves would encourage the commission to exercise its discretion with regard to the depth and extent of the inquiry, especially when it is likely to reveal faults on both sides. But this discretion is not unlimited, the prevailing view being that the commission of conciliation must accompany its proposals with a statement of reasons. If a dispute arises from a difference of opinion about alleged facts, the commission can hardly conceal the results of its examination into those facts. Indeed, as a rule the commission is precluded by the Regulations of the Institute of International Law from setting forth 'definitive' conclusions with reference to disputed facts. But what kind of 'non-definitive' conclusions are allowed in the statement of reasons? The suggestion is probably that the commission would bring out the weaknesses of one or other argument concerning the existence of the facts, without taking up an explicit position on them (above, p. 240). To do so, the commission must form an opinion, however general, on the basis of a substantial inquiry into the relevant circumstances. The Chaco example, although not involving a formal statement of reasons, well illustrates the role and form of fact-finding in this sense.

As far as the procedure for the acquisition of information is concerned, the tendency has been to emphasize the distinction between conciliation and 'inquiry' in the Hague sense. This tendency found expression in a reluctance to apply the procedural rules of the 1907 Convention to the fact-finding proceedings of conciliation commissions. Whereas the rapporteur of the Institute suggested in his final report applying Part III of the Convention to the consultation of experts, visits on the spot, and examination of witnesses, the plenary session limited such application to the examination of witnesses (Art. 5). It is even doubtful whether the automatic application of the Hague rules to the examination of witnesses is appropriate in all instances of conciliation. Thus a conciliation commission may consider that the examination of certain witnesses is likely to increase tension and therefore to prejudice the chances of reconciliation. If bound by the Hague rules, the commission would seem to be under the obligation to examine all the witnesses proposed by the parties. Similarly, the exigencies of conciliation may require, contrary to the relevant Hague rule, that certain witnesses, e.g. military or political prisoners, should be examined only by the neutral members of the commission and in their presence alone.[123]

---

[123]In the Franco-Moroccan case the commission refused to hear Ben Bella because it considered that his appearance might increase the tension between the parties and thus hinder the task of conciliation (see Cot, p. 203, & Nguyen-Quoc-Dinh, p. 614).

The present chapter concludes the examination of most of the problems that we have considered important for the comprehension of the institution of bilateral inquiry. In Chapter 9 we shall make some general observations about the nature of this institution in relation to other methods of peaceful settlement. It is perhaps appropriate at this stage to raise the question why bilateral recourse to inquiry or conciliation has been so rare. While hundreds of treaties have been signed, only a limited number have been implemented.

The first observation which stems from our analysis is that treaties have often been concluded under the influence of men of vision, whether statesmen or scholars, without any particular consideration of the overall needs of international society. The urge for a global network of treaties has led to the conclusion of treaties between geographically remote countries whose pattern of relations could hardly give rise to disputes suitable for settlement by the relevant treaties. Another reason for the rare application of some treaties may be found in their narrow scope. Thus, to the extent that the treaties exclude the settlement of questions involving vital interests, or honour, or independence, and to the extent that the interpretation of these reservations is in the hands of the contracting parties, the way is open for a state to avoid the undesirable (from its own point of view) intervention of a third party. Many treaties provide for the handling only of matters relating to facts in dispute, whereas in practice most disputes involve additional issues, often more basic than the issues of fact. In such circumstances, the isolation and handling only of the issues of fact may not contribute effectively to the solution of the dispute.

Perhaps the main explanation for the reluctance of states to have recourse to bilateral commissions of inquiry or commissions of conciliation is the identification of such commissions with the legal process. Our study has shown the pertinent similarities, both as regards procedure and the implications of the commissions' reports for the determination of legal rights. Since states generally perceive inquiry or conciliation as a form of arbitration, they prefer not to put their faith in a body which is unlikely to take account of their interests. As Northedge and Donelan have recently pointed out,[124] the burden of the settlement of international disputes must rest on political rather than legal institutions and devices, on balancing conflicting interests, on negotiation, bargaining, and the search for a mutually acceptable solution, rather than on a trial in a court of law 'from which one side emerges the victor and the other the vanquished'.

To the above considerations may be added the influence of universal or regional organizations which limit the application of bilateral inquiry or conciliation, either in a passive way—by providing a more attractive forum for the promotion of particular interests—or by virtue

[124]*International disputes; the political aspects* (1971), p. 320.

of active intervention at the outset of disputes between member states.

It follows that the application of bilateral inquiry or conciliation would be most appropriate in technical matters where the political element is absent or minimal. As we stated with reference to the activities of the United States–Canada International Joint Commission (above, p. 112), a treaty for the establishment of a commission of inquiry is more likely to serve as a basis for the successful solution of disputes when the subject-matter is technical and when both states parties enjoy good neighbourly relations.

CHAPTER 8

Inquiry in the Framework of the UN

INTRODUCTORY NOTE

In Chapter 1 we noted the distinction made between bilateral inquiry and inquiry in the framework of international organizations. The main difference between the two kinds of inquiry is the extensive involvement of third parties in the handling of a dispute by universal or regional organizations. This phenomenon entails, in turn, the influence of international politics in many aspects of the inquiry process.

The method of inquiry, as practised in international organizations, is held to comprise the establishment of various bodies, charged exclusively, or together with other duties, with the gathering of information on matters relating to the maintenance of peace and security, human rights, technical and economic co-operation, education, labour relations, and other specific fields. A thorough examination of the relevant practice would require a separate study, including the experience of the League of Nations,[1] the UN and its specialized agencies, and the various regional organizations.[2] The present chapter is not designed as a substitute for such a study. We have confined our examination to three topics which illustrate, it is believed, the main practical and theoretical problems relevant to the present study. The first two topics, peace observation and human rights, involve the analysis of UN 'fieldwork', while the third deals with the search for ways and means of improving the UN inquiry machinery.

PEACE OBSERVATION

The first report of the Secretary-General on methods of fact-finding draws attention to a number of UN bodies charged with observing and reporting the security situation in various parts of the world. Among the bodies mentioned are peacekeeping forces, observer groups, personal representatives of the Secretary-General, and special committees set up to examine a particular incident or situation.[3]

[1]See, in particular, Conwell-Evans, *The League Council in action* (1929), pt II: *League commissions of inquiry*.

[2]See generally Shore, *Fact-finding in the maintenance of international peace* (1970).

[3]To the latter category may be added four missions set up in pursuance of SC resolutions adopted on 22 Nov. 1970 (S/289), 15 July 1971 (S/294), 3 Aug. 1971 (S/295), and 2 Feb. 1973 (S/326) respectively. The first mission was sent to the Republic of Guinea, following

For the purposes of the present study, it would seem that a special examination of the organization and functions of military observer groups is warranted for the following two reasons: first, there is already an established pattern of deployment of military observers, especially in connection with the supervision of the cessation of hostilities; secondly, the main task of military observers often entails the continuous ascertainment of facts disputed by the parties. In this latter respect, the findings of the observers are designed to assist in the handling of the dispute either by the local observation machinery or by the Security Council. The investigation of border incidents by teams of military observers reminds us in particular of the fact-finding objectives of the Hague commissions of inquiry. We propose to confine our observations to UN experience on the Indian subcontinent and in the Middle East.[4]

Military Observer Groups in India and Pakistan (UNMOGIP and UNIPOM)

UNMOGIP has its origins in the activities of UNCIP, set up by the Security Council in 1948 with the dual task of investigating the fighting in Kashmir and mediating between India and Pakistan.[5] UN military personnel took an active part in the supervision of the ceasefire agreed upon by India and Pakistan in response to UNCIP's resolution adopted on 13 August 1948.[6]

Secretary-General Trygve Lie appointed in December 1948 a Belgian officer, Lt-General M. Delvoie, as Military Adviser to UNCIP. Delvoie was to organize a group of military observers and act as their 'Chief'. In January 1949 the Secretary-General dispatched to the subcontinent the first group of observers from the United States, Canada, Belgium, Norway, and Mexico.[7] The observers were divided into two groups, one attached to each army. Control Headquarters were established by the

---

a finding of the Council that external armed forces and mercenaries had committed an armed attack against the republic. The second mission was called upon to examine the situation along the border between Guinea (Bissau) and Senegal, following Senegal's allegations of acts of aggression committed by Portuguese forces. The third mission was charged to go to the Republic of Guinea and report on the situation, following Guinea's complaint of imminent Portuguese attacks. The fourth mission visited London, Lusaka, Dar es Salaam, and Nairobi, following Zambia's charges concerning acts of provocation by Southern Rhodesia. See respective reports of the missions, S/10009 & Add. 1, 2 Dec. 1970, S/10308, 16 Sept. 1971, S/10309, 15 Sept. 1971, S/10896, 5 Mar. 1973, Corr. 1 & Add. 1, 6 Mar. 1973.

[4]The following presentation is largely based on Dr Higgins's most valuable volumes: *UN peacekeeping, 1946–67*; *Documents and commentary*, i: *The Middle East* (1969); ii: *Asia* (1970).

[5]For background of the fighting see Lord Birdwood, *Two nations and Kashmir* (1956), ch. 4. UNCIP was established by virtue of SC res. S/654 of 20 Jan. 1948. For an account of the commission's work by its former member, see Korbel, *Danger in Kashmir* (1954), ch. 6.

[6]For text see Higgins, ii. 323–5.

[7]Only Mexico was not a member of the Security Council at the time.

senior officer of each group. These headquarters were under the direct command of the Military Adviser and in close liaison with the commander of the operations theatre on his side. Each group was divided into teams of two observers, attached to the tactical formations in the field and directly responsible to Control Headquarters. Accommodation, transport, and communication facilities were placed at the disposal of the observers by the two armies.[8]

According to 'Instructions for the Observers',[9] issued by Lt-General Delvoie, all observers were to make a thorough reconnaissance of the area of the unit to which they were attached. When breaches of the ceasefire occurred in their respective areas, the observers were to accompany the local authorities in their investigations and gather as much information as possible. Thereupon the observers were to report 'as completely, accurately and impartially as possible' to the officer in charge of the section or group to which they belonged.

On 27 July 1949, following UNCIP's initiative, India and Pakistan signed the Karachi Agreement on a ceasefire.[10] According to the agreement, the ceasefire line agreed upon was to be verified on the ground by local commanders on each side with the assistance of the UN military observers, so as to eliminate any no-man's land. If the local commanders were unable to reach agreement, the matter was to be referred to the commission's Military Adviser, whose decision was to be final. Section 1 provided that UNCIP would station observers where it deemed necessary. By virtue of other provisions, troops were to remain at least 500 yards from the ceasefire line and there was to be no increase in forces or strengthening of defences in areas where no major adjustments were involved by the determination of the ceasefire line.

The military observers proceeded with the verification on the ground of the ceasefire line—which was more than 500 miles long—and then supervised the forward movement or withdrawal of the troops adjacent to the new line. Thereupon, the observers could devote their main efforts to observation and the handling of complaints. The procedure for handling complaints—according to a former member of UNCIP's staff, S. Lourié—has been as follows:[11] Each complaint is promptly and thoroughly investigated. The team of observers goes to the place of the incident and tries to obtain all relevant details. It may call on witnesses, provided that the interview is informal and no oath is administered. After the investigation the team reports to the UN Control Headquarters, setting out in three distinct chapters its factual findings, its conclusions, and its recommendations regarding the action to be taken by either army or by the Chief Military Observer. The next step is for

[8]S/AC.12/MA/13 (Higgins, ii. 354).   [9]For text see S/AC.12/MA/1 (ibid., 353).
[10]For text see Higgins, ii. 334–7.
[11]See Lourié, 'The UN Military Observer Group in India and Pakistan', *Int. Org.*, 9 (1955), p. 20.

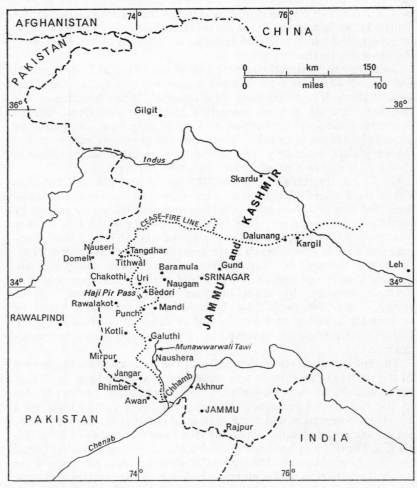

6 The Kashmir ceasefire line

(Reproduced from S/6651, 3 September 1965, as unofficial map showing approximate location of the ceasefire line.)

the Chief Military Observer to convey his recommendations to military observers in the field and if the matter is not settled at the local level, he takes it up with army headquarters in Delhi or Rawalpindi.

For the efficient performance of its duties UNMOGIP has kept a continuous record of the disposition of units of the two armies. Relevant information has been periodically submitted to the Chief Military Observer and has been treated by UN observers as 'Top Secret'.[12]

UNMOGIP's duties have included, in addition to observation of the ceasefire line, 'the competence to decide whether or not there is a violation of the Cease-Fire Agreement by either side'.[13] This adjudicative function has been carried out discreetly. It has not been customary to publish the 'awards' of the Chief Military Observer, and in this way an attempt has been made to keep military facts distinct from political propaganda.[14]

On 14 March 1950 the Security Council replaced UNCIP with a UN Representative (res. S/1469). The new Chief Military Observer, Brigadier Angle of Canada, had no duties towards the UN Representative.[15] Brigadier Angle reorganized the Military Observer Group under a single Control Headquarters which was located on one side of the ceasefire line for six months, and on the other side of the line for the next six months. General Nimmo (Australia), who succeeded Brigadier Angle in September 1950, continued the system of a single Control Headquarters.

The situation in Kashmir began to deteriorate in 1964. In mid-June 1965 General Nimmo reported that, during the previous five months, a total of 2,231 complaints from both sides had been submitted to UNMOGIP. Most of these alleged firing across the ceasefire line, while some alleged crossings of the line by armed men. As of that date, 377 violations in all categories had been confirmed by the observers, who found that 218 violations were committed by Pakistan and 159 by India.[16]

On 5 August 1965 major hostilities broke out in and outside Kashmir. According to the Indian version, 5,000 regular Pakistani soldiers, disguised as civilians, crossed the ceasefire line on that day. The government of Pakistan denied the allegation and pointed out that the conflict had escalated owing to Indian crossings of the ceasefire line in May and June, and the shelling of a Pakistani town. General Nimmo reported to

[12]Lourié notes (at p. 29) that both armies have co-operated to the fullest in giving the military observer group an extensive and up-to-date picture of their military establishment and positions in Kashmir.

[13]S/5450, 1 Nov. 1963, para. 5 (Higgins, ii. 343).

[14]In 1964–5, when the situation seriously deteriorated, the parties referred in statements or letters to the Security Council to 'awards' given by the Chief Observer. For examples, see Higgins, ii. 333–4.

[15]Lt-Gen. Courtney Hodges was appointed as personal Military Adviser of the UN Representative.

[16]Report of the Secretary-General on the situation in Kashmir, S/6651, 3 Sept. 1965 (Higgins, ii. 388).

the Secretary-General that armed men, generally not in uniform, had crossed the ceasefire line from the Pakistan side and had attacked Indian military positions on the Indian side of the line.[17] On 9 August General Nimmo cabled the Secretary-General that the situation along the ceasefire line was deteriorating. The Secretary-General promptly met the permanent representative of Pakistan and indicated to him Pakistan's responsibility for the events, as it emerged from the reports of the Chief Military Observer. The Secretary-General urged that the ceasefire line be observed. On the same day he conveyed to the Indian government his urgent appeal for restraint as regards any retaliatory action. In order to be better appraised of the situation on the sub-continent, he asked General Nimmo to come to New York for consultations.[18] Upon his return General Nimmo lodged with the Pakistani chief of staff an 'official protest and urgent request' for the withdrawal of Pakistani troops from the Chhamb sector. His action remained unheeded.[19]

Following repeated appeals by the Security Council,[20] India and Pakistan agreed at the end of September 1965 to stop fighting. After the ceasefire went into effect the Secretary-General appointed as his representative Brigadier-General Marambio of Chile and instructed him to meet with representatives of India and Pakistan for the purpose of formulating an agreed plan for the withdrawal of forces. At the same time the Secretary-General created a new group of observers— UNIPOM—charged with the supervision of the ceasefire outside Kashmir. UNMOGIP and UNIPOM were to be closely coordinated, administratively and operationally.[21]

According to instructions issued by the Secretary-General to Major-General Bruce F. Macdonald (Canada), the Chief Officer of UNIPOM, the responsibility of UNIPOM was limited to the area of conflict between India and Pakistan outside Kashmir and beyond the Kashmir ceasefire line; UNIPOM was an observation mission with the primary duty of observing and reporting; the reports submitted by the observers were to be thoroughly objective and as accurate and complete as possible. The observers in the field, in supervising the observance of the ceasefire, were to do all that they reasonably could to persuade local commanders to restore and observe the ceasefire in cases where firing occurred. Observers, however, had no power or authority to order an end to firing. Where their persuasive efforts failed, they were to report

[17]Ibid.

[18]S/6651, 3 Sept. 1965 (Higgins, ii. 389–90).

[19]S/6661, 6 Sept. 1965 (Higgins, ii. 391–2). Reporting on the events since 5 Aug. 1965, the Secretary-General stated that each instance of violation was protested by the UN observers who demanded that troops on the wrong side of the line be withdrawn (S/6651, 3 Sept. 1965; Higgins, ii. 389).

[20]Res. S/209 of 4 Sept. 1965; S/210 of 6 Sept. 1965; & S/215 of 20 Sept. 1965.

[21]Aide-mémoire of 25 Sept. 1965 from the Secretary-General to the representative of India, S/6738, 2 Oct. 1965 (Higgins, ii. 347).

fully to the Chief Officer on the circumstances leading to the breach of the ceasefire, on their efforts, and on the results.[22]

On 18 October 1965 the Secretary-General reported to the Security Council that there had been numerous confirmed breaches of the ceasefire of varying seriousness and that tension remained high in most sectors. Each side claimed that the other side had occupied new positions after the ceasefire and local commanders threatened to retake such positions by force. UNMOGIP and UNIPOM could not effectively supervise a ceasefire line which extended for almost 1,500 miles, because of the limited number of observers and the inadequate transportation and communication facilities. If the observers did not happen to be on the spot during the disputed events, they found it extremely difficult to arrive at a firm assessment of the blame for a particular incident.[23]

The following two examples may illustrate the handling of incidents by UN observers at that period:

1. An incident involving artillery fire took place on 24 September 1965 in the Lahore area, outside Kashmir. Colonel Gauthier, who was in charge of a team of observers, reported:

... Shelling started at 17.15 hours on 24 September from the Indian side with medium and field artillery, recoilless rifle, tank and small arms fire. ... This heavy firing went on for half an hour, forcing us to take cover. On returning to Lahore I immediately asked UNMOGIP to pass a strong protest to the Vice-Chief of Staff of the Indian Army, which was done. I then visited the local command who assured me that no Pakistan artillery had fired. It is difficult to state categorically if Pakistan artillery did retaliate, but the considered opinion is that the Indian started the firing, and I believe some shots were returned. I consider this situation explosive and I am experiencing great difficulty in preventing the Pakistan side from retaliating.[24]

2. In early October agreement was reached that certain bunkers south of Dograi (in the area of Lahore) would not be occupied by either party. However, on 5 November Pakistani forces occupied the bunkers. The Indian local commander complained, and the observers attempted to persuade the Pakistani forces to move, but without success. The Indian command agreed to refrain from action until 16.30 local time. At 15.20 observers who arrived in the area found firing in progress. Despite the observers' strenuous efforts, the firing escalated. The

---

[22]S/6649/Add. 7, 4 Oct. 1965 (Higgins, ii. 428).

[23]S/6710/Add. 4, 18 Oct. 1965 (Higgins, ii. 399). At the beginning of Sept. 1965 there were 43 UNMOGIP military observers. At the height of the crisis in Sept.–Oct. 1965 their number rose to 102. Of this total 13 were temporarily detailed to UNIPOM. As of 6 July 1966 the following countries contributed observers to UNMOGIP: Australia, Belgium, Canada, Chile, Denmark, Finland, Italy, New Zealand, Norway, Sweden, and Uruguay. By 30 Sept. 1965 UNIPOM was at its final complement of 90 observers. Contributing countries were: Brazil, Burma, Canada, Ceylon, Ethiopia, Ireland, Nepal, Netherlands, Nigeria, and Venezuela. Following the US promise to provide military assistance to Pakistan (Feb. 1954), India objected to the stationing of US observers (see Higgins, ii. 358, 362, & 440–1).

[24]S/6710/Add. 1, 26 Sept. 1965 (Higgins, ii. 396).

observer team was forced to take cover until about 17.30 hours, when it was able to withdraw. At 18.15 hours UNIPOM headquarters in Lahore negotiated by telephone a ceasefire on both sides as of 18.30 hours. Both sides agreed. At 18.30 hours Indian forces claimed that they had ceased fire, and that the Pakistani forces had not. UNIPOM headquarters advised patience. By 18.45 hours both sides announced that firing had ceased. On 6 November, at 14.17 hours, the Khasa observer team reported that Pakistani forces had vacated the disputed bunkers.[25]

On 10 January 1966, during a summit meeting held in Tashkent at the initiative of the Soviet government, the president of Pakistan and the prime minister of India signed a Declaration[26] expressing their agreement to restore peaceful relations between the two countries. To achieve that end they agreed, i.a., that all armed personnel should be withdrawn not later than 25 February to the positions held by them before 5 August 1965. UNIPOM and UNMOGIP helped the parties to complete the withdrawal by the target date. At a joint meeting convened by the Secretary-General's Special Representative, General Marambio, on 29 January 1966, military representatives of India and Pakistan signed an agreement[27] for the disengagement and withdrawal of their armed personnel. As regards disengagement, the parties agreed to request the 'good offices' of UNMOGIP and UNIPOM to ensure that the relevant actions to be taken by both parties are 'being implemented in letter and in spirit . . .'. In the event of a disagreement, the decision of UNMOGIP and UNIPOM was to be final and binding on both sides. So far as withdrawal of troops was concerned, the agreement provided that any matter on which there was disagreement was to be referred to the C.-in-C. Pakistan Army and COAS India for their joint decision. If the issue was still not resolved by them, the 'good offices' of General Marambio were to be requested and his decision was to be final and binding on both parties.

Annexed to the agreement were 'Ground Rules of Procedure' which laid down that 'opposing commanders', accompanied by UN representatives, would daily discuss plans for the lifting of mines and the dismantling of defences. Military observers carried out aerial and ground reconnaissance in order to confirm the veracity of certificates of mine clearance and the dismantling of defence works.

UNIPOM was withdrawn in the spring of 1966, soon after its tasks had been fulfilled,[28] while UNMOGIP continues to perform its functions regarding the Kashmir ceasefire line.

On 21 November 1971 India launched a large-scale invasion of East Pakistan. On 29 November the president of Pakistan requested the

---

[25]S/6710/Add. 8, 6 Nov. 1965 (Higgins, ii. 463–4).
[26]For text see Higgins, ii. 412–13.
[27]For text see ibid., pp. 407–9.
[28]The responsibilities of General Marambio also came to an end with the completion of the withdrawals.

Secretary-General, 'in order to obviate a threat to peace and to arrest the deteriorating situation', to consider stationing a force of UN observers on the Pakistan side of the East Pakistan border, to observe and report upon violations of Pakistan territory.[29] The Secretary-General immediately brought the Pakistan request to the attention of the Security Council. He noted that the stationing of observers on the territory of a sovereign state, even at the request of that state, should be authorized by the Security Council.[30]

On 3 December 1971 India and Pakistan accused each other of having initiated hostilities across the Western frontier and the ceasefire line in Kashmir (S/10410, Add. 1, 4 Dec. 1971). The Secretary-General was quick to supply the Security Council with up-to-date information based on reports from Lt-General Gonzales, the Chief Military Observer of UNMOGIP.[31] The Secretary-General recalled that UNMOGIP was charged with the supervision of the Karachi ceasefire agreement of 27 July 1949, and that the UN had no military observation machinery in any other part of the subcontinent.

The Chief Military Observer reported that, as of 29 November 1971, forces of both sides were deployed in battle positions for the stated purpose of meeting a threat from the opposite side. Both parties had contravened the Karachi Agreement by strengthening their forward defended localities, by laying minefields, constructing new unauthorized positions, and constructing additional defences in authorized positions. In addition, both India and Pakistan had strengthened their forces in Jammu and Kashmir in excess of the authorized number of troops. In respect of all these actions the Chief Military Observer 'had awarded "over-all" violations' to both India and Pakistan. In view of the admissions of the parties that they had consciously accepted responsibility for these breaches, UNMOGIP did not, as a rule, make the appropriate investigations in such cases. On the other hand, investigations were conducted following complaints in relation to alleged ceasefire violations, overflights, entering the 500-yard zone, crossing the ceasefire line, firing and use of explosives within five miles of the ceasefire line, and construction of new positions in the 500-yard zone or increase of defences in existing positions in that zone.

The Secretary-General stated further that at 13.00 hours West Pakistan time, on 3 December 1971, UN military observers reported movement of tanks and infantry in the Bhimber (Indian-held) sector of the ceasefire line. Shortly thereafter, the Pakistan Liaison Officer informed UNMOGIP that Indian forces had launched attacks along the ceasefire line and along the border. Thereafter the Chief Military

---

[29]See report of the Secretary-General to the Security Council, S/10410, 3 Dec. 1971, para. 12.
[30]Ibid., para. 13.
[31]See report on the situation along the ceasefire line in Kashmir, S/10412, 4 Dec. 1971.

Observer was currently informed by the various UNMOGIP field stations of the development of the fighting during the same day. Realizing that hostilities along the ceasefire line had commenced, the Chief Military Observer instructed the observers to remain at their stations. He was thus able to convey to the Secretary-General the detailed information received from the field of action. The Secretary-General, in turn, supplied the Security Council with up-to-date information.[32]

Hostilities on the subcontinent ended in the middle of December 1971 after the surrender of Pakistani forces in East Pakistan.

On 29 January 1972 the Secretary-General reported to the Security Council (S/10467/Add. 3) that the situation in Kashmir was generally stable. The High Commands of the Indian and Pakistan armies had provided the Chief Military Observer with information regarding the claimed locations of the lines of control of the respective military forces as of the time when the ceasefire went into effect. The lines claimed by the two sides did not coincide in all cases. UN observers were unable to verify the locations of the lines of control because, at the request of the High Commands of both parties, they were restricted from the beginning of the hostilities to the immediate areas of their field stations. For the same reason reports from the field stations have been based on information supplied to the observers by the respective local military authorities, confirmed so far as possible by such general visual and auditory observations as could be made from the immediate field station areas.

In a report covering the period 29 January to 12 May 1972 (S/10467, Add. 4, 12 May 1972) the Secretary-General stated that the situation concerning the functioning of the observers remained the same. As a result, he was not in a position to keep the Security Council fully informed. The Pakistani local military authorities continued to submit to UNMOGIP field stations complaints of alleged ceasefire violations by Indian armed forces. The Indian local military authorities submitted no such complaints, although Indian officials had referred publicly to ceasefire violations said to have been committed by Pakistani armed forces. A parliamentary statement by the Indian minister of defence alleging that Pakistani troops had attacked an Indian post on 5 May had been transmitted to the Secretary-General by the permanent representative of India. The Secretary-General forwarded the statement to the Chief Military Observer, who reported back his observations.

The permanent representative of Pakistan had communicated to the Secretary-General a number of complaints which were similarly transmitted to the Chief Military Observer. On 5 May 1972 the chief of the

[32]See S/10412/Add. 1, 5 Sept. 1971; Add. 2, 6 Dec. 1971; and report of the Secretary-General, A/8556; S/10432, 7 Dec. 1971, & Add. 1–11, 8–18 Dec. 1971. Following a deadlock in the Security Council, the General Assembly, on 7 Dec., called on India and Pakistan to cease hostilities and withdraw forces to their own side of the borders (res. 2793 (XXVI)).

Pakistani army staff handed to the Chief Military Observer a complaint of alleged ceasefire violations in two sectors. The Chief Military Observer, 'acting in the exercise of good offices', promptly transmitted the complaint to the Indian chief of army staff.

The Secretary-General further drew attention to 'flag meetings' at which local commanders met with the purpose of settling incidents. In the Indian view, flag meetings between local commanders provided effective bilateral machinery for maintaining the ceasefire; such meetings were successfully used on 32 occasions in the months of March–April alone, on the initiative of one or the other side. In the Pakistani view, flag meetings, in order to be acceptable and effective, would have to be held under the auspices of the UNMOGIP military observers. The Secretary-General asserted that the machinery of UNMOGIP continued to be available to the parties 'if desired'.

Conclusions. The nature of the military observation machinery was at first auxiliary. The observers were in the service of UNCIP, which was mainly concerned with the promotion of a political settlement. When it became clear that such a settlement was not forthcoming, and the responsibility for the conduct of negotiations on behalf of the UN was conferred successively on a number of individual representatives, the military-observation machinery developed as a separate and elaborate mechanism.

The continuous maintenance of the UN supervision machinery on the Indian subcontinent has been made possible because of the co-operation of the parties. The degree of mutual trust prevailing most of the time found expression in the willingness of both India and Pakistan to supply UNMOGIP headquarters with up-to-date information on the disposition of their forces (above, p. 251). The latest UN documentation indicates that since the 1971 war India is inclined to dispense with the services of UN observers in the field, while maintaining routine contacts at higher UNMOGIP level.[33] The reserved attitude of India may perhaps be an expression of her disappointment with the stand adopted by the UN, including the Secretary-General, in respect of India's responsibility for the war. It is also conceivable that, having gained confidence in their military superiority, the Indian military authorities expect to achieve better results by promoting a procedure of direct contact between local commanders.

An overall appraisal of the peacekeeping role of the UN observer groups on the Indian subcontinent must take into account the importance of the prompt and accurate information that has been reaching UN headquarters in New York, especially in time of crisis. Our analysis

[33]It is conspicuous that the Simla agreement of 3 July 1972, which provides for the withdrawal of Indian and Pakistani forces to their side of the international border and for respect of the 'line of control' in Kashmir, makes no mention of the UN machinery (see *International legal materials*, Sept. 1972, pp. 954 & 958).

shows that the observers in the field have been indispensable for the diplomatic initiatives of the Secretary-General. Of particular significance has been the ability of United Nations personnel stationed along the ceasefire line in Kashmir to provide the data necessary to determine which side initiated major hostilities, e.g. in August 1965 (above, pp. 251–2). The impartial ascertainment of facts prevents interested states from distorting the events and provides at least a moral justification for the aggrieved party. It will be recalled that, when Indian troops invaded East Pakistan, the president of Pakistan requested the stationing of observers on the Pakistan side of the East Pakistan frontier.

The immediate results of the observers' contact with the opposing armies have varied at different periods. Writing in 1954, Korbel asserted (at p. 162) that the presence of the UN observers contributed considerably to the calming of hostile spirits. In 1955 Lourié noted (at pp. 30–1) that after almost six years of cessation of hostilities, the two armies, with the active assistance of the UN Group, had been able not only to limit violations considerably but to settle all incidents quickly; in the absence of UN observers local flare-ups would have multiplied, with each side accusing the opposing one of violations of the Karachi Agreement. Lord Birdwood, who visited the area in 1955, related (at p. 155) that both sides used the observers as 'safety-valves to receive their complaints or listen to their soliloquies on Kashmir'.

Following the outbreak of hostilities in August 1965, the limitations of the observers' scope of action and influence came to the fore. Similarly, when fighting broke out in Kashmir, on 3 December 1971, UNMOGIP's role was confined to observing and reporting. The cessation of hostilities was the result of India's overall strategic and political considerations, rather than the intervention of the UN peace observation machinery.

UNTSO in the Middle East[34]

The elaborate peace-observation machinery in the Middle East has undergone several institutional changes, corresponding to the different categories of 'peace' prevailing in the area. Broadly speaking, three periods of peace observation may be distinguished: (1) the period of the two truces between the outbreak of the Arab-Israeli war in May 1948 and the conclusion of the armistice agreements in 1949; (2) the armistice period from 1949 to the outbreak of the six-day war in June 1967 (so far as relations between Egypt and Israel are concerned, this period, in effect, came to an end with the Sinai hostilities of 1956); and (3) the ceasefire period from 1967 onwards.

The continuous responsibility for peace observation in the area of conflict has been conferred on UNTSO which spontaneously grew out

[34]This section was set up in type before the war of October 1973. At present UNTSO's field organization is uncertain, pending disengagement of forces.

of the observation machinery established in the period of the two truces. Our examination will be confined primarily to the structure and functions of UNTSO since the Arab-Israeli war of June 1967.[35] By way of introduction, it may be noted that, following the conclusion of the Armistice Agreements, the Security Council distinguished between two functions of UNTSO personnel: first, observing and maintaining the ceasefire order contained in the Council's resolution of 15 July 1948 (this function involved the duty of the Chief of Staff of UNTSO to report directly to the Security Council); and second, assisting the four Arab states and Israel in supervising the implementation of the terms of the Armistice Agreements.[36]

The present role of UNTSO has to a large extent been determined by Security Council resolutions adopted during and after the six-day war of June 1967. On 6 June 1967, the day following the outbreak of the war, the Security Council called upon the governments concerned to take forthwith all measures for an immediate ceasefire and for a cessation of all military activities in the area. The Council requested the Secretary-General to keep it promptly and currently informed on the situation (res. S/233). While Israel, Jordan, and Lebanon accepted the call, Egypt and Syria did not comply at that stage. On 7 June the Council demanded that the governments concerned should cease fire and discontinue all military activities at a fixed time (20.00 hours GMT on 7 June). The Secretary-General was again requested to supply information (res. S/234). Egypt accepted the call, whereupon the Council turned its attention to the continuous fighting on the Israel-Syria front. On 9 June the Council demanded the immediate cessation of hostilities and requested the Secretary-General to make immediate contacts with the governments of Israel and Syria to arrange immediate compliance (S/235). In the course of the same day both countries accepted the demand for a ceasefire, but the fighting continued. The Secretary-General gave current oral reports to the Security Council on the development of the fighting. His reports were based on information supplied by UNTSO chief of staff, General Bull, who, in turn, was kept abreast of the situation by UNTSO observers in the area. The Secretary-General noted that the reports on the hostilities were fragmentary since General Bull and the observers operated under extremely difficult conditions.

On 11 June 1967 the Security Council adopted resolution S/236, which provided explicitly for the role of UNTSO personnel. The Council condemned 'any and all' violations of the ceasefire; requested the

---

[35]With regard to the truce and armistice periods see, generally, Higgins, i, Pt I. A comprehensive account of UNTSO's activities in 1948 is given in A/648: 'Progress report of the UN Mediator on Palestine', GAOR, 3rd sess. (1948), Suppl. 11. The report is dated 16 Sept. 1948. The armistice supervision machinery is the subject of Excursus I of my book *The Israel-Syrian armistice* (1967), pp. 293–317.

[36]See SC res. S/1376 (II) of 11 Aug. 1949.

Secretary-General to continue his investigations and to report to the Council as soon as possible; affirmed that its demand for a ceasefire and discontinuance of all military activities included a prohibition of any forward military movements subsequent to the ceasefire; called for the prompt return to the ceasefire positions of any troops which might have moved forward subsequent to the time of ceasefire; and called for 'full co-operation with the Chief of Staff of the United Nations Truce Supervision Organization in Palestine and the observers in implementing the cease-fire, including freedom of movement and adequate communication facilities'.

By the end of the war Israel forces had occupied Gaza and the Sinai peninsula, the West Bank of Jordan, and the Golan Heights in Syria. The armistice demarcation lines, as defined in the four Armistice Agreements, remained well within the occupied territories, with three exceptions: (1) the line between Israel and Lebanon; (2) the southern part of the Israel-Jordan line below the Dead Sea; and (3) the northern part of the Israel-Jordan line—south of Lake Tiberias.

In the changed military and political circumstances the question arose whether the Armistice Agreements, including their provisions for supervision with the assistance of UNTSO personnel, were still valid or not. Israel declared in 1956 that, on account of Egypt's active belligerence, the Israel-Egypt Armistice Agreement was no longer valid. In June 1967 Israel considered that Jordan's and Syria's attack on her put an end to the continuous validity of the Armistice Agreements with these two countries.[37] Lebanon's declared position of being at war with Israel had the same effect on the Israel-Lebanon Agreement. The Arab states, on the other hand, have maintained that the Armistice Agreements are still in effect, and that Israel had no right to terminate them unilaterally. This has also been the official position of the UN.[38] However, UN organs have, as a rule, refrained from asserting the validity of the armistice regime, probably bearing in mind that some basic provisions of the Armistice Agreements have been rendered obsolete, e.g. the obligation to respect the armistice demarcation lines. There is at the moment a wide consensus of opinion, shared by UNTSO,[39] that in effect the task of UNTSO personnel is to assist in observing and maintaining a new military status quo created as a result both of the changed military relationship between the parties, and the resolutions of the Security Council.

UN military observers assisted in the implementation of the Security Council resolutions of June 1967. Thus Israel and Syria accepted

[37]On the morning of 5 June Israel's prime minister Eshkol transmitted through the chief of staff of UNTSO a message to King Hussein, urging him not to join the hostilities between Israel and Egypt. The king did not heed the appeal.

[38]See ch. V of U Thant's annual report on the work of the organization for the period 16 June 1966 to 15 June 1967 (*UN monthly chronicle*, Oct. 1967, pp. 93–137).

[39]According to information obtained from UNTSO's headquarters in Jerusalem.

suggestions made by General Bull for the cessation of all firing and troop movements at 16.30 on 10 June, and for the deployment of UN observers on both sides of the line. Fighting stopped and, by 12 June, UN observers were deployed in the area. Thereupon UNTSO officers embarked on the important task of mapping the respective positions of the so-called 'forward defended localities' of the two armies. This led to the signing of two documents: the one stating the map references of the Israeli forward defended localities, signed on 15 June 1967 by a representative of UNTSO's chief of staff and a representative of the Israeli army, and the other stating the map references of the Syrian forward defended localities, signed on 26 June 1967 by a representative of UNTSO's chief of staff and a representative of the Syrian army.[40] The chief of staff informed both sides that any firing across the ceasefire lines thus established, as well as any movement beyond the lines and any overflight across the lines, would be considered as violations of the ceasefire, and would be immediately reported to the Secretary-General. By 27 June the observation of the ceasefire was being carried out by 110 UN observers, manning a total of 16 observation posts on both sides, and a reinforced control centre at Quneitra on the Golan Heights.[41]

With a view to discharging further his responsibilities, the Secretary-General suggested to the governments of Israel and Egypt that UN observers might be similarly deployed on both sides of the Suez Canal. The Security Council endorsed this initiative by means of a statement of consensus made by the president of the Council at the Council's meeting on 9–10 July 1967.[42] On 10 August 1967 the Secretary-General was able to report to the Council that 2 observation groups were patrolling between 3 observation posts on the Egyptian side and 4 observation posts on the Israeli side respectively.[43] Each group consisted of 16 observers. The number of observers in this sector was increased to 90, following the sinking of the Israeli ship *Eilat* and the retaliatory shelling of the refineries of Port Suez. The authorization for the increase was effected by means of a new consensus, agreed upon by the members of the Security Council in December 1967.[44] By November 1972 the

[40]The latter emphasized that the line is a purely practical arrangement for the specific purpose of facilitating the observation by the UN of the ceasefire and should not affect or prejudice the claims and positions of the Syrian government.

[41]S/7930/Add.18, 1 July 1967 (Higgins, i. 206–8).

[42]The president made reference to resolutions 233, 234, 235, & 236 (1967) of the Security Council and expressed the view that the Secretary-General should request the chief of staff of UNTSO to work out with the governments of Egypt and Israel, as speedily as possible, the necessary arrangements to station UN military observers in the Suez Canal sector under the chief of staff of UNTSO (S/8047, 10 July 1967; Higgins, i. 58). It will be noted that no reference to the armistice machinery was made.

Advanced parties of observers arrived in Ismailia and Kantara on 15 July and were instructed by General Bull to begin observation operations on both sides of the sector on the following day (S/7930/Add. 23, 17 July 1967).

[43]S/8053/Add. 1, 10 Aug. 1967 (Higgins, i. 132).

[44]See S/8053/Add. 3, 31 Oct. 1967 & S/8289, 8 Dec. 1967 (Higgins, i. 63 & 71).

number of observation posts rose to 7 on the Egyptian side and 8 on the Israeli side.

No special arrangements were made with respect to the posting of observers in the Israel-Jordan sector,[45] but observation posts were established in the Israel-Lebanon sector as late as 1972.[46] In pursuance of a consensus of the Security Council reached in April 1972,[47] 3 observation posts were established during the same month on Lebanese territory. The Secretary-General reported on 25 April that the effectiveness of the 3 observation posts might be increased, since the Lebanese authorities intended in appropriate circumstances to request the observers to move to areas from which a given incident could be better observed. In addition, more recourse might be made to the Mixed Armistice Commission for inquiries into incidents. The number of observers was increased from 7 to 21.[48] In compliance with a Lebanese request of 23 October 1972 for an increase in the number of observation posts and of UN observers, 2 additional observation posts became operational on 2 November 1972, and 4 additional observers were recruited.[49]

By May 1973 a total of 220 UN observers were distributed as follows: at UNTSO Headquarters in Jerusalem—10; along the Suez Canal—47 on the Israeli side and 41 on the Egyptian side; in the Israel-Syria sector—43 on the Israeli side and 48 on the Syrian side; in the Israel-Lebanon sector—29 on the Lebanese side; one liaison officer in Amman and one in Cairo. The countries represented were Argentina (8), Australia (6), Austria (12), Belgium (7), Canada (20), Chile (4), Denmark (12), Finland (25), France (24), Ireland (21), Italy (8), Netherlands (15), New Zealand (5), Norway (11), Sweden (33), and USA (9).[50]

[45]The absence of UN observation posts along the Jordan river seems to be due to Jordan's apprehension lest the formal recognition of the river as a ceasefire line would prejudice her legal position as regards sovereignty over the West Bank.

[46]On 16 Aug. 1969 Secretary-General U Thant addressed identical letters to the permanent representatives of Israel and Lebanon, in which he proposed 'that United Nations Observers, in adequate number to observe effectively, be stationed on both sides, with the function of observing and maintaining the Security Council cease-fire'. After stating that there was only token UN observer representation on the Lebanese side and none at all on the Israel side, he expressed his belief that the establishment of an observation operation would provide an important means 'of deterring incidents and of maintaining the cease-fire'. The permanent representative of Lebanon indicated that his government would welcome the strengthening of the observation machinery in the framework of the Armistice Agreement. The Israeli representative replied, with reference to the Lebanese response, that his government was not prepared to consider the matter on the basis of the armistice (see S/9393 & Add. 1, 18 Aug. 1969; Add. 2, 25 Aug. 1969).

[47]According to S/10611 (19 Apr. 1972), the consensus was reached without a formal meeting of the Council. It appears that the Secretary-General held consultations without convening the Council.

[48]See S/10617, 25 Apr. 1972. Israel withheld co-operation since the action was taken in response to a Lebanese request based on the Armistice Agreement of 1949 (see S/10611, 19 Apr. 1972, Annex, para. 8).

[49]See S/10818, 30 Oct. 1972; S/10824, 2 Nov. 1972; Add. 1, 22 Feb. 1973 & Add. 2, 2 Apr. 1973.

[50]This information has been obtained from UNTSO Hq.

Having outlined the main developments regarding the establishment of the UN observation machinery after the six-day war, we propose to examine the present structure and functions of UNTSO with particular emphasis on the procedure of inquiries. It will be noted that the relevant terminology used by UNTSO reflects the formal position of the UN whereby the armistice regime is still in existence, and the factual position according to which the main effective function of UNTSO is the observation of the ceasefire demanded by the Security Council in June 1967.[51]

The two diagrams below describe the staff and field organizations of UNTSO, while the map on p. 265 shows the disposition of the observation posts in the various sectors. The Israel-Lebanon, Israel-Syria, Israel-Egypt, and Israel-Jordan Armistice Commissions have their headquarters in Beirut, Damascus, Ismailia, and Amman respectively. The chairman of the Israel-Lebanon Commission is responsible for the observation posts on the Lebanese side of the Israel-Lebanon sector. The chairman of the Israel-Syria Commission is responsible for the observation posts on the Syrian forward defended localities and for the Tiberias Control Centre which, in turn, is responsible for the outstation at Quneitra (on the Golan Heights) and the observation posts on the Israel forward defended localities.

The chairman of the Israel-Egypt Commission is the officer-in-charge of the Ismailia Control Centre. He is responsible for the observation posts on the western side of the Suez Canal. Kantara Control Centre had its headquarters at Kantara East (occupied by Israel), but as a result of fierce fighting it was removed several kilometres eastward. This Centre is responsible for the observation posts on the eastern side of the Suez Canal. The chairmen of the Mixed Armistice Commissions, the officer-in-charge of Kantara Control Centre, the liaison officer in Cairo, and the liaison officer in Gaza are all directly responsible to the chief of staff.

A UN military observer assigned to a Mixed Armistice Commission or a Control Centre is under the exclusive control of the chairman of the commission or the officer-in-charge of the Control Centre. One of the main tasks of an observer is to assist the chief of staff in the observation and maintenance of the ceasefire. Whenever a ceasefire has been broken or whenever there is a likelihood of a ceasefire violation, the observer must endeavour to assist in restoring peace and tranquillity as soon as possible. Breaches of the ceasefire are to be reported immediately to the appropriate Mixed Armistice Commission or Control Centre. Similarly, observers are to inform their nearest headquarters of any threat, implied or actual, to the ceasefire.

Observation posts are continually manned whenever possible by two

---

[51]The discussion that follows is based on the Standing Operation Procedure of UNTSO, issued by the then chief of staff, Lt-Gen. Odd Bull, on 1 Aug. 1968 (as amended).

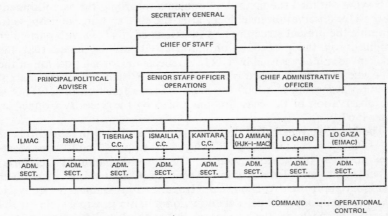

UNTSO field organization

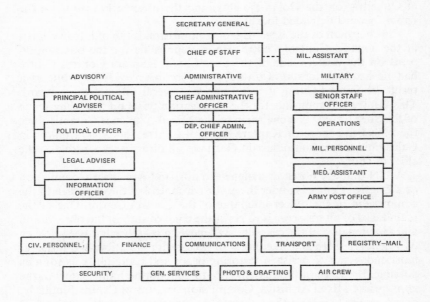

UNTSO staff organization

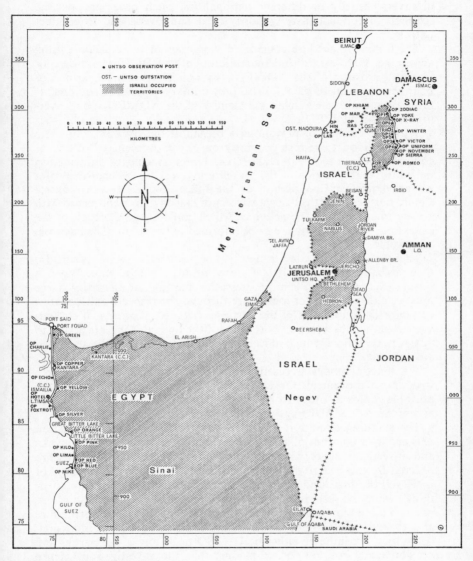

7 UNTSO area of operations

(Based on map included in UNTSO Standing Operation Procedure, 1968, and on S/7930/Add. 1788, 2 November 1972.)

observers, usually of different nationalities. Such observers may be required to conduct investigations, effect handovers, and to conduct patrols.

The following acts are considered violations of the ceasefire: firing across the ADL (armistice demarcation line) or FDL (forward defence locality), crossing of the ADL/FDL by military personnel, armed or unarmed; crossing of the ADL/FDL by military vehicles or equipment; firing of anti-aircraft guns in the vicinity of the ADL/FDL; and over-flights of the ADL/FDL.

With the purpose of preventing a breach of the ceasefire, observers are called upon to report promptly on any movement of troops or equipment close to the ADLs/FDLs. Upon receipt of information indicating that a breach of the ceasefire may occur, the chairman of a Mixed Armistice Commission or the officer-in-charge of a Control Centre must contact the delegate or senior liaison officer concerned with a view to suspending the activities which could cause a breach of the ceasefire. The chief of staff is to be informed of the action taken as soon as possible.

As a rule, ceasefires are arranged either through the Mixed Armistice Commissions, or the Control Centre, or the chief of staff. When a serious exchange of fire is in progress, the chairman or officer-in-charge must establish a time for a ceasefire through the respective delegations or senior liaison officers of the parties concerned. However, if circumstances allow, observers on both sides of the line must initiate action to achieve a ceasefire through officers of the parties who have the appropriate authority.

When acting under a ceasefire order observers must claim complete freedom of movement. Observers sent on ceasefire duties must take portable radios in order to be able to communicate with one another across the ADLs/FDLs and with at least one observation post.

The standing operation procedure of UNTSO makes a distinction between investigations of alleged breaches of the Armistice Agreements and investigations of incidents involving breaches of the ceasefire ordered by the Security Council in June 1967. In the terminology of UNTSO, the first kind of investigations are referred to as 'investigations', while the second kind are called 'enquiries'. 'Investigations' are pursued upon requests by either party and follow the rules of procedure and the practice developed by each Mixed Armistice Commission. 'Enquiries' are initiated either by UNTSO or by any of the parties and are conducted in a less formal manner than the 'investigations'. Since the armistice regime has in effect been superseded by the ceasefire regime, we may turn our attention to the inquiry procedure.

When one of the parties has requested an inquiry into an incident, the chairmen of the Mixed Armistice Commissions and the officers-in-charge of the Control Centres are to use their discretion in complying or not complying with the request. If, in their opinion, an inquiry would not assist them to obtain relevant facts, they are not bound to conduct it.

Observers conducting an inquiry are instructed to be strictly impartial and not to yield to pressure exercised by a party. If such pressure is applied, the observers must report the circumstances to the chairman or officer-in-charge. Throughout the inquiry the observers must exercise discretion and courtesy and make every effort to minimize unpleasant incidents and local friction.

The UN flag must always be flown on the UN vehicles, or carried by the observer when he leaves his vehicle if the inquiry takes place between the forward defended positions, in the vicinity of the ADLs/FDLs, or along the Suez Canal.

The party delegate or liaison officer is to be present in a 'liaison capacity' in the interest of the party and in order to assist the observers, for instance, by arranging for witnesses to be present, by acting as interpreters, and by producing evidence. The observers alone conduct the inquiry and are responsible for the inquiry report.

As a rule, inquiries are to be conducted in the area in which the incident has occurred. If this is not practical, the inquiry should take place in an area from which the scene of the incident can be observed. On arrival at the area of inquiry the observer should record the description of the scene of the incident, indicating the map references (as determined by him, not by the party concerned), the terrain, the location of the ADL or the FDL, and the surroundings. Greater value is to be attributed to physical than to oral evidence. Since oral evidence is not taken under oath, it is always open to question. On the other hand, physical (material) evidence is important and every opportunity must be taken to obtain it while still fresh and clear. Observers should bear in mind that if they search for material evidence first, witnesses may formulate their statements according to what has been found.

Witnesses are to make a statement, whereupon the observers must carefully consider the relevance of the statement to the complaint under inquiry. The observers may then ask the witness questions in order to clarify any points in the testimony, and to elicit additional information that would tend to prove or disprove the complaint. Leading questions are to be avoided. Observers should not permit any interference in the questioning by a representative of the parties. A delegate or liaison officer should not present evidence as a witness unless he has actually witnessed the incident. He may, however, give the observers an oral or written statement. Written reports from observers who have witnessed the incident are to be annexed to the inquiry report. The witnesses are to be heard separately. Once interrogated, a witness is not to be permitted to mix with other witnesses awaiting interrogation. Witnesses should be requested to remain available until the end of the inquiry in order to permit further questioning if necessary.

Physical evidence is of two kinds: material and documentary. Observers must request from the representative of the party physical evidence of an appropriate nature for inclusion in the inquiry report. Material evidence seen but of such nature as to prevent its inclusion in the report (e.g. unexploded projectiles) should be photographed or sketched and carefully described. In the case of a wounded person, the observer should, if practical, inspect the wound. A medical certificate or a statement of the attending physician which describes the point of entry and exit of the projectile and condition of the wounded person should always be obtained. Documentary evidence may include extracts of log sheets, medical certificates, post-mortem reports, death certificates, and photographs not taken by UNTSO but produced as evidence. Photographs of physical evidence and the scene of the incident should be taken, subject to the approval of the delegate or the liaison officer. Whenever appropriate, overlays to scale and sketches should be made regardless of whether photographs are taken.

Observers are to report only facts, describing carefully what they have seen and heard. They should avoid lending credence to unsubstantiated allegations of witnesses or to the complaint. Accordingly, they should refer to material of this nature as 'alleged'. However, at the conclusion of the report the observers must give a brief finding based on the evidence. If appropriate, observers may submit with the inquiry report a confidential letter to the chairman or to the officer-in-charge. This letter may include views regarding the veracity of the complaint or conclusions as to which party is at fault or has committed a violation.

The above procedure for the conduct of inquiries has been applied in relation to numerous incidents that occurred since the six-day war.[52] In the absence of any prospect of a political settlement (the Jarring mission, pursued by virtue of Security Council resolution 242 of 11 November 1967, experienced repeated deadlocks), the security situation in the whole area has deteriorated. UN observers performed their duties under severe strain and personal danger.[53]

[52]For an example of inquiry, see S/7930/Add. 74 & Corr. 1, 29 Aug. 1968 and S/7930/ Add. 76, 4 Sept. 1968. Israel complained that on 26 Aug. 1968 a patrol car had been mined and ambushed by Egyptian forces which had crossed the Suez Canal. Two Israeli soldiers were killed and one kidnapped. The inquiry conducted by UN military observers on 27 Aug. found that an Israeli army patrol had been mined and ambushed. The Egyptian authorities stated that no Egyptian forces had taken part in any action on the Israeli side. The observers asked to see the bodies of the two Israeli soldiers reported to have been killed, but were told that the bodies had been removed for burial. The observers could not therefore verify that two Israeli soldiers had been killed. However, the observers saw blood stains and three damaged steel helmets at the scene of the incident and took photographs of them.

On 2 Sept. 1968 Israel requested a meeting of the Security Council to discuss the incident. The Council dealt with a number of incidents in the area and on 18 Sept. 1968 adopted a resolution (S/258) in which it 'insisted' that the ceasefire ordered in its resolutions must be rigorously respected.

[53]On casualties among observers and on damage to UN installations, see S/9188,

Particularly serious was the situation in the Suez Canal sector where the Egyptian forces initiated the so-called 'war of attrition' designed to dislodge the Israel forces from the area. The frequent reports of the UN observers conveyed in the documentary series S/7930 (supplementary information received by the Secretary-General from the chief of staff of UNTSO)[54] revealed both the intensity of the fighting and the vigilance of the observers. On 21 April 1969 the Secretary-General issued a special report 'on the critical situation in the Suez Canal sector' (S/9171). He stated that since 8 April 1969, particularly, observance of the Security Council ceasefire resolutions S/233 (1967) and S/234 (1967) (above, p. 259) had been degenerating steadily. The weapons employed ranged from small arms to heavy mortars, rockets, tank fire, and heavy artillery. The only conclusion to be drawn from the observers' reports was that the Security Council ceasefire had become almost totally ineffective and that a virtual state of active war existed in that sector. In a special report on the 'increasing ineffectiveness of the cease-fire in the Suez Canal sector', dated 5 July 1969 (S/9316), the Secretary-General noted that heavy-weapons fire was initiated almost daily, especially from the west side of the Canal, in many areas of that sector. The pattern of acts of violence and reprisal, including a pronounced increase in aerial activity, had become almost routine. The Secretary-General asked the parties to return to observance of the ceasefire and also appealed to the members of the Security Council, individually and collectively, as well as to all members of the UN, to assist in making the ceasefire effective.

Intensive fighting in the Suez Canal area continued until 8 August 1970 when a standstill ceasefire agreement initiated by the United States entered into effect.[55]

In the Israel-Syria sector firing incidents have been frequent. According to information distributed by the Secretary-General during the period from early April until 15 July 1969, UN military observers reported firing incidents in which machine-gun, mortar, heavy-weapon, tank and anti-aircraft fire, as well as mine explosions, were heard.[56] Also reported were two aerial engagements watched by the military observers.[57] Reports covering the period 1 March–15 June 1970 related that incidents involving the use of artillery, tank, mortar and rocket fire were taking place on an almost daily basis and that aerial activity had

---

2 May 1968; S/9825, 8 June 1970; S/9368, 30 July 1969; S/7930/Add. 839, 16 July 1970; & S/7930/Add. 874, 7 Aug. 1970.

[54] 2,105 additions to the original document S/7930 of 5 June 1967 were issued by the end of Aug. 1973. Most of them deal with firing incidents.

[55] See Note by the Secretary-General on the Jarring mission for the information of the Security Council, S/9902, 7 Aug. 1970.

[56] S/7930/Add. 152, 9 Apr. 1969; Add. 178, 28 Apr. 1969; Add. 196, 14 May 1969; Add. 210, 27 May 1969; Add. 212, 28 May 1969; Add. 225, 7 June 1969; Add. 243, 24 June 1969; Add. 259, 29 July 1969.

[57] S/7930/Add. 214, 29 May 1969 & Add. 258, 9 July 1969.

increased.[58] While all firing virtually stopped on the Suez Canal after 8 August 1970, light and sporadic firing incidents continued to take place in the Israeli-Syrian sector after that date.

The Israel-Jordan and Israel-Lebanon sectors have been the scenes of many ceasefire violations. El Fatah irregulars operating from bases in both countries have crossed into Israel or Israel-occupied territory, and have caused numerous casualties. Occasionally rockets have been fired on Israel settlements. Consistent with its policy during the armistice regime, the Israeli government has authorized forceful counter-actions, including several armed incursions into the so-called Fatahland in southern Lebanon. Following precedent, the Security Council has condemned the Israeli attacks, while deploring (though not always) all acts of violence.

The Secretary-General has not been in a position to provide the Security Council with adequate information about the situation in the Jordan River area, and has repeatedly expressed his regret for the lack of observation machinery there (above, p. 262). On 21 March 1968 he reported that during the previous days there had been indications 'from various sources' of increasing tension in the Israel-Jordan sector, relating to terrorist activities on the Israeli side and threats of retaliatory action on Israel's part. There had also been reports of an unusual build-up of Israeli military forces in the Jordan valley area. Unfortunately, he stated, little or no verified information on these developments was available, because no UN observers were deployed there (S/7930/ Add. 64, 21 Mar. 1968). On 30 March 1968 the Secretary-General informed the Security Council that, according to accounts presented by both parties, heavy and prolonged firing, including artillery exchanges and aerial activity, took place on 29 March between the armed forces of Israel and Jordan. UNTSO's chief of staff, Lt-General Odd Bull, advised the Secretary-General that 'it is practically impossible for me to report on the developments in the Israel-Jordan cease-fire sector due to the fact that no United Nations observation is operating in the area' (S/7930/Add. 66).

The situation along the Jordan river gradually came under control. By the middle of 1970 Israel succeeded in virtually sealing off the ceasefire line and thus preventing infiltration. In September 1970 Jordan's King Hussein launched an armed struggle against the El Fatah groups stationed in Jordan, because he felt that they threatened his regime. Since then southern Lebanon has become the centre of El Fatah assaults against Israel.

On several occasions the Security Council was called upon to deal with ceasefire violations in the Israel-Lebanon sector. The recurring pattern has been: Lebanese allegations of large-scale air and ground attacks by Israeli forces in southern Lebanon resulting in casualties

[58]See, generally, from S/7930/Add. 571, 2 Mar. 1970 to Add. 775, 15 June 1970.

among Lebanese military and civilians; and Israeli assertions that the actions of the Israeli forces against terrorist bases in Lebanon were taken as measures of self-defence prompted by previous murderous attacks on Israeli civilians and border policemen.[59] At its discussions in June 1972 the Council was able to benefit for the first time from the peace-observation arrangements effected in that sector in April 1972.[60]

Conclusions. The UN peace-observation machinery in the Middle East has proved to be indispensable both for the world organization and for the parties involved. The presence of the UN has been considered essential for the maintenance of the truces in the first period, the armistice in the second, and the ceasefire in the third.

For the Secretary-General and the Security Council, UNTSO has been the only continuous reliable source of information on armed clashes and the immediate causes underlying them. Time and again members of the Security Council have felt that they could not proceed to a competent discussion of a particular complaint without being supplied with adequate and up-to-date data through UNTSO channels. In most instances, the information has been promptly delivered and accepted without any significant challenge.

The success in objective reporting has to be appreciated against the need for UNTSO to secure the confidence and co-operation of the parties. Indeed, there were instances, especially at the beginning of the armistice period, where UNTSO was apprehensive lest its reports would antagonize one or other of the parties, and therefore refrained from presenting a comprehensive picture of the situation. Gradually, however, UNTSO gained confidence and its reports contained all available particulars necessary to determine the responsibilities involved.[61]

One of the factors permitting the effective exercise of the fact-finding tasks seems to have been the separation of the mediatory endeavour to promote a political settlement from the peace observation function. As Count Bernadotte pointed out (A/648, 16 Sept. 1948), his position and decisions as truce supervisor could not, in the minds of the disputants,

[59]In res. 280 (1970), adopted on 19 May 1970, the Council condemned Israel for her premeditated military action on 12 May and deplored the loss of life and damage to property inflicted as a result of violations of resolutions of the Council. On 28 Feb. 1972 the Council demanded that Israel immediately desist and refrain from any ground and air military action against Lebanon and forthwith withdraw all her military forces from Lebanese territory (res. 313 (1972)). A preambular paragraph under which the Council would have deplored all actions that resulted in the loss of innocent lives failed to be adopted. On 26 June 1972 the Council called upon Israel to refrain from all military acts against Lebanon. While profoundly deploring all acts of violence, the Council condemned the repeated attacks of Israeli forces on Lebanese territory and population (res. 316 (1972)). A resolution couched in similar terms was adopted by the Council on 21 Apr. 1973 (res. 332).

[60]See S/7930/Add.1584, 26 Apr. 1972 to Add.1640, 21 June 1972, particularly Add.1641–1648 of 21, 22, 23, & 24 June 1972.

[61]I have treated this problem in *The Israel-Syrian armistice*, pp. 112, 213, 242, 261, 268, & 289.

be easily dissociated from his role in the more fundamental task of mediation.

In addition to fact-finding, UNTSO has performed a useful function in helping the parties to define their legal relationship through the delineation of truce, armistice, and ceasefire lines, demilitarized zones, no-man's lands, and areas of cultivation. As a consequence, the parties have been well aware of the respective spheres of their military authority, and the possibility of violations resulting from a legal vacuum (e.g. in relation to movements of boats on the Suez Canal) has been reduced. The same considerations apply to the role of UNTSO in securing agreed interpretations of basic rules, e.g. what constitutes a violation of the truce, armistice, or ceasefire.

As far as deterrence is concerned, it is doubtful whether UNTSO's presence has prevented serious breaches. In many instances the parties have acted according to their convictions, notwithstanding the negative evidence which UNTSO is likely to submit to the judgement of world opinion. On the other hand, UNTSO has had relative success in restoring peace when the initiation of fighting has not been prompted by governmental policy having broad military and political objectives. In particular, during the armistice regime, the arrangement of local ceasefires through the observers on the spot, or through the chief of staff, was a matter of routine.

A further comment on the observers' functions concerns the degree of their responsibility towards the parties, or towards the UN. Experience in the Middle East has shown that observation in the service of the parties, especially with regard to the conduct of inquiries, has suffered greatly from the breakdown of the armistice supervision machinery, which, in turn, was brought about by the general deterioration of the security situation.

On the other hand, observation pursued primarily in the service of the UN by means of observation posts, has proved to be most valuable even in times of crisis. The observers manning observation posts in the Middle East, both during the armistice and during the ceasefire period, have collected and conveyed a stream of adequate information. The inquiries conducted during the ceasefire period at the request of only one of the parties demonstrate the usefulness of the presence of UN observers when all direct contact between the parties is excluded.

The advantages of reducing the dependence of the observation machinery on the parties have prompted Dr Bowett to propose the following measures for improving peace observation of the UNTSO type:[62] (1) the terms of reference of the fact-finding bodies should be defined by the Security Council or by another review organ, and not be

---

[62]See 'Reprisals involving recourse to armed force', 66 *AJIL* (1972), 30–1. While the author refers to 'specific improvements to any fact-finding machinery likely to be concerned with reprisals', he has undoubtedly in mind overall supervision concerned also with 'initiating activities likely to cause reprisals' (ibid., p. 32).

dependent upon the agreement of the parties; (2) decisions on the interpretation and application of these terms should rest with the review
organ, not with the parties; (3) the fact-finding process should not be
confined to inquiries after the event but should evolve on a continuous
basis; (4) observers should have the non-compulsory power of investigation of witnesses; and (5) the observers should be accorded freedom of
movement on both sides of the dividing line. Dr Bowett points out that
these improvements might not be sufficient when frequent violations of
frontiers or ceasefire lines are occurring. The Middle East experience
suggests, he writes, that the various forms of machinery for observation,
fact-finding, limited deterrence, and even intermediate review of
responsibility, operate adequately only when both parties have an overriding interest in maintaining local peace.[63] We may add that if both
parties have such an interest, the need for the suggested improvements
is greatly reduced. The experience of the Israel-Lebanon Mixed Armistice
Commission shows that the existing legal framework was sufficient for
the smooth performance of armistice supervision functions.

Another observation, of a more general character, stems from our
study. Any process of inquiry, to be effective, needs the active and
continuous co-operation of the parties involved. To diminish the role
of the parties by establishing a rigid, quasi-arbitral system of peace
observation may reduce the prospect of success. As we shall see in the
next section, the need to secure the constructive co-operation of the
parties is not confined to peace observation only.

HUMAN RIGHTS

The UN has expressed varying degrees of concern with the maintenance
of human rights in dependent territories and South Africa on the one
hand, and in the rest of the world on the other. One of the main
features of the UN trusteeship system has been the dispatch by the
Trusteeship Council of periodic visiting missions to the territories concerned. During their tours in trust territories these missions have met
officials of the administering authorities and have held public or private
meetings in order to learn the views of the inhabitants.[64] In addition to
regular missions, special missions dealing with important constitutional
matters have been employed. For example, a commissioner appointed
by the General Assembly in November 1957 supervised, with the assistance of a team of UN observers, the elections held in April 1958, in the
trust territory of Togoland under French administration. Although the
government of South Africa refused to place the territory of South-West
Africa (Namibia) under the UN trusteeship system, it enabled a Special

---

[63]Ibid., pp. 31–2.
[64]See, for instance, *Report of the UN Visiting Mission to the Trust Territory of New
Guinea, 1971*, TCOR, 38th sess., Suppl. No. 2 (1971).

Representative of the Secretary-General to visit the territory in 1972 and to ascertain the wishes of the people on their future political status.[65]

With regard to non-self-governing territories, the main body charged with routine investigatory functions was, until 1963, the General Assembly Committee on Information. Since then the functions of examining information transmitted by the administering states have been conferred on the 'Special Committee on the situation with regard to the implementation of the Declaration on the Granting of Independence to Colonial Countries and Peoples',[66] also known as the 'Special Committee on Decolonization', or the 'Committee of Twenty-Four'. That committee, established by the General Assembly in November 1961, has become the only body responsible for matters relating to all dependent territories.[67] Its methods of work include examination of petitions, hearing of petitioners, and dispatch of visiting groups. With special reference to the right of self-determination, mention should be made of the mission sent in 1963 by the Secretary-General to ascertain the wishes of the people of Sabah (North Borneo) and Sarawak prior to the establishment of the Federation of Malaysia.[68] In 1970, following an agreement between Iran and the United Kingdom, the Secretary-General sent a personal representative to Bahrain to ascertain the true wishes of the people regarding the future status of the islands. The success of the mission gave hopes that the good offices of the Secretary-General could be usefully resorted to in the settlement of international disputes.[69]

In order to deal more effectively with the problem of racial discrimination in South Africa, the General Assembly established in December 1952 a commission 'to study the racial situation in the Union of South Africa' in the light of relevant provisions of the Charter and previous Assembly resolutions on racial persecution and discrimination. Not being allowed to enter South African territory, the commission based its findings on an analysis of the relevant legislation in force in South Africa, on oral and written statements made by non-governmental organizations and private individuals, and on memoranda communicated by certain member states. The commission submitted three reports to the Assembly, in 1953, 1954, and 1955, whereupon it ceased to function. In November 1962 the General Assembly set up the 'Special Committee on the Policies of Apartheid of the Government of the Republic of South Africa', entitled since 1970 'Special Committee on Apartheid', with the purpose of keeping the racial policy of the South

---

[65]See report of the Special Representative, S/10832, 15 Nov. 1972, Annex II.

[66]The Declaration was adopted by the General Assembly on 14 Dec. 1960.

[67]See report of the Secretary-General on methods of fact-finding, A/6228 (1966), para. 37.

[68]See report of the Secretary-General on methods of fact-finding, A/5694 (1964), paras 320–4.

[69]See Gordon, 'Resolution of the Bahrain dispute', 65 *AJIL* (1971), 560–8.

African government under review and reporting either to the Assembly or to the Security Council, or both. This committee examines official documents, press reports, memoranda from individuals and organizations, and conducts hearings. It works in close co-operation with the Committee of Twenty-Four and with the Council for Namibia established by the General Assembly in May 1967. The UN Commission on Human Rights established in 1967 an Ad Hoc Working Group of Experts to investigate charges of ill treatment of prisoners in South Africa. The group's mandate subsequently included the examination of manifold conditions in South Africa, Namibia, Southern Rhodesia, and the Portuguese territories in Africa (below, pp. 276 ff.).

UN inquiries into alleged violations of human rights elsewhere than South Africa and dependent territories have been narrow in scope.[70] In January 1957 the General Assembly established a committee to report on the situation in Hungary following the armed intervention of the Soviet Union in that country. The committee heard witnesses and received information from certain member states but was unable to secure the permission of the Hungarian government to enter its territory.[71]

In 1963 the president of the General Assembly sent a fact-finding mission to South Vietnam to investigate charges concerning the persecution of Buddhists. This mission proved to be exceptional in UN practice in so far as it was invited by the government directly concerned and received its continuous co-operation.[72] Another object of UN consideration has been the position of the Arab population in the territories occupied by Israel during the June 1967 war. A special working group of the Commission on Human Rights and a Special

[70]On the reluctance of the Commission on Human Rights to initiate inquiries in the rest of the world, see, generally, Carey, *UN protection of civil and political rights* (1970). The most recent procedure for dealing with complaints of private persons and groups concerning violations of human rights was established by res. 1503 (XLVIII) adopted by ECOSOC on 27 May 1970. The resolution provides for an investigation of situations that appear to reveal a consistent pattern of gross and 'reliably attested' violations, by an ad hoc committee appointed by the Commission on Human Rights. So far this provision has not been implemented.

The International Convention on the Elimination of All Forms of Racial Discrimination of 1965 and the International Covenant on Civil and Political Rights of 1966 provide for the setting up of ad hoc conciliation commissions with investigatory powers. No such commission has yet been set up under the convention on racial discrimination which came into force on 4 Jan. 1969. (The covenant is not yet in force.)

[71]See report of the Secretary-General on methods of fact-finding, A/5694 (1964), paras 198–202, and report of the committee, GAOR, 11th sess. (1957), Suppl. 18.

[72]The procedure followed by the mission is considered a model of the objective and impartial pursuit of factual evidence (see Bailey, 'UN fact-finding and human rights complaints', *Int. Aff.*, 48 (1972), p. 265). See also report of the mission, A/5630, GAOR, 18th sess. (1963), Annexes, a.i. 77.

It is significant that the mission did not offer its own conclusions concerning the veracity of the allegations. One possible explanation may be that, in its view such conclusions would serve no useful purpose because the Diem regime had been overthrown while the mission was still in South Vietnam, and the question of the persecution of Buddhists did not arise any more.

Committee of the General Assembly have examined allegations that the Israeli government violated human rights in the occupied territories (below, pp. 283 ff.).

The above non-exhaustive survey of UN institutional devices for the protection of human rights may serve as a background for the analysis of two major UN investigations into the condition of the non-white population in southern Africa and into the condition of the population in the territories occupied by Israel.

Investigation of conditions in Southern Africa

These investigations have been carried out by the Ad Hoc Working Group of Experts, established in pursuance of resolution 2 (XXIII), adopted by the Commission on Human Rights on 6 March 1967.[73] The original mandate of the group was to investigate the charges of torture and ill-treatment of prisoners and detainees in South Africa and to recommend action in concrete cases.[74] Subsequently this mandate was enlarged to include the investigation of allegations regarding infringements of trade union rights in South Africa,[75] South West Africa, and Southern Rhodesia;[76] capital punishment in southern Africa; treatment of political prisoners and captured freedom fighters in southern Africa; conditions of Africans in the 'Transit Camps' and on the 'Native Reserves' in South Africa, Namibia, and Southern Rhodesia; grave manifestations of colonialism and racial discrimination in South Africa, Namibia, Southern Rhodesia, Angola, Mozambique, and Guinea (Bissau);[77] the question of apartheid from the point of view of international penal law;[78] labour conditions in the Portuguese colonies in Africa;[79] and the system of recruitment of African workers in Namibia, Southern Rhodesia, and territories under Portuguese administration.[80] The group consisted at the outset of Ibrahima Boye (Senegal), Procureur-général of Senegal (chairman—rapporteur); Felix Ermacora (Austria), professor of public law at the University of Vienna; Branimir Janković (Yugoslavia), rector of the University of Nis (Yugoslavia); Luis Marchand Stens (Peru), professor of international law and deputy

[73]For text see report of the Commission on Human Rights, 23rd sess. (1967), ESCOR, 42nd sess. (1967), Suppl. 6, p. 76.
[74]Ibid.
[75]ECOSOC res. 1216 (XLII), adopted on 1 June 1967. For text see ESCOR, 42nd sess. (1967), Suppl. 1, p. 12.
[76]Res. 1302 (XLIV), adopted on 28 May 1968 (ESCOR, 44th sess. (1968), Suppl. 1, p. 11).
[77]Res. 21 (XXV) of the Commission on Human Rights, adopted on 12 Mar. 1969. For text see report of the commission. 25th sess. (1969), ESCOR, 46th sess. (1969), E/4621, p. 196.
[78]Res. 8 (XXVI) of the Commission on Human Rights, adopted on 18 Mar. 1970. For text see report of the commission, 26th sess. (1970), ESCOR, 48th sess. (1970), Suppl. 5, p. 78.
[79]ECOSOC res. 1509 (XLVIII), adopted on 28 May 1970 (ESCOR, 48th sess., Suppl. 1A, p. 9).
[80]ECOSOC res. 1599 (L), adopted on 21 May 1971 (ESCOR, 50th sess., Suppl. 1, p. 22).

permanent representative of Peru to the UN Office in Geneva; Waldo Emerson Waldron-Ramsey (Tanzania), barrister and economist, counsellor at the permanent mission of Tanzania to the UN.[81]

Since South Africa and Portugal withheld co-operation, on the grounds of illegality of the mandate and political bias,[82] the group was not able to visit South Africa, Namibia, or the Portuguese territories in Africa. As far as Southern Rhodesia is concerned, the United Kingdom was not in a position to ensure the entry of the group into that country. Consequently, the group was precluded from conducting 'on-the-spot' inquiries, but instead it collected evidence in neighbouring African countries, as well as in Europe and the United States. The names of most of the witnesses heard by the group were sent by various non-governmental organizations concerned with human rights in southern Africa, and by many liberation movements.

Generally, the group arrived at extremely negative findings, which were endorsed by the Commission on Human Rights, ECOSOC, and the General Assembly. The following findings may be given as an example: all political prisoners and opponents of apartheid detained under the '90-day' and '180-day' laws were tortured under interrogation in the hope of extracting confessions and information;[83] the South African government was continuing its policy of exterminating coloured people who opposed apartheid;[84] the cleaning up of the Caprivi strip in Namibia and the forced removal of the African population were elements of genocide;[85] the conditions in the Southern Rhodesian reserves were appalling and nothing was being done to improve the standards of hygiene, nutrition, health, and education;[86] Portuguese reprisals, in the form of taking of hostages, following a scorched-earth policy, massive and continued aerial bombardments and indiscriminate killing, were a normal phenomenon of the war in Angola, Mozambique, and Guinea Bissau;[87] and 'according to evidence', the most inhuman form of forced labour prevailed in the Portuguese colonies in Africa.[88]

By way of exception, the tone of the report (E/CN. 4/1076, 15 Feb. 1972) on new developments in southern Africa, submitted to the twenty-

[81]The Commission on Human Rights decided at its 29th session (Feb.–Apr. 1973) that the Ad Hoc Working Group would be composed of Kéba M'Baye (Senegal), chairman; Felix Ermacora (Austria), A. S. Mani (India), Branimir Jancović (Yugoslavia), Mahmud N. Rattansey (Tanzania), and Humberto Diaz-Casanueva (Chile).

[82]See letter of 17 Apr. 1967 from the permanent representative of South Africa to the Secretary-General, in report of the group, E/CN.4/950, 27 Oct. 1967, p. 28. See also letter of 19 Mar. 1970 from the Portuguese chargé d'affaires *a.i.* to the Secretary-General, E/CN.4/1036, 20 Mar. 1970.

[83]Report E/CN.4/950, 27 Oct. 1967, pp. 415–17.

[84]Report E/CN.4/984/Add. 8, 25 Feb. 1969, pp. 19–20.

[85]Report E/CN.4/1050, 2 Feb. 1971, p. 194.

[86]Report E/CN.4/1020/Add. 3, 16 Feb. 1970, p. 4.

[87]Report E/CN.4/984/Add. 17, 28 Feb. 1969, p. 14.

[88]Report E/CN.4/1020/Add. 3, 16 Feb. 1970, p. 4.

K

eighth session of the commission (March–April 1972), is moderate. This report, based not on hearings but on information made available to the group by the UN Secretariat, contains data describing some positive policies or impressions, e.g. Portuguese legislation for autonomy of the overseas territories, and opinions of correspondents who were not critical of the situation in Ovamboland (Namibia). For the most part, the report specifies the exact source of information.

The attitude of the members of the Commission on Human Rights towards the investigations has been ambivalent. At the outset some representatives, especially of the western powers, doubted the advisability of appointing a special commission of inquiry, since the group's activities would not be effective without the co-operation of the South African government. Reservations were also made on legal-constitutional grounds.[89] However, when the results of the first inquiry were submitted to the commission there was a widespread feeling that the group had acquired useful information.[90] Nevertheless, the question was raised whether an independent personality of unimpeachable international reputation would not be more suitable for the purpose of obtaining remedial measures.[91]

By 1971 the attitude of many members of the commission showed signs of exasperation. During the discussion of the report submitted to the twenty-seventh session in 1971, the representative of the Soviet Union saw no purpose in inviting the group 'to lengthen the list of suffering noted'. The time had come for the commission either to bring the work of the group to an end on the grounds that it had completed its task, or to set it a specific objective to help the commission in its fight against apartheid.[92] The US representative said that the activities of the ad hoc group, however valuable they might be, could not continue indefinitely.[93] At its twenty-eighth session in 1972 the Commission on Human Rights did not conduct any concentrated discussion on the last two reports of the group: on new developments in southern Africa (E/CN. 4/1076, 15 Feb. 1972) and on the question of apartheid from the

[89]See statements of the representatives of Tanzania (E/CN.4/SR.900, mtg of 23 Feb. 1967), France (SR.902, mtg of 24 Feb. 1967), Italy (ibid.), the UK (SR.910, mtg of 2 Mar. 1967), and the USA (SR.916, mtg of 7 Mar. 1967).

[90]See e.g. statements of the representatives of the UK (E/CN.4/SR.949, mtg of 8 Feb. 1968), USA (SR.955, mtg of 12 Feb. 1968), New Zealand (SR.955, mtg of 13 Feb. 1968), and Italy (SR.958, mtg of 15 Feb. 1968).

[91]The idea of dispatching a special representative was supported by the delegations of the USA (E/CN.4/SR.953, mtg of 12 Feb. 1968), New Zealand (SR.955, mtg of 13 Feb. 1968), Austria (SR.956, mtg. of 14 Feb. 1968), Chile (SR.957, mtg of 14 Feb. 1968), the Philippines (ibid.), the UK (SR.958, mtg of 15 Feb. 1968), and Italy (ibid.).

On the other hand, the representative of the UAR contended that private negotiations between a UN representative and a South African official were likely to lead not to progress 'but to a hushing up of the worst features of apartheid'. Moreover, the UN should not send any person to beg for human rights. (E/CN.4/SR.955, mtg of 13 Feb. 1968.) See, to the same effect, statement of the representative of the Soviet Union (ibid.).

[92]E/CN.4/SR.1107, mtg of 4 Mar. 1971.

[93]E/CN.4/SR.1111, mtg of 8 Mar. 1971.

point of view of international penal law (E/CN. 4/1075, 15 Feb. 1972). No proposals were made or decisions adopted with regard to the future activities of the group. The trend was to decrease the group's role in the continuing struggle against apartheid, while making use of its reports in order to activate other bodies. This trend found expression in resolution 2 (XXVIII) of 17 March 1972,[94] whereby the commission, 'having studied with appreciation the two reports', recommended that the Sub-Commission on Prevention of Discrimination and Protection of Minorities should appoint a special rapporteur 'to make special studies of policies and practices of discrimination on the basis of colour faced by people of African origin in all countries, and of the measures being taken and to be taken to combat such policies and practices . . .'. The commission further requested ECOSOC to transmit to member states, the Special Committee on Apartheid, and the International Law Commission the report of the group on the question of apartheid from the point of view of international penal law.

The relatively moderate attitude adopted by both the working group and the Commission on Human Rights may be attributed not only to the conviction that the continuous exposure and condemnation of flagrant violations would serve no useful purpose, but also to the current consultations between the UN Secretary-General and the South African government. It is pertinent that when the chairman of the working group introduced the 'fact-finding' report, he reminded the members of the commission that the Secretary-General was at the time in South Africa and had visited Namibia, 'and that it was important that nothing should be done which might hinder his mission'.[95]

Apparently, the commission accepted the views, advanced by some of its members several years before, that an independent personality might possibly achieve better results than the Ad Hoc Working Group of Experts.[96]

Conclusions. The inquiries into alleged violations of human rights in southern Africa have been of an essentially juridical character. The Ad Hoc Group of Experts took the UN Charter, the Universal Declaration of Human Rights, the two international covenants on human rights, the convention on racial discrimination, and the standard minimum rules for the treatment of prisoners, as a juridical basis for evaluating the facts. In this respect the practice of the group deviates from the pro-

---

[94]For text see report of the Commission on Human Rights, 28th sess. (1972) (ESCOR, 52nd sess. (1972), Suppl. 7, p. 50).

[95]E/CN.4/SR.1143, mtg of 9 Mar. 1972.

[96]On 31 July 1972 the Ad Hoc Working Group of Experts began a one-month field mission to Europe and Africa. The group received communications and heard testimonies in London, Geneva, Nairobi, Dar es Salaam, Lusaka, Brazzaville, Kinshasa, and Dakar. This was the group's fourth visit to Africa and its first since 1970 (*UN monthly chronicle*, Aug.–Sept. 1972, p. 84).

visions of the Hague Conventions of 1899 and 1907, which request the commission of inquiry to confine its findings to the ascertainment of facts, without entering into their legal implications.[97]

Another deviation from the Hague rules is the mandate of the group to make recommendations. Thus the Commission on Human Rights charged the group to recommend 'action to be taken in concrete cases'. This authorization bears on the very nature of the dispute and the wider purpose of the inquiry under consideration.

At its origin the dispute concerning the treatment of the non-white population in southern Africa was between many members of the UN, notably the newly independent states of Africa on the one hand, and South Africa, Southern Rhodesia, and Portugal on the other. Ideally, in the terms of the Hague Convention of 1907, the parties to the dispute could have agreed to appoint an impartial commission of inquiry to investigate the charges and ascertain the facts. The members of such a commission could be chosen from a panel of UN experts, whether existing or specially constituted for the purpose of the investigation. Another possible course could have been for both parties to ask the UN Commission on Human Rights to appoint such a commission. Neither of these courses was followed, because the accusing states excluded any dialogue with the three 'defendant' countries and because they wanted to ensure such control over the investigation as would serve their political purposes in combating racialism and colonialism. In practice the accusing states wanted the UN Organization to espouse their cause by identifying itself with their claims and charges. The second step would be for the UN to appoint an investigating body which would assemble as much incriminating evidence as possible. This evidence would then be widely published for the purpose of exposing the policies in question. Eventually, world public opinion would bring about the desired changes either by moral pressure or by stimulating drastic sanctions against the governments concerned.

As it turned out, the UN, by means of the Commission on Human Rights, responded favourably to the initiative of the most virulent anti-apartheid and anti-colonialist states. The Organization became in effect a party to the dispute because the Commission on Human Rights endorsed the original allegations made against South Africa as being well founded, while at the same time instituting the group to investigate the allegations. The posture thus assumed by the Commission on

---

[97]The Ad Hoc Group of Experts is generally considered a commission of inquiry, like the commissions provided for in the Hague Conventions. Ermacora points out that the group of experts, while being in fact an 'investigation commission' was not entitled so for two reasons: (1) to avoid coming into 'open conflict' with the terms of para. 7 of Art. 2 of the Charter, and (2) to prevent coming into conflict with the terms of ECOSOC res. 9 (II), authorizing the Commission on Human Rights 'to call in ad hoc working groups of non-governmental experts in specialized fields or individual experts . . .' ('International enquiry commissions in the field of human rights', *Revue des droits de l'homme*, I-2 (1968), pp. 188-9.)

Human Rights had its effects on the composition of the group and the conduct of its activities. The then Ukrainian president of the Commission on Human Rights contacted only the governments represented on the commission to ask them if they wanted or were able to propose experts to serve on the group. The South African government was not consulted and no attempt was made to establish a long list of experts as the panel for inquiry envisaged in Assembly resolution 268 D (III).[98] Although the members of the group were appointed in their personal capacities, the fact that, out of six, four held at the time of their appointment senior positions in the foreign services of their countries, was per se prejudicial to the impartiality of the inquiry. Moreover, the group included no prison experts, as stipulated in the relevant ECOSOC resolution and in the resolution of the Commission on Human Rights by virtue of which the group was established.

As regards the collection of evidence, the proceedings were characterized by the predominance of 'witnesses for the prosecution', which is natural in view of the background and purposes of the inquiry. The non-co-operation of the 'defendant' countries had a marked influence in this respect. It appears that no adequate attempt was made on the part of the group of experts to compensate for the absence of South Africa, Southern Rhodesia, and Portugal at the hearings. While witnesses were sometimes examined in true cross-examination fashion, they were not intensively questioned with the purpose of evaluating the credence of their evidence. As stated by Carey (pp. 121–2) with reference to the first inquiry, in the absence of representatives of respondent governments, 'the devil's advocate technique could have been used to advantage'. This gap could have been filled by appropriate rules of procedure. However, the Ad Hoc Working Group of Experts for many years conducted its inquiries with a very narrow set of rules concerning the keeping of records and the taking of an oath or making of a declaration of truthfulness by the witnesses.

The absence of rules of procedure, particularly rules on the admission of evidence, led to the admission of testimonies which did not bear on the specific terms of reference.[99] An additional consequence of the lack of rules was the uncertainty about the quorum needed for the proceedings. As late as 1 April 1969 the three members (out of six) then attending a session of the group decided that, because the group was an expert body, a quorum could be less than a majority. According to the same decision, each member was to be given an opportunity to signify his approval of the report.[100]

Another problem deserving our attention relates to the presentation of the views of the 'parties' in the report of the investigating body. In

[98]Ibid., p. 190. For res. 268 D (III), see below, App. III, p. 344.
[99]For examples, see Carey, p. 113.
[100]Ibid.

accordance with the Covenant of Civil and Political Rights, the Human Rights Committee to be set up under it is to submit to the parties to the dispute a report containing 'a brief statement of the facts', namely facts as ascertained by the committee and facts as presented by each of the parties.[101] In our case the group made no effort adequately to present the position of the accused parties. This is the result, to a certain extent, of the non-co-operation of the 'defendant' parties. However, if any favourable evidence reached the ad hoc group, it rarely found expression in its reports.[102] Perhaps a formal rule requesting the investigating body to present, to the best of its ability, the point of view of all parties concerned, would have contributed to the objectivity of the inquiry and would have enhanced the prestige of this and similar commissions of inquiry.

Despite certain drawbacks in the conduct of the inquiry, the Ad Hoc Working Group of Experts was able to provide convincing evidence that serious violations of human rights did in fact occur in the countries concerned. The practical effect of the group's findings, if any, has been negligible. While there has been some amelioration of conditions,[103] it is not easy to assess whether they are the result of the recommendations of the ad hoc group, as endorsed by the Commission on Human Rights, ECOSOC, and the General Assembly. Similarly, it is a matter of conjecture whether the public exposure of particular excesses has had a deterrent effect. What is certain is that the general policies and practices denounced by the UN have not come to an end. Consequently, there has been a feeling of frustration in the Commission on Human Rights at the end of four years of inquiries.

Given the strong emotional involvement, the clearly political objectives of the investigations, and the need for proceeding on a permanent basis, and also keeping in mind the non-co-operation of the parties concerned, the use of a commission of experts does not seem to be warranted. The pressure upon the authorities of the countries concerned could be maintained by other UN bodies, such as the Special Committee on the situation with regard to the Implementation of the Declaration on the Granting of Independence to Colonial Countries

[101]See Schwelb, 'Civil and political rights: the international measures of implementation', 62 *AJIL* (1968), 855.

[102]Carey notes disapprovingly (at p. 100) that the group omitted from its report a 'significant document'—report from Dr Hoffman—Delegate General of the ICRC on conditions in South African prisons. The group seemed to distrust Dr Hoffman's findings, which were in part favourable to South Africa. It may be added that, conversely, the group mentioned, on one occasion, that there had been some improvement in the condition of white political prisoners after conviction (see report E/CN.4/1050, 2 Feb. 1971, p. 192).

[103]e.g. the Portuguese Security Bureau had been disbanded. One of the witnesses testifying on the situation in Portuguese colonies stated that, following pressure by the UN, arbitrary arrests were decreasing rapidly and the living conditions in prisons were somewhat improving. He also said that the Portuguese authorities had begun to take 'equitable' decisions as regards prisoners arbitrarily arrested and that many persons had been freed (E/CN.4/1020, Add.1, 30 Jan. 1970, p. 64).

and Peoples, which has conducted similar inquiries and which has equal, if not wider, possibilities of obtaining and disseminating relevant information.[104]

Investigation of Israeli practices in the occupied territories

In pursuance of Security Council resolution 237 of 14 June 1967, the Secretary-General sent a Special Representative, Mr Nils-Göran Gussing to the Middle East to report on conditions affecting the civilian population and prisoners of war. Mr Gussing received full co-operation in the countries he visited. The report on his mission (A/6796; S/8158, 15 Sept. 1967)[105] provides a balanced analysis of the situation prevailing in the area at that time. The Special Representative related what he had seen and heard, as well as his own impressions. He was careful to convey the views of both parties, as testified by the memoranda of the Israeli and Jordanian authorities, appended to the report. Occasionally, the Special Representative acknowledged that the data at his disposal did not enable him to form an opinion. Following the failure of the Secretary-General to appoint a successor to Mr Gussing (on account of differences of opinion regarding inquiry into the position of Jews in Arab countries), the task of establishing special bodies to investigate the conditions in the occupied territories fell to the General Assembly and the Commission on Human Rights.

Two bodies, generally regarded as commissions of inquiry, were set up: the Special Committee to Investigate Israeli Practices Affecting the Human Rights of the Population of the Occupied Territories, established in pursuance of a resolution of the General Assembly adopted in December 1968, and the Special Working Group of Experts, established by virtue of a resolution adopted by the Commission on Human Rights in March 1969. The duplication of efforts may be explained by the delay in the formation of the Assembly's committee (see p. 284). It appears that those states which proposed the establishment of that committee were anxious lest it might fail to come into being, and took a similar initiative at the twenty-fifth session of the Human Rights Commission in February-March 1969.

The Special Working Group of Experts was charged with investigating allegations concerning Israel's violations of the Geneva Convention relative to the Protection of Civilian Persons in Time of War (the Fourth

---

[104]It will be noted that in pursuance of General Assembly resolution 2764 (XXVI) of 9 Nov. 1971, the Special Committee on Apartheid prepared a report on 'Maltreatment and torture of prisoners in South Africa' (ST/PSCA/SER.A/13 (1973)).

[105]The author of the report is the Secretary-General. In his Introduction he states that the report 'is based on the information contained in the final report of Mr Gussing to the Secretary-General'. In view of the nature of Mr Gussing's 'fact-finding' mission, it would perhaps have been desirable for the Secretary-General to publish Mr Gussing's final report in full. In the present report it is not easy to distinguish whether certain findings have been formulated by Mr Gussing or represent the Secretary-General's interpretation of Mr Gussing's findings.

Geneva Convention) of 12 August 1949.[106] Israel withheld co-operation since she did not recognize the competence of the group to inquire into the working of the Geneva Convention.

The group was composed of the following members: Ibrahima Boye (Senegal), chairman; Felix Ermacora (Austria); Branimir Janković (Yugoslavia); N. N. Jha (India); Luis Marchand Stens (Peru) and Waldo E. Waldron-Ramsey (Tanzania). During July and August 1969, the group held a total of twenty-nine meetings in New York, Geneva, Beirut, Damascus, Amman, and Cairo. In Syria and in Jordan the group visited refugee camps. It heard 103 persons, five of whom testified in closed meeting at their own request. In addition, the group consulted with a representative of the ICRC, Mr Claude Pilloud.[107]

In the conclusions of its report (E/CN 4/1016/Add. 2, 11 Feb. 1970), the group stated that it was not in a position to verify juridically the allegations received. Moreover, not being able to visit the territories, it received one-sided evidence. Nevertheless, the group was able to evaluate it. Thus it appeared that Israel was interested in ensuring the collaboration of the civilian population even against its will. It also appeared, 'according to certain witnesses', that whenever a person was suspected of endangering the security of the state, means of coercion were applied to extract information and confessions. The group reiterated, in this connection, that it was not in a position to verify these allegations juridically.

The Special Committee of the General Assembly was established in pursuance of Assembly resolution 2443 (XXIII) adopted on 19 December 1968 under the title 'Respect for and implementation of human rights in occupied territories'. By its terms the committee was to be composed of three member states—not individuals. The Assembly requested its president to appoint the members of the committee. The president, Mr Arenales of Guatemala, despite the 'most diligent efforts' on his part, did not succeed in finding 'three delegations willing to undertake what was universally regarded as a difficult, controversial, and unpleasant task'.[108] His untimely death created a constitutional problem which was solved on 23 January 1969, when the vice-presidents of the twenty-third session conferred the task of appointment on Mr Alvarado, chairman of the delegation of Peru to the same session. On 12 September 1969 Mr Alvarado appointed Ceylon (now Sri Lanka), Somalia, and Yugoslavia to serve on the Special Committee. The respective governments assigned the following persons as members of

---

[106]Res. 6 (XXV) adopted by the Commission on Human Rights on 4 Mar. 1969. For text see report of the commission, 25th sess. (1969) (ESCOR, 46th sess. (1969), E/4621, p. 183).

[107]See report of the group, E/CN.4/1016, 20 Jan. 1970, p. 10.

[108]See Amerasinghe, 'The work of the Special Committee to Investigate Israeli Practices Affecting the Human Rights of the Population of the Occupied Territories', *UN monthly chronicle*, May 1973, p. 73.

the committee: H. S. Amerasinghe, permanent representative of Ceylon to the UN, Abdulrahim Abby Farah, permanent representative of Somalia to the UN,[109] and Dr Borut Bohte, associate professor of the Faculty of Law of Ljubljana University and member of the Yugoslav Federal Assembly. Israel refused to co-operate with the committee on the grounds that resolution 2443 attempted to prejudge the very allegations the Special Committee was to investigate, that the resolution ignored the plight of the Jewish communities in certain Arab countries, and that the composition of the committee automatically guaranteed its anti-Israel bias: Somalia refused to recognize Israel, Yugoslavia broke off diplomatic relations with Israel, and Ceylon, while maintaining limited diplomatic relations with Israel,[110] had generally voted in favour of Arab resolutions at the UN.[111]

In 1970 the Special Committee held hearings in London, Beirut, Damascus, Amman, Cairo, Geneva, and New York. A second series of hearings was conducted in 1971 in Amman and Beirut. After the renewal of its mandate on 20 December 1971, the committee decided not to undertake another field mission. It continued to follow developments in the occupied territories through the press of Israel and of other countries, pertinent UN documents, as well as information from the ICRC.

Up to July 1973 the Special Committee produced three reports. In the first report (A/8089, 26 Oct. 1970) the committee stated the following conclusions: Israel was pursuing a conscious and deliberate policy calculated to depopulate the occupied territories of their Arab inhabitants; there was a policy of collective and area punishment in the form of destruction of houses, curfews, and mass arrests; in several prisons inmates were regularly ill-treated; civilians were treated with unnecessary severity in a number of instances; certain Arab villages were destroyed; the occupation had a disruptive effect on the economy of the occupied territories; there was a distinct lack of respect for the religious susceptibilities of the inhabitants of the occupied territories; there was interference by the Israeli authorities in educational matters, as well as interference with the judicial system, including legal aid.

The second report of the Special Committee (A/8389, 5 Oct. 1971, Corr. 1 & 2) differed from the first in two main respects. Less emphasis

[109]On 24 June 1971 the government of Somalia informed the Secretary-General that Mr Hussein Nur-Elmi, ambassador extraordinary and plenipotentiary, had been appointed to act instead of Mr Farah on the Special Committee.

[110]Ceylon broke off relations in Aug. 1970.

[111]See letter of 6 Jan. 1970 by the permanent representative of Israel to the Secretary-General, A/8089, 26 Oct. 1970, p. 12.

Rodley states that the composition of the Special Committee left something to be desired. All three states members of the committee had voted for res. 2443 (XXIII) (which condemned the practices to be investigated), a factor that, together with their general anti-Israel attitude, 'would hardly be expected to breed confidence in the intentions of the Special Committee' ('The UN and human rights in the Middle East', *Social research*, Summer 1971, p. 232).

was placed on allegations of individual ill-treatment and no detailed or numerous testimonies to that effect were included. On the other hand, the committee expanded its evaluation of allegations concerning policies of depopulation, annexation, and the denial of the right of self-determination. The committee concluded[112] that the policy of the Israeli government was designed 'to effect radical changes in the physical character and demographic composition of several areas of the territory under occupation by the progressive and systematic elimination of every vestige of Palestinian presence in these areas'. Summing up, the committee expressed the view that the fundamental violation of human rights lay in the very fact of occupation.[113]

In its third report (A/8828, 9 Oct. 1972) the committee stated that the 'alleged improvement' of the economic situation during the occupation was the natural consequence of an underdeveloped economy being brought into close relationship with a more developed economy. Even though the standard of living in the occupied territories may have risen, the question of the dependence of the occupied territories on the economy of Israel caused the Special Committee serious misgivings (paras 75–77). In addition, the committee confirmed that there was a deliberate Israeli policy of annexation and settlement of the occupied territories. It further noted that in the course of 1972 there had been some relaxation in security measures. With regard to allegations of ill-treatment while under detention, the committee was still unable, 'despite the compelling nature of the evidence it has received', to reach a conclusive finding. Such finding would only be possible after a free investigation by the committee carried out inside the occupied territories (para. 90).

Conclusions. The investigations of Israeli practices in the occupied territories, like those relating to southern Africa, were prompted by strong political motivations. The general aim of the Arab states was to use UN investigatory machinery as one of the means of bringing Israeli occupation to an end, without any concessions on their part. Unlike the states which initiated the southern African investigations, the Arab states and their supporters had no particular interest in entrusting the inquiries to a committee of experts acting in their personal capacity. The Special Group of Experts of the Commission on Human Rights was employed at the outset by default, and soon after the General Assembly Special Committee began to act, the services of the experts were dispensed with. This approach enhanced the political character of the inquiries. It is significant in this respect, that while the Special Group of Experts formulated its findings in a guarded manner, the

[112]See ch. IV of the report, entitled 'Findings'.

[113]In December 1971 the Special Committee submitted to the Secretary-General a supplementary report (A/8389/Add.1, 9 Dec. 1971, Corr. 1 & 2), dealing largely with the possibility of entrusting the tasks of a protecting power to the ICRC.

Special Committee of the Assembly, composed exclusively of countries hostile to Israel, used extreme language in evaluating the same issues.

The attitude of UN members towards the investigations of Israeli practices was, on the whole, different from that expressed in the southern African investigations. In the present instance a great number of states doubted whether there was prima facie evidence to substantiate the charges made, especially in view of first-hand information to the effect that Israel's policy in the occupied territories was basically liberal.[114] Moreover, many states which maintained normal relations with Israel felt that they should not support an initiative which was part of the political warfare in the Middle East. These attitudes would account for the refusal of 'neutral' states to take part in the Special Committee, as well as for the great number of abstentions on all resolutions concerning the investigations of Israeli practices in the occupied territories.

When the Special Committee started its investigations, it was able to take advantage of the model rules of procedure for UN bodies dealing with violations of human rights (E/CN 4/1021, 18 Feb. 1970 & Rev. 1, 30 Oct. 1970). The rules the committee adopted follow the model rules closely. However, the committee did not use any formal rules of evidence allowing it to determine the relevance of the evidence presented to it. As a consequence, the committee considered 'a wide range of evidence of varying degrees of probative force', including hearsay.[115] It appears that the committee realized this drawback, especially after Israel refuted the allegations in the Debras case of alleged ill-treatment,[116] and discontinued its practice of collecting indiscriminately evidence of alleged ill-treatment.

The Special Committee rarely resorted to cross-examination in order to test the validity of anti-Israeli allegations. This was a serious gap in its procedure, seeing that most witnesses appeared on the initiative of the Arab states. Moreover, the active involvement of Israel was acknowledged by the rules of procedure of the Special Committee in so

---

[114]Cf. Sherman, 'Israel's occupation problems' (*World today*, Nov. 1967, p. 491): 'By and large, however, it is true to say that rarely has an occupation been ruled with so light a rein and with so much attention to welfare. True, problems abound and complaints are numerous. But the smoothness with which life and contacts proceed has surprised not only the Arabs but even the Israelis, who have come to expect the unusual.'

In an article generally unfavourable to Israel's activities in the occupied territories, Dr Epp writes: 'To be sure, the Israeli military occupation is one of the most liberal and enlightened military occupations in history, but the fact remains that in the latter half of the twentieth century an enlightened military occupation is a contradiction in terms. The awareness of occupied peoples, the conscience of humanity, and international law do not allow for any unilateral military occupation, however generous' ('The Palestinians . . . a hi-jacked people', *World federalist*, world edn, Nov.–Dec. 1970, p. 7).

[115]See Bender, 'Ad hoc committees and human rights investigations: a comparative case study in the Middle East', *Social research*, Summer 1971, p. 257.

[116]Witness Mohammed Debras testified that after the June 1967 war he had been castrated against his will by Israeli medical personnel. Israel proved by means of medical reports that, for medical reasons, Mr Debras had undergone two operations for the removal of his testicles by Arab surgeons in Gaza before 1967 (see A/SPC/PV 799, 25 Feb. 1972).

far as they provided for the participation of representatives of the country concerned in the inquiry, and particularly for their right to cross-examine witnesses. It was to be expected that in order to compensate for the absence of Israeli representatives, the committee would have provided for methodological cross-examination.[117]

The reports of the Special Committee were not full and reasoned.[118] Within its mandate the committee could have presented and evaluated evidence favourable to Israel. Instead, the committee suppressed such evidence[119] and highlighted negative evidence. Moreover, by way of generalization, negative evidence submitted with regard to a number of persons or places was extended to the whole population and the whole area of the occupied territories. In certain instances, the committee accepted as facts allegations which could have been easily refuted by proper inquiries.

Thus, in its first report (A/8089, 26 Oct. 1970, p. 60) the committee asserts that the transfer of the Court of Appeal from Jerusalem to Ramallah has brought its activities to a standstill. The fact is that this court has functioned normally ever since its transfer, and that during the period covered by the report it issued over 2,000 judgments, including judgments on important questions of principle.[120]

Similarly, the concern of the Special Committee 'at the lack of legal assistance for persons who are in detention', and its impression that only three or four lawyers were available for this purpose is ill founded. Several witnesses appearing before the committee testified either that they personally had been defended by lawyers of their own choice or that other detainees had been so defended.[121] This evidence alone should have prompted the committee to make further investigations about the extent of legal aid, before drawing its extreme conclusion.

[117]See Bender, p. 259. Sometimes the chairman expressed bewilderment at some prima facie baseless allegations and prompted the witnesses concerned to reconsider their statements, e.g. A/AC.145/RT.13, 8 June 1970, mtg of 11 Apr. 1970, pp. 33–6; RT.14, 26 June 1970, mtg of 11 Apr. 1970, pp. 78–80; RT.21, 2 July 1970, mtg of 17 Apr. 1970, p. 17.

[118]It may be of interest to note that the chairman of the Special Committee regarded that body as a 'tribunal'. Cf. RT.29, 13 July 1970, p. 61.

[119]A former Israeli deputy-governor of the Gaza district, with special responsibility for the normalization of civilian life, sent the Special Committee a letter in which he enumerated various activities of the military government designed to improve conditions in the Gaza Strip, and offered to give evidence. The committee did not mention his letter in its report and did not invite him as a witness (see statement of the Israeli representative before the Special Political Committee, A/SPC/SR.748, 14 Dec. 1970, mtg of 10 Dec. 1970).

[120]See annual reports of the West Bank Command, *June 1967–June 1968*, p. 191; *April 1968–March 1969*, p. 180; *April 1969–March 1970*, p. 150; *April 1970–March 1971*, p. 138. I am grateful to Mr Y. Tweig, representative of the Israeli Ministry of Justice in the West Bank Command, for his explanations on the practice of the Ramallah Court of Appeals.

[121]See A/AC.145/RT.19, 1 July 1970, mtg of 16 Apr. 1970, p. 41; RT.21, 2 July 1970, mtg of 17 Apr. 1970, pp. 86 and 101; RT.22, 10 July 1970, mtg of 17 Apr. 1970, pp. 23–25; RT.32, 14 July 1970, mtg of 25 Apr. 1970, p. 76.

Had it pursued such an investigation, the committee would have been satisfied that no less than ninety lawyers had appeared before military tribunals in defence of the accused.[122]

The committee failed to present an objective appraisal of the situation pertaining to legal defence by omitting to mention in its findings that, with a few exceptions, local lawyers in the West Bank were on strike.[123] Many witnesses testified to that effect[124] and on several occasions members of the committee expressed their concern lest the boycott might adversely affect the legal aid for persons in the occupied territories.[125] Yet the fact of the Arab lawyers' strike was not taken into consideration in the final analysis of the evidence. The committee obviously wanted to lay the blame on Israel for whatever shortage of lawyers might have been felt. In accordance with this basic approach, the committee failed to mention the Israeli legislation designed to provide sufficient legal aid.[126]

Similar considerations are valid with regard to the committee's findings that there exists 'a distinct lack of respect for the religious susceptibilities of the inhabitants of the occupied territories'. The evidence produced before the committee does not warrant such a sweeping statement.[127] The committee did not mention that the Israeli

[122]In response to my inquiry on the subject, the legal adviser of the Military Command for Judea and Samaria (the West Bank) supplied me with a list of 90 lawyers who appeared before military tribunals in the area up to Oct. 1970—the period covered by the Special Committee's report. The list includes 13 lawyers from the occupied territories, the rest being Arab and Jewish lawyers from Israel. In only a limited number of cases were lawyers appointed by the tribunal.

To the above list must be added other lawyers who had continuously appeared before military tribunals in Gaza.

[123]A strike of Arab lawyers was called by the Bar Council in Amman immediately after the six-day war. The strike did not affect the lawyers in Gaza who have continued their practice, including appearance before military courts.

[124]e.g., A/AC.145/RT.7, 30 Apr. 1970, mtg of 6 Apr. 1970, p. 47; RT.10, 11 May 1970, mtg of 8 Apr. 1970; RT.18, 26 June 1970, mtg of 15 Apr. 1970, p. 67. Mr Nabulsi, an advocate from the West Bank, stated before the committee that the advocates on the West Bank decided to strike because the Israelis changed some of the laws and because they transferred the Jerusalem Court to Ramallah. He said that in 1969 there were about 100 or more advocates in the occupied territories and that the boycott comprised 95 per cent (RT.7, above).

[125]e.g., A/AC.145/RT.22, 10 July 1970, mtg of 17 Apr. 1970, pp. 33 ff. and RT.32, 14 July 1970, mtg of 25 Apr. 1970, pp. 74–5.

[126]See Order No. 145 of 23 Oct. 1967, relating to the West Bank in the compilation *Proclamations, orders and appointments of the Israel Defence Forces Command in the region of Judea and Samaria* (in Hebrew & Arabic) (1967–8), p. 306. Similar compilations are published with regard to the commands in the Golan Heights, the Gaza Strip and Northern Sinai, and Central Sinai.

I am grateful to Lt-Colonel D. Shefi, Acting Military Advocate-General, for providing me with various data and comments on the administration of justice in the occupied territories.

[127]The committee relied to a great extent on the evidence of Shaikh Sayegh, former president of the Shari'a (Muslim) Court of Appeal (A/AC.145/RT.17, 26 June 1970, mtg of 15 Apr. 1970, pp. 62 ff.). Shaikh Sayegh was asked several times to cite the Israeli orders or regulations which imposed, in his view, restraints on the functioning of the Shari'a courts. He gave evasive answers and in its report the committee was not able to elaborate on the subject.

Knesset immediately after the six-day war adopted a special law for the protection of the holy places in Jerusalem[128] and that subsequently the military commanders of the occupied areas promulgated orders for the protection of the holy places.[129] Any proper inquiry into the matter would have brought to the attention of the committee the public notices instructing visitors of the occupied territories to refrain from certain actions which violate the sanctity of the holy places. The committee, which relied on a great variety of sources, must have come across some favourable impressions of responsible religious leaders with regard to respect for religious feelings. However, statements to that effect found no expression in the reports.[130] Similarly, the committee ignored the statement of a witness, 'who left no doubt in the minds of the members of the Special Committee to his credibility' (A/8089, 26 Oct. 1970, p. 27), that generally, the policy of the Israeli authorities was 'to take very much care that the Holy Places should be respected'.[131] The committee chose to rely only on the negative evidence of the same witness in relation to other issues.

The approach of the Special Committee in the matter stands in marked contrast to that of Ambassador Thalmann, the Secretary-General's Personal Representative in Jerusalem, who related various grievances of Muslim religious leaders but also reported the text of the Holy Places Law 5727—1967, as well as the views of various religious representatives who had told him spontaneously that 'so far the Israel authorities had conformed to the principles which had been laid down and that there was therefore no ground for complaint'.[132]

The conclusions reached by the Special Committee in its second report with regard to the economic conditions in the occupied territories are not substantiated. According to the committee, the evidence indicated that the occupation had a disruptive effect on the economy. The committee added that, in the view of an Israeli witness, the economic conditions had actually improved (A/8089, 26 Oct. 1970, p. 59). The committee made no attempt to analyse the evidence received in both directions and to supplement it with its own independent inquiries. Instead, the committee gave full credence to negative evidence

[128]According to the Protection of Holy Places Law, 5727—1967, adopted on 27 June 1967, whoever desecrates or otherwise violates a Holy Place is liable to imprisonment for a term of seven years; whoever does anything that is likely to violate the freedom of access of the members of the various religions to the places sacred to them or their feelings with regard to those places, is liable to imprisonment for a term of five years.

[129]See, e.g. Order No. 66 of 10 Aug. 1967 issued by the Commander of the West Bank. Mr Farah mentioned the existence of this order at the meeting of the committee held on 8 Apr. 1970, RT.10, 11 May 1970, p. 41.

[130]See, e.g., statement made on 5 June 1969 by Mr Salih Ututalum, Muslim member of the Philippines cabinet, quoted in the pamphlet *Moslem religious life in Jerusalem*, published by the Israeli Ministry of Religious Affairs (Mar. 1970).

[131]Testimony of Mr Abileah, of the Israeli League for Human and Civil Rights, A/AC.145/RT.40, 23 July 1970, mtg of 12 June 1970, p. 24.

[132]See report on Thalmann's mission, paras 140 & 141 (S/8146; A/6793, 12 Sept. 1967).

and expressed reservation and scepticism in relation to positive evidence.[133] The committee was obviously not inclined to pursue a thorough inquiry into the economic conditions of the occupied territories. In such circumstances it should perhaps have refrained from expressing opinions on the subject. Its effort to restore the balance in the third report can hardly compensate for its earlier failure.[134]

The committee's repeated findings that Israel was seeking the depopulation of the territories of their Arab inhabitants has, likewise, not been supported by any adequate data. Any conscientious analysis of the policy of Defence Minister Dayan in the occupied territories would have led the committee to believe that it is based not on 'depopulation' but on coexistence and co-operation between the Arab inhabitants of the occupied territories and the population of Israel. The Special Committee itself quoted in its second report a series of statements of the defence minister in which he called for improving the standard of living of the Gaza refugees, coexistence between Arabs and Jews in Hebron and, in general, the promotion of 'dialogue' and 'common life' between the Arab population of the occupied territories and the Israel population (A/8389, 5 Oct. 1971, pp. 30–1). The committee intended to show, on the basis of these quotations, that Dayan seeks the annexation of the occupied territories. Whatever the merits of such an assertion, the evidence brought in support ran counter to the committee's findings that the Israeli government is pursuing a policy of oppression designed to force the population of the occupied territories to leave.

So far as the subject of annexation is concerned, the committee failed to mention the attitude of many Israeli leaders, and for that matter a large part of the Israeli population, who oppose annexation, either on account of consideration for the Palestinian right of self-determination, or because of the detrimental demographic implications of annexation, or both.[135] It is conspicuous that in its analysis of the 'Allegations of annexation and settlement' (A/8389, pp. 27–41) the committee did not mention the plan of Israel's vice-premier Allon which, rather than

---

[133]See, in particular, A/AC.145/RT.10, 11 May 1970, mtg of 8 Apr. 1970, p. 61; & A/AC.145/RT.37, 16 July 1970, mtg of 1 May 1970, p. 16.

[134]For an account of Israel's success in improving the economic situation and welfare of the occupied territories, see, generally, *Four years of military administration, 1967–71; data on civilian activities in Judea and Samaria, the Gaza Strip and Northern Sinai*, published by the Israeli Ministry of Defence (n.d.). See also Lifshitz, *The economic development in the administered areas, 1967–9* (1970) (in Hebrew), in particular pp. 16, 23–4, & 88. David Caute wrote in *The Guardian* of 26 Apr. 1970, that 'By and large, the Israeli presence has boosted rather than depressed the economy of Judea and Samaria'. According to an Arab journalist, 'Israel has been successful in these years of conquest in making restitution to these people for their sense of depression through economic abundance which has almost made them forget the territories . . .' (Nabil Khury in the Beirut *al-Hawadess*, 23 Apr. 1971).

[135]According to E. Silver (*The Observer*, 27 Aug. 1972), 'Foreign Minister Abba Eban, who believes that it is wrong to impose a Zionist destiny on unwilling Arabs, contents himself with the demographical argument (if Israel keeps the West Bank the Arabs will have an effective political majority by 1990)'.

advocating the 'depopulation' and 'annexation' of the West Bank with its 600,000 Arab inhabitants,[136] favours the exclusion of the bulk of that area from Israel.[137]

In sum, the political factors underlying the establishment and composition of the Special Committee have prevented it from conducting a thorough inquiry into all relevant aspects relating to Israel's practices in the occupied territories.

General observations on human rights inquiries

The practice of the UN with regard to inquiries into alleged violations of human rights reveals the following basic differences from the Hague system: joint initiative of the parties in dispute is not necessary for the appointment of a commission of inquiry; the state requesting an inquiry need not claim direct injury; the consent of the accused state is not a prior condition for the conduct of the inquiry; the accused state is not necessarily consulted on the membership of the commission, or its mode of operation; the commission of inquiry is responsible not to the states in conflict, but to the UN organ that has appointed it; the scope of investigations includes legal, as well as factual, issues; the report contains not only findings but also recommendations; action on the report is expected, not only by the state or states directly concerned, but also from the competent UN organs.

The internationalization of the institution of inquiry has been characterized by the overwhelming influence of political factors, which has led to an ever-increasing estrangement from the Hague system of genuine fact-finding. One of the results has been that investigations are not made in those countries which have sufficient political influence to prevent the adoption of any decision to that effect. Conversely, states which command strong voting power have been instrumental in initiating inquiries in other places with the general purpose of furthering a broad political aim. This explains the concentration of UN investigations into alleged violations of human rights in southern Africa and the Israeli occupied territories.

Another feature of the politicization of human rights investigations is the influence of the political organs of the UN in the formulation of the terms of reference and composition of the commissions of inquiry.

[136] At the end of Dec. 1971, the population of the West Bank was 623,000 and that of the Gaza Strip and North Sinai 379,300. The figures for Dec. 1967 are 595,900 and 389,700, respectively (see *Four years of military administration*, pp. 15 & 144).

[137] Israel's minister for foreign affairs is reported to have told US Secretary of State Rogers in Apr. 1972 that there is full agreement in the Israeli government on the Allon Plan and that from the point of view of Israel the plan could be the basis of an Arab–Israel settlement. The agreement on the Allon Plan was not based on a formal government decision; however, it emerged from the stand taken by the majority of ministers (*Ha'aretz*, 26 Apr. 1972).

As regards the Gaza Strip, Israel does not seem to claim its incorporation within her boundaries as a *conditio sine qua non* of the future political settlement. Cf. statement of Israel's minister for foreign affairs, Mr Eban, in *The Observer* of 7 May 1972.

In some instances issues have been prejudged at the outset[138] and no safeguards have been taken to ensure the independence of the commissioners. The most extreme case is that of the General Assembly Special Committee investigating Israeli practices in the occupied territories. The Assembly appointed three states (not individuals) which had minimal or no diplomatic relations with Israel. Similar problems arise in the case of the Ad Hoc Special Group of Experts, where members of the group have also functioned as members of the Commission on Human Rights.[139]

The use of commissions of inquiry in political struggles has resulted in the enlargement of their terms of reference and in a tendency to perpetuate their activities until the objectives of that struggle are obtained. Unlike the Hague commissions, the UN Ad Hoc Committee of Experts and the Assembly Special Committee have not confined their task to narrowly defined specific charges, but exercise review functions over a broad range of issues. The disadvantages of this approach have been felt by many representatives in the UN.

The political background of the inquiries of the above two commissions has found another expression in the non-cooperation of the parties concerned. It would seem that, in the minds of the initiators of the inquiries, the co-operation of the 'respondent' countries was to be confined, primarily, if not exclusively, to the agreement of these countries to an on-the-spot investigation. The accusing states did not make any attempt to create an atmosphere of mutual trust which could possibly lead to the co-operation of the accused parties in the establishment of the respective commissions and their day-to-day activities. The accused countries, for their part, withheld co-operation because of fears that the inquiry was calculated to discredit them. As a result of the non-co-operation of the parties, the commissioners had to rely mostly on one-sided evidence detrimental to the authors of alleged violations of human rights. This limitation has been recognized by the Special Committee of the General Assembly which has repeatedly pointed out the advantage

---

[138]While noting with disapproval this phenomenon, Sydney Bailey states that 'there would at least be something to be said for putting in separate resolutions decisions to engage in fact-finding, and decisions to deplore or condemn or otherwise pronounce on the facts which are to be sought' (*Int. Aff.*, 48 (1972), p. 261).

[139]Professor Ermacora, who has been in this position for several years, doubts the advisability of allowing persons to serve in such a double capacity. In his view, the separation of the individual's behaviour as an expert and as a state delegate has never been achieved. 'Partiality and impartiality of human rights enquiry commissions', in *René Cassin amicorum disciplorumque liber*, i: *Problèmes de protection internationale des droits de l'homme* (1969), p. 70.

The Netherlands representative stated, during a discussion of one of the reports of the special group of experts by the Commission on Human Rights, that his delegation questioned the wisdom of combining independent fact-finding with political decision-making, 'since it was doubtful whether persons who had acted in an individual capacity as experts should also act as representatives of their Governments when the report of their findings came to be discussed' (E/CN.4/SR.1104, mtg of 3 Mar. 1971).

of being superseded by a protecting power chosen by an arrangement mutually acceptable to Israel and the Arab states.[140]

An additional consequence of the politicization of the inquiries is the often extreme formulation of the findings and the recommendations of the commissions of inquiry. In bilateral commissions of inquiry and conciliation we noted the predominant principle of endeavouring to reach a solution mutually acceptable to the parties. This endeavour found expression not only in the diplomatic contacts of the commission with the disputing parties, but also in the moderate tone of the reports. In the present instance the attempt to reach an agreement has been excluded from the outset. The reports of the commissions of inquiry have been used by the political organs of the UN to bring public pressure upon the parties. The extreme language of the reports has been a convenient basis for condemnatory resolutions of the Commission on Human Rights, ECOSOC, and the General Assembly.

It must be emphasized that the above observations on the role of political factors relate to two specific inquiries.[141] The political background of an international inquiry need not necessarily prejudice its impartiality and thoroughness. For instance, the actions of Ghana against Portugal, and of Portugal against Liberia regarding alleged violations of labour conventions, were politically motivated. Nevertheless, the standards applied by the ILO in the conduct of the inquiries ensured the submission of objective reports accepted by all the parties concerned.[142] Similar considerations apply to the activities of the European Commission of Human Rights. This body, described by one of its members (now president), Mr J. E. S. Fawcett, as 'a commission of

---

[140]See, e.g. report A/8389/Add.1, 9 Dec. 1971, p. 3, and press releases |Nos 1971/179, 13 July 1971; 1971/183, 19 July 1971, & 1971/185, 26 July 1971, issued by the UN Information Centre for Greece, Israel, Turkey, and Cyprus.

[141]In the practice of the UN there have been such balanced inquiries conducted with the co-operation of the parties, e.g. the mission to South Vietnam or the mission of Mr Gussing to the Middle East. It is pertinent that many of the provisions on implementation of the convention on racial discrimination and the covenant on civil and political rights are designed to exclude political influences in the process of ascertaining facts. Generally, the two instruments envisage the active co-operation of the parties throughout the proceedings.

[142]See report of the Ghana–Portugal commission of inquiry in ILO, *Official Bull.*, 45/2, Suppl. II (Apr. 1962). See also report of the Portugal–Liberia commission of inquiry, ibid., 46/2, Suppl. II (Apr. 1963). The high standard of the ILO investigatory bodies has been associated with their 'judicial' or 'quasi-judicial' nature (see Vignes, 'Procédures internationales d'enquête', *AFDI, 1963*, p. 458, and Valticos, 'La commission d'investigation et de conciliation en matière de liberté syndicale et le mécanisme de protection internationale des droits syndicaux', ibid., *1967*, p. 466.

Cf. Jenks: 'An international inquiry into human rights may not always be, though it may sometimes be, a judicial proceeding in the sense of being a proceeding which finally determines the rights of the parties to a contested case; but it should always be judicial in the sense that all affected by the enquiry have a full opportunity of expressing their views and commenting on any allegations, evidence or information relating to them before the commission proceeds to formulate any conclusions' ('The international protection of trade union rights', in Luard, ed., *The international protection of human rights* (1967), p. 241).

inquiry, with certain limited advisory and mediatory functions',[143] applied the most rigorous standards of proof in its handling of the Greek case.[144]

The difficulties created by the politicization of international investigations into alleged violations of human rights have prompted the Secretary-General to question the advisability of continued reliance on ad hoc bodies like the Special Committee of the Assembly and the Special Working Group of Experts of the Commission on Human Rights. Conditions may be ripe, he wrote in his report on 'Respect for human rights in armed conflicts' (A/8052, 18 Sept. 1970, para. 246),

to encourage consideration of the idea of gradually moving away from the ad hoc approach, which might be viewed as somewhat precarious and liable to inspire a lesser degree of confidence, towards setting up, on a durable standing basis, an agency of implementation under the aegis of the United Nations.

Such an agency 'would have to be scrupulously non-political and it should strive to offer all guarantees of impartiality, efficiency and rectitude'.

The attempt of the UN to establish a system of international inquiry, based on the principles outlined by the Secretary-General, will be examined in our next section.

CONSIDERATION OF METHODS OF 'INQUIRY', 'CONCILIATION', AND 'FACT-FINDING' BY THE UN

Various UN organs dealt, in two successive stages, with problems directly connected with the subject of our study. In the first stage, the UN endeavoured to promote the use of what were defined as 'procedures of inquiry and conciliation' by means of 'commissions of inquiry or of conciliation'. The second stage was devoted to consideration of an item which was eventually defined as 'Question of Methods of Fact-Finding'. In certain respects the discussions at the UN resemble those of the League of Nations (above, pp. 121–2).

---

[143]*The application of the European convention on human rights* (1969), p. 259.

[144]See report of the commission (in 2 mimeo. vols, Strasbourg 1970), ii, pt 1, pp. 14–17: 'Standards and means of proof'. I am grateful to Mr Fawcett for drawing my attention to the report.

The activity of the European Commission of Human Rights in the above case prompted Mr Carey, former member of the UN Commission of Human Rights, to observe (at p. 90): 'The Greek situation was being handled by the Council of Europe with an array of procedures for exceeding anything yet devised by the UN. . . . investigation was being applied in a manner bound to inspire persons wishing to see the UN more active in the field.' The same comment would seem to apply to the other cases handled by the European Commission on Human Rights, including those emanating from petitions of individuals (see, in particular, Monconduit's analysis of the *Lawless Case: La commission européenne des droits de l'homme* (1965), pp. 444–68).

The question whether the establishment of special and permanent fact-finding bodies would not prejudice the peaceful functions of the Security Council and the General Assembly was raised with as much emphasis as was the parallel question during the discussions in the League.

The UN deliberations culminated in the adoption by the General Assembly of two resolutions providing for the creation of machinery designed to further the implementation of the respective methods. By its resolution of 28 April 1949 (268 D (III)), the Assembly invited member states to designate persons to form a Panel for Inquiry and Conciliation, and by a resolution of 18 December 1967 (2329 (XXII)) it requested the Secretary-General to prepare a Register of Experts. The persons included in the Register were to be available explicitly for fact-finding tasks.

Establishment of a Panel for Inquiry and Conciliation (1949)

In its resolution 111 (II), adopted on 13 November 1947, the General Assembly instructed the Interim Committee to examine how the Assembly might implement its responsibility to consider the general principles of co-operation in the maintenance of international peace and security (Art. 11, para. 1, of the Charter), and to promote international co-operation in the political field (Art. 13, para. 1 (*a*)). The Interim Committee prepared a report entitled 'Study on Methods for the Promotion of International Co-operation in the Political Field',[145] which served as the basis for the adoption by the General Assembly on 28 April 1949 of resolution 268 (III) relating to our subject. In section A of the resolution the General Assembly instructed the Secretary-General to prepare a revised text of the General Act for the Pacific Settlement of International Disputes of 1928 (above, p. 128 & below, App. II, p. 340). Section D, entitled 'Creation of a Panel for Inquiry and Conciliation', consists of a Preamble outlining the reasons for the proposed action, two operative paragraphs concerning the role of member states in the creation of the Panel, and an Annex of ten articles relating to the composition and use of the Panel (below, App. III, p. 344).[146]

The Preamble envisages the future Panel as having a double function: to help states to settle their disputes outside the UN, and to assist the UN organs in their activities for the promotion of international peace. So far as the first function is concerned, the General Assembly 'deems it desirable' to facilitate in every practicable way the compliance of

[145]See Reports of the Interim Committee of the General Assembly (5 January–5 August 1948), A/605: GAOR, 3rd sess., Suppl. 10 (1948).

[146]Besides sections A and D, which concern us directly, the resolution contains section B whereby the Assembly recommended that the Security Council consider appointing rapporteurs or conciliators in disputes and situations brought before it. The resolution does not mention the possibility of the rapporteur or conciliator having fact-finding functions. Section C dealt with proposed amendments to the rules of procedure of the General Assembly.

member states with the obligation in Article 33 of the Charter (above, p. 134) first of all to seek solutions to their disputes by peaceful means of their own choice. With regard to the second function, the General Assembly 'notes the desirability', as shown by the experience of UN organs, of having qualified persons available to assist those organs in the settlement of disputes and situations by serving on 'commissions of inquiry or of conciliation'. In the final paragraph of the Preamble, the General Assembly 'concludes' that the establishment of a Panel of qualified persons available to states or to the General Assembly, the Security Council, and their subsidiary organs, would promote the use and effectiveness of procedures of inquiry and conciliation.

In the operative paragraphs of the resolution, the General Assembly invites each member state to designate from one to five persons who, by reason of their training, experience, character, or standing, are suitable to serve as members of 'commissions of inquiry or of conciliation'. It further directs the Secretary-General to take charge of the administrative arrangements connected with the composition of the Panel. The articles relating to the composition and use of the Panel for Inquiry and Conciliation provide, i.a., as follows: members of the Panel must be designated for a term of five years, the designations being renewable. The Panel must be available at all times to UN organs (the organs are not specified here, as they are in the Preamble) in case they wish to select from it members of commissions to perform tasks of inquiry or conciliation in connection with disputes or situations in respect of which the organs are exercising their functions. The Panel must also be available at all times to all states, whether or not members of the UN, which are party to any controversy, for the purpose of selecting from the Panel members of commissions to perform tasks of investigation or conciliation with a view to settlement of the controversy.

The method of selecting members of a 'commission of inquiry or of conciliation' is to be determined in each instance by the organ appointing the commission or, in the case of a commission appointed by or at the request of states parties to a controversy,[147] by agreement between the parties. Members of commissions constituted by or at the request of the parties are to receive appropriate remuneration, each party contributing an equal share. Subject to any determination to the contrary made by the organ or parties concerned, the commissions may meet at the seat of the UN or at such other place as they may determine to be necessary for the effective performance of their functions.

The Secretary-General must assign to each commission constituted by a UN organ adequate staff and must, if necessary, seek expert assistance from the Specialized Agencies. He is also charged with entering

[147]The parties may jointly req uest the Secretary-General, the president of the General Assembly, or the chairman of the Interim Committee to appoint a member or members of a commission.

into suitable arrangements with the appropriate state authorities in order to assure to the commission, so far as it may find it necessary to exercise its functions within their territories, full freedom of movement and all the facilities necessary for the performance of its functions. With regard to commissions constituted by the parties to a controversy, such assistance by the Secretary-General is to be rendered, to the extent possible, at the request of the commission.

Upon completion of its proceedings, each commission appointed by a UN organ is to render such reports as may be determined by the appointing organ. Each commission appointed by or at the request of the parties to a controversy must file a report with the Secretary-General. If a settlement of the controversy is reached, such report will normally merely state the terms of the settlement.

It will be observed that the employment of inquiry or conciliation by commissions appointed by the parties is envisaged only with regard to disputes or controversies, while the use of these methods by UN bodies is envisaged also with regard to the adjustment of situations, i.e. differences of a less serious character (below, p. 314, n. 169).

The above resolution does not give a clear indication, not to speak of a definition, of the task of the commissions to be established. Is each commission to be either a commission of inquiry or a commission of conciliation? Or is it to be a commission of inquiry and conciliation, in the sense of the Gondra treaty as modified (above, pp. 129 ff.). The phrase used throughout section D of the resolution is 'commissions of inquiry or of conciliation', which would suggest that a single commission would have the task either of inquiry or of conciliation. However, the principle that the commission appointed by the parties is expected to include in its report the terms of settlement, if a settlement is reached, would indicate that in all cases the commission would be a conciliation commission, i.e. a commission could be either a commission of inquiry and conciliation, or a commission of conciliation alone. In view of the expressed wish of the General Assembly to promote the use of both inquiry and conciliation, there are no grounds for believing that the relevant provisions of the resolution imply a tendency to subordinate the inquiry process. It will be noted that the facilities to be given to the commissions include freedom of movement for fact-finding purposes. Moreover, in all cases the commissions are under an obligation to submit a report. If it is provided that, should a settlement be reached, the report will normally 'merely' state the terms of settlement, we may assume, on the basis of our previous analysis of treaty provisions to the same effect, that in this case it is not necessary for the commission to present in the report an elucidation of the question in dispute, including an appraisal of the facts. The word 'merely' implies that such an elucidation is a preliminary condition of the solution reached.

The relationship between the commissions appointed by the parties and the UN Organization is ambivalent. Basically, these commissions are independent of the UN: they are set up by the parties; their terms of reference are defined by the parties; and the endeavour to reach a solution is made without participation of UN officials. Nevertheless, various provisions of the resolution indicate the desire of its authors for the investigatory and conciliatory process not to escape the vigilance of the UN. Thus the Secretary-General is in charge of the administrative arrangements connected with the composition and 'use' of the Panel. Like the president of the General Assembly and the chairman of the Interim Committee, the Secretary-General may appoint members of the commissions, if requested by the parties to do so. Moreover, at the request of a commission he must make available a variety of facilities which involve close contact with the parties and with the commission in the course of the proceedings. Finally, the commission must file its report with him.

The creation of the Panel for Inquiry and Conciliation expresses a renewed interest in the use of inquiry by commissions set up by the parties to the dispute and responsible only to those parties. It is significant that the General Assembly did not confine itself to keeping in force the General Act of 1928, which put less emphasis on inquiry than did earlier conciliation treaties. Section D of resolution 268 (III) repeatedly uses the term 'inquiry' and, unlike the General Act, provides for the submission of a report.

Experience has shown, however, that states have not been forthcoming, either as regards the designation of members of the Panel or as regards its use. According to a list published by the Secretary-General on 20 January 1961 (A/4686; S/4632), the Panel as of that date consisted of fifty-one persons, designated by the following fifteen states: Austria, Brazil, Ceylon, Denmark, the Dominican Republic, Ecuador, El Salvador, Greece, Haiti, Israel, the Netherlands, Pakistan, Sweden, the UAR, and the United Kingdom.[148] The failure of the great majority of states, including the United States, the Soviet Union, and France, to designate members to the Panel,[149] and the absence of any initiative, either by UN organs or by individual states, to use the Panel so far, seem to show that the new institution is not considered practical for the solution of current disputes. The following analysis of subsequent UN debates on the specific question of fact-finding will, it is believed, throw some light on the attitude of states in the matter.

Establishment of a Register of Experts on Fact-Finding (1967)
(*a*) *General framework of the debates.* Discussions on fact-finding took

---

[148]On 28 Feb. 1973 the UN Information Centre for Greece, Israel, Turkey, and Cyprus at Athens informed the author that the list of the Panel was still the same.
[149]With regard to the possible designation of members of the Panel by the USA, see below, p. 312, n. 166.

place during the 17th–21st sessions of the General Assembly (1962–6)[150] within the framework of agenda item 'Consideration of principles of international law concerning friendly relations and co-operation among States in accordance with the Charter of the United Nations', and during the 22nd session (1967) under the item 'Question of methods of fact-finding'.

The subject was examined mainly with reference to a Netherlands proposal for the establishment of a permanent UN fact-finding organ. The proposal was first raised at the 758th meeting of the Sixth (Legal) Committee, held on 13 November 1962, and served as the basis for the following resolution—1967 (XVIII)—adopted by the General Assembly on 16 December 1963:

The General Assembly,
Recalling that in its resolution 1815 (XVII) of 18 December 1962 the principle that States shall settle their international disputes by peaceful means in such a manner that international peace and security and justice are not endangered is mentioned as one of the principles to be studied at the eighteenth session of the General Assembly,

Recognizing the need to promote further development and strengthening of various means of settling disputes, as described in Article 33 of the Charter of the United Nations,

Considering that, in Article 33 of the Charter, inquiry is mentioned as one of the peaceful means by which the parties to any dispute, the continuance of which is likely to endanger the maintenance of international peace and security, shall seek a solution,

Considering further that inquiry, investigation and other methods of fact-finding are also referred to in other instruments of a general or regional nature,

Believing that an important contribution to the peaceful settlement of disputes and to the prevention of such disputes could be made by providing for impartial fact-finding within the framework of international organizations and in bilateral and multilateral conventions,

Taking into account that, with regard to methods of fact-finding in international relations, a considerable practice is available to be studied for the purpose of the progressive development of such methods,

Believing that such a study might include the feasibility and desirability of establishing a special international body for fact-finding or of entrusting to an existing organization fact-finding responsibilities complementary to existing arrangements and without prejudice to the right of parties to any dispute to seek other peaceful means of settlement of their own choice,

1. *Invites* Member States to submit in writing to the Secretary-General, before 1 June 1964, any views they may have on this subject and requests the Secretary-General to communicate these comments to Member States before the beginning of the nineteenth session;

---

[150]The subject was not discussed at the 19th session. Many pending issues were not dealt with at that session because of a crisis over the financing of peacekeeping operations.

2. *Requests* the Secretary-General to study the relevant aspects of the problem under consideration and to report on the results of such study to the General Assembly at its nineteenth session and to the Special Committee on Principles of International Law concerning Friendly Relations and Co-operation among States established under Assembly resolution 1966 (XVIII) of 16 December 1963;

3. *Requests* the Special Committee to include in its deliberations the subject-matter mentioned in the last preambular paragraph of the present resolution.

Following the adoption of this resolution, the discussions on the question of fact-finding were mainly held in the Special Committee on Principles of International Law concerning Friendly Relations and Co-operation among States (1964 session)[151] and in the Sixth Committee of the General Assembly (1965, 1966, and 1967 sessions). A number of governments offered written comments and the Secretary-General submitted the two studies on methods of fact-finding, which we have discussed in Chapter 1.

(*b*) *Main approaches to the question of fact-finding.* While all the delegations recognized the usefulness of fact-finding, differences of opinion arose with regard to its importance and with regard to the necessity for its promotion by new machinery. Three main trends of thought may be distinguished:

1. Enthusiastic support for the use of fact-finding, based on the claim that fact-finding is designed to play a significant role in the settlement and the prevention of international disputes. This trend of thought was consistently propounded by the Netherlands government, which proposed the establishment of an authoritative UN fact-finding body capable of dealing with a variety of disputes.

2. Recognition of the usefulness of fact-finding, coupled with strong opposition to its promotion by the establishment of a special fact-finding body as envisaged in the Netherlands proposal. This was the firm attitude of the socialist countries, led by the Soviet Union.

3. Hesitant and vague support for the method of fact-finding, accompanied by considerable reservations with regard to its promotion by way of impressive international machinery. This approach found particular expression in the statements made on behalf of the United States, the United Kingdom, and France.

With regard to the desirability of establishing new machinery for fact-finding, a Finnish proposal (A/6686, Add. 3, 5 Oct. 1967), put forward as late as 1967, proved to be crucial for the outcome of the debates. The government of Finland expressed the view that it was very important to consider the possibility of compiling a list of experts similar to the register of experts and scholars in international law which had been prepared on the initiative of the Secretary-General to further

[151]See its report, A/5746, GAOR, 20th sess., a.i. 90 & 94, Annexes (1965).

the appreciation of international law by providing technical assistance.[152]

According to the Netherlands government, in almost every international dispute there was at some point a difference between the parties concerning the facts of the case. If an impartial third party with sufficient expert knowledge and with recognized authority were enabled to establish what really had happened, it would then be possible—even though the dispute itself would perhaps not be resolved—to establish a factual basis for discussion and judgement. The removal of the difference of view regarding the facts would no doubt, in itself, promote a peaceful settlement.

The existing procedures, such as those provided for in the Hague Conventions of 1899 and 1907, the General Act of 1928 as revised in 1949, and General Assembly resolution 286 D (III), were seldom used because they envisaged a combination of inquiry and conciliation, thus linking fact-finding to the peaceful solution of the dispute. If bodies established under these instruments were called upon to function, their mandate would be a broad one and they would be authorized to make recommendations to the parties on all the legal and political questions involved. As conciliation in international relations between sovereign states so often gave rise to difficulties, the phases of fact-finding and conciliation ought to be separated. Another disadvantage was that most of the existing instruments provided for ad hoc commissions of inquiry. However, once a dispute had arisen between two states, the general climate was not conducive to co-operation and agreement between them. Even if the parties were willing to be informed about the facts, they were apt to raise difficulties concerning the composition, competence, terms of reference, and rules of procedure of the body to be established.[153] A permanent body, on the other hand, would accumulate experience which would make it more efficient, while the results of ad hoc fact-finding commissions were usually filed away and were not generally available.[154]

[152]On 20 Dec. 1965 the General Assembly established a programme of assistance in the teaching, study, dissemination and wider appreciation of international law (res. 2099 (XX)). As part of the programme, a register of experts and scholars in the field of international law was issued by the Secretariat in 1967 (see *YBUN, 1967*, p. 761).

[153]Carl Schurmann (then permanent representative of the Netherlands to the UN) writes that in the field of conflicts concerning alleged international torts the fact-finding function of commissions, committees, observers, and mediators has very often been combined with, or formed part of, the broader tasks of conciliation or arbitration. It may be, he observes, that this blurring of the line between fact-finding and efforts to bring the parties to a settlement has made many governments wary of agreeing to the former through fear of the latter. Another reason for the comparative rarity of resort to commissions of inquiry may well be that, once a dispute has arisen, the parties are suspicious of one another as well as, at times, of third parties, whom they may suspect of having an interest in a settlement, and thus find it difficult to agree on a body of investigators in whose integrity and disinterestedness they would have full confidence (*A center for international factfinding: a review and a proposal* (1963), p. 26).

[154]See statement of the Netherlands representative at the 989th mtg of the Sixth Committee, on 2 Nov. 1967.

The government of the Netherlands suggested the establishment of a permanent organ, whose activities should be governed by the following three principles:

1. The organ should supplement the existing institutions. As could be seen from the second study by the Secretary-General, various inter-governmental organizations already had their own procedures for examining facts in specific spheres. The new organ must not detract from the existing machinery, but must complement it.

2. The co-operation of states should be voluntary. The organ should institute inquiries only when requested to do so. States not themselves submitting a request should as a rule be free to limit their co-operation in the inquiry or to withhold it altogether.

3. The organ should employ a flexible procedure.

The terms of reference of the proposed organ should be limited to the establishment of facts. Although it was not always easy to separate the ascertaining of a fact from an evaluation of it, it was apparent from earlier inquiries that the investigators had managed to keep within proper limits. The terms of reference should be determined by the organ's statute and by the mandate issued to it for each separate inquiry. The appraisal of the scope of the terms of reference should be left to the organ itself.

The services of the organ could be used for the establishment of the following categories of facts: (*a*) concerning disputes; (*b*) relevant to the execution of international agreements. The ascertainment of facts in this respect may be instrumental in preventing disputes. Not only may the refutation of alleged facts remove tensions, but the possibility of an early ascertainment of facts may help to prevent neglect of obligations; (*c*) required for purposes of information when decisions at the international level are being taken. This function covers the need for reporting on situations and circumstances which are being dealt with by an international body, and may relate to various matters which need not issue from a dispute nor be concerned with the execution of international obligations.

As regards composition, the organ would have to take the form of a standing body, composed of independent persons of high moral standing and acknowledged impartiality, designated for a specific period. Fifteen members would be a suitable number. Membership of the organ need not preclude the discharge of other functions. Provision could be made to enable the organ to form chambers among its members, on the analogy, i.a., of Articles 26–9 of the Statute of the International Court of Justice.

The organ should be placed at the disposal of the UN and the Specialized Agencies and of any two or more states.

The initiative to institute an inquiry should rest not with the organ but solely with states or intergovernmental organizations. On the other hand, the determination of the means, methods, and procedures for fact-finding would have to be left to the organ, which should be able to engage the services of experts in a specific specialized field, as the International Court may do under Article 50 of its Statute.

The granting of admission to the territories of states and of other facilities necessary for the execution of a fact-finding mandate would as a rule be mentioned or implied in the inquiry agreement concluded by the states concerned.

The report on the findings must be adopted by the organ by a majority vote, and must mention any differences of opinion of members who wish such mention to be made.

The organ could be established and its statute adopted by a resolution of the General Assembly.[155]

In reply to reservations regarding the proposal for a new fact-finding body, the Netherlands representative stressed in the Sixth Committee that recourse to it should be voluntary. There was no attempt whatsoever to establish a central fact-finding body with compulsory jurisdiction. The fact that the Security Council had primary responsibility in connection with the investigation of certain disputes or situations did not imply that the parties to the dispute and others, for example regional organizations, were not under the obligation to make all possible efforts, including fact-finding, to reach a settlement. The proposed body would deal with matters within the competence of the Security Council only at the latter's request and could therefore never usurp the functions of the Council. Moreover, fact-finding in international relations should be regarded as applicable to many more situations than those likely to endanger international peace and security (989th mtg, 2 Nov. 1967).

The Soviet Union, together with the other socialist countries, voted against resolution 1967 (XVIII) of 16 December 1963, which provided, i.a., for the study of the feasibility and desirability of establishing a special international body for fact-finding (above, p. 300).[156] In the view

[155] See in particular A/AC.119/L.9 & A/AC.119/L.29.

[156] The resolution on fact-finding was adopted by the General Assembly by a vote of 65 to 15, with 27 abstentions. The following distribution of votes indicates the attitudes of various states, or groups of states, on the subject:

In favour: Argentina, Australia, Austria, Belgium, Bolivia, Brazil, Canada, Central African Republic, Chad, Chile, Nationalist China, Colombia, Congo (Leopoldville), Costa Rica, Cyprus, Denmark, Dominican Republic, Ecuador, El Salvador, Finland, France, Gabon, Greece, Guatemala, Haiti, Honduras, Iceland, Iran, Ireland, Israel, Italy, Jamaica, Japan, Lebanon, Liberia, Luxembourg, Madagascar, Malaysia, Mauritania, Mexico, Morocco, Nepal, Netherlands, New Zealand, Nicaragua, Niger, Norway, Pakistan, Panama, Paraguay, Peru, Philippines, Rwanda, Senegal, Sierra Leone, Spain, Sweden, Thailand, Trinidad and Tobago, Tunisia, Turkey, UK, Uruguay, USA, Venezuela.

Against: Albania, Bulgaria, Byelorussian SSR, Cuba, Czechoslovakia, Ethiopia, Hungary, India, Indonesia, Mongolia, Poland, Romania, Ukrainian SSR, USSR, Yugoslavia.

Abstaining: Afghanistan, Algeria, Burma, Burundi, Cambodia, Cameroon, Ceylon, Congo (Brazzaville), Dahomey, Ghana, Guinea, Iraq, Ivory Coast, Jordan, Kuwait, Laos, Libya, Mali, Nigeria, Saudi Arabia, Somalia, Sudan, Syria, Tanganyika, Togo, UAR, Uganda (see *YBUN, 1963*, p. 519).

of the Soviet government, the General Assembly had resolved in its resolution 1815 (XVII) to undertake, pursuant to Article 13 of the Charter, a study of the principles of international law concerning friendly relations and co-operation among states with a view to their progressive development and codification, not a study of measures by which these principles might be applied.[157]

At a subsequent stage of the consideration of the question of fact-finding, the Soviet government pointed out that it had consistently supported the idea that, when an international dispute arises, all the factual circumstances of that dispute should be ascertained in a thorough and objective manner. At the same time, the Soviet Union took the view that, in order to do this, fuller use should be made of the possibilities and methods which already exist under multilateral agreements and also under the Charter. The proposal to establish a permanent UN body for fact-finding gave rise, in the view of the Soviet government, to many serious objections on both practical and legal grounds. From the practical point of view, the Security Council had in the past established appropriate commissions to investigate the factual aspect of an international dispute whenever this had proved necessary. There was nothing to prevent the Security Council from establishing commissions of this kind in the future if the need arose. From the legal point of view, the proposal by the Netherlands was aimed at usurping the rights and powers of the Security Council, which, under the UN Charter, had been given responsibility for investigating 'any dispute, or any situation which might lead to international friction or give rise to a dispute' (Art. 34). Although it was stated in the proposal of the Netherlands that a permanent UN fact-finding body should merely supplement the functions of existing institutions, its effect would actually be to remove many important functions from the jurisdiction of the Security Council and to take the place of the Security Council in the carrying out of the function of investigating disputes which had been entrusted to it by the Charter.[158]

In the opinion of the Soviet government, the proposal to establish, within the framework of the UN, an international fact-finding body which would operate on a permanent basis and have the same powers as were assigned to the Security Council, was not consonant with the basic provisions of the Charter. Moreover, the establishment of such a permanent body by a decision of the General Assembly or of the Secretary-General was open to objection. Under Articles 29 and 34 of

[157]See statement of the representative of the Soviet Union at the 831st mtg of the Sixth Committee, held on 9 Dec. 1963.

[158]In the statement referred to in the previous footnote, the Soviet representative said that in order to appreciate the legal and political implications of the establishment of a new fact-finding body, one need only imagine a situation in which—despite the competence of the General Assembly—the questions of apartheid or of the Portuguese colonies, for instance, were referred for consideration to an international fact-finding centre acting in isolation and holding a veritable monopoly.

the Charter the setting up of bodies of this kind was within the competence of the Security Council, or, if the dispute were of a legal nature, within the jurisdiction of the International Court. The General Assembly was given no such powers under the Charter.[159]

In the initial stages of the debate, the US representative thought the suggestion of the Netherlands worthy of serious consideration, but expressed doubts as to the desirability of creating further machinery for the peaceful settlement of disputes. An abundance of such machinery already existed, and greater use should be made of it. The International Court of Justice and the Permanent Court of Arbitration could be extremely useful, and states should be encouraged to make use of regional institutions and of the Panel for Inquiry and Conciliation.[160]

On a later occasion, the US representative made a statement which may be interpreted as supporting the Netherlands initiative. Refuting a Soviet assertion, he said that the establishment of a special body for fact-finding would be perfectly in keeping with the Charter and, more specifically, with Articles 10, 14, 22, 33, and 34.[161] However, subsequent discussions did not show any inclination on the part of the United States to support the proposal of the Netherlands. Speaking before the Special Committee, the US representative drew a distinction between the need for increased employment of existing fact-finding techniques and the need to establish new institutional devices or procedural rules. This observation, he said, was not intended to prejudge the question of new procedures or institutions. While no procedure was of any use without the requisite will to employ it in good faith, the mere availability of well-designed machinery set up for the specific purpose of fact-finding might induce states or UN organs to use it. He suggested exploring the question whether to establish new machinery, or to make increased use of existing machinery, to perform fact-finding functions in spheres other than those relating to the settlement of disputes. Perhaps the improvement of fact-finding techniques in areas where national interests did not clash so sharply would serve to increase the international community's confidence in fact-finding procedures to be employed in connection with

[159]See comment of the Soviet Union in A/6686/Add.1 of 31 Aug. 1967.

[160]See statement at the 814th mtg of the Sixth Committee on 19 Nov. 1963.

[161]831st mtg of the Sixth Committee, 9 Dec. 1963. In reply to the Soviet objection that the establishment of an international fact-finding centre would violate the Charter, the Canadian representative pointed out that if the General Assembly should eventually decide to create an international fact-finding centre as a subsidiary organ of the Assembly, it had express authority to do so under Art. 22 of the Charter. Under Art. 34 such a body could legitimately be used by the Security Council for the purpose of investigating a dispute, and under Art. 50 of the ICJ Statute it could be entrusted by the Court with the task of carrying out an inquiry or giving an expert opinion. Moreover, even if the General Assembly, after careful study of a recommendation for the creation of such an organ, should decide at some time in the future to convene a conference of member states for the purpose of establishing it outside the UN in order to complement existing arrangements, there was nothing in the Charter to preclude such action (834th mtg of the Sixth Committee, 11 Dec. 1963).

disputes falling under the provisions of Chapters VI and VII of the Charter (see A/AC.119/SR.36, mtg of 25 Sept. 1964).

During the further discussions the US representative reiterated that states failed to resort to international fact-finding either because adequate machinery for impartial fact-finding did not exist or because states lacked the requisite will to resort to it when their own interests were at stake. He thought that perhaps the Panel for Inquiry and Conciliation should be reconstructed, and perhaps greater use should be made of rapporteurs and conciliators in disputes before the Security Council and the General Assembly (990th mtg of Sixth Committee, 3 Nov. 1967).

The approach of the United Kingdom was similar. The UK representative stated in the initial stages of the debates that the existing machinery for peaceful settlement could be improved, particularly in the field of fact-finding, and a greater degree of co-ordination might also be necessary. But it was questionable whether the reluctance of states to submit their disputes to independent bodies was due to these imperfections. The problem was bound up with the attitude of states towards the judicial role in the solution of disputes (825th mtg of Sixth Committee, 3 Dec. 1963).

During the deliberations of the Special Committee, the UK representative asserted that the establishment of the true facts underlying international disputes was of cardinal importance. Wherever the facts were in dispute, states unfortunately tended to interpret the situation so as to suit their own ends. Greater resort to the procedure of fact-finding, and perhaps the very existence of some new international fact-finding machinery, might lead to higher standards in the presentation of their cases by states. The UK delegation was therefore interested in the suggestions made by the Netherlands. It agreed in particular that fact-finding should be kept separate from decision-making functions. Fact-finding must be recognized as a distinct operation, and should not be regarded as a commitment to further procedures. At the same time, the independent and impartial determination of the facts might assist the settlement of disputes through negotiations or lead the parties to agree to some further third-party procedure (A/AC.119/SR36).

The UK government, in its written comment (A/6686 & Corr. 1, 15 Aug. 1967), submitted in pursuance of General Assembly resolution 2182 (XX) of 12 December 1966, observed that the Security Council had made good use of fact-finding in the past, and could well have resorted to this means of investigation more frequently or even as a matter of regular practice. The Security Council might similarly have considered more often the possibility of recommending to the parties to a dispute resort to impartial fact-finding. The UK government wondered whether the failure to use the existing machinery was due to lack of knowledge or lack of goodwill, or to some other cause. In any event, in the light of experience, it had some doubts whether, at the present time, the creation of a new international organ for fact-finding would be fruitful. It believed that a more critical study of existing instruments should be made. For example, it was quite likely that the Permanent Court of Arbitration already provided the foundation for whatever might be required, at least in the realm of the settlement or prevention of international disputes. The increase in the membership of that Court from forty-five members in 1946 to sixty-five members in 1966, as well as the direct experience of the United Kingdom in the use of the machinery of the Court in the case of the *Red Crusader*, was encouraging in this respect.

The French government was also of the opinion that attention should be concentrated on the reasons for the failure of the existing machinery. The representative of France in the Special Committee asked various questions which, in his view, needed to be answered before any substantive action on the matter was taken. Why were the existing means inadequate for the needs of the world community? To the extent that they had not led to satisfactory results, what were the reasons for their failure? What grounds were there for thinking that a special organization, to which recourse would be optional, would succeed where previous attempts had failed or produced insufficient results? Was the method of fact-finding possible without the simultaneous determination of the political content of the facts, and was it reconcilable with the almost universal refusal of states to submit political disputes to judgement? (see A/AC.119/SR.36).

During the discussions in the Sixth Committee in 1967, the representative of France reiterated that, while in some cases the establishment of the facts at issue could contribute to the peaceful settlement of a dispute between states, there were other instances where the dispute turned not on the facts of the situation but on the legal or political interpretation of those facts. Thus fact-finding procedures could not usefully be applied in all cases, and their utilization could therefore not be made compulsory. His delegation was against a permanent organ for fact-finding. As the studies by the Secretary-General showed, there already existed well-established procedures for fact-finding which were used by states and were adapted by them to suit the circumstances of each individual situation or dispute. The success of such procedures rested on their flexibility and diversity. It would be a mistake to attempt to centralize or codify them (991st mtg, 7 Nov. 1967).

The above opinions and attitudes of the Netherlands, the Soviet Union, and the western powers represent the main trends of thought expressed at the UN. In order to complete the picture, a few additional opinions of other states will be considered.

As regards the general role of fact-finding, the Bulgarian government observed that disputes between states arose and continued not simply because of differences in their way of conceiving facts as such, but also because of differences in the evaluation of those facts and their moral or juridical implications. In many cases the point at issue was not whether an act had been committed or not but the conditions in which the act had occurred, whether it was not provoked, over-emphasized, or utilized in a tendentious manner. In attempting to solve international disputes by juridical means it appeared neither possible nor useful to make a rigid separation of the functions of fact-finding from those of settlement proper. The introduction of a body not familiar with the relationship between the parties and with the legal, moral, and political aspects of the case, did not seem likely to improve relations or to promote the solution of the dispute. Bulgaria objected to the establishment of a special international fact-finding body on the grounds, i.a., that its very existence might be used in certain cases as a means of exerting pressure. Unwillingness to have recourse to it might, to say the least, be used as an excuse for unfavourable and possibly tendentious interpretations of the conduct of the party concerned, with the aim of discrediting it in the eyes of world opinion.[162]

According to the representative of Thailand, disputes often arose out of a misunderstanding of the facts, elucidation of which could show that neither party was to blame and that the situation was the creation of an outside power which had an interest in fostering ill will (991st mtg of Sixth Committee).

The Iraqi representative considered that the main issue raised by the question of fact-finding was political rather than legal, since resort to fact-finding methods depended on the will of states. If states wished to establish the facts of a dispute, they would find no difficulty in agreeing on the body and the procedures for performing that task (ibid.).

In the opinion of the government of Sweden, impartial fact-finding was needed. Unless all the facts of a controversy were available and correctly assessed, it was very unlikely that a rational solution could be found. A further consideration was that controversies were sometimes accompanied and aggravated by influential public opinion, which might be calmed by an authoritative and impartial establishment of the facts.[163]

Referring to the proposal for the establishment of a fact-finding body, the Polish representative felt that the question must be considered primarily from the standpoint of state sovereignty. His delegation was therefore opposed to the establishment of a new organ for fact-finding, the actual result of which would be to deprive the parties to a dispute of

---

[162]See written comment, A/5725, GAOR, 20th sess., a.i. 90 & 94, Annexes (1965). A reservation similar to the last mentioned was expressed in the Special Committee by the representative of India. He feared that certain states would misuse a permanent fact-finding body by invoking its services as a matter of course, whether or not the complaint was adequately substantiated (see A/AC.119/SR.36).

[163]See written comment, A/5725/Add.2, GAOR, 20th sess., a.i. 90 & 94, Annexes (1965).

L

their freedom to choose the most appropriate methods for carrying out the necessary inquiries.[164]

(c) *The outcome of the debate.* The reconciliation of the different views expressed in the course of the five years during which the question of fact-finding was considered, was finally entrusted to a working group of the Sixth Committee, set up in November 1967. This group, composed of sixteen states, considered three working papers, produced by Finland, the Netherlands, and Czechoslovakia, respectively (A/6995, Annex 1, 15 Dec. 1967).

According to the draft resolution contained in the Finnish working paper, the General Assembly was to ask the Secretary-General to prepare a register of experts nominated by member states, to be used as a basis for the selection of ad hoc fact-finding organs. The Assembly would request member states to nominate not more than five of their nationals, who would be competent in legal and other fields, for inclusion in the register; the Assembly would further invite member states, in the event of a dispute, to agree to have recourse to the register of experts for the purpose of establishing an ad hoc fact-finding organ; one person from the register would be nominated by each state party to the dispute; the persons nominated would in turn select a chairman, who need not necessarily be drawn from the register. (The possibility was envisaged that individual members of the International Court might be asked to act as chairmen of the fact-finding bodies.) The task of the fact-finding organ so established would be to ascertain the facts relating to the dispute and to submit a report to the states concerned. The organ would be precluded from making proposals for a solution. The expenses would be divided between the opposing parties in a way to be assessed by the organ.

The text submitted by the Netherlands consisted of a draft resolution according to which the General Assembly would recommend, as alternatives, either the establishment of the fact-finding organ previously suggested by the Netherlands, or the creation of a panel as suggested by Finland. The Assembly would urge member states and UN organs in appropriate cases to make use of the existing fact-finding machinery with a view to facilitating the settlement of disputes and compliance with multilateral and bilateral agreements. The General Assembly would also call upon member states to make nominations to the Panel for Inquiry and Conciliation and to keep in mind the possibility of using the Panel in appropriate instances. The General Assembly would further invite the Secretary-General to consider suggestions for the setting up of

---

[164] 990th mtg of Sixth Committee, 3 Nov. 1967. In a written comment dated 8 Aug. 1966, the government of Poland expressed its support of all means for the peaceful settlement of disputes, including the methods of fact-finding, which are not contrary to the principle of the sovereignty of states and which do not interfere in matters within their domestic competence (A/6373 & Add.1, GAOR, 21st sess., a.i. 87, Annexes (1966)).

special facilities in the Secretariat to assist states wishing to use methods of fact-finding.

The Czechoslovak working paper was also in the form of a draft resolution to be submitted to the General Assembly. According to its preamble, the General Assembly would take into account, i.a., that ad hoc bodies are one of the methods of fact-finding, and would reaffirm its belief that an important contribution to the peaceful settlement of disputes and to the prevention of such disputes could be made by recourse to the methods of fact-finding within the framework of international organizations or under appropriate arrangements. According to the first operative paragraph, the Assembly would invite states to consider the possibility of entrusting the ascertainment of facts relating to the dispute 'to the existing competent organizations or to ad hoc bodies in conformity with the principles of international law and the Charter of the United Nations, and without prejudice to the right to seek other peaceful means of settlement of their own choice'.

With regard to the above formulation, some delegations requested that a reference should be made to permanent fact-finding organs, if only through the use of the wording 'ad hoc or other bodies'. However, this proved unacceptable to other delegations.

As a result of its deliberations, the working group recommended the adoption of the following draft resolution (A/C.6/L.642), which was based mainly on the Finnish proposal:

Question of Methods of Fact-Finding

The General Assembly,

Recalling its resolutions 1967 (XVIII) of 16 December 1963, 2104 (XX) of 20 December 1965 and 2182 (XXI) of 12 December 1966 on the question of methods of fact-finding,

Noting the comments submitted by Member States pursuant to the above-mentioned resolutions and the views expressed in the United Nations,

Noting with appreciation the two reports submitted by the Secretary-General in pursuance of the above-mentioned resolutions,

Recognizing the usefulness of impartial fact-finding as a means towards the settlement of disputes,

Believing that an important contribution to the peaceful settlement of disputes and to the prevention of disputes could be made by providing for impartial fact-finding within the framework of international organizations and in bilateral and multilateral conventions or other appropriate arrangements,

Affirming that the possibility of recourse to impartial methods of fact-finding is without prejudice to the right of States to seek other peaceful means of settlement of their own choice,

Reaffirming the importance of impartial fact-finding in appropriate cases for the settlement and the prevention of disputes,

Recalling the possibility of the continued use of existing facilities for fact-finding,

1. *Urges* Member States to make more effective use of the existing methods of fact-finding;

2. *Invites* Member States to take into consideration, in choosing means for the peaceful settlement of disputes, the possibility of entrusting the ascertainment of facts, whenever it appears appropriate, to competent international organizations and bodies established by agreement between the parties concerned, in conformity with the principles of international law and the Charter of the United Nations or other relevant agreements;

3. *Draws special attention* to the possibility of recourse by States in particular cases, where appropriate, to procedures for the ascertainment of facts, in accordance with Article 33 of the Charter of the United Nations;

4. *Requests* the Secretary-General to prepare a register of experts, in legal and other fields, whose services the States parties to a dispute may use by agreement for fact-finding in relation to the dispute, and requests Member States to nominate up to five of their nationals to be included in such a register.

On 13 December 1967 the draft resolution proposed by the working group was adopted unanimously[165] by the Sixth Committee, and five days later the General Assembly also unanimously adopted the same text (res. 2329 (XXII)). Thus came to an end the prolonged consideration of the question of fact-finding by the UN.

In pursuance of the resolution of the General Assembly of 18 December 1967, the Secretary-General, in a circular letter dated 16 January 1968, requested member states to submit to him the names of up to five of their nationals for inclusion in the Register of Experts. By 27 December 1972 the following forty-two member states had responded to that request: Argentina, Austria, Burma, Cameroon, Canada, Nationalist China, Colombia, Democratic Republic of Congo, Cyprus, Denmark, Ecuador, Finland, France, Ghana, Greece, Guatemala, Guinea, Iceland, Ireland, Italy, Jamaica, Japan, Jordan, Kenya, Laos, Madagascar, Morocco, Netherlands, Nigeria, Norway, Pakistan, the Philippines, Portugal, Saudi Arabia, Senegal, Sudan, Sweden, Thailand, Turkey, Uganda, United Kingdom, and Zambia.[166]

Conclusions

'*Fact-finding*' versus '*inquiry*'. One of the most significant phenomena in the UN deliberations is the universal acknowledgement of the independent role and importance of genuine inquiry (fact-finding) in

[165]Speaking in explanation of his vote, the Soviet representative expressed his delegation's understanding that the draft resolution was based on the premise that the majority of the committee was opposed to the establishment of a permanent fact-finding body. Thus, he had supported it in the belief that it reflected his delegation's position, as stated n the committee and in the working group.

The representative of Italy said that his delegation had voted for the draft resolution on the understanding that it did not establish any machinery for compulsory fact-finding.

[166]See A/7751, 7 Nov. 1969 & A/8108, 18 Nov. 1970. On 30 Sept. 1970 the US representative, Charles W. Yost, declared during the general debate in the General Assembly that his government would soon nominate qualified individuals to both the Panel of Inquiry and Conciliation and the 'register of fact-finding experts' (A/PV.1854).

the sense of the Hague Conventions, as opposed to the enlarged inquiry, envisaged in numerous other treaties. While, in the first stage of the debates, the prominence of enlarged inquiry employed in conjunction with conciliation was paramount, in the second stage all the participants focused their attention on the desirability of ascertaining facts in the settlement or prevention of disputes, as well as on the most suitable fact-finding machinery. The item of discussion was specifically defined as 'Question of Methods of Fact-Finding', and in the final resolution on the subject the General Assembly recognized the usefulness of impartial 'fact-finding' as a means towards the settlement of disputes, reaffirmed the importance of impartial 'fact-finding' for the settlement and prevention of disputes, invited states to take into consideration the possibility of entrusting the 'ascertainment of facts' to competent international bodies, and provided for a Register of Experts whose services could be used for 'fact-finding' in relation to disputes.

Apart from the enthusiastic approach of the Netherlands, the singling out of fact-finding from enlarged inquiry and from conciliation does not signify any revolutionary step in international thinking. On the contrary, the outright opposition of many states to the continued discussion of the subject, the similar opposition to the Netherlands proposal for the creation of a permanent fact-finding body, and the reservations expressed with regard to the limitations of fact-finding, show that states were not prepared to raise fact-finding to the status of a primary method for the settlement or prevention of disputes. Nevertheless, the continued emphasis on fact-finding proper signifies a considerable revival of the Hague theoretical framework.

The role of 'inquiry' and 'fact-finding' in the prevention of disputes or in preventing aggravation of disputes. The Hague conception, and that permeating the treaties examined in the present study, envisaged inquiry as a means of settling disputes. The deliberations in the UN, on the other hand, laid increasing emphasis on the preventive function of inquiry. This was largely due to the dichotomy, established by the Netherlands, between the settlement and the prevention of disputes. For the proper understanding of this dichotomy we propose to draw attention to two conflicting definitions of the term 'dispute': a narrow definition in the sense of serious controversy;[167] and a wide definition, comprising disagreements of a milder character.[168] To the latter category

---

[167]'Dispute' conceived in this sense is defined in the *Dict. de la terminologie du droit international* (1960), prepared under the auspices of Basdevant, as follows: 'Opposition entre des prétentions ou des intérêts se traduisant dans la vie pratique par l'affirmation respective de vues opposées, la prétention élevée de part et d'autre de les faire prévaloir, le désaccord existant dépassant ainsi l'ordre intellectuel pour passer dans l'ordre pratique et devenir un élément de trouble' (at p. 209).

[168]A dispute, writes Kelsen, exists if one party makes a claim against another party and the other party rejects the claim (*The law of the UN* (1951), p. 360). The term 'dispute' is used in many international agreements in a wider sense. Thus, Art. 1 of the General

314 The Handling of International Disputes

may be included differences with regard to the 'adjustment of situations'.[169]

If the narrow definition of 'dispute' is adopted, the preventive role of fact-finding would mean the prevention of the aggravation of those milder differences and tense situations into a (serious) dispute. If the wider definition is used, it would be more accurate to speak of the prevention of the aggravation of disputes, rather than the prevention of disputes.

To these two forms of preventive fact-finding must be added the routine flow of information where no differences of opinion exist. The requests for information by the investigative body are designed to deter the parties from violations likely to lead to a dispute, whether mild or serious.

The government of the Netherlands suggested, it will be recalled, that the proposed fact-finding body should be used for three categories of facts: (a) concerning disputes; (b) relevant to the execution of international agreements; and (c) required for purposes of information in taking decisions at international level. In the opinion of that government, the ascertainment of the second category of facts could be instrumental in preventing disputes, since 'not only may the refutation of

---

Act of 1928 speaks of 'disputes of every kind'. The term as employed in the Hague Convention of 1907 comprises 'international difference' (Art. 1), serious difference endangering peace (Art. 8), disputes involving neither honour nor essential interests (Art. 9), 'a dispute arising from contract debts claimed from one Power by another Power due to its nationals, (Art. 53), dispute as to the interpretation and execution of an arbitral award (Art. 82).

See also Feinberg's discussion of the *Mavromatis Palestine Concessions Case* (*PCIJ*, Ser. A, No. 2), where the Court held that whereas the dispute under consideration was at first between a private person (Mavromatis) and a state (Great Britain), when the Greek government took up the case, the dispute entered the domain of international law and became a dispute between two states. 'La juridiction et la jurisprudence de la Cour permanente de Justice internationale en matière de mandats et de minorités', in 59 *Hague Recueil* (1937), i. 609–12.

[169]Lauterpacht writes that while the distinction between disputes and situations is probably of little consequence in practice, it is significant that not only disputes, but also situations not involving an actual dispute between two or more parties, can be brought before the UN. Possibly, he states, under that head the UN may concern itself with situations such as those envisaged under Art. 19 of the League Covenant, which provided that 'the Assembly may from time to time advise the reconsideration by members of the League of treaties which have become inapplicable and the consideration of international conditions whose continuance might endanger the peace of the world' (see Oppenheim, ii. 112). See to the same effect the commentary on Art. 14 of the Charter in Goodrich & others, pp. 142 & 271, n. 50, and Russell, *A history of the UN Charter* (1958), pp. 459, 608 f., 666–8).

Art. 14, empowering the General Assembly to recommend measures for the peaceful adjustment of any situation, regardless of its origin, which it deems likely to impair the general welfare or friendly relations among nations, was specifically invoked by the General Assembly when it called upon Portugal to submit information on its non-self-governing territories (res. 1542 (XV) of 14 Dec. 1960). In its resolutions of 8 Dec. 1946 regarding the treatment of persons of Indian origin in South Africa and of 2 Nov. 1947 on the future government of Palestine, the Assembly used the language of Art. 14 without making express reference to it. These 'situations' would be regarded as 'disputes' under the wide definition of the term.

alleged facts remove tensions, but the possibility of an early ascertainment of facts may help to prevent neglect of obligations' (above, p. 303).

The above assertion seems to be based on a narrow definition of the term 'dispute', in the sense of a serious controversy, not involving the 'simple' refutation of alleged facts. The intention of the Netherlands government was probably to distinguish between fact-finding designed to settle a dispute conceived as a serious controversy, and fact-finding designed to supervise the execution of an agreement either for the purpose of avoiding its violation, by means of requests for routine information, or for the purpose of adjusting situations which had not yet developed into a serious controversy, i.e. a dispute.

Recognition of the preventive function of fact-finding also came from the government of Czechoslovakia, which urged the General Assembly to reaffirm its belief that an important contribution could be made towards the peaceful settlement of disputes and the prevention of such disputes by recourse to methods of fact-finding within the framework of international organizations or under appropriate arrangements (above, p. 311). Similarly, the US representative suggested exploring the question whether fact-finding might be employed in spheres other than those relating to the settlement of disputes. He thought that the improvement of fact-finding techniques in areas where national interests did not clash so sharply might increase confidence in the employment of fact-finding in the actual settlement of disputes (above, pp. 306–7). It should be noted that the role of fact-finding in spheres other than those relating to the settlement of disputes was regarded, in the context of the UN discussions, as tantamount to its role in preventing disputes.[170]

The examination of the preventive function of fact-finding was particularly endorsed in the General Assembly resolution of 20 December 1965 (above, p. 8), whereby the Secretary-General was asked to supplement his first study so as to cover the main trends of international inquiry as a means for ensuring the execution of certain treaties. The second study by the Secretary-General on methods of fact-finding (above, pp. 8–9) gives expression to a broad concept of the

[170]During the debate in the Sixth Committee on the final draft resolution subsequently adopted by the Assembly, the New Zealand representative stated that his delegation would have wished the proposal of the working group to be bolder and to pay more attention to fact-finding as an instrument for doing other things than settling disputes, although there was some recognition in the 5th and 7th preambular paragraphs of fact-finding in that role. In these paragraphs the Assembly affirms the importance of fact-finding in the prevention of disputes (see above, p. 311).

In the Special Committee, the representatives of Ghana and the UAR objected to the consideration of fact-finding not related to the settlement of international disputes. The Netherlands representative replied that from the outset his delegation had recognized that there were two separate aspects of the question: first, fact-finding with a view to the peaceful settlement of disputes, and secondly, fact-finding not concerned with the peaceful settlement of disputes.

institution of international inquiry, since it includes, as examples of the application of such methods, two categories of 'fact-finding': (1) the reporting of specific phenomena which do not necessarily involve any difference of opinion, not to speak of a dispute, or adjustment of a situation (see n. 169), and (2) fact-finding employed in the adjustment of situations.[171] Thus mention is there made of the obligation of states parties to the Convention relating to the Status of Refugees (189 UNTS (1954), 137), the Convention relating to the Status of Stateless Persons (360 UNTS (1960), 117), and the Supplementary Convention on the Abolition of Slavery, the Slave Trade, and Institutions and Practices Similar to Slavery (266 UNTS (1957), 3), to provide UN bodies with information regarding pertinent national legislation and the steps taken to implement the respective conventions. Similarly, the study mentions the ECOSOC resolution of 23 July 1953 requesting the states parties to the Convention on the Political Rights of Women (193 UNTS (1954), 135) to report every two years on the measures taken by them to implement the provisions of the convention. The methods of fact-finding employed by the International Atomic Energy Agency consist, in the view of the Secretary-General, in the right of the agency, i.a. to review the design of the principal nuclear facilities, to arrange for the keeping of records and the submission of records, to send inspectors to determine whether there is compliance with the undertaking not to use atomic energy for military purposes, and to ensure that agreed radiation levels are not exceeded.

The above examples may be construed as illustrating the preventive function of 'fact-finding', in so far as regular information on the implementation of certain agreements prevents their violation and, consequently, prevents the occurrence of disputes.

Other arrangements included in the Secretary-General's study concern adjustments of 'situations' which in his view do not seem to have the character of disputes. The study states, for example, that the Committee of Ministers and the Consultative Assembly of the Council of Europe 'may deal with the fact-finding aspects of any situation' which may affect the attainment of the aims of the Council. The Consultative Assembly has acted as 'a fact-finding body' on two occasions: first, during the years 1952–4, when a working group of the Political Committee of the Assembly drew up proposals for the settlement of the Saar question between France and the Federal Republic of Germany; and secondly, when another working group of the Political Committee

---

[171]The Secretary-General explained in his first study that his object was to describe the use of 'international inquiry as a peaceful means for settling disputes or adjusting situations' (above, p. 5). He noted (in para. 7) that, owing to lack of time, the study would not deal with international inquiry as envisaged in certain treaties as a means for ensuring their execution. The second study filled the gap, and it appears that in the view of the Secretary-General, the role of international inquiry in the adjustment of situations is particularly pertinent in the context of the execution of treaties.

examined the 'difficulties' which had arisen between Austria and Italy over the status of the German-speaking minority in northern Italy. In each instance these working groups attempted to collect factual information (para. 99 of the report). In so far as the 'situations' described above are not regarded as disputes, but as being of a nature likely to give rise to a dispute, fact-finding undertaken with a view to their settlement may be considered as preventing the occurrence of a dispute.

In spite of considerable emphasis in the debates and in the second study of the Secretary-General on the preventive function of fact-finding, the final resolution of the General Assembly (below, App. IV, p. 347) does not mention this function in its operative section. According to that section, states are invited to resort to fact-finding when 'choosing means for the peaceful settlement of disputes', and the experts included in the Register are to render fact-finding services 'in relation to a dispute'.[172] The function of fact-finding in preventing disputes is mentioned only in the Preamble. In the fifth recital, following the Czechoslovak proposal, the General Assembly expressed its belief that impartial fact-finding within the framework of international organizations and in conventions or other arrangements would make an important contribution to the peaceful settlement of disputes and to the prevention of disputes. In the seventh recital, the General Assembly reaffirmed the importance of impartial fact-finding 'for the settlement and the prevention of disputes' (below, App. IV, p. 347).[173]

The records do not reveal any arguments in favour of the subordination of the preventive function of fact-finding. One possible explanation is that the substantial number of states which objected to the increased role of fact-finding or, specifically, to the creation of new fact-finding machinery, and which accepted only half-heartedly the establishment of the Register of Experts, endeavoured to limit the competence of any future commissions of experts, over whose composition and activities they might have no control.

Commissions established by states v. commissions established by international organizations. The consideration by the UN of the methods of

---

[172]In certain instances the purpose of fact-finding bodies established 'in relation to a dispute' may be regarded as seeking the prevention of a dispute or the prevention of the aggravation of a dispute. The first report of the Secretary-General deals, i.a., with bodies set up by the principal organs of the UN for the purposes of observation. These bodies include UNMOGIP, UNTSO, and UNOGIL. To a great extent the task of such bodies is not to settle a dispute but to prevent violations and adjust situations the continuance of which is likely to give rise to a dispute. Nevertheless, they have been established *in relation* to a dispute which had passed the critical stage. In this respect they are to be distinguished from fact-finding bodies or procedures established without reference to a particular dispute. It is doubtful whether the General Assembly used the phrase 'in relation to a dispute' in the sense here described.

[173]With regard to the settlement of 'disputes', 'controversies', or 'situations' by members of the Panel for Inquiry and Conciliation, see above, pp. 296-7, and below, App. III (Arts 3 & 4), p. 345.

'inquiry' and 'fact-finding' revealed another twofold purpose of these methods: (1) to assist states directly, and (2) to assist international organizations. The resolution of the General Assembly on the establishment of the Panel of Inquiry and Conciliation is explicit in this respect. On the one hand, the Panel is designed to assist states in seeking solutions to their disputes by peaceful means of their own choice. On the other hand, the Panel is available to assist UN organs in the settlement of disputes and situations. Members of the Panel may be chosen to serve on a 'commission of inquiry or of conciliation', either by the states or by the UN organs concerned. While each commission is responsible to the states or the UN organs which appointed it, there exists, as we have noted (above, pp. 298–9), an ambivalent relationship between commissions appointed by the parties and the UN Organization.

As far as consideration of the specific question of fact-finding is concerned, the General Assembly in its resolution of 16 December 1963 (above, p. 300) expressed its belief in the importance of fact-finding 'within the framework of international organizations and in bilateral and multilateral conventions'. The Netherlands suggested that the proposed fact-finding organ should be placed at the disposal of the UN and the Specialized Agencies and of any two or more states (above, p. 303). The Soviet government noted with approval the system of international bodies for investigation and fact-finding established in accordance with the Charter and other international agreements (above, p. 305). The US representative in the Special Committee thought that the mere availability of well-designed fact-finding machinery might induce states or UN organs to use it (above, p. 306). The UK government was in favour of the use of fact-finding by the Security Council as a matter of regular practice, and referred with pride to its own experience in the direct settlement of its dispute with Denmark in the *Red Crusader* case (above, pp. 307–8). The representative of France in the Sixth Committee expressed approval of the 'well-established procedures for fact-finding' described in the two reports by the Secretary-General (above, p. 308). The 'procedures' referred to relate to commissions established either by international organizations, including regional organizations, or by two or more states.

While the above twofold purpose was revealed throughout the discussions, the overall impression is that most of the oral statements and written comments, as well as the two studies by the Secretary-General, emphasized the employment of fact-finding by the UN. However, it is significant that when the time came to sum up the debate, there was a reversal. The role of fact-finding in assisting UN organs was virtually disregarded, and attention was centred on fact-finding in the direct service of individual states. The Finnish working paper (above, p. 310), on which the final resolution was based, envisaged the use of fact-finding only by states in dispute. As far as the final resolution is concerned, the

General Assembly asserted, in the Preamble, the importance of fact-finding within the framework of international organizations; it did not deem it necessary to promote this category of fact-finding in the operative section of the resolution. That section, it will be recalled, urged 'member states' to make more effective use of fact-finding, invited 'member states' to entrust the ascertainment of facts to competent international organizations and bodies established by agreement between the parties concerned, and drew attention to recourse to procedures for the ascertainment of facts under Article 33 of the Charter. Finally, the experts comprised in the Register were to be at the service of the 'states parties to a dispute'.

The reference to competent international organizations is not clear but, even if UN organs are meant, the distinctive feature of the provision is that the choice of these organizations is left to the parties, i.e. the reference is not to the ordinary fact-finding practice of UN organs.[174]

The records do not contain any explanation of the reasons which prompted the delegations to minimize the use of fact-finding by international organizations, and by the UN in particular. Again, it may be submitted that as a whole they were apprehensive about the innovation embodied in the Register of Experts. If the Register is confined to the use of individual states, they may or may not use it, according to their wish. If, however, the Register is at the disposal of UN organs, some members of those organs may invoke its services against the wishes of other members. The recurring argument of the Soviet Union against the establishment of the fact-finding body proposed by the Netherlands was that it would undermine the position of the Security Council or the General Assembly. The reason for this opposition, apparently, was that the existence of the proposed body might limit the power of these two organs to influence the composition and tasks of fact-finding missions. The Soviet Union and the countries supporting her attitude accepted the Register as the lesser evil, but they retained their suspicions (above, p. 312, n. 165). It was therefore not unnatural for them to try to limit its scope of action.

The reserved attitude of many socialist and non-aligned states can be understood, to a certain extent, by reference to a statement by the representative of the Netherlands, made at the 489th meeting (13 December 1965) of the Special Political Committee of the General Assembly during a discussion of the peaceful settlement of disputes. He said that the UN had successfully applied the method of fact-finding. However, there were also many cases in which impartial investigations

---

[174]During the discussion of the final draft in the Sixth Committee, the New Zealand representative said that in the view of his delegation the possibility of UN organs making use of the Register of Experts was not excluded, and it would therefore vote for the draft resolution. The representative probably relied on the preambular provision referred to above.

of the facts had been impossible or had not been undertaken. That method would have been very effective if, for example, one country had accused another of pursuing alleged invaders on its territory and molesting the local population, or complaints had been made of foreign intervention or subversion in the form of aid given to rebels or intruders. In all such cases, fact-finding on the spot could settle the dispute, at least as far as the facts were concerned.

If the Netherlands representative's concepts of 'foreign intervention', 'subversion', or 'rebels' happened to differ from those held by many socialist or non-aligned countries, then such countries would fear that the Netherlands delegation, and other delegations sharing its views, might attempt to use any new fact-finding machinery, including the Register of Experts, for the suppression of what those countries regarded as national liberation movements. It would follow that, as far as many socialist and non-aligned countries were concerned, it was preferable for the new Register not to be employed by the UN.

The western powers, though less outspoken, were similarly concerned. Their repeated insistence on the need to improve existing institutions did not conceal their apprehensions regarding the Netherlands proposal. The services of an impressive fact-finding agency might be invoked by rival states and used as a weapon in the cold war. Thus, for the western powers also, the Register was a compromise solution. They would have preferred the institutional status quo. It follows that it would have suited their interests if the services of the new body of experts were rendered only at the entirely free request of individual parties to a dispute.

Observations on the handling of the problem by the UN. The deficiencies of the General Assembly resolution concerning the Panel for Inquiry and Conciliation have been pointed out in the relevant part of this chapter (above, pp. 298–9). We should like now to note some aspects of the manner in which the 'question of fact-finding' was considered by various UN organs.

The discussions were unnecessarily prolonged, repetitious, and often purposeless. In the course of five years, the various representatives restated once and again their unchanged positions, often quoting whole passages from statements made by themselves or their predecessors. Instead of trying to wind up the discussion as soon as the main views were known, the deliberations were postponed from year to year through lack of time. The issues were not well defined, and the discussion was not systematic. In its initial resolution of 16 December 1963 (above, p. 300) the General Assembly enumerated as methods of fact-finding 'inquiry, investigation and other methods' referred to in instruments of a general and regional nature. This formulation is misleading. Our study has revealed ample evidence that 'inquiry' and 'investigation' are not necessarily methods of fact-finding. They may be identical with fact-finding, or may involve fact-finding in conjunction with other methods. Moreover, what other methods of fact-finding, besides 'inquiry' and 'investigation', are referred to in the various instruments?

In fact, the deliberations did not concentrate on the study of such methods, but on the Netherlands proposal for the establishment of a permanent fact-finding body. Even when it became apparent in the early stages of the discussions that the overwhelming majority of participant states was definitely opposed to the proposal, the delegation of the Netherlands put it forward again and again under different forms, many of which raised additional questions as to the nature of the proposed body. It must be recognized, however, that the persistence of the Netherlands eventually led to the compromise solution of the Register of Experts, which satisfied the Netherlands request for the explicit separation of fact-finding from conciliation. This separation is of considerable theoretical value, and should be kept in mind in the final conclusions of this study.

CHAPTER 9

General Conclusions

An overall attempt will now be made to evaluate the effect which the theoretical and practical developments examined in this study have had on the nature of the Hague institution of inquiry. We should first question the validity of the following views relating to the nature of the method of inquiry: (1) that the enlarged inquiry of the Bryan commissions is one of the forms of the method of inquiry (see, generally, ch. 1); (2) that conciliation commissions are also commissions of inquiry (above, pp. 136–7); (3) that the method of inquiry is one of the elements of the method of conciliation (above, pp. 15, 121, n. 43); and (4) that inquiry is subordinate in status to other methods, in the sense that it is not an independent method but one whose function is to assist those other methods (above, p. 17).

As regards the tendency to include the enlarged inquiry of the Bryan treaties in the concept of inquiry, our analysis leads to the conclusion that to investigate a dispute in all its aspects represents not a simple modification of the Hague institution, but an entirely different phenomenon. The whole raison d'être of the Hague commissions of inquiry was their limited application to a particular set of disputes arising out of differences of opinion on points of fact. The Bryan treaties have not brought about any change in the conceptual framework of the Hague system of inquiry. The four commissions of inquiry established after the conclusion of the first Bryan treaties had the exclusive object of ascertaining the facts in dispute.

On the other hand the Bryan system can hardly be described as an established method in its own right. The complete failure of its application has prevented the crystallization of any recognized system of 'enlarged inquiry' or 'comprehensive examination' which could have been construed as an independent new method for the settlement of disputes. The practical significance of the Bryan system of all-inclusive examination lies in its adoption as the basis of conciliation. This type of examination became typical for commissions of conciliation, not for commissions of inquiry, which continued their parallel, though tenuous, separate existence.

As far as commissions of conciliation are concerned, we have a sufficiently broad theoretical and practical background to be able to answer the question whether commissions of conciliation may validly be considered as commissions of inquiry which have assumed the additional power of making recommendations. The answer to that question must be in the negative, not only because of their general competence to examine all aspects of the dispute, but also for the following reasons. First, in practice, the examination conducted by conciliation commissions is often concentrated on the legal aspects of the dispute—and here the contrast with the original Hague institution is obvious. Second, in spite of the prevailing view of the necessity for a two-stage process of elucidation of the questions in dispute coupled with efforts (often informal) to effect conciliation, the conciliation commissions are not precluded from making the latter efforts at the initial stages of their examination. If they do so, and succeed in formulating, at that early stage, terms of settlement acceptable to both parties, the nature of their work would bear hardly any resemblance to the Hague commissions. Third, in those exceptional circumstances, where conciliation commissions deal primarily with the elucidation of facts, the conduct of the examination is subordinated to the main purpose of reconciling opposing views. The fact-finding process in conciliation serves the purpose of securing agreement, perhaps based on a compromise, even if the examination of the facts is not complete and the whole truth is not brought to light. (In principle, it will be recalled, the commission of conciliation is not required to submit a report incorporating its findings of fact.) Here again, the character and purpose of the inquiry into the facts are intrinsically different from those of the Hague commissions.

Our conclusion therefore is that commissions of conciliation should not be regarded as commissions of inquiry. In this respect the method of bilateral inquiry remains confined to inquiry commissions established in accordance with the Hague Conventions.

We come now to the question whether inquiry conducted by genuine inquiry commissions should be regarded as one of the forms in which the method of conciliation is applied.

It should be emphasized that, while procedures designed to ascertain facts may be employed in the course of conciliation, there is no room for conciliatory efforts in the work of commissions of inquiry. The latter—contrary to commissions of 'inquiry and conciliation' or of 'conciliation' proper—are not expected to suggest, even by implication, a solution 'susceptible of being accepted' by both parties. Commissions of inquiry established in conformity with the Hague Conventions must elucidate the facts by a thorough, impartial, and conscientious investigation, and must submit to the parties a complete report on the result of their investigation. A fact should not be concealed for fear that one party may appear in the wrong and refuse, for that reason, to co-operate in the settlement of the dispute.

In the *Tavignano*, *Tiger*, and *Red Crusader* cases, the commissions of inquiry were called upon to determine where a certain incident took place. In all three cases the commissions strove to accomplish their task with the greatest thoroughness, in the knowledge that if their efforts were successful the claim of one party would be totally substantiated and the claim of the other party would be found baseless. There was no room to satisfy both parties by way of a report on the facts likely to meet, even partially, the claims of both. Indeed, as a result of a detailed inquiry, the *Tiger* and the *Red Crusader* commissions ascertained the place of the respective incidents, thus vindicating the claim of one of the parties only. And if the *Tavignano* Commission could not ascertain the exact location of the main incident, it was not because of any wish to avoid giving a finding in favour, as it were, of one of the parties, but because of technical limitations beyond its control. As far as the *Tubantia* case is concerned, the question whether the Dutch vessel was or was not torpedoed by a German submarine called for a straight-forward answer. In submitting the case to the commission, the two governments did not expect it to engage in a liberal interpretation of the facts (above, p. 222) with a view to bridging the gap between the opposing claims. As it turned out, the report on the facts was accepted by Germany as proving her legal responsibility, and she paid the compensation due. Even in the Dogger Bank case, the way in which the commissioners acquitted themselves of their task showed, it is believed, that they were not prompted by any desire to allay the susceptibilities of Great Britain and Russia.

Reference may also be made to the *Maine* and Schnaebelé cases (above, pp. 33–5), which were in the minds of the promoters of the Hague institution of inquiry. If commissions of inquiry had been set up in these cases, they would have had to ascertain whether or not the *Maine* was sunk at the instigation of the Spanish authorities or, in the second case, whether or not Schnaebelé was arrested on German territory. It is difficult to conceive the work of such commissions as entailing any element of conciliation. The same would have been the position if a commission of inquiry had been established by Albania and the United Kingdom to ascertain the cause of the explosions which damaged British warships in the Corfu Channel in 1946 (above, p. 4, n. 8).

We may conclude that the method of bilateral inquiry is not an element in the method of conciliation. To be sure, bilateral inquiry may lead to a reconciliation, but it should not for that reason be confused with conciliation. Inquiry remains, in this respect also, a distinct pro-cedure in its own right.

The fourth question, relating to the allegedly subordinate status of bilateral inquiry as regards other bilateral methods, arises out of the general attitude of many writers, and more specifically from the analysis by Cot (pp. 44–5), to which we have referred in the introductory chapter (p. 17). According to Cot, the Hague Conventions conferred on the commissions of inquiry two functions: (1) quasi-arbitral—to state the facts; and (2) quasi-mediatory—to promote the settlement of the dispute. Since the successful pursuit of an inquiry might, in spite of all precautions, have the effect of a judgment (*chose jugée*), the parties were inclined to give the commissions a wider but less precise mandate. Thus the report would not appear as an element of proof, but as the possible basis for a compromise. The experience of commissions of inquiry established within the framework of the Hague Conventions confirmed, he writes, the uncertainty of their task. In respect of the four incidents which were the object of an inquiry, only the commission set up to clarify the torpedoing of the *Tubantia* followed the scheme of Part III of the conventions. In the Dogger Bank and *Red Crusader* cases, the commissions were not content to present only the facts, but also made an appraisal regarding the responsibilities of the parties. In the case of the *Tavignano*, the procedure of inquiry was linked to the procedure of arbitration and took a different direction. If the international commission of inquiry, concludes Cot, appears to be permanently 'unbalanced', it is because its very conception is based on an ambiguity. Inquiry is not a method for the pacific settlement of disputes, but an instrument in the service of various possible methods. Therefore the pattern of inquiry changes in accordance with the particular method which it is called upon to serve, i.e. mediation or arbitration.

Our study shows, it is believed, that Cot's observations are not justified. The learned author would doubtless agree that the Hague system of genuine inquiry or fact-finding, was followed not only in the *Tubantia* case but also in the *Tiger* case. The remaining three cases were also not of a nature to support his premise. The *Tavignano* case did not take a different direction because of what is described as its link with arbitration. The *Tavignano* Commission exercised a purely fact-finding task, in the best tradition of the Hague Conventions, the parties agreeing to have recourse to an arbitral tribunal only if it were eventually deemed necessary.

The *Tavignano* agreement on inquiry made no reference to subsequent recourse to arbitration. The task of the commission was to 'investigate, mark and determine' certain geographical points and to determine the hydrography, configuration, and nature of the Tunisian coast and neighbouring banks (above, p. 146). The commission pursued its work uninfluenced by any arrangement for possible recourse to arbitration. Moreover, the agreement of the two parties to refer the case to arbitration if they could not settle the dispute on the basis of the report of the commission of inquiry should not, in principle, detract from the independent status of inquiry as a peaceful method for the settlement of disputes. Inquiry is generally considered as a diplomatic method, together with negotiations, good offices and mediation, and conciliation. None of these other methods is held to be a subsidiary device because states having recourse to its use choose to bring their case to arbitration or judicial settlement as a last resort.

As far as the *Red Crusader* case is concerned, the fact that the commission expressed an opinion regarding the responsibilities of the parties does not mean that the inquiry was intended to serve, or that it in fact served any procedure of arbitration. Our analysis seems to show that the commission did not have to express opinions in law in order to comply with its terms of reference. The detailed 'inquiry' designed to determine the geographical location of the *Red Crusader* did not serve any 'arbitral' process concerning the lawfulness of the Danish commander's action. The pronouncement in law did not indicate any inherent instability of the inquiry method. It must be emphasized again that if the dispute had been confined to determining the location of the *Red Crusader*, as has happened in similar cases (above, p. 145), an inquiry commission on the Hague model would have been fully equipped to perform that task, independently of any legal considerations. Similarly, the approach of the Dogger Bank Commission should not be interpreted as indicating an inherent incapacity of commissions of inquiry to provide a solid basis for the settlement of disputes by the confining of their examination to issues of fact. The conferment of the additional task of establishing responsibility was regarded as an express deviation from the Hague rules, necessitated by Great Britain's insistence in the matter. The best proof that even at the time of the Dogger Bank incident commissions of inquiry were not expected to concern themselves with legal questions, is the preservation of the exclusively fact-finding function of inquiry commissions in the Hague Convention of 1907. Moreover, as has been shown in the present study, the Dogger Bank Commission refrained from formulating its report in legal terms, thus acting in fact as a genuine inquiry commission.

It follows from the above considerations and from our study as a whole that international inquiry is an independent method in its own right. Its similarity to arbitration does not derogate from its separate status, just as the similarity between arbitration and judicial settlement, or between mediation and good offices, does not affect the definition of either of these processes as a separate method for the pacific settlement of disputes. International inquiry has its own distinctive characteristics and features. It combines the benefits of diplomacy and legal settlement, inasmuch as the parties obtain a competent, impartial report on the facts at issue while preserving their freedom of action.

Practice has shown that the method of inquiry contains all the necessary components enabling it to settle a dispute once and for all. Voluntary recourse to a commission of inquiry composed of members chosen by the parties is in itself an indication of a desire on the part of the states in dispute to co-operate with the commission and to respect its findings. The issues are clear-cut, and the expert knowledge of the commissioners is considered sufficient to enable them to make definitive findings on questions of fact. These findings indicate in themselves where the legal responsibilities lie. Little room is therefore left for any reserve by the parties after the submission of the report, and the disputes are settled on the basis of the respective reports. The successful outcome of the inquiries must also be attributed to the non-dangerous character of the disputes. As noted in Chapter 6 (p. 195), it would appear that the inquiry method is particularly apt for disputes which, although creating tension, are unlikely to lead to hostilities.

Having thus conceived the nature of inquiry as a method, distinct from the other recognized methods, for the peaceful settlement of disputes, we wish to stress the difference between inquiry so conceived and procedures of 'inquiry' or 'fact-finding', such as examination of witnesses or 'visits on the spot', used by commissions of inquiry, commissions of conciliation, arbitral or judicial tribunals, or international organizations.

We have noted that a commission of conciliation does not acquire the status of a commission of inquiry by virtue of its competence to elucidate the questions in dispute or its 'inquiry' into the facts of the dispute. The same is true of arbitral and judicial tribunals. The examination of witnesses and inquiries on the spot are specific techniques for acquiring evidence (above, p. 4, n. 8). As such, they should be regarded as elements of the arbitral or judicial process and not as an application of the method of inquiry in the settlement of international disputes.

So far as the use of 'inquiry' or 'fact-finding' procedures by international organizations is concerned, the position may be different. We may refer here to the various views, outlined in the introductory chapter, suggesting the extension of the method of inquiry within the framework of international organizations. Our study of bilateral inquiry tends to support only those approaches which conceive the establishment of 'commissions of inquiry' as an evolution of the method of inquiry or, as we would prefer to call it, the institutionalization of a parallel method of inquiry. Many other 'methods of fact-finding' are prima facie so remote from the original institution that they can hardly be placed in the same category. This seems to be particularly true of 'fact-finding' missions whose primary task is to reduce tension by means of diplomatic negotiations with the authorities of the states concerned. Similarly, the overall examination of disputes by the Council and Assembly of the League of Nations and the corresponding organs of the UN have little in common with the Hague institution, especially having regard to the predominance of the political factors underlying the debates.[1] Finally,

[1] According to Claude, a major difficulty in the General Assembly has been the tendency of governments to insist upon using the committees of the whole and the plenary body

exception must be taken to the inclusion in the method of inquiry of a variety of 'reporting systems' designed to supply information as a matter of routine practice. It is doubtful whether this way of preventing disputes could validly be viewed as an application of the method of inquiry, since this would lead to such an elastic notion of inquiry as would empty it of all meaning. Every communication of facts within the framework of the UN for example, is ultimately designed to further the aims of the Organization in the prevention or settlement of disputes. Does it follow that each and every instance of such communication of facts is to be regarded as a development or application of the method of inquiry? Here again, we should keep in mind the distinction between inquiry as a method for the settlement of disputes and particular devices for obtaining information.

In the light of the foregoing observations relating to bilateral inquiry as an independent method on the one hand, and the employment of inquiry techniques by other methods on the other, we may conclude that the institution of international inquiry as envisaged in the Hague Conventions of 1899 and 1907 has remained essentially intact. The development of conciliation out of inquiry has not affected the theoretical postulates of the Hague institution, or its application in appropriate instances. Similarly, the structure of the inquiry method as defined by the Hague Conventions does not seem to have been influenced by the development of international organizations. As with conciliation or judicial settlement, international organizations have employed certain techniques for acquiring factual information and have possibly developed their own system of inquiry commissions, while allowing and even encouraging the parallel use of the Hague system by individual states. Article 33 of the Charter has acknowledged the separate role of international commissions of inquiry established on the pattern of the Hague Conventions (above, p. 134). Moreover, in 1967 the General Assembly drew special attention to the 'procedures for the ascertainment of facts, in accordance with Article 33 of the Charter'—the method of inquiry is here clearly envisaged—and established the Register of Experts on fact-finding. This reassertion of the usefulness of the inquiry method in its genuine form reflects not only an acknowledgment of the shortcomings of the UN but also a certain reliance on the potentialities of international inquiry. Whether or not this reliance will be followed

---

for full-scale public debate and formal voting upon international disputes. This is virtually equivalent to saying that they reject the whole idea of pacific settlement, for a massive international conference is as inappropriate a place, and a general counting of votes as unpromising a method, of achieving pacific settlement as can be devised. To the extent that states have renounced the concept of the General Assembly as a creator and sponsor of specialized bodies and intimate procedures for mediation and have made it a forum for their contentions and a registrar of their political victories, they have undermined its usefulness as an instrument for pacific settlement. The General Assembly has largely become a battlefield rather than a peace conference (*Swords into plowshares*, 3rd edn (1964), p. 219).

by actual recourse to bilateral inquiry is a matter of conjecture. Just as the practice of bilateral conciliation has recently increased, it is possible that states will find it convenient to take advantage of the services of commissions of inquiry in appropriate disputes and in favourable conditions of international co-operation and trust.[2] Experience, though limited, has been by no means disappointing in this respect. The institution of international inquiry has stood the test. It has proved both stable and sufficiently elastic to allow of adjustments necessitated by particular circumstances.

[2]Hyde considers that it may sometimes be preferable to employ commissions of inquiry rather than commissions of conciliation. In his view, a state may find itself embarrassed if foreign commissioners make a strong recommendation which, not being necessarily based on law, is adverse to its policy and interests; it may also resent the efforts of a non-judicial body to induce it to relinquish its legal rights or to pursue a course which may entail sacrifice of those rights. For that reason, it is not impossible that the narrower and more modest efforts of a commission of inquiry which is not endowed with authority to conciliate may prove, at least in certain circumstances, to be more acceptable to states which fail to adjust their controversy by direct negotiation (*International law*, ii. 1579).

Hyde's observations seem to be relevant to disputes concerning alleged facts whose legal implication is clear.

APPENDIX I

Convention pour le Règlement Pacifique des Conflits Internationaux (1907)

[Authentic text][1]

Titre III. Des Commissions internationales d'enquête

Article 9

Dans les litiges d'ordre international n'engageant ni l'honneur ni des intérêts essentiels et provenant d'une divergence d'appréciation sur des points de fait, les Puissances contractantes jugent utile et désirable que les Parties qui n'auraient pu se mettre d'accord par les voies diplomatiques instituent, en tant que les circonstances le permettront, une Commission internationale d'enquête chargée de faciliter la solution de ces litiges en éclaircissant, par un examen impartial et consciencieux, les questions de fait.

Article 10

Les Commissions internationales d'enquête sont constituées par convention spéciale entre les Parties en litige.

La convention d'enquête précise les faits à examiner; elle détermine le mode et le délai de formation de la Commission et l'étendue des pouvoirs des Commissaires.

Elle détermine également, s'il y a lieu, le siège de la Commission et la faculté de se déplacer, la langue dont la Commission fera usage et celles dont l'emploi sera autorisé devant elle, ainsi que la date à laquelle chaque Partie devra déposer son exposé des faits, et généralement toutes les conditions dont les Parties sont convenues.

Si les Parties jugent nécessaire de nommer des assesseurs, la convention d'enquête détermine le mode de leur désignation et l'étendue de leurs pouvoirs.

Article 11

Si la convention d'enquête n'a pas désigné le siège de la Commission, celle-ci siégera à La Haye.

Le siège une fois fixé ne peut être changé par la Commission qu'avec l'assentiment des Parties.

Si la convention d'enquête n'a pas déterminé les langues à employer, il en est décidé par la Commission.

Article 12

Sauf stipulation contraire, les Commissions d'enquête sont formées de la manière déterminée par les articles 45 et 57 de la présente Convention.[2]

---

[1]Netherlands, *Deuxième Conférence Internationale de la Paix, La Haye, 15 juin–18 octobre 1907, Actes et documents*, i: *Séances plénières de la conférence* (1907), pp. 604–19. See also PCA, *Convention pour le règlement pacifique des conflits internationaux, conclue à La Haye, le 18 octobre 1907* (1908); Cd 3857 (1908), pp. 39–52, and Martens, *Nouveau recueil*, 3rd ser., iii (1910), pp. 360–413.

[2]See above, p. 96, n. 40.

Article 13

En cas de décès, de démission ou d'empêchement, pour quelque cause que ce soit, de l'un des Commissaires, ou éventuellement de l'un des assesseurs, il est pourvu à son remplacement selon le mode fixé pour sa nomination.

Article 14

Les Parties ont le droit de nommer auprès de la Commission d'enquête des agents spéciaux avec la mission de Les représenter et de servir d'intermédiaires entre Elles et la Commission.

Elles sont, en outre, autorisées à charger des conseils ou avocats nommés par Elles, d'exposer et de soutenir leurs intérêts devant la Commission.

Article 15

Le Bureau international de la Cour permanente d'arbitrage sert de greffe aux Commissions qui siègent à La Haye, et mettra ses locaux et son organisation à la disposition des Puissances contractantes pour le fonctionnement de la Commission d'enquête.

Article 16

Si la Commission siège ailleurs qu'à La Haye, elle nomme un Secrétaire-Général dont le bureau lui sert de greffe.

Le greffe est chargé, sous l'autorité du Président, de l'organisation matérielle des séances de la Commission, de la rédaction des procès-verbaux et, pendant le temps de l'enquête, de la garde des archives qui seront ensuite versées au Bureau international de La Haye.

Article 17

En vue de faciliter l'institution et le fonctionnement des Commissions d'enquête, les Puissances contractantes recommandent les règles suivantes qui seront applicables à la procédure d'enquête en tant que les Parties n'adopteront pas d'autres règles.

Article 18

La Commission règlera les détails de la procédure non prévus dans la convention spéciale d'enquête ou dans la présente Convention, et procèdera à toutes les formalités que comporte l'administration des preuves.

Article 19

L'enquête a lieu contradictoirement.

Aux dates prévues, chaque Partie communique à la Commission et à l'autre Partie les exposés des faits, s'il y a lieu, et, dans tous les cas, les actes, pièces et documents qu'Elle juge utiles à la découverte de la vérité, ainsi que la liste des témoins et des experts qu'elle désire faire entendre.

Article 20

La Commission a la faculté, avec l'assentiment des Parties, de se transporter momentanément sur les lieux où elle juge utile de recourir à ce moyen d'information, ou d'y déléguer un ou plusieurs de ses membres. L'autorisation de l'État sur le territoire duquel il doit être procédé à cette information devra être obtenue.

Article 21
Toutes constatations matérielles, et toutes visites des lieux doivent être faites en présence des agents et conseils des Parties ou eux dûment appelés.

Article 22
La Commission a le droit de solliciter de l'une ou l'autre Partie telles explications ou informations qu'elle juge utiles.

Article 23
Les Parties s'engagent à fournir à la Commission d'enquête, dans la plus large mesure qu'Elles jugeront possible, tous les moyens et toutes les facilités nécessaires pour la connaissance complète et l'appréciation exacte des faits en question.

Elles s'engagent à user des moyens dont Elles disposent d'après leur législation intérieure, pour assurer la comparution des témoins ou des experts se trouvant sur leur territoire et cités devant la Commission.

Si ceux-ci ne peuvent comparaître devant la Commission, Elles feront procéder à leur audition devant leurs autorités compétentes.

Article 24
Pour toutes les notifications que la Commission aurait à faire sur le territoire d'une tierce Puissance contractante, la Commission s'adressera directement au Gouvernement de cette Puissance. Il en sera de même s'il s'agit de faire procéder sur place à l'établissement de tous moyens de preuve.

Les requêtes adressées à cet effet seront exécutées suivant les moyens dont la Puissance requise dispose d'après sa législation intérieure. Elles ne peuvent être refusées que si cette Puissance les juge de nature à porter atteinte à Sa souveraineté ou à Sa sécurité.

La Commission aura aussi toujours la faculté de recourir à l'intermédiaire de la Puissance sur le territoire de laquelle elle a son siège.

Article 25
Les témoins et les experts sont appelés à la requête des Parties ou d'office par la Commission, et, dans tous les cas, par l'intermédiaire du Gouvernement de l'Etat sur le territoire duquel ils se trouvent.

Les témoins sont entendus, successivement et séparément, en présence des agents et des conseils et dans un ordre à fixer par la Commission.

Article 26
L'interrogatoire des témoins est conduit par le Président.

Les membres de la Commission peuvent néanmoins poser à chaque témoin les questions qu'ils croient convenables pour éclaircir ou compléter sa déposition, ou pour se renseigner sur tout ce qui concerne le témoin dans les limites nécessaires à la manifestation de la vérité.

Les agents et les conseils des Parties ne peuvent interrompre le témoin dans sa déposition, ni lui faire aucune interpellation directe, mais peuvent demander au Président de poser au témoin telles questions complémentaires qu'ils jugent utiles.

Article 27

Le témoin doit déposer sans qu'il lui soit permis de lire aucun projet écrit. Toutefois, il peut être autorisé par le Président à s'aider de notes ou documents si la nature des faits rapportés en nécessite l'emploi.

Article 28

Procès-verbal de la déposition du témoin est dressé séance tenante et lecture en est donnée au témoin. Le témoin peut y faire tels changements et additions que bon lui semble et qui seront consignés à la suite de sa déposition.

Lecture faite au témoin de l'ensemble de sa déposition, le témoin est requis de signer.

Article 29

Les agents sont autorisés, au cours ou à la fin de l'enquête, à présenter par écrit à la Commission et à l'autre Partie tels dires, réquisitions ou résumés de fait, qu'ils jugent utiles à la découverte de la vérité.

Article 30

Les délibérations de la Commission ont lieu à huis clos et restent secrètes. Toute décision est prise à la majorité des membres de la Commission.

Le refus d'un membre de prendre part au vote doit être constaté dans le procès-verbal.

Article 31

Les séances de la Commission ne sont publiques et les procès-verbaux et documents de l'enquête ne sont rendus publics qu'en vertu d'une décision de la Commission, prise avec l'assentiment des Parties.

Article 32

Les Parties ayant présenté tous les éclaircissements et preuves, tous les témoins ayant été entendus, le Président prononce la clôture de l'enquête et la Commission s'ajourne pour délibérer et rédiger son rapport.

Article 33

Le rapport est signé par tous les membres de la Commission.

Si un des membres refuse de signer, mention en est faite; le rapport reste néanmoins valable.

Article 34

Le rapport de la Commission est lu en séance publique, les agents et conseils des Parties présents ou dûment appelés.

Un exemplaire du rapport est remis à chaque Partie.

Article 35

Le rapport de la Commission, limité à la constatation des faits, n'a nullement le caractère d'une sentence arbitrale. Il laisse aux Parties une entière liberté pour la suite à donner à cette constatation.

Article 36

Chaque Partie supporte ses propres frais et une part égale des frais de la Commission.

Convention for the Pacific Settlement of International Disputes (1907)

[*Unofficial translation*][1]

Part III. International Commissions of Inquiry

Article IX

In disputes of an international nature involving neither honour nor vital interests, and arising from a difference of opinion on points of fact, the Contracting Powers deem it expedient and desirable that the parties who have not been able to come to an agreement by means of diplomacy, should, as far as circumstances allow, institute an International Commission of Inquiry, to facilitate a solution of these disputes by elucidating the facts by means of an impartial and conscientious investigation.

Article X

International Commissions of Inquiry are constituted by special agreement between the parties in dispute.

The Inquiry Convention defines the facts to be examined; it determines the mode and time in which the Commission is to be formed and the extent of the powers of the Commissioners.

It also determines, if there is need, where the Commission is to sit, and whether it may remove to another place, the language the Commission shall use and the languages the use of which shall be authorized before it, as well as the date on which each party must deposit its statement of facts, and, generally speaking, all the conditions upon which the parties have agreed.

If the parties consider it necessary to appoint Assessors, the Convention of Inquiry shall determine the mode of their selection and the extent of their powers.

Article XI

If the Inquiry Convention has not determined where the Commission is to sit, it will sit at The Hague.

The place of meeting, once fixed, cannot be altered by the Commission except with the assent of the parties.

If the Inquiry Convention has not determined what languages are to be employed, the question shall be decided by the Commission.

Article XII

Unless an undertaking is made to the contrary, Commissions of Inquiry shall be formed in the manner determined by Articles XLV and LVII of the present Convention.[2]

---

[1]Cd 3857, pp. 52–64. This text is used by the PCA, which has published it in a pamphlet entitled *Convention for the pacific settlement of international disputes concluded at The Hague on October 18th, 1907* (May 1957). The same text appears also in Scott, *The Hague conventions and declarations of 1899 and 1907* (1915), pp. 45–55, and in TCIA, ii. 2220–47. The wording of Part III in the above sources differs from the wording in Scott's *Proceedings, 1907*, i. 599–615. On the different versions of Arts IX & XXXV see above, p. 93, n. 24 and p. 95, n. 37 respectively.

[2]See above, p. 96, n. 40.

Article XIII

Should one of the Commissioners or one of the Assessors, should there be any, either die, or resign, or be unable for any reason whatever to discharge his functions, the same procedure is followed for filling the vacancy as was followed for appointing him.

Article XIV

The parties are entitled to appoint special agents to attend the Commission of Inquiry, whose duty it is to represent them and to act as intermediaries between them and the Commission.

They are further authorized to engage counsel or advocates, appointed by themselves, to state their case and uphold their interests before the Commission.

Article XV

The International Bureau of the Permanent Court of Arbitration acts as registry for the Commissions which sit at The Hague, and shall place its offices and staff at the disposal of the Contracting Powers for the use of the Commission of Inquiry.

Article XVI

If the Commission meets elsewhere than at The Hague, it appoints a Secretary-General, whose office serves as registry.

It is the function of the registry, under the control of the President, to make the necessary arrangements for the sittings of the Commission, the preparation of the Minutes, and, while the inquiry lasts, for the charge of the archives, which shall subsequently be transferred to the International Bureau at The Hague.

Article XVII

In order to facilitate the constitution and working of Commissions of Inquiry, the Contracting Powers recommend the following rules, which shall be applicable to the inquiry procedure in so far as the parties do not adopt other rules.

Article XVIII

The Commission shall settle the details of the procedure not covered by the special Inquiry Convention or the present Convention, and shall arrange all the formalities required for dealing with the evidence.

Article XIX

On the inquiry both sides must be heard.

At the dates fixed, each party communicates to the Commission and to the other party the statements of facts, if any, and, in all cases, the instruments, papers, and documents which it considers useful for ascertaining the truth, as well as the list of witnesses and experts whose evidence it wishes to be heard.

Article XX

The Commission is entitled, with the assent of the Powers, to move temporarily to any place where it considers it may be useful to have recourse to this means of inquiry or to send one or more of its members. Permission must be obtained from the State on whose territory it is proposed to hold the inquiry.

Article XXI

Every investigation, and every examination of a locality, must be made in the presence of the agents and counsel of the parties or after they have been duly summoned.

Article XXII

The Commission is entitled to ask from either party for such explanations and information as it considers necessary.

Article XXIII

The parties undertake to supply the Commission of Inquiry, as fully as they may think possible, with all means and facilities necessary to enable it to become completely acquainted with, and to accurately understand, the facts in question.

They undertake to make use of the means at their disposal, under their municipal law, to insure the appearance of the witnesses or experts who are in their territory and have been summoned before the Commission.

If the witnesses or experts are unable to appear before the Commission, the parties will arrange for their evidence to be taken before the qualified officials of their own country.

Article XXIV

For all notices to be served by the Commission in the territory of a third Contracting Power, the Commission shall apply direct to the Government of the said Power. The same rule applies in the case of steps being taken on the spot to procure evidence.

The requests for this purpose are to be executed so far as the means at the disposal of the Power applied to under its municipal law allow. They cannot be rejected unless the Power in question considers they are calculated to impair its sovereign rights or its safety.

The Commission will equally be always entitled to act through the Power on whose territory it sits.

Article XXV

The witnesses and experts are summoned on the request of the parties or by the Commission of its own motion, and, in every case, through the Government of the State in whose territory they are.

The witnesses are heard in succession and separately, in the presence of the agents and counsel, and in the order fixed by the Commission.

Article XXVI

The examination of witnesses is conducted by the President.

The members of the Commission may however put to each witness questions which they consider likely to throw light on and complete his evidence, or get information on any point concerning the witness within the limits of what is necessary in order to get at the truth.

The agents and counsel of the parties may not interrupt the witness when he is making his statement, nor put any direct question to him, but they may ask the President to put such additional questions to the witness as they think expedient.

Article XXVII

The witness must give his evidence without being allowed to read any written draft. He may, however, be permitted by the President to consult notes or documents if the nature of the facts referred to necessitates their employment.

Article XXVIII

A Minute of the evidence of the witness is drawn up forthwith and read to the witness. The latter may make such alterations and additions as he thinks necessary, which will be recorded at the end of his statement.

When the whole of his statement has been read to the witness, he is asked to sign it.

Article XXIX

The agents are authorized, in the course of or at the close of the inquiry, to present in writing to the Commission and to the other party such statements, requisitions, or summaries of the facts as they consider useful for ascertaining the truth.

Article XXX

The Commission considers its decisions in private and the proceedings are secret.

All questions are decided by a majority of the members of the Commission.

If a member declines to vote, the fact must be recorded in the Minutes.

Article XXXI

The sittings of the Commission are not public, nor the Minutes and documents connected with the inquiry published except in virtue of a decision of the Commission taken with the consent of the parties.

Article XXXII

After the parties have presented all the explanations and evidence, and the witnesses have all been heard, the President declares the inquiry terminated, and the Commission adjourns to deliberate and to draw up its Report.

Article XXXIII

The Report is signed by all the members of the Commission.

If one of the members refuses to sign, the fact is mentioned; but the validity of the Report is not affected.

Article XXXIV

The Report of the Commission is read at a public sitting, the agents and counsel of the parties being present or duly summoned.

A copy of the Report is given to each party.

Article XXXV

The Report of the Commission is limited to a statement of facts, and has in no way the character of an Award. It leaves to the parties entire freedom as to the effect to be given to the statement.

Article XXXVI

Each party pays its own expenses and an equal share of the expenses incurred by the Commission.

Note on the Parties to the Hague Conventions of 1899 and 1907 for the Pacific Settlement of International Disputes[1]

The Convention of 1899 was signed at The Hague on 29 July 1899 by the representatives of the following twenty-six states: Austria-Hungary, Belgium, Bulgaria, China, Denmark, France, Germany, Great Britain and Ireland, Greece, Italy, Japan, Luxembourg, Montenegro, Netherlands, Persia, Portugal, Romania, Russia, Serbia, Siam, Spain, Switzerland, Turkey, United Kingdoms of Sweden and Norway, United Mexican States, and United States of America. Between 29 July 1899 and 12 June 1907 all the signatory states ratified the convention. The government of the Socialist Federal Republic of Yugoslavia in a note of 27 March 1969, received by the Netherlands Ministry for Foreign Affairs, confirmed that it considers itself a party to the Hague Treaties and Declarations of 29 July 1899 which had been ratified by Serbia.

The following states adhered to the convention: Argentina, Bolivia, Brazil, Chile, Colombia, Cuba, Dominican Republic, Ecuador, El Salvador, Guatemala, Haiti, Nicaragua, Panama, Paraguay, Peru, Uruguay, and Venezuela (1907); Honduras (1961), Lebanon (1968), and Iraq (1970).

The following states have declared that they consider themselves parties to the convention: India and Pakistan (1950); Ceylon, Iceland, Laos, and USSR (1955); Cambodia (1956); New Zealand (1959); Australia and Canada (1960); Cameroon, Democratic Republic of Congo and Upper Volta (1961); Byelorussian SSR and Ukrainian SSR (1962); Mauritius (1970); and Fiji (1973).

The Convention of 1907 was signed at The Hague on 18 October 1907 by the representatives of the following forty-three states: Argentina, Austria-Hungary, Belgium, Bolivia, Brazil, Bulgaria, Chile, China, Colombia, Cuba,

[1] Based on *Tableau officiel des signatures, ratifications, adhésions et dénonciations concernant les conventions et déclarations élaborées à La Haye en 1899 et 1907 au cours des deux Conférences Internationales de la Paix*, published (in typewritten form) in June 1973 by the Netherlands Ministry for Foreign Affairs in its capacity as depositary. I am grateful to Miss F. Y. van de Wal, assistant legal adviser at the Netherlands Ministry for Foreign Affairs and to Miss H. J. M. Bredt, Head of the Treaties Publication Section, for supplying me with this official list (as revised).

See also Bardonnet, 'L'état de ratifications des conventions de La Haye de 1899 et de 1907 sur le règlement de conflits internationaux', in *AFDI, 1961*, pp. 726–41.

Denmark, Dominican Republic, Ecuador, El Salvador, France, Germany, Great Britain, Greece, Guatemala, Haiti, Italy, Japan, Luxembourg, Mexico, Montenegro, Netherlands, Norway, Panama, Paraguay, Peru, Persia, Portugal, Romania, Russia, Serbia, Siam, Spain, Sweden, Switzerland, Turkey, United States, Uruguay, and Venezuela.

Of these states, the following twenty-nine ratified the convention: Austria-Hungary, Bolivia, China, Denmark, El Salvador, Germany, Mexico, Netherlands, Russia, Sweden, and the United States (1909); Belgium, France, Haiti, Norway, Siam, and Switzerland (1910); Guatemala, Japan, Panama, and Portugal (1911); Cuba, Luxembourg, and Romania (1912); Spain (1913); Brazil (1914); Paraguay (1933); Dominican Republic (1958); and the United Kingdom (1970).

The following states adhered to the convention: Nicaragua (1910); Czechoslovakia, Finland, and Poland (1922); Honduras and Israel (1962); Sudan and Uganda (1966); Lebanon, Malta, and the UAR (1968); Iraq and Swaziland (1970).

The following states have declared that they consider themselves parties to the convention: Iceland, Laos, and USSR (1955); Cambodia (1956); Cameroon, Democratic Republic of Congo, and Upper Volta (1961); Byelorussian SSR and Ukrainian SSR (1962).

By virtue of its Article 91, the Convention of 1907 replaces the Convention of 1899 as between the contracting parties.

APPENDIX II

Revised General Act for the Pacific Settlement of International Disputes. Adopted by the General Assembly of the United Nations on 28 April 1949[1]

CHAPTER I

Conciliation

Article 1

Disputes of every kind between two or more Parties to the present General Act which it has not been possible to settle by diplomacy shall, subject to such reservations as may be made under article 39, be submitted, under the conditions laid down in the present chapter, to the procedure of conciliation.

Article 2

The disputes referred to in the preceding article shall be submitted to a permanent or special conciliation commission constituted by the parties to the dispute.

Article 3

On a request to that effect being made by one of the Contracting Parties to another party, a permanent conciliation commission shall be constituted within a period of six months.

Article 4

Unless the parties concerned agree otherwise, the Conciliation Commission shall be constituted as follows:

(1) The Commission shall be composed of five members. The parties shall each nominate one commissioner, who may be chosen from among their respective nationals. The three other commissioners shall be appointed by agreement from among the nationals of third Powers. These three commissioners must be of different nationalities and must not be habitually resident in the territory nor be in the service of the parties. The parties shall appoint the President of the Commission from among them.

(2) The commissioners shall be appointed for three years. They shall be re-eligible. The commissioners appointed jointly may be replaced during the course of their mandate by agreement between the parties. Either party may, however, at any time replace a commissioner whom it has appointed. Even if replaced, the commissioners shall continue to exercise their functions until the termination of the work in hand.

(3) Vacancies which may occur as a result of death, resignation or any other cause shall be filled within the shortest possible time in the manner fixed for the nominations.

[1] 71 UNTS (1950), 102–10.

Article 5

If, when a dispute arises, no permanent conciliation commission appointed by the parties is in existence, a special commission shall be constituted for the examination of the dispute within a period of three months from the date at which a request to that effect is made by one of the parties to the other party. The necessary appointments shall be made in the manner laid down in the preceding article, unless the parties decide otherwise.

Article 6

1. If the appointment of the commissioners to be designated jointly is not made within the periods provided for in articles 3 and 5, the making of the necessary appointments shall be entrusted to a third Power, chosen by agreement between the parties, or on request of the parties, to the President of the General Assembly, or, if the latter is not in session, to the last President.

2. If no agreement is reached on either of these procedures, each party shall designate a different Power, and the appointment shall be made in concert by the Powers thus chosen.

3. If, within a period of three months, the two Powers have been unable to reach an agreement, each of them shall submit a number of candidates equal to the number of members to be appointed. It shall then be decided by lot which of the candidates thus designated shall be appointed.

Article 7

1. Disputes shall be brought before the Conciliation Commission by means of an application addressed to the President by the two parties acting in agreement, or in default thereof by one or other of the parties.

2. The application, after giving a summary account of the subject of the dispute, shall contain the invitation to the Commission to take all necessary measures with a view to arriving at an amicable solution.

3. If the application emanates from only one of the parties, the other party shall, without delay, be notified by it.

Article 8

1. Within fifteen days from the date on which a dispute has been brought by one of the parties before a permanent conciliation commission, either party may replace its own commissioner, for the examination of the particular dispute, by a person possessing special competence in the matter.

2. The party making use of this right shall immediately notify the other party; the latter shall, in such case, be entitled to take similar action within fifteen days from the date on which it received the notification.

Article 9

1. In the absence of agreement to the contrary between the parties, the Conciliation Commission shall meet at the seat of the United Nations, or at some other place selected by its President.

2. The Commission may in all circumstances request the Secretary-General of the United Nations to afford it his assistance.

M

Article 10

The work of the Conciliation Commission shall not be conducted in public unless a decision to that effect is taken by the Commission with the consent of the parties.

Article 11

1. In the absence of agreement to the contrary between the parties, the Conciliation Commission shall lay down its own procedure, which in any case must provide for both parties being heard. In regard to enquiries, the Commission, unless it decides unanimously to the contrary, shall act in accordance with the provisions of part III of the Hague Convention of 18 October 1907[2] for the Pacific Settlement of International Disputes.

2. The parties shall be represented before the Conciliation Commission by agents, whose duty shall be to act as intermediaries between them and the Commission; they may, moreover, be assisted by counsel and experts appointed by them for that purpose and may request that all persons whose evidence appears to them desirable shall be heard.

3. The Commission, for its part, shall be entitled to request oral explanations from the agents, counsel and experts of both parties, as well as from all persons it may think desirable to summon with the consent of their Governments.

Article 12

In the absence of agreement to the contrary between the parties, the decisions of the Conciliation Commission shall be taken by a majority vote, and the Commission may only take decisions on the substance of the dispute if all its members are present.

Article 13

The parties undertake to facilitate the work of the Conciliation Commission, and particularly to supply it to the greatest possible extent with all relevant documents and information, as well as to use the means at their disposal to allow it to proceed in their territory, and in accordance with their law, to the summoning and hearing of witnesses or experts and to visit the localities in question.

Article 14

1. During the proceedings of the Commission, each of the commissioners shall receive emoluments the amount of which shall be fixed by agreement between the parties, each of which shall contribute an equal share.

2. The general expenses arising out of the working of the Commission shall be divided in the same manner.

Article 15

1. The task of the Conciliation Commission shall be to elucidate the questions in dispute, to collect with that object all necessary information by means

[2]*British and Foreign State Papers*, C.298; 54 LNTS, 435 & 134 LNTS, 453.
[The text of the Convention of 1907 does not appear in the LNTS. The pages referred to contain only short notes on the accession of four states to the convention.]

of enquiry or otherwise, and to endeavour to bring the parties to an agreement. It may, after the case has been examined, inform the parties of the terms of settlement which seem suitable to it, and lay down the period within which they are to make their decision.

2. At the close of the proceedings the Commission shall draw up a *procès-verbal* stating, as the case may be, either that the parties have come to an agreement and, if need arises, the terms of the agreement, or that it has been impossible to effect a settlement. No mention shall be made in the *procès-verbal* of whether the Commission's decisions were taken unanimously or by a majority vote.

3. The proceedings of the Commission must, unless the parties otherwise agree, be terminated within six months from the date on which the Commission shall have been given cognizance of the dispute.

Article 16

The Commission's *procès-verbal* shall be communicated without delay to the parties. The parties shall decide whether it shall be published.

APPENDIX III

Resolution of the UN General Assembly on the Establishment of a Panel for Inquiry and Conciliation (1949)[1]

D

CREATION OF A PANEL FOR INQUIRY AND CONCILIATION

The General Assembly,

Mindful of its responsibilities, under Articles 13 (1a) and 11 (1) of the Charter, to promote international co-operation in the political field and to make recommendations with regard to the general principles of the maintenance of international peace and security,

Deeming it desirable to facilitate in every practicable way the compliance by Member States with the obligation in Article 33 of the Charter first of all to seek a solution of their disputes by peaceful means of their own choice,

Noting the desirability, as shown by the experience of organs of the United Nations, of having qualified persons readily available to assist those organs in the settlement of disputes and situations by serving on commissions of inquiry or of conciliation,

Concluding that to make provision for a panel of persons having the highest qualifications in this field available to any States involved in controversies and to the General Assembly, the Security Council and their subsidiary organs, when exercising their respective functions in relation to disputes and situations, would promote the use and effectiveness of procedures of inquiry and conciliation,

1. *Invites* each Member State to designate from one to five persons who, by reason of their training, experience, character and standing, are deemed to be well fitted to serve as members of commissions of inquiry or of conciliation and who would be disposed to serve in that capacity;

2. *Directs* the Secretary-General to take charge of the administrative arrangements connected with the composition and use of the panel;

3. *Adopts* the annexed articles relating to the composition and use of the Panel for Inquiry and Conciliation.

ANNEX

ARTICLES RELATING TO THE COMPOSITION AND USE OF THE PANEL FOR INQUIRY AND CONCILIATION

Article 1

The Panel for Inquiry and Conciliation shall consist of persons designated by Member States who, by reason of their training, experience, character and standing, are deemed to be well fitted to serve as members of commissions of inquiry or of conciliation and who would be disposed to serve in that capacity. Each Member State may designate from one to five persons, who may be private persons or government officials. In designating any of its

[1]Res. 268 (III) of 28 Apr. 1949, entitled 'Study of Methods for the Promotion of International Cooperation in the Political Field'.

officials, a State shall agree to make every effort to make such person available if his services on a commission are requested. Two or more States may designate the same person. Members of the panel shall be designated for a term of five years and such designations shall be renewable. Members of commissions appointed under these articles shall not, in the performance of their duties, seek or receive instructions from any Government. Membership in the panel shall not, however, render a person ineligible for appointment, as representative of his Government or otherwise, on commissions or other bodies not formed under these articles.

Article 2
The Secretary-General of the United Nations shall have general responsibility for the administrative arrangements connected with the panel. Each Government shall notify him of each designation of a person for inclusion in the panel, including with each notification full pertinent biographical information. Each Government shall inform him when any member of the panel designated by it is no longer available due to death, incapacity or inability to serve.

The Secretary-General shall communicate the panel and any changes which may occur in it from time to time to the Member States, to the Security Council, the General Assembly and the Interim Committee. He shall, where necessary, invite Member States promptly to designate replacements to fill any vacancies on the panel which may occur.

Article 3
The panel shall be available at all times to the organs of the United Nations in case they wish to select from it members of commissions to perform tasks of inquiry or conciliation in connexion with disputes or situations in respect of which the organs are exercising their functions.

Article 4
The panel shall be available at all times to all States, whether or not Members of the United Nations, which are parties to any controversy, for the purpose of selecting from the panel members of commissions to perform tasks of inquiry or conciliation with a view to settlement of the controversy.

Article 5
The method of selecting members of a commission of inquiry or of conciliation from the panel shall be determined in each case by the organ appointing the commission or, in the case of commissions appointed by or at the request of States parties to a controversy, by agreement between the parties.

Whenever the parties to a controversy jointly request the Secretary-General, the President of the General Assembly or the Chairman of the Interim Committee to appoint under these articles a member or members of a commission to perform tasks of inquiry or conciliation in respect of the controversy, or whenever such request is otherwise made pursuant to the provisions of a treaty or agreement registered with the Secretary-General of the United Nations, the officer so requested shall appoint from the panel the number of commissioners required.

Article 6

In connexion with the constituting of any commission under these articles, the Secretary-General shall give the United Nations organ concerned or the parties to the controversy every assistance, by the performance of such tasks as ascertaining the availability of individuals selected from the panel, and making arrangements for the time and place of meeting of the persons so selected.

Article 7

Members of commissions constituted pursuant to these articles by United Nations organs shall have the privileges and immunities specified in the General Convention on the Privileges and Immunities of the United Nations. Members of commissions constituted by States under these articles should, so far as possible, receive the same privileges and immunities.

Article 8

Members of commissions constituted under these articles shall receive appropriate compensation for the period of their service. In the case of commissions constituted under article 4, such compensation shall be provided by the parties to the controversy, each party providing an equal share.

Article 9

Subject to any determinations that may be made by the United Nations organ concerned or by the parties to a controversy in constituting commissions under articles 3 and 4 respectively, commissions constituted under these articles may meet at the seat of the United Nations or at such other places as they may determine to be necessary for the effective performance of their functions.

Article 10

The Secretary-General shall assign to each commission constituted by a United Nations organ under these articles, staff adequate to enable it to perform its duties and shall, as necessary, seek expert assistance from specialized agencies brought into relationship with the United Nations. He shall enter into suitable arrangements with the proper authorities of States in order to assure the commission, so far as it may find it necessary to exercise its functions within their territories, full freedom of movement and all facilities necessary for the performance of its functions. The Secretary-General shall, at the request of any commission appointed by parties to a controversy pursuant to article 4, render this assistance to the commission to the extent possible.

Upon completion of its proceedings each commission appointed by a United Nations organ shall render such reports as may be determined by the appointing organ. Each commission appointed by or at the request of parties to a controversy pursuant to article 4, shall file a report with the Secretary-General. If a settlement of the controversy is reached, such report will normally merely state the terms of settlement.

APPENDIX IV

Resolution of the UN General Assembly on the Establishment of a Register of Experts on Fact-Finding (1967)[1]

The General Assembly,

Recalling its resolutions 1967 (XVIII) of 16 December 1963, 2104 (XX) of 20 December 1965 and 2182 (XXI) of 12 December 1966 on the question of methods of fact-finding,

Noting the comments submitted by Member States pursuant to the above-mentioned resolutions and the views expressed in the United Nations,

Noting with appreciation the two reports submitted by the Secretary-General in pursuance of the above-mentioned resolutions,

Recognizing the usefulness of impartial fact-finding as a means towards the settlement of disputes,

Believing that an important contribution to the peaceful settlement of disputes and to the prevention of disputes could be made by providing for impartial fact-finding within the framework of international organizations and in bilateral arrangements,

Affirming that the possibility of recourse to impartial methods of fact-finding is without prejudice to the right of States to seek other peaceful means of settlement of their own choice,

Reaffirming the importance of impartial fact-finding in appropriate cases for the settlement and the prevention of disputes,

Recalling the possibility of the continued use of existing facilities for fact-finding,

1. *Urges* Member States to make more effective use of the existing methods of fact-finding;

2. *Invites* Member States to take into consideration, in choosing means for the peaceful settlement of disputes, the possibility of entrusting the ascertainment of facts, whenever it appears appropriate, to competent international organizations and bodies established by agreement between the parties concerned, in conformity with the principles of international law and the Charter of the United Nations or other relevant agreements;

3. *Draws special attention* to the possibility of recourse by States in particular cases, where appropriate, to procedures for the ascertainment of facts, in accordance with Article 33 of the Charter of the United Nations;

4. *Requests* the Secretary-General to prepare a register of experts, in legal and other fields, whose services the States parties to a dispute may use by agreement for fact-finding in relation to the dispute, and requests Member States to nominate up to five of their nationals to be included in such a register.

[1]Res. 2329 (XXII) of 18 Dec. 1967 entitled 'Question of Methods of Fact-Finding'.

BIBLIOGRAPHY

AMERASINGHE, H. S. The work of the Special Committee to Investigate Israeli Practices Affecting the Human Rights of the Population of the Occupied Territories. *UN monthly chronicle*, May 1973.

L'Affaire du F.OABV. *1958*.

Annuaire de l'Institut de Droit International, 1959, 48/I; *1961*, 49/II.

ASBECK, F. M. VAN. La tâche et l'action d'une commission de conciliation. 3 *Ned. tijd. int. recht* (1956).

—— La procédure suivie par la commission permanente de conciliation franco-suisse. 3 *Ned. tijd. int. recht* (1956).

BAILEY, S. D. *Peaceful settlement of disputes; ideas and proposals for research.* London, 1970.

—— UN fact-finding and human rights complaints. *Int. aff.*, 48 (1972).

BARDONNET, D. L'état de ratifications des conventions de La Haye de 1899 et de 1907 sur le règlement de conflits internationaux. *AFDI, 1961*.

BAR-YAACOV, N. *The Israel-Syrian armistice; problems of implementation, 1949–66*. Jerusalem, 1967.

BASTID, S. La commission de conciliation franco-siamoise. *Etudes en l'honneur de Georges Scelle*, i. Paris, 1950.

—— La commission de conciliation franco-suisse. *AFDI, 1956*.

BAXTER, R. R., ed. Documents on the St Lawrence Seaway. Special suppl. of *ICLQ*, 1960.

—— *The law of international waterways*. Cambridge, Mass., 1964.

BEAUCOURT, A. *Les commissions internationales d'enquête*. Arras, 1909.

BENDER, J. C. Ad hoc committees and human rights investigations: a comparative case study in the Middle East. *Social research*, 38/2 (Summer 1971).

BIRDWOOD, LORD. *Two nations and Kashmir*. London, 1956.

BLOOMFIELD, L. M. & FITZGERALD, G. F. *Boundary water problems of Canada and the United States (the International Joint Commission, 1912–58)*. Toronto, 1958.

BOKANOWSKI, M. *Les commissions internationales d'enquête*. Paris, 1908.

Boundary waters between the United States and Canada. 4 *AJIL* (1910).

BOWETT, D. W. Reprisals involving recourse to armed force. 66 *AJIL* (1972).

—— *United Nations forces*. London, 1964.

BURNS, E. L. M. *Between Arab and Israeli*. London, 1962.

BUSTAMENTE Y SIRVÉN, A. S. DE. *La Seconde Conférence de la Paix réunie à La Haye en 1907*. (Trans. from the Spanish by Georges Scelle.) Paris, 1909.

CAREY, J. *UN protection of civil and political rights*. Syracuse, 1970.

CHACKO, C. J. *The International Joint Commission between the United States of America and the Dominion of Canada*. New York, 1932.

Chronique des faits internationaux: Danemark et Royaume-Unie . . . Affaire du *Red Crusader.* 65 *RGDIP* (1961); Règlement de l'incident du *Red Crusader.* 66 *RGDIP* (1962).

Chronique des faits internationaux: Turquie; La question arménienne; Intervention européenne. 3 *RGDIP* (1896).

CLAUDE, I. *Swords into plowshares.* 3rd edn. New York, 1964.

Les commissions de conciliation et la SDN. 29 *RGDIP* (1922).

Commission de conciliation franco-siamoise. *Rapport* (27 juin 1947). *La documentation française, notes documentaires et études,* No. 811, 23 Jan. 1948.

Commission internationale d'enquête constituée à Malte en vertu de la convention d'enquête signée à Rome entre la France et l'Italie le 20 mai 1912. *Incidents du vapeur français 'Tavignano' et des mahonnes 'Camouna' et 'Gaulois' arrêtés et visités par les contre-torpilleurs 'Fulmine' et 'Canopo' de la marine royale italienne; documents et procès-verbaux.* n.d.

Commission Internationale d'Enquête constituée en vertu de la Déclaration du 12/25 novembre 1904 échangée à Saint-Pétersbourg entre les Gouvernements de Grande-Bretagne et de Russie. *Procès-verbaux des séances.* FO confidential paper No. 8376.

Commission Internationale d'Enquête constituée par la Déclaration russo-anglaise du 12/25 novembre 1904. *Documents y relatifs. Arch. dipl.,* 93, 3rd ser., No. 1 (i) 1905; *Procès-verbaux des séances (22 décembre 1904–25 février 1905).* Ibid., 94, 3rd ser., No. 4 (ii), 1905.

Commission Internationale d'Enquête pour examiner le cas du vapeur 'Tiger' [Germany–Spain, 1917]. Procès-verbaux (typewritten). The Hague, Library of the Peace Palace, n.d.

Commission to Study the Organization of Peace (chairman: Professor L. B. Sohn). *Twentieth report: the United Nations; the next twenty-five years.* New York, 1970.

CONWELL-EVANS, T. P. *The League Council in action.* London, 1929.

COT, J.-P. *La conciliation internationale.* Paris, 1968. (Eng. trans: *International conciliation.* London, 1972.)

Cour Permanente d'Arbitrage, *see* Permanent Court of Arbitration.

David Davies Memorial Inst. of International Studies. *Report of a study group on the peaceful settlement of international disputes.* London, 1966.

—— *International disputes; the legal aspects; report of a study group.* London, 1972.

Dictionnaire de la terminologie du droit international. Paris, 1960.

EPP, F. H. The Palestinians . . . a hi-jacked people. *World federalist,* world edn, Nov.–Dec. 1970.

ERMACORA, F. International enquiry commissions in the field of human rights. *Revue des droits de l'homme—Human rights journal,* I–2 (1968).

—— 'Partiality and impartiality of human rights enquiry commissions of international organisations', in *René Cassin amicorum disciplorumque liber,* i: *Problèmes de protection internationale des droits de l'homme.* Paris, 1969.

FAUCHILLE, P. *Traité de droit international public,* 8th edn of Bonfil's *Manuel de droit international public,* i, pt 3. Paris, 1926.

FAWCETT, J. E. S. *The application of the European convention on human rights.* Oxford, 1969.

FEINBERG, N. La juridiction et la jurisprudence de la Cour permanente de Justice internationale en matière de mandats et de minorités. 59 *Hague Recueil* (1937), i.

FENWICK, C. G. *International law.* 4th edn. New York, 1965.

FOSTER, W. F. Fact-finding and the World Court. 7 *Canadian yearbook of international law, 1969.*

FOURNIER, F. E. *La politique navale et la flotte française.* Paris, 1910.

FRANÇOIS, J. P. A. *Handboek van het Volkenrecht,* ii. 2nd edn. Zwolle (Netherlands), 1950.

—— Le Palais de la Paix en 1956. 4 *Ned. tijd. int. recht* (1957).

GOODRICH, L. M. & OTHERS. *Charter of the United Nations.* 3rd rev. edn. New York & London, 1969.

GORDON, E. Resolution of the Bahrain dispute. 65 *AJIL* (1971).

GRANT, A. J. & TEMPERLEY, H. *Europe in the nineteenth and twentieth centuries, 1789–1950.* 6th edn by Penson. London, 1952.

Great Britain:

    C. 7894: *Correspondence relating to the Asiatic provinces of Turkey,* pt I: *Events at Sassoon, and Commission of Inquiry at Moush.* (Turkey No. 1, 1895.)

    C. 7894-I: *Correspondence relating to the Asiatic provinces of Turkey,* pt II: *Commission of Inquiry at Moush: procès verbaux and separate depositions.* (Turkey No. 1, 1895.)

    Cd 2350: *Correspondence relating to the North Sea incident.* (Russia No. 2, 1905.)

GREENSPAN, M. Human rights in the territories occupied by Israel. 12 *Santa Clara lawyer* (1972).

GROS, A. Observations sur une enquête internationale: l'affaire du 'Tavignano'. *Mélanges offerts à Juraj Andrassy.* The Hague, 1968.

—— Remarques sur la conciliation internationale. *L'évolution du droit public; études offertes à Achille Mestre.* Paris, 1956.

GUGGENHEIM, P. *Traité de droit international public,* ii. Geneva, 1954.

HABICHT, M. *Post-war treaties for the pacific settlement of international disputes.* Cambridge, Mass., 1931.

HACKWORTH, G. H. *Digest of international law,* vi & vii. Washington, 1943.

HEENEY, A. D. P. Along the common frontier; the International Joint Commission. *Behind the headlines* (Canadian Inst. of International Affairs), July 1967.

HERSHEY, A. S. *The international law and diplomacy of the Russo-Japanese war.* New York, 1906.

Hertslet's commercial treaties, ix. London, 1856.

HIGGINS, R. *United Nations peacekeeping, 1946–67; documents and commentary,* i: *The Middle East;* ii: *Asia.* London, 1969 & 1970.

HILL, N. L. International commissions of inquiry and conciliation. *Int. conc.,* 278 (1932).

HOLLS, F. W. *The Peace Conference at The Hague.* New York, 1900.

HUDSON, M. O. Visits by international tribunals to places concerned in proceedings. 31 *AJIL* (1937).

HYDE, C. C. Commissions of conciliation and the Locarno Treaties. 20 *AJIL* (1926).

—— *International law, chiefly as interpreted and applied by the United States*, ii. 2nd edn. Boston, 1947.

—— The place of commissions of inquiry and conciliation treaties in the peaceful settlement of international disputes. 10 *BYIL* (1929).

The International Joint Commission between the United States and Canada. 6 *AJIL* (1912).

Inter-Parliamentary Union. *Official report of the Fourteenth Conference, held in the Royal Gallery of the House of Lords, London, July 23rd to 25th, 1906.*

Israel, Ministry of Defence. *Four years of military administration, 1967–71; data on civilian activities in Judea and Samaria, the Gaza Strip and Northern Sinai.* n.d.

JENKS, C. W. 'The international protection of trade union rights', in Luard, E., ed. *The international protection of human rights.* London, 1967.

KELSEN, H. *The law of the United Nations.* London, 1951.

KERLEY, E. The powers of investigation of the Security Council. 55 *AJIL* (1961).

KORBEL, J. *Danger in Kashmir.* Princeton, N.J., 1954.

KOREY, W. The key to human rights—implementation. *Int. conc.*, 570 (Nov. 1968).

LANDY, E. A. *The effectiveness of international supervision; thirty years of ILO experience.* London, 1966.

LA PENHA, R. DE. *La commission d'enquête sur l'incident anglo-russe de la mer du Nord.* Paris, 1906.

LA PRADELLE, A. DE. La conférence de la Paix (La Haye, 18 mai–29 juillet 1899). 6 *RGDIP* (1899).

—— & POLITIS, N. *Recueil des arbitrages internationaux*, iii. Paris, 1954; 2nd edn, i: *1798–1855.* Paris, 1957.

LAUTERPACHT, E. *The contemporary practice of the United Kingdom in the field of international law, 1962*, i (*January 1–June 30*). London, 1962. [The *Red Crusader* incident.]

LAUTERPACHT, H. *The development of international law by the International Court.* London, 1958.

LAWRENCE, T. J. *International problems and Hague conferences.* London, 1908.

—— *War and neutrality in the Far East.* London, 1904.

League of Nations. *Arbitration and security; systematic survey of the arbitration conventions and treaties of mutual security deposited with the League of Nations.* 2nd edn. 1927. LN Doc. C.653. M.216. 1927. V.

—— *Dispute between Bolivia and Paraguay; report of the Chaco Commission.* LN Doc. C.154. M.64. 1934. VII.

LE RAY, A. *Les commissions internationales d'enquête au XXe siècle.* Saumur, 1910.

LIFSHITZ, Y. *The economic development in the administered areas, 1967–9.* Tel-Aviv, 1970. [In Hebrew.]

LOURIÉ, S. The UN Military Observer Group in India and Pakistan. *Int. org.*, 9 (1955).

LOW, S. The International Conference of Peace. *NAR.* 169 (1899).

MACCALLUM, J. L. The International Joint Commission. *Canad. Geog. J.*, Mar. 1966.

MANDELSTAM, A. La commission internationale d'enquête sur l'incident de la mer du Nord. 12 *RGDIP* (1905).

MARTENS, F. DE. International arbitration and the Peace Conference at The Hague. *NAR*, 169 (1899).

—— *Nouveau recueil generale de traités.*

MÉRIGNHAC, A. *La Conférence Internationale de la Paix.* Paris, 1900.

MILLER, D. H. *The drafting of the Covenant.* London, 1928. 2 vols.

MONCONDUIT, F. *La commission européenne des droits de l'homme.* Leyden, 1965.

MOORE, J. B. *History and digest of the international arbitrations to which the United States has been a party*, i & ii. Washington, 1898.

—— *International adjudications*, modern ser. New York, 1929–30. Saint Croix river arbitration. Mixed commission under article V of the treaty between Great Britain and the United States of November 19, 1794.

—— The North Sea incident. *The collected papers of John Basset Moore*, iii. New York, 1944.

MURDOCK, J. O. Arbitration and conciliation in Pan America. 23 *AJIL* (1929).

MYERS, D. P. *The commission of inquiry: the Wilson-Bryan peace plan; its origin and development.* Boston, 1913.

—— The modern system of pacific settlement of international disputes. *Pol. Sci. Q.*, 46 (1931).

Netherlands, Ministry for Foreign Affairs. *Conférence Internationale de la Paix, La Haye, 18 mai–29 juillet 1899.* 1899. New edn 1907.

—— *Deuxième Conférence Internationale de la Paix, La Haye, 15 juin–18 octobre 1907, Actes et documents*, i: *Séances plénières de la conférence*, ii: *Première commission*, iii: *Deuxième, troisième et quatrième commissions.* 1907.

—— *Tableau officiel des signatures, ratifications, adhésions et dénonciations concernant les conventions et déclarations élaborées à La Haye en 1899 et 1907 au cours des deux Conférences Internationales de la Paix.* Published in typewritten form, June 1973.

NGUYEN-QUOC-DINH. Les commissions de conciliation sont-elles aussi des commissions d'enquête? 71 *RGDIP* (1967).

NORTHEDGE, F. S. & DONELAN, M. D. *International disputes; the political aspects.* London, 1971.

OPPENHEIM, L. *International law*, i, 8th edn by Lauterpacht; ii, 7th edn by Lauterpacht. London, 1955 & 1952.

Permanent Court of Arbitration. *Rapport de la commission internationale d'enquête concernant la perte du vapeur néerlandais 'Tubantia'.* 1922.

—— *Report of the commission of enquiry established by the government of the United Kingdom of Great Britain and Northern Ireland and the government of the Kingdom of Denmark on November 15, 1961; investigation of certain incidents affecting the British trawler 'Red Crusader' (the 'Red Crusader' incident).* March 1962.

PILLET, A. *La cause de la paix et les deux conférences de La Haye.* Paris, 1908.

PIPER, D. A significant docket for the International Joint Commission. 59 *AJIL* (1965).

PLUNKETT, E. A., JR. UN fact-finding as a means of settling disputes. 9 *Virginia journal of international law* (1968–9)

POLITIS, N. Les commissions internationales d'enquête. 19 *RGDIP* (1912).

Proceedings of the Commission of Inquiry and Conciliation, Bolivia and Paraguay, March 13, 1929–September 13, 1929. Baltimore, 1929.

De quelques règles de procédure appliquées en matière d'enquête internationale. 32 & 33 *Journal du droit international privé et de la jurisprudence comparée* (1905 & 1906).

REVON, M. *L'arbitrage international.* Paris, 1892.

RODLEY, N. S. The United Nations and human rights in the Middle East. *Social research.* Summer 1971.

ROLIN, H. Les pays de l'Est et le règlement pacifique des différends internationaux. 1 *RBDI* (1965).

—— L'heure de la conciliation comme mode de règlement pacifique des litiges. *Annuaire européen,* iii (1957).

—— Une conciliation belgo-danoise. 57 *RGDIP* (1953).

ROSENNE, S. *Israel's armistice agreements with the Arab states.* Tel-Aviv, 1951.

—— *The International Court of Justice.* Leyden, 1957.

ROUSSEAU, C. *Droit international public.* Paris, 1968.

RUSSELL, R. *A history of the United Nations Charter; the role of the United States, 1940–5.* Washington, 1958.

SALMON, J. La convention européenne pour le règlement pacifique des différends. 63 *RGDIP* (1959).

SANDIFER, D. V. *Evidence before international tribunals.* Chicago, 1939.

SCHURMANN, C. W. A. *A center for international fact finding; a review and a proposal.* New York, 1963.

SCHWARZENBERGER, G. *A manual of international law.* 5th edn. London, 1967.

SCHWELB, E. Civil and political rights: the international measures of implementation. 62 *AJIL* (1968).

SCOTT, J. B., ed. *The Hague conventions and declarations of 1899 and 1907.* New York, 1915.

—— ed. *The Hague Court reports.* New York, 1916; 2nd ser., New York, 1932.

—— *The Hague Peace Conferences of 1899 and 1907,* i. New York, 1909.

—— ed. *The proceedings of the Hague Peace Conferences; translation of the official texts:*
The conference of 1899. New York, 1920.
The conference of 1907, i: *Plenary meetings of the conference;* ii: *Meetings of the first commission;* iii: *Meetings of the second, third, and fourth commissions.* New York, 1920–1.

—— ed. *The reports to the Hague Conferences of 1899 and 1907.* Oxford, 1917.

—— ed. *Treaties for the Advancement of Peace between the United States and other powers negotiated by the Honorable William J. Bryan, Secretary of State of the United States.* New York, 1920.

Settlement of the Dominican-Haitian controversy. *Bulletin of Pan American Union,* 72 (Mar. 1938).

SHERMAN, A. Israel's occupation problems. *World today,* Nov. 1967.

SHORE, W. I. *Fact-finding in the maintenance of international peace.* New York, 1970.

SIMPSON, J. L. & FOX, H. *International arbitration.* London, 1959.

SMITH, F. E. & SIBLEY, N. W. *International law as interpreted during the Russo-Japanese war.* 2nd edn. London, 1907.

STARKE, J. C. *An introduction to international law.* 6th edn. London, 1967.

STONE, J. *Legal controls of international conflict.* Sydney, 1959.

STUYT, A. *Survey of international arbitrations, 1794-1970*. Leyden, 1972.
Switzerland:
Messages du Conseil fédéral à l'Assemblée fédérale:
(a) Concernant l'approbation des traités de conciliation conclus, le 2 juin 1924, avec la Suède et, le 6 juin 1926, avec le Danemark (du 28 octobre 1924). *Feuille fédérale suisse, 1924*, iii.
(b) Concernant l'approbation du traité de conciliation et d'arbitrage conclu, le 18 juin 1924, entre la Suisse et la Hongrie (du 28 octobre 1924). *Feuille fédérale suisse, 1924*, iii.
(c) Concernant l'approbation du traité de conciliation et d'arbitrage obligatoires conclu, le 6 avril 1925, entre la Suisse et la France (du 15 mai 1925). *Feuille fédérale suisse, 1925*, ii.
(d) Concernant la question de l'accession de la Suisse à la Société des nations (du 4 août 1919). *Feuille fédérale suisse, 1919*, iv.
Rapport du Conseil fédéral à l'Assemblée fédérale concernant les traités internationaux d'arbitrage (du 11 décembre 1919). *Feuille fédérale suisse, 1919*, v.

TAYLOR, A. J. P. *The struggle for mastery in Europe, 1848–1918*. Oxford, 1954.
TIMSIT, G. Le fonctionnement de la procédure d'enquête dans l'affaire du 'Red Crusader'. *AFDI, 1963*.
United Nations. *A survey of treaty provisions for the pacific settlement of international disputes, 1949–62*. 1966.
—— *Systematic survey of treaties for the pacific settlement of international disputes, 1928–48*. 1948.
—— *Reports of the Secretary-General on methods of fact-finding:*
(a) 1 May 1964, A/5694 (GAOR, 20th sess., a.i. 90 & 94, Annexes, 1965).
(b) 22 April 1966, A/6228 (GAOR, 21st sess., a.i. 87, Annexes, 1966).
—— *Multilateral treaties in respect of which the Secretary-General performs depositary functions; list of signatories, ratifications, accessions, etc., as at 31st December 1971*. ST/LEG/SER.D/5.
United Nations Conference on International Organization, San Francisco, 1945. *Documents*, vols iii & xii.
US Dept of State. *Papers relating to the foreign relations of the United States, 1929*, i (1943); *1930*, i (1945).
—— *Treaties in force; a list of treaties and other international agreements of the United States in force on January 1, 1972*. Washington, 1972.
—— Senate. Treaties, conventions, international acts, protocols and agreements between the United States of America and other powers:
i & ii, *1776–1909*, compiled by W. M. Malloy. 1910.
iii [*1910–13*], compiled by G. Charles (Pt 1: Conventions in force; pt 2: Conventions not in force). 1913. (Suppl. 1913 to Senate Doc. No. 357.)
iii, *1910–23* [preface by C. F. Redmond]. 1923.
iv, *1923–37*, compiled by E. J. Trenwyth.
VALTICOS, N. La commission d'investigation et de conciliation en matière de liberté syndicale et le mécanisme de protection internationale des droits syndicaux. *AFDI, 1967*.
VIGNES, D. Procédures internationales d'enquête. *AFDI, 1963*.
VISSCHER, CH. DE. *Aspects récents du droit procédural de la Cour Internationale de Justice*. Paris, 1966.

—— La procédure de conciliation devant la SDN. *Revue de droit international et de législation comparée* (1923).

—— *Théories et réalités en droit international public.* 4th edn. Paris, 1970.

VOLIO-JIMINEZ, F. International protection of human rights; balance sheet of a promising action. *UN monthly chronicle*, Dec. 1964.

WAINHOUSE, D. W. & OTHERS. *International peace observation.* Baltimore, 1966.

WHITE, A. D. *Autobiography of Andrew Dickson White.* New York, 1922. 2 vols.

WHITEMAN, M. M. *Damages in international law*, ii. Washington, 1937.

WITENBERG, J.-C. La théorie des preuves devant les juridictions internationales. 56 *Hague Recueil* (1936), ii.

WOOLSEY, L. H. The Bolivia–Paraguay dispute. 23 & 24 *AJIL* (1929 & 1930).

Index of Treaties

General Index

ABC Treaty, Bryan treaties distinguished from, 116
Agents: conciliation commissions, before, 212f., 342; duties of, 82–3, 155, 169, 172; inquiry commissions, before, 66ff., 81ff., 97–8, 106, 159f., 169, 172f., 186, 331, 335, 337f.
Åland islands dispute, 16n.
American states: Convention for the Establishment of International Commissions of Inquiry, 124f., 138; International Conference of, on conciliation, 129, 202, 210; *see also* General Convention of Inter-American Conciliation.
Amman, *see* Jordan.
Angola, UN sub-committee on, 7
Anti-War Treaty of Non-Aggression and Conciliation, 131
Arab-Israel Armistice Agreements, 258ff.; demarcation lines in, 260
Arbitral commissions, mixed: composition of, 41n.; Hague Commissions, comparison with, 41
Arbitral tribunals; arbitrators, appointment of, 32n.; award of, 43, 105; cases before 1905, 81n.; choice of umpire, 32n.; composition of, 43, 81n., 96n.; Dogger Bank and Hague Commissions, comparison with, 29, 42–4, 81, 94, 96, 106; inquiry by, 3n., 10; procedure of, 19, 29, 43, 81, 104, 106; reference to, after failure of conciliation, 127n., 139; *see also* Carthage case; Manouba case; Tavignano case; US–Canada International Joint Commission
Arbitration: compulsory, cases for, 21n.; conciliation, distinguished from and relationship with, 225f., 228ff., 231, 237; provisions for in League Covenant, 119–20, in treaties, 107, 113–14, 123ff., 131, 139, in UN Charter, 132ff., 140
Argentina: ABC Treaty, 116; Chile, boundary dispute with, 9
Armenian massacre, commission of inquiry: 33, 35–7, 77; Hague Commission, comparison with, 36–7; results of, 36f.

Bahrain, visit of representative of UN Secretary-General, 274
Bastid: conciliation, on, 231, 241
Batavia, Security Council Consular Commission in, 7
Belgian-Danish Commission: composition and conciliation functions of, 217, 219f.; fact-finding by, 219–20; facts and legal aspects of dispute, 216–19; inquiry functions of, 219–20; juridical approach of, 218, 227; proceedings, 217; settlement, terms of, 217, 219f.; terms of reference, 217
Benelux Economic Union, 8
Bogotá, Pact of, 8, 131–2, 138
Bolivia, *see* Chaco Commission
Border incidents, inquiry into, 5, 77, 117–19, 248
Borneo, UN Secretary-General's mission to, 274
Boundary waters, *see* US–Canada International Joint Commission
Brazil: ABC Treaty, 116; Great Britain, agreement with, 117
Bryan Commissions: Belgian-Danish Commission, similar to, 220; composition of, 115; conciliation, as basis of, 12, 322; enlarged inquiry by, 3, 136, 322; Franco-Siamese Commission, similar to, 215ff.; Hague Commissions, comparison with, 116, 136, 322; initiative, power of, 116; investigation by, 3, 115–16, 135f.; opinions of writers on, 6, 12–16; permanency of, 115; reference of disputes to, 115
Bryan Treaties: ABC Treaty distinguished from, 116; application of, no, 116; Brazil, Chile, and Great Britain, agreements between, 117; British Dominions with, 115; conciliation treaties and, 123ff., 134–5; Convention of American States, and, 124; designation of, 135; effect

—reports of, 122ff., 232f.; dispensing with, 230, 235, 238, 243; legal effect of, 123ff.

—settlement, proposed terms of: formulation of, 235, 242, 343; rejection of, 236n., 240n.; secrecy after acceptance, 236; statement of reasons accompanying, 230, 236, 240n., 242, 244

—*See also* Belgian-Danish Commission; Bogotá, Pact of; Chaco Commission; Conciliation; Dominican Republic; Franco-Moroccan Commission; Franco-Siamese Commission; Franco-Swiss Commission; General Act for the Pacific Settlement of Disputes; Greece–Italy dispute; League of Nations; Locarno treaties; Organization of African Unity

Commissions of inquiry: ad hoc, disadvantages of, 302; analysis of disputes handled by, 141, 196–7; competence of, classification of, 196–7; conciliation by, whether, 322ff.; conciliation commissions, distinguished from, 243, 322–3, 329n.; Convention for the Establishment of, 124f., 138; elucidation of facts by, 77, 323, 327; enlarged inquiry by, 109, 322; functions of, 76–8, 196–7, 323; legal character of, 245; limited recourse to, 245, 302n; mixed, 26, 34f.; nature of dispute, 19, 141, 196, 327; organization and procedure of, 19, 141; success of, 326ff.; technical matters, appropriate for, 112, 246; *see also* Armenian massacre; Belgian-Danish Commission; Bryan Commissions; David Davies Institute; Dogger Bank Commission; European Commission of Human Rights; Franco-Siamese Commission; Germany–Netherlands dispute; Gondra Treaty; *Igotz Mendi* dispute; Labour conventions; UN Panel for Inquiry and Conciliation; US–Canada International Joint Commission; *and under* Human rights; League of Nations; Taft (Knox) Treaties; UN; UN Secretary-General

Conciliation: American and European approaches to, 130; arbitration,

distinguished from and related to, 226, 228f., 231, 237; Baron van Asbeck on, 220ff., 224f., 230f.; council of, plans for, 119n.; definition of, 12n., 14n., 235, 237; disputes submitted to, 139; enlarged inquiry, role of, 225f.; fact-finding separation of, from, 302, 307, 321; failure of, reference to arbitration after, 127n., 139; Fenwick on, 14n.; Gros on, 226-8; Guggenheim on, 14–15; inquiry, distinguished from and related to, 134–5, 198, 225–34, 237, 322ff.; judicial settlement, distinguished from and related to, 225ff., 229, 231; Oppenheim on, 12–13; origin of, 119n., 198; Rolin on, 198, 228-30, 234; Rousseau on, 16

—*See also* American states; Bryan Commissions; Commissions of conciliation; Conciliation treaties; Institute of International Law; International Conciliation, Commission on; UN Panel for Inquiry and Conciliation; US–Canada International Joint Commission; *and under* League of Nations.

Conciliation treaties: conciliation, predominance of, in, 126, 128, 130ff., 138, 198; inquiry and conciliation balanced, 6, 119, 124f., 138, 198; limited recourse to, 245; narrow scope of, 245; UN Secretary-General report on, 6; *see also* American states; Anti-War Treaty of Non-Aggression and Conciliation; Bogotá, Pact of; Bryan Treaties; Conciliation; European Convention for the Peaceful Settlement of International Disputes; General Convention of Inter-American Conciliation; Locarno Treaties; Taft (Knox) Treaties *and under* Chile; Franco-Swiss Commission; Germany; League of Nations; Switzerland; USSR

Corfu Channel: case, inquiry in, 2n., 4n., 324; UN Security Council Sub-Committee on incidents in, 7, 10

Costa Rica and Nicaragua, investigations in dispute between, 7

Cot: inquiry on, 17, 325

Council of Europe: fact-finding by, 8,